W. His/Medizin

86
89/94

Renaissance Characters

Renaissance Characters

Edited by
Eugenio Garin

Translated by Lydia G. Cochrane

University of Chicago Press

Chicago and London

Eugenio Garin is professor emeritus at the Scuola Normale Superiore of Pisa.

Originally published as *L'uomo del Rinascimento,* © 1988 Gius.
Laterza & Figli Spa, Roma-Bari.

The chapters by John E. Law, Michael Mallett, Peter Burke, and
Margaret L. King are published from the authors'
original English language versions, revised.

The chapters by André Chastel and Tzvetan Todorov have been
translated from the authors' original French language versions.

The University of Chicago Press, Chicago 60637
The University of Chicago Press, Ltd., London
© 1991 by The University of Chicago
All rights reserved. Published 1991
Printed in the United States of America

00 99 98 97 96 95 94 93 92 91   5 4 3 2 1

ISBN 0-226-28355-0 (cl.)

Library of Congress Cataloging-in-Publication Data

Uomo del Rinascimento. English.
    Renaissance characters / edited by Eugenio Garin ; translated by
Lydia Cochrane.
        p.   cm.
    Translation of: L'uomo del Rinascimento.
    Includes bibliographical references and index.
    1. Renaissance.   2. Italy—Civilization—1268–1559.   I. Garin,
Eugenio, 1909–   .   II. Title.
CB361.U57   1991
940.2'1—dc20   90-27679
                                                                  CIP

∞ The paper used in this publication meets the minimum requirements of the
American National Standard for Information Sciences—Permanence of paper for Printed
Library Materials, ANSI Z39.48–1984.

Publisher's Preface to the Italian Edition

In 1988 we published *L'uomo medievale*, edited by Jacques Le Goff, a work that presented an overall view of the age in which the idea of Europe germinated. The book was received favorably by Italian readers and has been or will be published in translation in France, Germany, England, Spain, Portugal, and the United States.

This new volume on Renaissance man, edited by Eugenio Garin and written by major specialists in the field, attempts to portray one of the most luminous moments in Italian culture, a moment decisive for the genesis of the modern mind. In addition, it also hopes to make a contribution to our understanding of the formation and development of the idea of Europe.

Bringing a European common market into existence is no simple matter, nor is it easy to achieve full awareness of a common cultural matrix. This book, like its predecessor, hopes to provide a start.

To Eugenio Garin and to the authors who have collaborated with him toward the success of this volume we give thanks, in our own name and in that of its readers, both for what we stand to learn from it and for its contribution to the recognition of the cultural unity of Europe.

Editori Laterza

Contents

Introduction

Eugenio Garin

*T*HE widely used but somewhat ambiguous term "Renaissance Man" occurs in both literature and historiography in generally accepted interpretations of the specific historical period that extended roughly from the
mid-fourteenth century to the end of the sixteenth century and of trends that
originated in the Italian city states and spread throughout Europe. It almost
seems as if that age produced a number of human types or exemplars with
special characteristics, singular gifts and attitudes, and new functions.[1] Obviously, with the passage of time and as those human types and those characteristics moved from the Italian cities to other European cities and beyond,
they underwent changes, often notable ones. Thus the diffusion outside Italy
of ideas and themes proper to the Italian Renaissance occurred in a variety of
ways and over a long time span to reach beyond the chronological limits
assigned to the Renaissance well into the seventeenth century.

From the start of the Renaissance the idea of "rebirth," of being born to a
new life, accompanied various aspects of the movement, both as a program
and as a myth. The idea of the dawn of a new age and the birth of new times
circulated tenaciously during the fifteenth century, so much so that many
historians in the not too distant past belabored the point, ultimately considering that idea the distinguishing characteristic of the entire period.[2] If this
conclusion is highly debatable it is because what was reaffirmed, exalted, and
"reborn" was not only (and not overwhelmingly) the ancient world of classical Greek and Roman values to which those historians invariably returned.
The cultural revival that characterized the Renaissance from its outset was
above all a renewed affirmation of man and of human values in all fields of

1. On the concept of the "Renaissance man," see Ágnes Heller, *A Reneszansz Ember* (Budapest: Akadémiai Kaido, 1967), available in English as *Renaissance Man*, trans. Richard E. Allen
(London and Boston: Routledge & Kegan Paul, 1978; New York: Schocken Books, 1981).

2. For the theses of Herbert Weisinger (1944–45) and, in part, Franco Simone, see Wallace
K. Ferguson, *The Renaissance in Historical Thought: Five Centuries of Interpretation* (Boston:
Houghton Mifflin, 1948; New York: AMS Press, 1981).

endeavor from the arts to civic life. It is not by chance that from the start one of the most striking aspects of Renaissance writers and historians was their preoccupation with men, with their world, and with their activities in the world. Although Jacob Burckhardt's famous statement (which he borrowed from Michelet) that "the civilization of the Renaissance was the first to discover and throw light on the entire, the rich figure of man" is so imbued with rhetoric that it now seems nearly insufferable, it is nevertheless true that Renaissance culture was rooted in a historical reality in which men's life stories, their individual experiences, their types, and even their bodily presence were central; in which painters and sculptors made unforgettable portrayals of human figures and philosophers exclaimed "What a great miracle is man!" (*magnum miraculum est homo*).

If we go back to the analogous expression "medieval man" and consider its various configurations, we immediately realize (if we accept the customary chronological limits of the Renaissance) that everything—the complex of problems, even the terms involved—is different in the later age. To begin with, the spatial and temporal coordinates of the Renaissance are not only enormously different from those of the Middle Ages but are also closely connected with the specific cultural characteristics of an age that can be defined (at least in theory) on the level of people's activities and behavior patterns.

The Renaissance proper—the "great" Renaissance—was extremely short in comparison with the Middle Ages: it lasted slightly more than two centuries. Its origins were Italian. It should not be confused with seemingly analogous medieval phenomena such as the many renascences that flourished in other ways and outside Italy, even though the earlier revivals show similarities to and even had some influence on the Renaissance.[3] The shifts in sensibility and culture are already evident in Petrarch, and they are echoed by events of a profound resonance well beyond the confines of Italy and the boundaries of literary phenomena. Similarly, although Coluccio Salutati's contrast of the active life and the contemplative life was hardly a novelty and he used the well-worn rhetorical format of full argument from both sides of the question, he clearly argues in favor of the active life of involvement in this world, in politics, and in civic affairs (Pallas Athena springing fully armed from the head of Zeus), a position that a few decades later became fashionable

---

3. On this important point, which can only be mentioned in passing here, see Erwin Panofsky, *Renaissance and Renascences in Western Art* (Stockholm: Almqvist & Wiksell, 1960; New York: Harper & Row, 1972); and Eugenio Garin, *Rinascite e rivoluzioni. Movimenti culturali dal XIV al XVII secolo*, 2d ed. (Rome and Bari: Laterza, 1975), 3–47.

among the most refined intellectual circles in Tuscany. The quarrel over the Donation of Constantine certainly did not begin with Lorenzo Valla (we need only recall Nicholas of Cusa), but Valla no longer belonged to the Middle Ages and was not a "medieval man." It was precisely for his political and theological debates, for his praise of Epicurean *voluptas*, for his dialectic and his "elegances" that he was praised, anthologized, printed, and presented as the master teacher of the new age by his great "student," the prince of European humanists, Erasmus of Rotterdam. It was, in fact, from Valla's critical writings on the New Testament, which Erasmus edited and published as soon as he encountered the work, that Erasmus (who in many ways closely resembled Valla) drew the first inspiration for his own renowned writings on the Bible.

The Renaissance lasted roughly two and a half centuries, then, and a handful of Italian city states were its primary places of birth. These are the coordinates within which Renaissance man—if indeed such an entity existed with clearly defined traits—should be sought and placed. That is, we should seek him in a series of individuals who, through specific activities and in analogous ways, all brought new personages into being. Such was the artist, who not only created original works of art but, through his professional activities, transformed his position in society, participated in the life of the city, and defined his relationships with others; such were the humanist, the notary, and the jurist, who became their city's governing magistrates and whose writings influenced its political life; and such was the architect, who collaborated with the city's ruler to build the "physical" city.

Even though Jacob Burckhardt now seems remote and is often attacked and refuted, his name will recur frequently in these essays as one who constructed a lasting image of the Renaissance as a decisive moment in Italian civilization. Burckhardt himself, however, one of the fathers of the concept of the "Renaissance man," consistently mingled two closely connected but distinct themes, with equivocal results. The first of these themes is the Renaissance's intense and unequaled emphasis on man, describing him, praising him, and placing him in the center of the universe. This focus relies on the development of a philosophy of man, which in turn entails a theory of his upbringing and education, and it implies a new pedagogy not wholly free from political concerns.

Something quite different was also happening, however. In a society in crisis and in transformation, a singular wealth of human types came into being in connection with new forms of and variations on occupational activities. Original and sometimes exceptional figures sprang from both the artists' workshops and the humanists' schools. Activities evolved and at times were totally transformed. "New" men were born, and other types degenerated from models to objects of ridicule as the stock characters of masques and farces. There was, on the one hand, the exuberant or eccentric painter or sculptor, a man of quick and trenchant wit, capable of inventing extraordinary practical jokes that test personal identity and even the very bases of existence (as in *La novella del Grasso legnaiolo*).[4] Or, on the other hand, there was the other aspect of the learned man, the humanist become an insufferable pedant, transformed into an object of satire and farce.

Burckhardt tended to blend (indeed, to confuse) the elaboration of a new philosophy of man ("the discovery of man") and interest in the history of men in society. He even roots the typical Renaissance man's insatiable curiosity regarding man in a new conception of man in the world. The Italians, he observes, "were the first of all European nations who displayed any remarkable power and inclination accurately to describe man as shown in history, according to his inward and outward characteristics" (trans. Middlemore, 324). Italians "were not confined to the spiritual characteristics of individuals and nations; [man's] outward appearance was in Italy the subject of an entirely different interest from that shown in it by Northern peoples" (ibid., 338). Thus Burckhardt insists at length on the "artistic eye" needed to discern individuals and types in even the most unlikely sorts of documents.

If we keep in mind the distinction between the new philosophy of man, the history of men, and the delineation of new human types, we can appreciate Burckhardt's excellent grasp of the importance of the flowering of biography and autobiography during the Renaissance. He quite rightly emphasizes the exceptional success of the great collective biographies of classical antiquity, which were read endlessly and also circulated in vernacular versions for the use of readers of modest culture and social condition. The lives of Plutarch's heroes circulated, as did Diogenes Laertius's accounts of his philosophers, while small-format, popular illustrated editions of extracts and compendia (even medieval ones) of the anecdotes and sayings of the Greek philosophers were also published.

In other words, the philosophic focus on man in general took concrete form in histories of men (above all, in self-memorialization); in the record of one's own and one's contemporaries' terrestrial exploits in the here and now,

---

4. Available in English as "Fatso the Carpenter," trans. Janet Levarie Smarr, in *Italian Renaissance Tales*, Janet Levarie Smarr, ed. (Rochester, Minn.: Solaris Press, 1983), 105–33.

in "man, precisely, of the Renaissance." The archives of a number of Italian cities contain numerous *ricordanze*, hundreds of which have been printed, but many more of which are preserved in manuscript. Documents of all sorts—even tax declarations—contain memorable fragments of a life. For example, one impoverished Florentine woodcutter reports in the 1480 *catasto*, "I no longer keep a shop because I cannot pay the rent," adding that his son "serves at the hospital and is learning to medicate and does not have wages." Elsewhere in the tax records one Antonio di Balduccio, "infirm in his person and in his legs," reports a number of sons who were all apprentice laborers or were going to school *a legiere* (to read) except for the youngest, Balduccio, who "does nothing [for] he is little, six years old." Antonio was also burdened with responsibility for his mother, "seventy-two years old and gouty, and who cannot stand because [she is so] bent over, and cannot go [anywhere]. She is infirm and not well and makes the whole lot of us at home do her constant bidding." Antonio adds that fortunately "I live with my male children in the house of Bartolomeo di Nicholaio, a glassblower, my father-in-law, and I pay no rent, and they and I work for him."

Thus even a tax declaration (and there are so many of them!) becomes a draft page of an autobiography or a sketch for a portrait. To say nothing of the developing genre of letters—in Latin and the vernacular, simple and learned, written by women and children—that picture everyday happenings, continually interjecting presentations of the self or accounts of personality differences.

In her massive study, *Man in the Renaissance*, published in Budapest in 1967, Ágnes Heller, a pupil of Lukács, observed that the Renaissance was "the age of great autobiographies." This was, she adds, because so many exceptional personalities were formed by a society in the process of constructing itself, transforming itself, and telling its own story. A dynamic concept of man replaced a static one. For Heller, the new man—modern man—was a man in the making who constructed his own persona and was aware of doing so. This was "the man of the Renaissance."

Although we need to keep in mind the distinction between a philosophy of man that gradually became increasingly subtle and profound and a history of men who were changing in response to new models during a critical moment for society, it is also obvious that theoretical reflection on man—on his nature and his destiny, on his use of his senses, on his functions and his activities; on his relations with society on this earth, with the church, and with God—necessarily contributes to variations in man himself and in the society in which he lives. Human types changed as their functions changed. We need only reflect on the increasing influence that certain "intellectuals"—notaries, rhetoricians, and "humanists"—acquired in a number of fifteenth-century city states to have the many chancellors, secretaries, and *oratori* (ambassadors) spring to mind in their full variety, also reminding us of the changes they underwent, their deeds, and their functions.

Nor should we forget architects and their importance for Renaissance cities, many of which underwent radical restructuring. When Antonio Averlino (called Il Filarete) dedicated his treatise on architecture and politics first to Francesco I Sforza, the duke of Milan, then to Piero de' Medici, the son of Cosimo il Vecchio, he pointed to a special relationship between the technician who drew up the plans for the new city and all its structures and the ruling lord with whom he discussed the project on equal terms. At the same time, he underscored the interdependence of the building and the function or office for which it is destined.

Military architecture underwent equally radical change in an age when all men's activities and the means for pursuing them were evolving rapidly. Not only were wars fought in changing ways, reflecting new techniques in the art of war, new arms, and new "machines" that served military engineers and architects alike, but also military personnel from the condottiere down to the mercenary soldier changed. Guicciardini's perspicacious and subtle observations on the radical transformation of warfare in the fifteenth century (not only by the introduction of the "fury of the artillery") are frequently quoted. Defensive tactics changed, hence the architecture of cities changed. Above all, military personnel changed, as did leadership and even who went into combat. *Gli ingegni degli uomini* changed: Guicciardini notes in his *Storia d'Italia*, "then terrified by the ferocity of the attacks, men began to whet their wits and contrive more subtle means of defense" (*History of Italy*, trans. Alexander, 341).

Soldiers changed character as well. One chronicler calls the Spanish mercenaries at the Sack of Prato in 1512 "barbarian savages and unbelievers." Soldiers now were the *Lanzi* (*Landsknechten*) who sacked Rome. Soldiers were the sinister and often horribly mutilated *ceffi* who long populated drawings and prints, men thirsty for sack and for torture who took pleasure in inflicting pain. They were the men who massacred others out of cruelty and greed who crowd the pages of Erasmus, men he saw as universally present in a Europe by then devastated by wars ("Not a corner of the earth have they left unravaged by their hellish dissensions—wars, robberies, plagues" [*Ten Colloquies*, trans. Thompson, 113]). These too were "men of the Renaissance," soldiers of the Renaissance, like Pippo Spano before them and Francesco Ferrucci after them.

Nor were all Renaissance women devoted mothers like Alessandra Macinghi Strozzi, wholly devoted to the Strozzi family's commercial interests
and her children, or like the learned Isotta Nogarola and Cassandra Fedele, or
Alessandra Scala with her "pale violets," Battista Montefeltro, or even Margaret of Navarre. The women of the Renaissance were also Tullia d'Aragona
and her "colleagues"—a prostitute and the daughter of a prostitute, whose
refined prose we can read in the *Dialogo dell'infinità d'amore;* they were
Veronica Franco of Venice, with her letters and her poetry, who "conceded
herself," through her mother's good offices, for "two scudi" near the church
of Santa Maria Formosa, and who promised in her *Terze rime* "certain properties of infinite sweetness concealed in me will I discover to you." Not to
mention Nanna, Pippa, and the other heroines of Aretino's *Giornate,* who
discuss technical aspects of their profession, how good business is, and "job-
related" incidents with bitter and disenchanted competence.

Perhaps it is precisely in her autobiographical reflection, her capacity for
thought, memory, and social comparison—in short, in her attaintment of a
certain cultural rank—that the distinctive trait of the Renaissance courtesan
resides, or at least of some of the more famous courtesans of the Renaissance,
from Veronica Franco to Tullia d'Aragona and Gasparina Stampa, women
remembered by their writings just as Veronica Gambara and Vittoria Colonna were. Toward the end of the sixteenth century Montaigne admired the
"princely dress" (*les vestements de princesses*) of the many prostitutes he
encountered in Italy, and Veronica Franco, whose professional activities seem
to have been fairly modest in scale, carried on "literary" exchanges not only
with Cardinal Luigi d'Este but also with Henry III of France.

Just as the reader will find that the present volume in no way resembles
Ágnes Heller's historico-philosophical work on Renaissance man, he or she
will look in vain for a profile of the new "soldier of fortune" or the professional prostitute, even though both are figures who fully reflected the contradictions of their changing times. What the reader will find is nearly all the
figures that a canonical literature has by now fixed as typical of the epoch—
figures through whom the "new" age gave formal expression to its novelty
or whom we have become accustomed to seeing inextricably connected with
the Italian Renaissance in the titles of famous literary texts and universally
admired works of art. Such are the statues of condottieri that grace the public
squares of Italy, the works of artists like Donatello and Verrocchio; such are
the treatises on the prince, the cardinal (*De cardinalatu*), or the courtier; such
are the "lives of the most excellent painters, sculptors, and architects," and
so forth. Works like these are obvious inducements to emphasize the prince

and the military commander, the cardinal and the courtier, the artist and the philosopher, the merchant and the banker—even the sorcerer and the astrologer.

Doubtless a few typical figures are missing. One is that of the humanist chancellor, often a characteristic figure in both the cultural and political development of a number of Italian republics. Such men contributed much to the increasing importance of propagandistic techniques and activities that the more refined "rhetorical" instruments of men like Leonardo Bruni promoted and imposed on all of Europe. The most important of them—Salutati, Bruni, Bracciolini, Loschi, Decembrio—are to some extent included among the humanists, jurists, and intellectuals of a certain standing who joined in the political life of the courts of the new lords or mingled in circles close to the great church prelates and in the chancelleries of the later republics. Depending on the circumstances, these men were courtiers or curial functionaries who served and were the collaborators of princes or cardinals. It was they who systematically explored the ancient monastic libraries and founded new libraries, and they who circulated the manifestos of the new culture in literary texts of rare beauty in which they combined information on the recovery of classical authors with current concerns. It was they who laid the foundations for future philology. It was they who took charge—literally or informally—of the new schools. Thus a humanist as renowned as Leonardo Bruni, the chancellor of Florence, could write a treatise to further the education of the noble Battista Malatesta. Guarino da Verona founded his school in Ferrara for similar reasons, and Vittorino da Feltre his *casa dei giuochi* in Mantua. Although these were schools for "lords," they had a certain impact on education and spawned a number of imitators.

This is hardly the place to discuss the roots, the nature, and the later development of the new humanistic culture founded on a return to circulation of the high learning and great art of the major Greek and Latin sources. It is clear, however, that increasingly broad segments of the population came to participate in that culture, a notion that Lauro Martines expressed in the title of his work on the Italian city-states of the Renaissance, *Power and Imagination*. In reality, "merchant writers" (on whom Vittore Branca and Christian Bec have written so incisively) participated in the cultural movement of humanism as well.[5] Such men were scholars and patrons. They were also

5. Lauro Martines, *Power and Imagination: City-States in Renaissance Italy* (New York: Alfred A. Knopf, 1979; Random House Vintage Books, 1980); Vittore Branca, ed., *Mercanti scrittori* (Milan: Rusconi, 1986); Christian Bec, *Les marchands écrivians, affaires et humanisme à Florence, 1375–1434* (Paris and The Hague: Mouton, 1967).

booksellers and printers (like the printer-publishers who appear with merchants and bankers in one of the essays in the present work). Erasmus was welcomed as a friend in Aldo Manuzio's house near the Rialto in Venice when he went to that city to follow the printing of the *Adages*, a great book that was to spread throughout Europe the humanist culture reborn in Italy. The fare at Aldo's table was less than spectacular, but Venice was "the most splendid of cities" and there was lively conversation among Greek scholars and famous humanists, men like Janus Lascaris and Girolamo Aleandro, a great Greek scholar and a future apostolic nuncio. Manuzio's was one *bottega* among many. Alberto Pio of Carpi was its patron; not only Erasmus but also Reuchlin was a frequent visitor. Between 1495 and 1498, well before Erasmus's arrival in Venice, the Aldine presses had already produced one authentic masterpiece of culture and of the typographer's art, the splendid first printed edition of the Greek text of the complete works of Aristotle in five folio volumes. Petrarch and Poliziano followed, and, in 1500, Lucretius, a text truly irreconcilable with Christian doctrine that Aldo reprinted before his death in 1515 in a cleanly printed "pocket" edition. Aldo Manuzio's publishing house was a seedbed of humanism that attracted learned men from Greece and from all over Europe. Both an "academy" and a "shop," like the studios of the great painters, it also seems to have functioned as a sanctuary for the great humanists, who made use of the technological advance of printing to launch an operation of pan-European proportions and put into circulation much-needed editions not only of Plato and Aristotle but also of Poliziano and Erasmus, followed by grammars and dictionaries, the keys to both ancient and modern thought and knowledge.

If Aldo Manuzio's printshop was a *bottega d'umanisti*, so, in its own way, was Vespasiano da Bisticci's copyshop in Florence, which furnished elegant illuminated manuscripts not only for the collections of the Italian princes but also for the library of Matthias Corvinus, king of Hungary. Vespasiano's shop was a meeting place for humanists and merchant writers, men who were still closely linked to the humanistic atmosphere of the early quattrocento and to the "discovery" of Greek and Roman ancient writers. Not by chance, the first broad-ranging collection of biographies of "men of the Renaissance" was the work of the "paper merchant" Vespasiano da Bisticci. The work was already organized by types: popes, cardinals, and bishops; princes and commanders; magistrates and humanists; and so forth. In reality, all intellectuals and a notable proportion of the magistrates and the merchants, at least during the heroic phase of the Renaissance, were in some measure "humanists," sought to appear to be so, or frequented the humanists. Furthermore, Marsilio Ficino dedicated his Plato in Latin to various members of the Medici family (Cosimo, Piero di Cosimo, and Lorenzo) and to Federigo da Montefeltro, duke of Urbino—all of whom exemplified the Platonic ideal of the wise ruler.

Although humanism can be used as a common reference for "Renaissance man," it is also true that even simple schoolmasters of the time, teachers of grammar and rhetoric, declared themselves humanists. These were the men who guided the young in their first contact with ancient authors, when at last they replaced the medieval *auctores octo* who had been the bane of Erasmus's and Rabelais's schooling. "What times!" Erasmus exclaims, "when boys had explained to them with great pomposity and prolix glosses the moralizing versets of John of Garland." Rabelais wrote unforgettable passages on the radical changes in schooling that provided an emblematic education, although in practice change was not always easily effected. In the summer of 1443 in Ferrara, the city that hosted one of the greatest educators of the quattrocento, Guarino, and that contained the university of Rodolfo Agricola and Copernicus, anyone who wanted to teach was obliged to demonstrate possession of *bonae litterae* (that is, of *studia humanitatis*). Anyone failing to do so and continuing to spread barbarities was to be run out of the city like a wild beast (*de civitate ejiciatur, ut pestifera bellua*).

One after the other the *auctores octo*—the old, medieval school texts for children—disappeared from circulation and were no longer printed. The "simple grammar-school teachers" of the cinquecento already taught Latin with the aid of Erasmus's *Colloquies*. Moreover, they did so in vast numbers, soon restoring to the humanistic message its original impact as a message of liberty. In her study of the diffusion of Erasmus in Italy, Silvana Seidel Menchi describes and amply documents the case of the many minor humanist schoolmasters, one of whom inspired his judge to declare, "Under the cover of teaching grammar, he was teaching heresy."[6] That is another story, however.

We need to keep in mind one more point: the interpretation of the Renaissance as a historical period and a stage in the history of Western culture—its origins, its chronological limits, its contents, its nature, even its essence—has always prompted lively debate and continues to do so. Scholars have crossed swords and still disagree on how the Renaissance relates to the Middle Ages; whether polemical differences separate the two periods or they show essential continuity; whether moderately clear chronological limits can be set for the Renaissance; whether a crisis in civilization (for some, a radical one) coincided

---

6. Silvana Seidel Menchi, *Erasmo in Italia. 1520–1580* (Turin: Bollati Boringhieri, 1987) 122–42.

(or nearly coincided) with profound cultural change in the various sectors of human activity such as the arts and sciences, or politics and economics; whether the Renaissance, as it expanded beyond the confines of the Italian cities in which it had originated, retained some of its original characteristics, and if so, which ones. Other questions remain as well: What were the relationships between the various fields touched by the Renaissance? Were there technological and scientific conquests of equal importance to the greatness of artists like Michelangelo? To reverse the question, was the exceptional architectonic skill of someone like Brunelleschi conceivable without notable general advances in technology? In what measure did the ethical and political problems (which amounted to a full-blown political philosophy) raised by Machiavelli—who continues to trouble human minds—respond to concrete historical experience, and does an understanding of those events help us to understand Machiavelli?

In more general terms, to what extent are the canonical, time-honored myths and representations acceptable as still valid, given that their roots (which often date from the Renaissance itself) have been shown, with increasing clarity, to reflect a partisan agenda?

The unresolved questions are many and differences of interpretation can be acrimonious. Preconceived notions of all sorts, some deriving from ideology and even from national pride, inevitably and perhaps unconsciously converge in them. In 1751, in his introduction to the *Encyclopédie*, d'Alembert praised the Renaissance and thanked Italy: "It is from her that we have received the sciences, . . . the fine arts, and good taste, of which she has furnished us a large number of inimitable models" (*Preliminary Discourse*, trans. Schwab and Rex, 70). Yet there are historians today who speak of the "so-called Italian Renaissance," challenging both its existence and its importance.

The nine essays collected in this volume (the number nine is not to be taken as fraught with esoteric significance) have been written by specialists in their fields. While their authors have aimed at an accurate reflection of current scholarship, they do not necessarily concur on overall interpretations. Variations in emphasis may be helpful for comparing and if need be for discussing modes and methods for approaching the specific problems in such a way as to keep debate open and in touch with a concrete confrontation with real beings. There is a continuity from the description of any typical "figure" to the living examples offered by history. Furthermore, it is precisely in the nuances in the various types, in the way they oppose one another, impinge upon one another, or continually suggest still other types, that the men and women of the Renaissance emerge in all their living individuality.

O N E

The Renaissance Prince

John E. Law

INTRODUCTION

E ARLY in *Die Kultur der Renaissance in Italien* (1860), Jacob Burckhardt tells a story involving Pope John XXIII (Baldassare Cossa) and
the king of the Romans, Sigismund of Luxemburg. The spiritual and
secular leaders of Christendom met at Cremona in 1414 as part of the negotiations leading to the Council of Constance. Their host was the lord of the
city, Cabrino Fondulo, who took his distinguished guests to the top of one
of Cremona's most salient landmarks, the Torrazzo, to admire the view.
As they did so, their guide was tempted to push them to their deaths. In the
only slightly less melodramatic version told by John Addington Symonds (in
The Age of the Despots, the first volume of his *Renaissance in Italy* [1875])
following Antonio Campo's history of Cremona of 1645, Fondulo came to
regret not having disposed of the two men as he himself faced execution in
Milan in 1425.

Burckhardt does not reveal his source, which was possibly *Le Vite di
Huomini Illustri* of Paolo Giovio (1561), but in the context of his work the
significance of the story is largely historiographical. It expressed views of the
Renaissance prince and the Renaissance state—some positive, others negative—that Burckhardt shared with and encouraged in other historians of the
period.

In the first place, and certainly most dramatically, the Renaissance prince
is supposed to have displayed a ruthless, cynical self-interest in his dealings
with others, be they his subjects, his councilors, his fellow rulers, or members
of his own family. Second, he is often represented as showing contempt for
the medieval concept of Christendom and in particular for its acceptance of a
hierarchical and ordered society presided over by the "two swords" of papacy
and empire. The Renaissance ruler is no longer a prince in the feudal sense
but is rather, as Machiavelli and other political thinkers in the classical tradition saw him, an independent ruler relying on his own wits and resources
rather than on his superiors or his divinely allocated position in a pyramidal
society. Third, and perhaps more positively, the Renaissance prince is often

1

thought to have approached the business of government in a new spirit, being ready or even enthusiastic for change rather than conforming to custom. Thus he is often thought to have had a more creative influence on the development of the state.

I shall argue that historians have overstressed the case for a "Renaissance" prince, and that while changes can be detected during the period, they are often superficial rather than substantial, or the product of circumstance rather than choice. In support of this argument, most of the evidence will be drawn from fifteenth-century Italy, regarded by Burckhardt and others as a precursor and model for the rest of Renaissance Europe. Apart from this historiographical interest, fifteenth-century Italy also allows for the study of various types of principalities: signorial or "despotic" regimes and monarchies on the European model; regimes that are local in origin and influence and those of international significance; parvenu princes and those claiming ancient origins and even divine sanction.

VIOLENCE AND POWER

Even if both the Giovio-Burckhardt and the Campo-Symonds versions of the story of Cabrino Fondulo and the heads of Christendom are dismissed as legend or anecdote, they do reflect the fact that the lord of Cremona had a well-deserved reputation for violence and cruelty. Indeed, in his account of the encounter at Cremona, the well-informed and contemporary chronicler Andrea Redusio of Treviso records that it occurred to both the pope and Sigismund that, in the light of past events, it might be wiser not to overstay their welcome with such an untrustworthy and dangerous host. The incidents to which Redusio refers were those of July 1406, when Fondulo had seized power after murdering members of the previous ruling family of Cremona, the Cavalcabò, as they thought they were enjoying the hospitality of their erstwhile supporter at his castle of Maccastorno. The sinister role of the Torrazzo in the 1414 story may be explained by the fact that Cabrino did have two of his opponents flung from its summit in 1407.

Violence could indeed characterize the seizure, retention, and loss of power by the Renaissance prince. Violence could be used to dispose of rivals. In 1392 Jacopo d'Appiano overthrew and killed Pietro Gambacorta, his erstwhile patron, to gain the lordship of Pisa. Cesare Borgia disposed of many of the rulers who threatened Borgia dynasticism in the Papal States. In 1502 Giulio Cesare da Varano, lord of Camerino in the March of Ancona, and two of his sons were killed in prison.

Violence could also be used against subjects who threatened a ruler's control. After the castellan of Nocera had murdered two leading members of the

Trinci family of Foligno in 1421, their surviving brother Corrado stormed the castle and killed not only the guilty party but also his family and adherents. Ferrante of Naples tricked, imprisoned, and executed many of the leading members of the baronage who threatened his throne (1486). Perhaps most shocking of all, to contemporary as well as to later opinion, violence could be used within a ruling dynasty to seize power and eliminate rivals and pretenders. In 1381, shortly after he attained his majority, Antonio della Scala, lord of Verona, had his elder brother murdered, a drastic move possibly prompted by Antonio's fears as to his own fate. In 1385 Giangaleazzo Visconti deceived and imprisoned his uncle Bernabò to acquire the entire Visconti inheritance.

Finally, if violence could accompany the acquisition and retention of power, it could also characterize its loss. In May 1435 Tommaso Chiavelli, lord of Fabriano in the March of Ancona, fell victim—along with many of his family—to a citizens' conspiracy as he attended mass. The ascendancy of Corrado Trinci came to an end when Foligno was besieged by a papal army under the command of the determined and able cardinal Giovanni Vitelleschi and an internal rebellion delivered the ruling dynasty into his hands (1439). On 26 December 1476, in the church of Santo Stefano in Milan, Galeazzo Maria Sforza fell to the daggers of assassins who claimed tyrannicide as justification for their murder of the duke of Milan.

The strong and enduring impression of violence that such incidents can create appears to be reinforced by the warlike nature of the would-be or actual rulers of Renaissance Italy, many of whom were professional soldiers, or condottieri. Some were drawn from long-established ruling dynasties like the Este of Ferrara, the Gonzaga of Mantua, and the Montefeltro of Urbino. Others emerged during the period, seeing a state as an attractive, deserved, and prestigious reward. Not all were successful. Giovanni Vitelleschi built up a formidable army in the nominal service of the papacy, as well as an impressive collection of castles, lordships, and estates in the papal province of the Patrimony of St. Peter. He also acquired high ecclesiastical office—the archbishopric of Florence and the patriarchate of Alexandria (1435) and a cardinalate (1437)—and it was rumored that he had his sights set on the papal tiara itself. Possibly for these very reasons he was trapped in the Castel Sant'Angelo and died in prison in 1440. Eventually much more successful was Francesco Sforza, who came from a family of mercenary soldiers and who tried himself to amass lordships in the Papal States in the 1430s before acquiring the duchy of Milan in 1450, partly by inheritance (through his marriage to Bianca Maria Visconti), but more substantially due to military might and political skill.

Obviously there is a temptation to treat the violence often associated with power in Renaissance Italy in melodramatic terms. Contemporaries could do so themselves, and sudden downturns in fortune were favorite topics for chroniclers and moralists. The imprisonment of Bernabò Visconti inspired the composition of *lamenti* on the theme of the cruelty of fortune. When Francesco "Il Vecchio" da Carrara lost the lordships of Padua and Treviso through military defeat and popular insurrection in 1388, local chroniclers described how he stripped off his clothes and beat himself to fulfill a prophecy that he would leave Padua naked.

Incidents of this nature have also had their appeal for artists, composers, novelists, and "popularizers" in more recent times. Among the most inspirational (or notorious) in this regard are the Borgia: for example, the librettist Felice Romani used Victor Hugo's *Lucrèce Borgia* for an opera by Donizetti on the same heroine. Even relatively obscure or local incidents could excite the Romantic imagination. Corrado Trinci's massacre of his enemies at Nocera inspired a novel and a play. For the composer Bellini, Romani wrote the libretto for the opera *Beatrice di Tenda*. Beatrice was probably the daughter of one condottiere, Ruggero Cane, and married another, Facino Cane. After his death, she became the wife of Filippo Maria Visconti, in 1414. Although older than her new husband, her dowry of lordships inherited from Facino made her politically attractive to the duke as he sought to reconstruct the Visconti state, largely dismantled after the sudden death of Giangaleazzo in 1402. However, Beatrice did not retain her allure for her husband. In 1418 she was accused of adultery, tortured, and executed at night in the castle of Binasco.

But of course the Romantic imagination found a great deal of inspiration outside Italy. Among the libretti of Romani set to music by Donizetti was *Anna Bolena*, concerning another tragic heroine, while the career of a further victim of Tudor dynastic insecurity, Mary Queen of Scots, has proved an enduring and inspirational subject for writers, artists, and musicians. Fascinating though it is for the study of the history of taste and ideas about the past, the Romantic reading (or embroidering) of history can encourage a distorted view of the Renaissance prince as an amoral "Machiavellian" ogre.

It is also important to realize that the princes of Renaissance Italy had contemporary enemies with a vested interest in exaggerating their misdeeds and blackening their reputations. Hence for republican Florence Giangaleazzo Visconti was not a true *Conte di Virtù*—a title he had acquired through his marriage to Isabelle de Valois, countess of Vertus (1360)—but a cruel and unjust tyrant and a source of vice and treachery. For the propagandists of the Visconti state itself like the humanist Andrea Biglia, "reguli" like Cabrino

Fondulo were sowers of discord. Similar arguments were used on behalf of the restored papacy in the fifteenth and sixteenth centuries against turbulent subjects like the Trinci or the Bentivoglio lords. The Spanish origins and the aggressive dynasticism of the Borgia insured them a hostile press in Italy itself and in both Catholic and Protestant Europe.

Moreover, in the period under consideration conventional morality and political thought did not condone, let alone encourage, the violent ruler. Of course rebels were to be punished and foreign enemies defeated; for these reasons the Roman Senate in 1436 hailed Giovanni Vitelleschi as the third founder of Rome, after Romulus, and it contemplated erecting an equestrian statue in his honor after he had defeated the Colonna family. The military achievements of Francesco Sforza were applauded by the dynasty's propagandists and supporters, though they too failed to erect an equestrian monument to the duke's memory. But the lord who ruled by force alone, whose residence was a citadel rather than a palace, was a tyrant rather than a true prince. This article of conventional wisdom, which can be traced throughout medieval political thought and back to antiquity, can be found expressed in warnings to Alfonso V as he undertook the repair of the Castel Nuovo in Naples (ca. 1440), to Nicholas V as he strengthened the Castel Sant'Angelo (ca. 1450), and to Francesco Sforza as he restored and extended the Visconti castle at the Porta Giovia in Milan (ca. 1450).

The same theme emerges, if from a different angle, in the political thought and propaganda produced for such rulers as Giangaleazzo Visconti. For example, a tract (anonymous but almost certainly written by a Visconti courtier ca. 1396) makes a dramatic case for Genoa's acceptance of the duke's rule. The author claims to have had a vision of Giangaleazzo in a dream, enthroned in his "impregnable castle" at Pavia. But the duke's greatness, though "impe rial," "majestic," and "sublime," is expressed in terms of magnificence, wisdom, justice, and physical stature rather than in terms of military force. Genoa is admitted to his presence in the form of a woman suppliant who proceeds to catalogue the miseries suffered by that once-great city, central to which is "infernal and diabolical faction." From such disasters Giangaleazzo offers the sole hope of deliverance, and similar appeals in similar terms were addressed on Genoa's behalf to later Visconti and Sforza rulers.

The picture in the 1396 tract of the just ruler magnanimously presiding over a splendid court shows that even though the reputation of the Renaissance prince does have its darker, violent side, from another perspective he and his court can emerge as the epitome of good taste and Renaissance civilization. Even Cabrino Fondulo obtained an imperial privilege for the university of Cremona. Historiography has treated Federigo da Montefeltro, count and then duke (1474) of Urbino, as a personification of Renaissance culture and sensibilities. Although he came to power on the murder of his elder and legitimate brother Oddantonio (1444), and although he was a mercenary soldier in part responsible for the horrifying sack of Volterra (1472), Federigo is generally seen as a patron both of the arts and of his subjects. The civilized character of the Montefeltro court at Urbino has been immortalized in Baldassare Castiglione's *Courtier* (1528), while a sympathetic reading of the well-preserved and articulate correspondence that linked Urbino with the courts of Mantua, Ferrara, and elsewhere has inspired and informed a genre of biographically based studies from authors like Dennistoun and Cartwright, to cite only two pioneering British examples.

Such correspondence often reveals a conventional piety, which can be confirmed from other evidence. Niccolò d'Este (1393–1441) went on pilgrimages to Jerusalem and Vienne (to the shrine of St. Anthony the Abbot); his son Ercole (1471–1505) was a patron of church music. Moreover, even if the ruling dynasties of Renaissance Italy produced few saints, they could contribute men and women of conspicuous piety, a few of whom—Paolo Trinci (d. 1391) and Battista da Varano (d. 1524) for example—were later beatified. Galeotto Roberto Malatesta of Rimini had such a reputation for strict religious observance that a localized cult flourished briefly after his death in 1431. Of course, the display of piety could often be an expression of remorse or guilt. In 1446 Filippo Maria Visconti was apparently so troubled by the tax burden he had imposed on his subjects that he turned to a panel of theologians for advice. Bona of Savoy, the widow of Galeazzo Maria Sforza, confessed her husband's sins to the pope. The experience of military defeat and political rejection drove Alfonso II of Naples to a Sicilian monastery in 1494.

Acts of contrition and the support of the church by rulers who at the same time exploited its offices and its wealth can be traced throughout medieval Europe, raising doubts as to how far the political behavior of these princes can be regarded as specifically "Renaissance." As part of his propaganda campaign against Sigismondo Malatesta, Pius II accused the lord of Rimini of paganism and idolatry, and he devised for him an inverted canonization to ensure his enemy a place in hell (1461). But behind such invective there is little to suggest that the morality of the Renaissance prince, his attitudes toward religion, or his use of violence as a means to win and retain power were any different from that of his medieval predecessors in the rest of Europe. After all, the cult of St. Thomas of Canterbury, martyred by agents of Henry II of England (1170), was quite strong in Italy, and the vendetta between the houses of Plantagenet and de Montfort, leading to the murder of

Henry of Almain, son of Richard, earl of Cornwall and king of the Romans, by his cousin Guy de Montfort in the church of San Silvestro at Viterbo (1271), was preserved for the edification of later generations in Dante's *Divine Comedy* (*Inferno*, XII, 119–20). No Renaissance prince committed an act of sacrilege to equal that perpetrated by the agents of Philip IV against Boniface VIII at Anagni in 1303 (*Purgatorio*, XX, 86–87; *Paradiso*, XXX, 148).

THE SEARCH FOR LEGITIMACY

That the close association between violence and tyranny was a commonplace can be seen not only from the political treatises of the period but also in the formulas of government. For example, when the papacy granted fiefs or vicariates to its greater subjects, the award normally included standard clauses to the effect that the lord was expected to rule well, protecting his subjects and respecting their liberties and property, and similar exhortations were handed down by the *signori* themselves to the magistrates they appointed or approved.

Such evidence makes it unlikely that the story of Cabrino Fondulo's "revolutionary" thoughts or regrets should be taken too literally, let alone regarded as typical. In fact, the lord of Cremona benefited from precisely the hierarchical order he is alleged to have wished to destroy. In 1413 Sigismund, king of the Romans, made him imperial vicar in Cremona and confirmed titles already bestowed on him by the Visconti (the county of Soncino and the marquisate of Castellone). In March 1412, John XXIII promoted Costantino Fondulo to the bishopric of Cremona. These grants, the fact that Sigismund and his court stayed in Cremona for over a month, and the opinion of some sources that both pope and emperor were lavishly entertained argue that Cabrino saw the occasion as an opportunity to be exploited and enjoyed rather than squandered.

In this respect the lord of Cremona was not exceptional. It is true that some dynasties achieved an ascendancy which was never formally sanctioned or expressed in any explicit title. In contemporary political thought, families like the Bentivoglio of Bologna or the Baglioni of Perugia—or even the Medici of Florence before their acquisition of a feudal title (1532)—belonged to a category of "veiled tyrants," and modern research has tended to conclude that in economic and political terms such families shared power and are better described as *primi inter pares* than as princes.

But among those rulers whose ascendancy was less ambiguous, it is hard to find clear instances of Renaissance princes reacting against the traditional, medieval hierarchy. Filippo Maria Visconti mystified contemporaries by pointedly absenting himself from Sigismund's coronation with the iron crown of Lombardy in Milan (1431), a theatrical occasion which could possibly have enhanced his prestige, but it is more likely that Filippo Maria was fearful rather than defiant, and on other occasions he was anxious for Sigismund's support and his recognition of the Visconti duchy. That Francesco Sforza had himself acclaimed as duke by the people of Milan (1450)—a procedure which both he and his sons knew to be unorthodox, since they continued to try to acquire imperial investiture until 1493, when Lodovico "Il Moro" obtained the title from Maximilian for four hundred thousand ducats—shows a respect for rather than a disregard of tradition. In 1461 Francesco rejected the offer of a French peerage in exchange for acknowledging French rather than imperial overlordship.

But perhaps the most famous rejection of the medieval concept of authority in the period was Lorenzo Valla's demolition of the Donation of Constantine (1440), a document which was used by the papacy to justify its secular dominion over the states of the church and its feudal overlordship over the Kingdom of Naples and the islands of Sicily, Sardinia, and Corsica. Valla did not write in a spirit of pure historical and philological inquiry, as historians of humanism tend to suggest, but to please his patron, Alfonso V of Aragon, whose titles to Naples and the island kingdoms were compromised by claims to papal supremacy; once the papacy and the king had come to terms (1443), Valla's scholarship was forgotten by the politicians.

Indeed, so acknowledged was the traditional order in Renaissance Italy that it is more appropriate to approach the subject in a positive light. Throughout the period unabated curiosity and interest were shown in the royal and princely houses of Europe and in news connected with their courts—an interest that recent research has shown to have been as lively in republics as in other types of regimes, and that probably intensified as the affairs of Italy became more enmeshed with those of the rest of Europe. Sometimes this reflected military and political concerns, as, for example, in the various phases of the contest for the throne of Naples between the houses of Anjou-Durazzo, Anjou-Provence, and Aragon-Trastamara. On other occasions, an interest is shown in more distant events, such as the astounding victories of Henry V of England and the humiliation of the French kingdom, followed by the premature death of the king, the succession of the infant Henry VI, and the achievements of Joan of Arc. Lastly, royal visitors to the peninsula could create a stir, as demonstrated by the progress of the king of Denmark in 1474.

Closely related was the pride taken by Italian rulers in the honors and privileges they received from royal and princely hands. For example, the imperial registers that cover Sigismund's expeditions to Italy as king of the Romans and emperor are full of the favors he bestowed or sold: knighthood, membership in the household, feudal titles, the right to bear the imperial coats of arms. A conspicuous beneficiary was Amedeo VIII of Savoy, who was promoted from count to duke (1416). Another was Gianfrancesco Gonzaga, who was made marquis of Mantua in 1433.

Earlier Gianfrancesco had been granted the right to wear and bestow the English royal livery, a privilege confirmed by Henry VI in 1436. The portrait of Federigo da Montefeltro by Justus of Ghent and Pedro Berruguete shows the duke of Urbino wearing the order of the Ermine (from Ferrante of Naples) and the order of the Garter (from Edward IV of England). In a clumsy attempt to rival the latter honor, the da Varano lords of Camerino claimed that an ancestor had received the Garter as early as 1285, long before that order of chivalry had been founded. Lastly, Italian rulers were proud of their right to display imperial, royal, or princely emblems in their coats of arms: the Bentivoglio of Bologna were proud of their right to quarter their shield with the imperial eagle, a privilege granted in 1460.

Such evidence explains why it should come as no surprise that tastes closely associated with European court culture but once considered to be "medieval" or "foreign" in the context of Renaissance Italy were in fact so strongly represented there. Evidence of these tastes ranges from the illustrated Books of Hours and romances in the Visconti and Este libraries to the frescoes of the Labors of the Months commissioned by the prince-bishop of Trent (ca. 1400), Pisanello's Arthurian scenes for the Gonzaga palace in Mantua (ca. 1440), or the historical, mythological, and chivalric themes in the decoration of the Trinci palace at Foligno or the da Varano palace àt Camerino. Nor is it surprising that Italian rulers sought to establish close connections with the royal and princely houses of Italy and Europe. For example, the Este sent their children to be educated at the Aragonese court of Naples and established a number of marriage alliances with a dynasty that had greatly enhanced the role and influence of the southern monarchy in Italian affairs.

Of course, their enemies mocked or criticized dynasties with royal blood in their veins associating themselves with parvenu lords. The Florentine chronicler Matteo Villani belittled the marriage of Isabelle de Valois, countess of Vertus and daughter of John II of France, to Giangaleazzo Visconti in 1360: "What can be more extraordinary than to see princes of ancient and illustrious lineage bowing to the service of tyrants?" Wenceslas's sale of the ducal title to Giangaleazzo in 1395 contributed to his deposition as emperor in 1400. Cesare Borgia's acquisition of the duchy of Valentinois (1498) and his subsequent marriage to the sister of the king of Navarre (1499) did not silence sneering at the French court. But mockery of this kind only underlines the value of such marriages for the ruling families of Renaissance Italy. The Visconti family tree, for example, reveals a certain number of connections (authentic or presumed) with the royal or princely houses of Cyprus and Sicily and with the kings of France and England. Tradition has it that Beatrice "Tenda" was the daughter of Pietro II Balbo, count of Tenda in Piedmont, and hence a descendant of the Byzantine imperial Lascaris line. If this had indeed been the case, it is obvious that Filippo Maria Visconti could not have gotten rid of her so easily.

In constitutional terms, respect for the hierarchical order can be recognized from the fact that Renaissance princes disregarded the principles of popular sovereignty, totally superficial gestures aside. Popular enthusiasm and acclaim were accepted ingredients at moments of accession and coronation, but the idea of election had virtually disappeared. This applies to the ecclesiastical and secular principalities of the north (e.g., the prince-bishopric of Trent and the house of Savoy), the monarchies of the south and the islands, and the papacy alike.

The political and juridical situation was not the same in those areas of the peninsula where the legal basis of authority was more ambiguous, among the lordships of the Papal States and the Kingdom of Italy. There it was still considered important to maintain more of the semblance of acceptance on the part of the communes concerned. This can be seen particularly clearly in the case of the Sforza accession to the duchy of Milan. Despite his military ascendance, Francesco considered it valuable to preserve the idea that communities surrendered to him on terms, freely, and he stage-managed his acclamation as duke of Milan to compensate for the weakness of his hereditary claim. The same ideas can be seen at work in the Appiano lordship of Piombino: when the direct male line of succession failed in 1451, the commune was accorded a role in assigning the succession to Emanuele. Even Cesare Borgia, after his conquest of the Romagna in 1499, did not dispense with the acceptance of his rule by the province's communes.

In most of such cases, however, it is clear that genuine initiative rarely if ever rested with the subject population. The award of the title of standard-bearer of justice for life made to Giovanni II Bentivoglio was less a product of communal decision-making on the part of Bologna and more a consequence of the influence and protection of allied foreign powers. Generally, communal acceptance and titles were valued for propaganda purposes or because such a demonstration of "free will" bound subjects more completely to their incoming lord. It is also clear that even where some form of popular participation continued, the princes of Renaissance Italy preferred to base their titles to govern on other grounds.

The most obvious and traditional basis among the secular states of Italy, as elsewhere, was hereditary right, whose strong appeal can be gauged from the way ruling dynasties stressed (and fabricated) their ancient origins and the achievements of their ancestors. Continuity was often underlined by the use of a relatively restricted number of Christian names—Jacopo with the Appiano and Ugolino and Corrado with the Trinci, for example. Dynastic propaganda was a prominent aspect of the court culture of Italy, as it was of medieval and Renaissance Europe as a whole. In the late fifteenth century Giulio Cesare da Varano had family portraits added to the decorative scheme of his palace in Camerino. The belief in the hereditary principle could be given more practical expression when rulers associated their successors with them in government and tried to provide for the succession in their wills. Leonello d'Este had had a growing role in government for about ten years before the death of Niccolò III (1441); Rodolfo III da Varano made several attempts to settle the succession among his sons before his death in 1424.

The princes of Renaissance Italy also tried to acquire hereditary titles to govern from their overlords. Both in the Papal States and in imperial territory, rulers tried to broaden the grant of vicariates to provide for their succession. They were also prepared to expend a great deal of political, diplomatic, and financial effort in acquiring feudal titles that had a hereditary character. The most famous example of this in imperial territory (the Kingdom of Italy) is Giangaleazzo, who acquired the title of duke in 1395. Other dynasties followed suit, however: the Gonzaga were made marquises in 1433 and the Este dukes of Modena in 1452. A similar ambition can be detected among the vicars of the Papal States: the ducal title was acquired by the Este for Ferrara (1471), by the Montefeltro for Urbino (1474), and by the da Varano for Camerino (1515).

It would of course be a mistake to distort the significance of the search for titles and juridical legitimacy. Francesco Sforza bludgeoned the title of marquis out of Eugenius IV in 1434 to dignify his conquests in the March of Ancona, but it did little to reinforce his rule in practical military or political terms. As we shall see, the power of the Renaissance prince did not depend on his legitimacy as a ruler, and the achievement of hereditary succession and the award of a title did not guarantee political security from internal and external enemies.

Indeed, such "achievements" could prove a source of weakness. French claims to the Visconti succession threatened the Sforza even before the Italian Wars, and the same was even more true of the Kingdom of Naples, where the claims of the house of Anjou and acknowledged papal supremacy encouraged the baronage of the *Regno* to resist the Aragonese crown. The aggressive dynasticism practiced by many of the Renaissance popes left their kin exposed to their enemies on the death of their papal patron: Francesco Maria della Rovere, nephew of Julius II and duke of Urbino, was deprived of his principality in 1516 by the Medici Leo X in favor of Leo's own nephew Lorenzo, though Francesco Maria was able to return on Leo's death in 1521.

Finally, the acknowledgment of papal or imperial sovereignty explicit in the search for and acceptance of titles could expose their holders to such superior authority, as when Alexander VI attacked the lords of the Papal States for treason and the failure to make the obligatory census payments. For all their diplomatic efforts and the splendor of their court, the Sforza were no more able to acquire the prestige and security of a sovereign, royal, title than the dukes of Burgundy.

However, examples of this kind serve only to show that such titles were not empty of all significance, and that truly sovereign power eluded most of the princes of Italy. This conclusion has long been recognized for the Papal States in the later fifteenth century, a period when historians have seen successive popes deliberately extending and consolidating their authority in the provinces as well as in Rome itself, but even in the previous period, dominated by the Great Schism and conciliarism, the support and sanction of the papacy was prized, if the initiative more often rested with the pope's subjects.

Historians have tended to dismiss the notion of imperial authority in the north, seeing it as an anachronism that weakened and dissipated imperial power north of the Alps and as little more than a distraction in northern Italy. But this position ignores not only the efforts made to obtain imperial honors and titles and the eagerness with which families like the Gonzaga and the Este attended imperial progresses; it also disregards the fact that in a confused and fluid political situation, the emperors could still wield political and military influence. Sigismund's support of claimants to the della Scala inheritance in Verona and of Lodovico of Tek as patriarch of Aquileia threatened the expansion of the Venetian republic on the Italian mainland, and the imperial challenge to Venice became all the greater once the succession had passed to the Habsburgs.

ASPECTS OF GOVERNMENT

The award of honors and titles meant more than added prestige: it could confer on the recipient a means of patronage and strengthen his authority. Gianfrancesco Gonzaga's right to the English royal livery allowed him to invest up to fifty of his courtiers with the privilege. The title of count palatine liberally distributed by the emperors entitled the holder to legitimize bastards and create notaries. The award of feudal titles like that of marquis or duke increased the power of the ruler to make grants and enfeoffments, to initiate *quo warranto*-style enquiries into the rights held or claimed by his subjects, to adjudicate in disputes, and to invest favored or important subjects with lesser feudal titles. Filippo Maria Visconti's ducal title encouraged him to investigate the claims to jurisdiction and territory advanced by families like the Pallavicini and the Anguissola, leading to the disappropriation of the first (1428) and the advancement of the second (1438). In 1428 Sigismund ordered the great feudal families of the Malaspina, Fieschi, and Campofregoso to respect the authority of his representative, Filippo Maria Visconti.

The authority of the prince is a topic that has long interested historians, who detect in the Renaissance a period of rapid and radical transformation in the nature of the state leading to a marked increase in the effective authority of the ruler. For example, in military terms, the change is seen in the development of professional, permanent armies of increasing size. To support such commitments, governments are seen to have increased the burden of taxation and to have adopted mercantilist policies to boost the economy and deprive their enemies of resources. The Renaissance prince is also understood to have challenged the "medieval" liberties enjoyed by the nobility, the church, and the guilds and to have articulated his own aims and imposed his own authority through a larger, more professional bureaucracy.

This interpretation owes much in its origins to Burckhardt, who described the Italian state of the fifteenth and sixteenth centuries as "the outcome of reflection and calculation, the State as a work of art." In Burckhardt's view, Renaissance rulers, like contemporary artists and men of letters, were freed from the constraints imposed on them by the medieval world. Rulers became more dedicated in the pursuit of ends; their authority became less inhibited and more centralized; they displayed a growing mastery of the techniques and resources of government; they became more alert to the value of political propaganda and court and public ceremonial.

Doubts as to the validity of this thesis are almost immediately suggested by Burckhardt's treatment of the lordships of Renaissance Italy, which tends to be anecdotal and more concerned with personalities than policies. More recent research appears to have confirmed at least some of Burckhardt's conclusions, however—though as in the Swiss historian's work, such developments in the state are not seen as unique to princely regimes but as characteristic of republican governments as well. In the fifteenth century, for example, rulers can be found introducing legislation, instituting magistracies, and encouraging the efforts of their subjects to combat the threats posed by famine and disease. Alfonso V supported the construction of a large central hospital in Palermo in 1429, as did Francesco Sforza in Milan in 1456.

Again, rulers can be found trying to establish greater control over the distribution of ecclesiastical benefices in their territories. Filippo Maria Visconti threatened to support the Council of Basel to achieve greater cooperation from the papacy, and Nicholas V granted Francesco Sforza a bull in 1450 to allow him to present his candidates for office. The origins of mercantilism can be traced in efforts to strengthen the local economy. The Sforza, for example, encouraged the renowned arms industry of Milan, the construction of canals, and the introduction of the mulberry.

On the other hand, many recent studies would modify, if not reject entirely, the views of Burckhardt and his followers in respect to the allegedly changing nature of the state in the Renaissance. The means taken to control famine and disease can be shown to have been not only fundamentally unsound (in matters of hygiene and medicine, for example) but also to have been inconsistently applied: if the Renaissance papacy was anxious to encourage food production and imports in the area of Rome, it was also ready to issue export licenses.

Similar points can be made in the area of political economy. Repeated legislation—for example, to protect the woolen industry of Milan from foreign competition—is evidence of failure rather than planning. Much of the documentation cited to illustrate the economic policies of a regime on closer examination can be revealed to be the product of petitions rather than policy, and hence an expression of the opportunism of a subject rather than the initiative of a ruler. In ecclesiastical matters none of the princely regimes of Renaissance Italy established concordats with the papacy that allowed them to control the church within their frontiers. Relatively few of the ruling dynasties of the Papal States were allowed to establish a secure hegemony over the local church, and the bull of 1450 addressed to Francesco Sforza did not allow him uncontested control of the benefices within his dominions.

Again, the vigorous survival of privilege can be detected at all levels of society. In 1453 Francesco Sforza was told that the variety and extent of immunities claimed by the nobility of Piacenza were such that his own authority was only nominal. Moreover, perhaps most obviously in the case of fifteenth-century Italy, some regimes—like that of Cabrino Fondulo—were so short-lived and turbulent as to qualify for discussion in terms of war, politics, and diplomacy rather than of government and administration. Lastly, not only did virtually no Italian regime enjoy full jurisdictional sovereignty in the Renaissance, but many were also dependent on the patronage and protection of other powers. In the fifteenth century, the Appiano lords of Piombino existed as the clients, the *accomodati*, of Genoa, Florence, or Naples.

We need now to examine some key areas of government, public administration, and the rule of the court, taking illustrations from th. permanent and prominent Italian regimes.

TAXATION

The subject of public finance is central to the study of the Renaissance state, but if the demand for revenue grew in the period—largely due to escalating military budgets—the principal sources of revenue available to governments had been established earlier in the Middle Ages. Some derived from ancient rights claimed by the state. For example, Jewish communities were subject to special taxation. The property of rebels was liable to confiscation. The sale of salt was generally regarded as a state monopoly, and other regalian rights were more specific to particular states. The crown of Naples, like that of Castile, claimed the right to license the massive transhumant traffic in cattle and sheep. The papacy tried to enforce a monopoly of alum production from the mines at Tolfa discovered in 1462.

The levy of indirect taxation was more common and more central to public finance, but its value tended to decline just when governments needed it most—in times of war, plague, and famine. Hence rulers raised revenue by methods once regarded as "extraordinary" but well established by the Renaissance. Direct taxation was imposed by the regimes of northern and central Italy, while the feudal principality of Piedmont-Savoy and the kingdoms of Naples, Sicily, and Sardinia followed the procedure of obtaining consent through parliament. Requests for taxation could be justified before parliamentary assemblies in terms of traditional feudal aids, though with increasing frequency the defense of the realm was cited as a cause. For example, in 1500 the parliament of Sardinia voted Ferdinand a *donativo* for three years and an aid, ostensibly to cover the costs of the marriage of his daughter.

The range of financial resources open to governments and the surviving documentation on its assessment and collection might suggest that the history of public finance confirms the picture of the growing authority of the Renaissance prince. But high levels of taxation did not necessarily mean strong government: after the murder of Galeazzo Maria Sforza (1476) levels of taxation were reduced and the authority of his brother Lodovico "Il Moro" was weakened by rumors that the subjects of the king of France paid taxation only if they had consented to do so.

A closer scrutiny of the evidence reveals the difficulties facing a prince when it came to maintaining and exploiting the sources of revenue in theory available to him. When the Aragonese crown began the conquest (or reconquest) of Sicily, Sardinia, and Naples, the rights and revenues of the crown had been largely usurped. More generally, contraband undermined state monopolies (like the sale of salt), and the revenue from indirect taxation and the widespread practice of tax farming generally short-changed the state.

The massive amount of paper work generated by tax assessment and collection nowhere included regular budgets or financial reviews, but everywhere it reveals the difficulties encountered by the state. Reports presented to Charles V in 1517 and 1520 on the finances of Naples made clear the erosion of royal revenues. More generally and obviously, subjects were reluctant to pay taxes and quick to cite immunities or their own poverty as justification for not doing so. Requests for taxation presented to the parliaments of Piedmont-Savoy and the Aragonese kingdoms met with procrastination and haggling over petitions, and in 1522 Sicilian opponents of Charles V's tax demands attended the parliament at Messina armed.

It is hardly surprising, therefore, that the princes of Renaissance Italy made frequent recourse to expedients to raise desperately needed ready cash. The house of Savoy, the Sforza, and the crown of Naples were all forced to pawn jewelry; Alfonso V pawned his crown jewels in 1443, the year following his triumphant entry to the capital. Offices, titles, privileges, and sources of revenue themselves were often the price to be paid for contracting expensive loans: in 1461, Louis of Savoy settled his debts with his own chancellor in this way. By 1525 papal finances were largely controlled by Tuscan and Roman bankers.

ADMINISTRATION AND THE COURT

Important changes have also been detected in state bureaucracy and the court. For example, not only do the records of government survive in greater abundance for the Renaissance period, but their range of business appears to have expanded and their degree of specialization to have increased. Related phenomena are a multiplication of public offices and a growth in the degree of professionalism, long detected in the conduct of diplomacy and more recently in military administration.

Men with particular expertise were appointed to positions in government. In 1453 the duke of Savoy chose as one of his secretaries a man familiar with the institutions and administrative practices of other Italian states. A drive for efficiency and integrity among chancery and treasury officials is also apparent: the great Sforza chancellor, Cicco Simonetta, initiated reforms of his office and was at pains to make sure, for example, that the correct forms were observed in addressing foreign governments. A sign of increasing *esprit de corps* in the Milanese context is the account of Sforza administration written by the humanist Tristano Calco, while the chanceries of most Italian states put an increased emphasis on training, particularly to ensure that their formal correspondence could be expressed in a fashionable Latin style. This helps to account for the increasing appointment of humanists by regimes ranging from the da Carrara *signoria* of Padua to the crown of Naples.

Lastly, although the court is hard to define precisely as an institution, society, or event, it is generally considered to reflect the new authority and wider ambitions of the Renaissance prince. The urban palaces and suburban and rural villas built by dynasties like the da Varano, the Este, and the Montefeltro appear to have had more than a practical or social function—they served as a flattering mirror for the prince and as a means of propaganda. Not that the prince's message was confined within his palace walls. By tradition and by design, court ceremonial was often extremely public. Alfonso V commissioned banners proclaiming in heraldic terms his claims to the Neapolitan throne; in 1442 he entered Naples on a triumphant chariot, accompanied by the emblems of his many kingdoms and by processional floats celebrating such appropriate virtues as justice, the event being commemorated in a Renaissance-style triumphal arch placed around the entrance to the Castel Nuovo.

Neither the efficiency and competence of the Renaissance state nor the prince's control of his court or over propaganda should be exaggerated, however. Some regimes—most notably the house of Savoy—remained itinerant and lacked a settled base or court. Government archives have a miscellaneous character that, when taken in conjunction with a proliferation of public offices, suggests a lack of specialization and direction. Furthermore, the appreciation of the value of the written record was not a preserve of central government alone, and documents can reveal the difficulties faced by the prince rather than the deference of his subjects. For example, the statutes of guilds and subject communities, although issued under the prince's name, tend to reflect tradition and self-interest rather than the will of the ruler.

The proliferation of public appointments common to all princely regimes often reflects administrative confusion and a desire on the part of the ruler to reward his followers and supporters and to raise money or extend credit. Alfonso V's use of public office to reward his Spanish followers caused resentment, as the king himself realized, though not from would-be reforming champions of the Renaissance state but from his slighted Neapolitan and Sicilian subjects. Attempts at reform to counter abuses tended to be infrequent, unsustained, and ineffective: in 1455 and 1456 Alfonso was faced with petitions for a general pardon when he tried to curb corruption within the royal administration.

Lastly, much of what historians like to call propaganda was too personal or arcane to qualify properly for that description, a point that applies with particular force to some typically "Renaissance" forms. For example, the medal, clearly inspired by classical models and often expressing the ruler's aspirations as well as his likeness, was not intended for mass circulation but for the favored few, and many of the *imprese* adopted by Renaissance rulers were deliberately obscure or ambiguous and designed to be appreciated only by the initiated.

The court was far from being a clear statement of the ruler's will. Princes and their advisors often stressed the need to be generous to friends and supporters: *magnanimitas* was a traditional virtue expected of the ruler, as Francesco Sforza recalled (perhaps with regret) when he defended his wish to allocate the benefices in his dominions by citing the obligation to reward his friends and supporters. Treatises on the court could often underline this notion, explicitly and implicitly, as they flattered or idealized the ruler himself—often, of course, the dedicatee of the work. One good example is the early fifteenth-century *De Institutione Regiminis Dignitatum* addressed by the itinerant humanist Giovanni Tinto Vicini to the lord of Fabriano, Battistachiavello Chiavelli.

Such works could also conform to the medieval tradition in another sense, castigating or mocking the self-interest and intrigues of the courtier as he fed off a ruler's generosity or exploited his ignorance or good nature. This applies to the treatises that Giovanni Conversini of Ravenna (1343–1408) based on his own experiences at the da Carrara court. It can also be detected in the observations on the court contributed by two more obviously "Renaissance" figures, Leon Battista Alberti (1404–72) and Aeneas Sylvius Piccolomini (1405–64), both of whom combined personal experience with a reading of the works of John of Salisbury (ca. 1115–80). A report on the da Varano court of Camerino written in 1502–3 represents it as having been a source of food, work, gossip, entertainment, warmth, and sport for the lord's subjects rather than as a reverential theater for the proudly named *signore*, Giulio Cesare da Varano.

CONCLUSION

The report of 1502–3 was addressed to Alexander VI, on whose authority the da Varano had been ousted from Camerino in 1502. Almost as soon as the pope had died, the dynasty was restored, but after 1545 the small principality based in Camerino was finally absorbed into the Papal States. The decline in the number of autonomous states was a clear trend in the history of Renaissance principalities, and one that gave a marked sense of urgency and topicality to the historical and political writings of contemporaries like Machiavelli and Guicciardini. This does not mean that all the smaller principalities disappeared—the Este at Ferrara and the Gonzaga at Mantua survived until 1598 and 1708, respectively—but increasingly the political map of Italy and of Europe became dominated by the larger monarchies, reducing their smaller neighbors like the Appiano of Piombino or the Pio of Carpi to increasingly obvious client status.

That this had not occurred earlier was due in large measure to the internal divisions and foreign threats that the larger European states had experienced in the fifteenth century, and this may be one of the reasons the principalities of fifteenth-century Italy have acquired the reputation of being precocious examples of state-building and princely power. But a principal aim of this essay has been to argue that historians have exaggerated the degree of change experienced by this Italian "model." Efforts were made to maximize economic and fiscal resources. Armies were becoming larger, more permanent, and more professional. The size of bureaucracies increased and their actions were more fully documented. The cultural interests of the Renaissance colored court life and influenced the nature of the patronage and propaganda encouraged by the prince.

Appearances can be deceptive, though. For example, the archives of Renaissance governments are more likely to have survived than those of earlier periods and they are, thanks to the advent of printing and the greater use of the vernacular, more accessible to the modern historian. However, this is not evidence for a sudden or fundamental change in ideas about the state in particular or in a general "mentality," and the records of government are not per se evidence for growing authority on the part of the prince or greater efficiency on the part of his servants. Historians (and not only those of the Renaissance prince) have often been reluctant to recognize that much of their archival evidence was generated "from below" or shows the state on the defensive, struggling to deal with its stubborn, litigious, and opportunistic subjects.

Moreover, historians are also too prone to be the "king's friends," as K. B. McFarlane expressed it in the context of late medieval England. Such an allegiance—and the interpretation of the state in terms of the ruler—tends to exaggerate the efficiency and accept the aims of central government. Relatively neglected, on the other hand, are the "provincial" archives, the record of onlookers at the court spectacle and of such alleged representatives of reaction as the "feudal nobility."

Lastly, the warning issued by Charles Homer Haskins, in the context of the Norman and Hohenstaufen kingdom of Sicily, is often ignored: It is not the business of historians to award prizes for being "modern." Disregarding this advice can lead to a readiness to exaggerate or distort the nature of change. For example, as argued above in the context of the search for legitimacy, the change from "signoria" to "principate" often detected in Renaissance Italy was a move towards a more traditional, "medieval," understanding of government, although none of the new princes of northern and central Italy ever acquired the sacred authority claimed by such monarchies as the crowns of Naples and France and enjoyed by the papacy. Again, the reputation of Machiavelli's *Prince* is such that its novelty can be exaggerated and the extensive earlier literature on the subject can be ignored. As a consequence, the conservative, traditional nature of much of the political thinking of the Renaissance period is underestimated. Ambiguity—at least to modern eyes—continued to surround the concept of the state, which could be understood as both a geopolitical expression and a personal attribute of the ruler himself.

A good instance of the proprietary view of the state is provided by Ferrante of Naples, who used his authority as king to support speculation on the markets for grain, oil, and wool. His northern contemporary, Henry VII of England, shared Ferrante's reputation for astute rapacity. This point of similarity suggests that if the evidence for the "Renaissance" prince has been exaggerated in the case of Italy, the same might well be true for the rest of Europe. All the historiographical points raised above in the Italian context could be applied more widely. Furthermore, to many contemporary observers (Machiavelli and Castiglione, for example) and to later generations, the early sixteenth century was a period of political and military catastrophe for Italy, a period when the Renaissance came to an end, at least in certain respects.

This is not the case with France, England, Spain, or the Habsburg empire as a whole. Historians of these monarchies have seen the period traditionally as one of recovery and expansion of the authority and the frontiers (internal and external) of the state. The courts created and the propaganda produced by the new generation of rulers—monarchs like Isabella of Castile or Henry VIII of England—have been assiduously, even obsequiously, studied, and the idea that decisive changes in the direction of modernity took place has in some instances (certainly in the case of Britain) long been built into all levels of the educational program.

If the authority of the prince in the relatively small and homogeneous states of fifteenth-century Italy can be shown to have been more personal, circumscribed, variable, and compromised than Burckhardt suggested, have not historians perhaps exaggerated the novelty and strength of the "new monarchies" of sixteenth-century Europe?

BIBLIOGRAPHY

GENERAL

The Cambridge Medieval History. Vol. 8, *The Close of the Middle Ages*. Cambridge: Cambridge University Press; New York: Macmillan, 1936.

The New Cambridge Modern History. Vol. 1, *The Renaissance, 1493–1520*. Cambridge: Cambridge University Press, 1961.

Guenée, Bernard. *States and Rulers in Later Medieval Europe*, trans. Juliet Vale. Oxford and New York: Blackwell, 1985.

Hale, John H. *Renaissance Europe: Individual and Society, 1480–1520*. London: Collins, 1971; New York: Harper & Row, 1972.

Hay, Denys. *Europe in the Fourteenth and Fifteenth Centuries*. London: Longman, 1966.

Koenigsberger, H. G. and George L. Mosse. *Europe in the Sixteenth Century*. London: Longman; New York: Holt, Rinehart & Winston, 1968.

Mattingly, Garrett. *Renaissance Diplomacy*. London: Cape; Boston: Houghton Mifflin, 1955; Baltimore: Penguin Books, 1964; New York: Russell & Russell, 1970.

Shennan, J. H. *The Origins of the Modern European State, 1450–1725*. London: Hutchinson, 1974.

ITALY

Burckhardt, Jacob. *The Civilization of the Renaissance in Italy*. 2 vols. New York: Harper Torchbooks, 1958.

Galasso, Giuseppe, gen. ed. *Storia d'Italia*. Turin: UTET, 1976–. Vol. 4, Ovidio Capitani et al., *Comuni e signorie: istituzioni, società e lotte per l'egemonia* (1981); vol. 7, pts. 1, 2, Giorgio Gracco, Girolamo Arnaldi et al., *Comuni e signorie nell' Italia nordorientale e centrale* (1987); vol. 14, Mario Caravale and Alberto Caracciolo, *Lo stato pontificio da Martino V a Pio IX* (1978).

Hay, Denys and John Law. *Italy in the Age of the Renaissance, 1380–1530*. London and New York: Longman, 1989.

Law, John E. *The Lords of Renaissance Italy*. London: The Historical Association, 1981.

Martines, Laura. *Power and Imagination: City States in Renaissance Italy*. New York: Alfred Knopf, 1979; Random House, Vintage Books, 1980.

Valeri, Nino, ed. *Storia d'Italia*. 2d ed. rev. 5 vols. Turin: Union tipografico-editrice torinese, 1965. Vols. 1 and 2.

Pieri, Piero. *Il Rinascimento e la crisi militare italiana*. Turin: G. Einaudi, 1952; 2d ed. 1970.

T W O
The Condottiere
Michael Mallett

*A*NY image of the Renaissance is one of brilliant flashes and contrasting shadows, and about no group of Renaissance personalities is this more true than about the military captains of Italy. This is the way in which they are presented to us by their contemporaries.

The most articulate Italians of the fourteenth and fifteenth centuries were the humanists; they inherited from classical writing an admiration for military activity conducted in the interests of the community at large, an enthusiasm for heroes and deeds of battle, but an intense dislike of mercenaries. The mercenaries who were condemned by Aristotle and Plato and deplored by Vegetius were foreign soldiers imported by tyrants or necessitated by the decline of a civilization no longer able to defend itself. The mercenaries attacked by Petrarch were also largely foreign and non-Italian—the companies of German, Hungarian, French, and English troops common in Italy for much of the fourteenth century. For Petrarch, as for Salutati and Bruni, the gradual disappearance of these ultramontanes and their replacement by Italian captains in the later years of the fourteenth century were grounds for hope that the ancient military virtues would be restored. The rising tide of local civic pride and patriotism that accompanied the emergence of the Italian state system led fifteenth-century humanists to deplore the employment of mercenary captains from beyond the frontiers of the state, whether they were Italians or ultramontanes. The condottieri posed a potential threat to civil liberty, and the use of them deprived the state of the opportunity to develop its natural defenses and its own citizenry.

These ideas were particularly prevalent in Florence, where the city lived in perpetual fear of the activities of the rural nobility and of marauding armies. Elsewhere in Italy, where humanists were frequently the spokesmen of princely governments, there was a greater emphasis on the need for effective, faithful captains regardless of origins and a great worry about the obvious alternative—the arming of the civilian population. The humanists of the courts—Pier Candido Decembrio, Guarino Guarini, Flavio Biondo—

22

produced both panegyrics and denunciations of condottieri, fueled by classical precedents and contemporary political attitudes as well as by observation of the actual behavior of the captains themselves.

Many of these themes were picked up in the early sixteenth century by even more influential writers—Niccolò Machiavelli, Francesco Guicciardini, and Paolo Giovio. By this time the shadow of foreign domination was threatening even the proudest and strongest of the Italian states, and the emphasis was not just on the extent to which entrusting defense to mercenary arms debilitated the citizenry but also on the apparent failure of the mercenaries to fulfill their role at all. With Machiavelli and Guicciardini the denunciation of the condottieri reached a new crescendo as even the heroic deeds and military professionalism reluctantly recognized by Bruni and his contemporaries appeared to have been forgotten in the disgrace of Charles VIII's march on Naples and Louis XII's easy conquest of Milan.

The mercenary captains are either excellent soldiers or they are not: If they are, you cannot trust them because they will always aspire to their own greatness either by oppressing you who are their master, or by oppressing others whom you had no intention of oppressing; However, if the captain is not skillful, he will as a result ruin you. (*The Prince*, 12; trans. Musa, 101)

Machiavelli's biting criticism has been a lasting antidote to the visual impression created by great condottiere monuments like the equestrian statues of Gattamelata and Colleoni. All of them are one-sided images, containing more rhetoric than truth. There is no way that they can be reconciled into some sort of composite image of the condottiere.

But what of the condottieri as "men of the Renaissance"—as representatives of that individualism, that quest for fame and achievement so persuasively argued by Burckhardt and Symonds? Modern historians are less inclined to write in these terms than their nineteenth-century predecessors. They tend to emphasize the extent to which men of the Renaissance were fettered and constrained by the institutions, structures, and circumstances of their time, rather than the ways in which they appear to have broken away from the traditions and preconceptions of the past. While it is true that the Italian Renaissance was represented by a remarkable "cluster" of geniuses in many fields (and this tells us something about the opportunities and stimuli of the period), it is also true that the lives and fortunes of most men and women continued to be dominated by traditional—in some cases new—restraints. This applied as much to condottieri as it did to artists in the *bottega*, to humanists in the chancelleries, or to merchants in the counting houses. The fortunes of a condottiere depended more on birth, on membership in a military clan, on the vagaries of state service, and on the oscillations of the Mediterranean economy than they did on personal qualities or military expertise. Advancement was charted more by an additional ten lances in the contract or an extra half-florin a month per lance in pay than by the conquest of cities and the acquisition of palaces. The condottiere had a degree of control over his own company, but in the last resort his fortune was directed by the capabilities, needs, objectives, and resources of the prince or the state that he served.

War was conducted in Italy by means of contracts, and hence by condottieri, for more than two hundred years. There can be no single image of condottiere warfare—no snapshot or even a series of snapshots of condottieri that will be a satisfactory synthesis of such a time span. What follows can be no more than a personal attempt to resolve these problems.

While we normally associate the condottieri with the fourteenth and fifteenth centuries, the conditions that encouraged the development of mercenary traditions in European warfare are to be found in the thirteenth century. It was then that mercenaries first began to appear in significant numbers in feudal armies and in the armies of the early communes. In northern and central Italy in particular the rapid growth of the economy, of towns, and of urban wealth produced both more to fight for and more with which to fight. Urban rivalries, initially economic but increasingly territorial, led to a situation of permanent tension and small-scale warfare. During the thirteenth century urban communities found it increasingly difficult to recruit a sufficient number of their citizens for aggressive campaigns against neighbors at a time when economic growth continued to foster both other preoccupations and the resources to hire professional troops. The defense of the walls of a city was one thing; prolonged siege and devastation campaigns were quite another. At the same time, population growth, the crusading tradition, and a shift towards primogeniture among the landowning classes of certain parts of Europe were beginning to create a surplus of skilled but frequently unemployed fighting groups. These groups began to drift towards Italy, where the possibilities of employment and of booty seemed most likely.

Initially, a majority of the groups of mercenaries available were non-Italian. The Angevin conquest of southern Italy brought in large numbers of French troops, which were soon available for hire in other parts of Italy. Catalans also were prominent among the early mercenary companies. The arrival of Henry VII and a renewal of imperial ambitions and interest in Italy brought many Germans in the early fourteenth century, while in the 1340s the marriage of Joanna I of Naples to the younger brother of the king of Hungary and the subsequent murder of her Hungarian husband led to the arrival of large contingents of Hungarian troops. Finally, the 1360s saw the appearance of organized English and French companies, unemployed after the peace of Bretigny brought a temporary lull in the Hundred Years War.

At first these foreign companies were relatively small. The first *condotte* that survive date from the 1260s and 1270s, and the captains who signed them were soon known as condottieri. There was inevitably a tendency for these foreign mercenaries to operate as companies rather than sell their services as individuals: it was natural both for the leaders to collect as many followers as possible and for the employing governments to seek to provide for their military needs with as few contracts as possible. By the 1320s, some very large companies were operating in Italy, and the sheer professionalism and experience of these groups made it increasingly difficult for states to attempt to conduct wars without resort to their services. To some extent these companies developed an *esprit de corps*, along with mechanisms for collective decision-making and distribution of booty, which made them appear more like corporations than the retinues of military captains. Nevertheless, the leader, while often not the sole signatory of the contract of employment for the company, as he became in the fifteenth century, was crucial to the success and reputation of the company, and it is unrealistic to draw too clear a dividing line between an age of companies and an age of condottieri.

It is equally unrealistic to draw such a dividing line between a period in which mercenary warfare in Italy was dominated by foreigners and one in which Italians emerged as the leading condottieri. For a variety of reasons, foreign mercenary companies were readily available in Italy up to the 1370s: they tended to be larger and more experienced than Italian companies, and employment of them often seemed less risky politically. A foreign captain was thought to be less likely to aspire to lordship of an Italian state than an Italian noble. For all these reasons there was a tendency during much of the fourteenth century for foreign captains and foreign companies to hold the center of the stage. But the great foreign companies contained many Italians, and there were Italian condottieri with their own companies alongside the foreign companies. Pandolfo Malatesta, fighting for the Florentines, defeated the Great Company of Corrado Lando in 1359 at Campo delle Mosche, twenty years before the famous victory over the Bretons of Alberico da Barbiano at Marino. What happened in the last three decades of the century was that the ultramontanes gradually began to disappear, leaving Italian captains unchallenged by the end of the century. Therefore, the question is Why did the foreigners depart? rather than What induced Italians to take up arms?

To some extent the answer to this question lies in renewed opportunities for fighting elsewhere in Europe; to some extent it lies in the depressed state of the Italian economy in the second half of the fourteenth century and in a certain reduction in wealth and in economic opportunities. More importantly, the answer to the problem is to be sought in a growth of xenophobic feeling in Italy linked to a strengthening of the Italian states. The rhetoric of Petrarch and the humanists, the letters and preaching of St. Catherine of Siena, the determination of the cardinals to elect an Italian pope in 1378, the willingness of the Italian states even to combine with each other in order to expel the foreign companies—all these came together toward the 1370s to produce a much more difficult situation for the foreign captains. At the same time, skilled Italians were already available. Cardinal Albornoz's solution of settling the Romagna by the installation of local nobles as papal vicars served also to encourage the development of a group of captains whose social and territorial pretensions were already partly satisfied and who possessed the resources to raise effective companies. Here, then, was the background for a gradual transition—a background in which the growing power and determination of the state was playing a part.

The period that followed (from the outbreak of the Schism and the battle of Marino to the battle of Aquila in 1424 and the deaths of Sforza and Braccio) is often seen as the golden age of the condottieri. It was certainly a period of political confusion, partly resulting from the Schism, but more from the process by which Milan, Venice, and Florence, and eventually the Papal State and Naples, strengthened themselves at the expense of their small neighbors. It was a period that offered great opportunities to resourceful captains, but at the same time, as the number of employers was reduced and the captains found themselves serving larger, more powerful, and more unified states, those opportunities became more restricted.

This was by no means a steady political development, however. Giangaleazzo Visconti was able in the last two decades of the century to create an expanding state with the help of a group of prominent captains including Jacopo del Verme, Facino Cane, Alberico da Barbiano, and Pandolfo and Carlo Malatesta. But this state fell apart at his death in 1402, and the condottieri temporarily divided up the inheritance. The work of consolidating the Milanese state had to be done again, and this time it was Carmagnola who played a key role. The success of Giangaleazzo Visconti forced Florence and eventually Venice to become more consistent employers and rewarders of captains. Until Hawkwood's death in 1394 he remained the main defense of Florence, which thereafter found it difficult to establish a stable relationship with a leading condottiere, even while spending huge sums on war. It was often said that condottieri preferred the service of princes, and certainly Florence evinced a distrust and suspicion of its captains that was a permanent barrier to effective military strength in the Renaissance. Venice, however, moved determinedly after 1404 toward the creation of such strength, although initially through the creation of a cadre of long-serving minor condottieri rather than by attracting the attention and fidelity of major figures. This was partly because the focus of attention of the more ambitious captains shifted to central and southern Italy in the first three decades of the fifteenth century.

The divisions in the Papal States and in Naples as a result of the accelerating crises of the Schism and the Angevin-Aragonese rivalry produced the best opportunities for the sort of ambition and independent action that we so often associate with the condottieri. It was in these circumstances that the rivalries between the two schools of condottiere warfare, the Sforzeschi and the Bracceschi, seemed to be more important than those between Rome and Avignon or between Anjou and Aragon. The entry of Martin V into Rome in 1420 as unchallenged pope was undoubtedly the beginning of a new chapter in the history of the Papal State, although initially the new pope was very dependent on his captain general, Braccio da Montone. Similarly, the gradual ascendancy of Alfonso V of Aragon in Naples created a new situation in which the more enterprising condottieri resumed their search for employment elsewhere.

The new opportunities came in the sustained struggle between Milan and Venice (aided for much of the period by Florence) that dominated the period 1425–54. However, the very fact that this was an almost continuous series of wars meant that, while it led to plenty of work for condottieri, it led also to the formal development of permanent armies and continuity of service, which bridled whatever political ambitions the soldiers might have entertained. Some of the great captains of this period were indeed condottiere princes, but they were princes before they were condottieri, and their value as condottieri depended on the resources of their states. Guidantonio Manfredi, Giovanfrancesco Gonzaga, Niccolò d'Este, Sigismondo Malatesta, and Federigo da Montefeltro all filled this role during the prolonged wars of these decades. Until the emergence of the last two in the 1440s, however, the leading commanders were not actually condottiere princes but captain generals authorized by the warring states to raise huge companies of two to three thousand men. Niccolò Piccinino, Carmagnola, Gattamelata, Michele Attendolo, Francesco Sforza, and Bartolomeo Colleoni made their reputations in this way. Francesco Sforza graduated, as it were, by marrying the daughter of Filippo Maria Visconti and becoming, as duke of Milan, the greatest condottiere prince of all. On the whole, however, this period provided the condottieri with work, honor, and even great wealth, but limited scope for political advancement.

After 1454 and the peace of Lodi a period of relative calm descended on Italy. There were wars and rumors of wars during the next forty years, but they flared up over relatively minor issues and tended to be resolved quickly, as much by diplomacy as by military confrontation. The political map of Italy had been largely settled, and the attention of governments was concentrated on organizing the states that had been created. The permanent armies were retained at reduced levels; some of the condottieri fretted, but most settled on their estates or in their capitals. Some of the leaders in the previous wars continued to exercise great political influence: Federigo da Montefeltro's advice was sought by Italian rulers on a wide variety of problems, although he was rarely called upon to fight; Roberto da Sanseverino and Bartolomeo Colleoni continued to be influential in northern Italy for a further twenty years, just as Braccio Baglioni and Napoleone Orsini were in the Papal States and Diomede Carafa was in Naples. By the 1480s a new generation of condottieri was coming forward: men for whom war was an occasional and carefully prepared enterprise rather than a continuous preoccupation; men who increasingly had interests that went beyond the career of arms. Niccolò Orsini, count of Pitigliano; Bartolomeo d'Alviano; Giangiacomo Trivulzio; Gasparo and Giovanfrancesco da Sanseverino; and Prospero and Fabrizio Colonna all appear to have been more rounded personalities than their predecessors. Among the condottiere princes of this and the next generation the change is even more apparent, as their preoccupations as rulers tended to outweigh their occasional activities as soldiers. They, in particular, were moving toward the position in which military contracts meant raising and supporting troops rather than necessarily leading them.

At the heart of the condottiere system was the *condotta*, or contract, that laid down the conditions of service under which the captain and his men served. *Condotte* were not, of course, peculiar to military service: they were used in business and industrial contracting, in the hiring of teachers and university professors, and in the creation of a court or an entourage. Similar military contracts were used on both the French and the English sides in the Hundred Years War. *Condotte* were largely dictated by the employer and not demanded by the employee, and increasingly in fourteenth-century Italy they conformed to carefully laid-down formulas. It is true that the formal wording of the contract could mask secret agreements by which the terms of the contract were abrogated or modified, but it would be absurd to assume that all the hundreds of *condotte* that have survived and the thousands more that have not were no more than token agreements. It is also true that the attention of the historian must focus on the mechanisms devised by states for the enforcement of the terms of the contract in order to judge the effectiveness of the controls imposed upon captains and soldiers. But the fact remains that it is in the breakdowns in the system that the independence of the condottiere lies rather than in the system itself.

The contract specified the nature of the service expected (full pay, half pay, or pay *in aspetto*); the size, equipment, and quality of the company with which the service was to be rendered; the pay scales, additional allowances, and standard retentions that would be enforced; and the length of service expected. It was in this last area that some of the most significant changes took place in contracts over the fourteenth and fifteenth centuries. In the fourteenth century the contract period was geared very specifically to the immediate military circumstances: service was required for a particular campaign and ranged between a month and six months at the most. There was little or no prospect of any extension or renewal of the contract, particularly beyond the normal campaigning season. Condottieri became free agents again at the end of each contract. By the fifteenth century the possibility of renewing a contract was built in specifying a grace period (*rispetto* or *beneplacito*) added to the normal term (*ferma*), thus giving the employer an option period in which he could decide whether to renew the contract or to authorize the condottiere to begin to seek service elsewhere.

The option to retain the service of companies through the winter—and eventually in a situation of permanence—became reflected in longer contract periods. By the mid-fifteenth century most states had moved over to *condotte* of at least a year's initial duration, and most condottieri found themselves expecting permanent service. The renewal of contracts became more of a formality, and the contracts themselves became more flexible and less restrictive. One of the signs of this flexibility was the use of the same contracts for peace or for war service, with different pay rates and different company sizes stipulated in the contract. Thus a condottiere in winter quarters in peacetime could be called out for war, authorized to recruit more troops, and then paid at higher rates, all within the same contract.

The system was equally important in its reverse operation, when a degree of demobilization and reduction of military expenses could be achieved within the contract system and without incurring the risks involved in large-scale demobilization. The problems of the free companies and the pressures imposed on states at the end of wars by condottieri facing disengagement were the main stimuli for the more flexible contract system of the fifteenth century. The condottiere had exchanged a degree of independence for security of employment at quite an early stage, and this must be an important aspect of the context in which we view him.

Theoretically, any soldier who signed a *condotta* for military service was a condottiere, and the term was used to apply to men at arms who contracted to provide five followers as much as to great captains who commanded two thousand men. However, it is the captains of significant bodies of mounted troops to whom we usually refer when we use the title "condottiere." Captains of infantry were hired in the same way but were normally described as constables, not condottieri. However, much of what can be said about condottieri applies to them, even when referring to social prestige.

The great majority of condottieri were of noble birth. The skills, status, and economic base required to raise and lead troops in the late Middle Ages were essentially those of the noble class, and few outside that class were able to succeed in a military career. There were of course exceptions: Muzio Attendolo, known as Sforza, was one of a clan of minor Romagnol landowners who were not noble although they possessed estates and connections that gave them a great advantage in recruiting. Muzio achieved nobility, giving his son, Francesco—often regarded as the embodiment of the prototypical condottiere success story—a good start in his career. Francesco inherited one of the best organized and most feared companies in Italy, as well as the support of a whole clan of Attendolo captains. At the same time, his success in becoming duke of Milan and founding a princely dynasty was exceptional by any standards. Niccolò Piccinino and Erasmo da Narni, known as Gattamelata, were examples of men of no social standing who made their way by skill in arms and by good fortune. They both rose to positions of high command and great prestige, but they were unusually successful. The vast majority of their colleagues bore noble names: Orsini and Colonna, Baglioni and Fortebracci, Malaspina, Sanseverino, and Trivulzio. During the fourteenth century, many had come to dominate cities as signori or papal vicars, and thus owed their achievements as soldiers to both domination of a town and landed wealth. But the Manfredi, Malatesta, Montefeltro, Este, Gonzaga, and Bentivoglio were all successful military families whose noble origins preceded their emergence as fourteenth-century signori.

The fourteenth century (and particularly the later fourteenth century) was a difficult period for the landed nobility. The value of land and of the products of land declined after the Black Death, and the practice of multiple inheritance left the nobility of northern and central Italy with few resources other than the diminishing manpower of their estates. At the same time, the pressures exerted by the expansion of the cities had threatened their prestige and their life-style. These were the men who were tempted to enter the turbulent and, at first, risky world of mercenary warfare in the late fourteenth century. They were mostly men who had a natural following from their estates and a base to which to withdraw between contracts. They had the resources to maintain their companies for short periods when contracted pay—or indeed employment at all—was not forthcoming.

Effective military companies were much more often inherited than created: Piccinino and Gattamelata, although both self-made men in the military sense, owed their companies to Braccio da Montone, in whose service they had risen and whose mantle they divided. A successful marriage was also often an important component of a condottiere's career. Piccinino married the daughter of his first commander; subsequently, after murdering his first wife for adultery, he married a niece of Braccio. Gattamelata married into the Brunoro da Leonessa family, which gained him the lifelong support of that Umbrian noble clan. The marriage and family links between condottieri were often important guides to their allegiances. Also important in assessing the motivation and background of a particular captain was the incidence of political exile in Renaissance Italy. Exiles made good potential recruits to the career of arms, and exile groups were to be found everywhere in the unstable world of Italian politics.

Condottieri, then, were for the most part scions of a landed nobility, but the profession of arms gave them opportunities not only to enrich themselves but also to gain prestige and standing outside the normal hierarchical patterns. While lands and social position could ensure a good start in the career, achievement and success depended on more personal qualities. However, these qualities were not necessarily the obvious ones of bravery and physical strength. In the list of classical military virtues *prudentia* came before *fortitudo*, and in Renaissance assessments of successful military commanders, the qualities of military and political prudence also figured high. Obviously, a record of military success was important for an ambitious commander seeking either new employment or promotion, but the reputation of a condottiere, on which his future really depended, was created as much by his ability to recruit and control good troops and by his political judgment as by his strictly military skills. A Florentine report on the advisability of giving a major *condotta* to Sigismondo Malatesta in the 1450s commented: "It would be of greatest moment to retain Sigismondo at the city's expense for the men he has, for his skill in arms, and for the authority he enjoys with everyone." In fact, Sigismondo did not possess political prudence to the same degree as his contemporary Federigo da Montefeltro, and as a result he was a good deal less successful in his quest for remunerative and sustained employment. By the mid-fifteenth century the quality that appealed most to employing states was a record of fidelity and strict observance of contract. These were the qualities of the long-serving captain whose duties were as much concerned with maintaining reliable troops in peacetime as with leading them in war.

Much, in fact, of the traditional view of the ruthless, arrogant, and ambitious condottiere needs to be revised in light of fifteenth-century developments. There were always ambitious soldiers, but their ambitions were limited, on the whole, to the creation of a secure base and the achievement of a measure of respect and social standing. An extensive estate or fief and a secure income, rather than signorial control of a city, were the limits of the ambition of the average condottiere by the middle of the fifteenth century. But there were still restless figures like Roberto da Sanseverino who seemed, even in the 1480s, unable to accept any position of inferiority either in military command or in political councils.

The majority of captains learned to balance opportunism with concern for their reputation and bravura with caution. War might mean improved pay, a larger company, and the opportunity for excitement, valorous deeds, and occasionally extra profit. But it also brought the danger of substantial losses in limited resources, damage to a hard-earned reputation, and potential threat to life and limb. It is interesting that leading Italian condottieri had little enthusiasm for fighting the Turks in the Balkans in the fifteenth century. This was not just because conditions were likely to be more arduous and the danger greater, but also because such fighting would take them out of the system and the limited but assured rewards available in it. When Sigismondo Malatesta agreed to command the Venetian army in the Morea in 1463, after several leading condottieri had refused the honor, he found that in his absence his position in Rimini was threatened by the pope.

One element in the increasing stability of the condottiere system was the companies themselves. The company represented the capital of the condottiere, and his reputation and his chances for long-term and lucrative employment depended on his ability to maintain an effective and loyal company. It was for this purpose that a secure base was so important. The condottiere needed to have his own winter quarters area where his company could be billeted safely when winter quarters were not offered by the employing state. Even before he was assured of continuous employment himself, he needed, if possible, to retain the members of his company in permanent service. This he did by issuing *condotte* to his squadron commanders and many of his men at arms, which tied them to him for set periods of service and were constantly renewable. The contracts within the company usually bore no chronological relationship to the contracts under which the condottiere and the whole company served. By this system and by the care with which the condottiere fostered loyalty and provided for the needs of his company a coherent unit was created that was passed from father to son or to a chosen successor. It is not surprising that a condottiere prince like Federigo da Montefeltro should have been able to achieve this sort of continuity, with his control over a substantial recruiting and billeting area and the focus of his court at Urbino as an added incentive to long-term service.

What is more surprising is the example of the company of Michele Attendolo in the period between 1425 and 1448. Attendolo did not have a permanent base in this period other than his family estates in the Romagna, and his company moved around in the service of the papacy, Florence, and Venice, spending several years at a time in each employment. The records of this company have survived quite remarkably, and they show that during those twenty-three years the company normally numbered about six hundred lances and that Attendolo signed contracts with 512 lesser condottieri. More than one hundred of these spent more than ten years in the company; only thirty-one deserted Attendolo's service before the end of a particular contract. Twenty-five of these condottieri died in his service, fifteen of them in battle. There is no reason to believe that Michele Attendolo's was an exceptional company: Jacopo Piccinino, Gattamelata, Roberto da Sanseverino, and Bartolomeo Colleoni must also have had very similar arrangements for the retention of their large companies over long periods, without the advantage of a small state to maintain them (until Colleoni got the fief of Malpaga from Venice in the mid-1450s).

Clearly a company such as this developed its own commissariat and provisioning system. A substantial part of the pay received by the condottiere for his company was retained by him to provide food, clothing, arms and equipment, etc. This was one of the ways in which military contracting was already big business and condottieri could become rich men. But at the same time, reasonable pay to the troops over and above the services provided was essential if the loyalty of the company was to be retained. Again, the evidence of the Attendolo documents is that his troops were paid regularly and were not dependent on occasional windfalls of booty for cash in their pockets.

All this suggests that to see the condottiere company as a band of rapacious mercenaries living on the fringes of society is very misleading. Such a company more normally lived in permanent billets where it sank roots deep into the local economy and society. It was often well-organized and disciplined and quite capable of providing its own services and support structures. To what extent it was reasonably paid was as much in the hands of the employing state as in those of the condottiere himself. A condottiere frequently found himself using his own capital or borrowing from bankers in order to pay his troops while he waiting for the often tardy payment from the employing state. This was just one of the many problems that blighted the relations between condottieri and their employers, and at times it led to violent reactions from the former and vicious denunciations from the latter.

The condottiere was, by the very nature of the term, a contracted soldier, and therefore the relationship that he had with his employer and the extent to which the contract was honored on both sides are the keys to an understanding of his historical role. Undoubtedly, fourteenth- and fifteenth-century Italian states, particularly commercial city states, were vulnerable to blackmail and bullying by large army companies. By 1400 the difference in skill and expertise between professional mercenary troops and hurriedly raised urban or rural militias was such as to make it difficult for a state to resist, on the basis of its own resources, the demands of a determined condottiere. The damage that a company could do to trade routes and to the countryside, even though it could usually be prevented from entering and sacking a major city, was bound to cause grave concern. The danger of civil unrest provoked by shortages of food or more directly by military depredations was a constant fear of governments.

However, to place too much weight on that side of the balance is to underestimate the growing strength of the Italian states by the late fourteenth century and the growing emphasis on continuity and permanent structures. While a small city-state could be bullied by a large mercenary company in the fourteenth century, the expanded states of the fifteenth century were less susceptible to that sort of threat. They developed mechanisms for controlling and disciplining the condottieri; they employed troops on a larger scale, which enabled them to resist threats from individual captains or companies; they strengthened their static defenses. All this deterred the potential military coup. More significantly, however, states began to provide sufficient long-term rewards to make bad faith of any sort a less attractive proposition.

Of all the supervisory mechanisms devised by Italian states for controlling the condottieri, the best known is the use of civilian commissaries to accompany mercenary armies in the field. There was a long tradition of such commissaries going back into the thirteenth century. They were always senior members of the political class of the employing state, and their role was to advise the captains on matters of policy in war and to report on the behavior of the army to the employing government. But such men obviously had little chance of controlling a condottiere who was determined to break his contract, nor could they do more than report on bad behavior by the troops. Without a substantial support structure of civilian officials responsible for recruiting, drawing up contracts, inspections, pay, billets, provisions, and so forth, the commissaries had a very limited role to play.

That support structure was coming into place in most Italian states in the late fourteenth and early fifteenth centuries. It was part of a general extension of bureaucracy and centralized administration. The appearance of large numbers of experienced civilian military officials, often known as *collaterali*, coincided with the growing permanence of the system as a whole. The condottieri found themselves not only accompanied on campaigns by senior commissaries but supervised and assisted by a bevy of lesser officials at all times. Treatises on military organization of the second half of the fifteenth century, particularly Chierighino Chiericati's *Trattatello della milizia*, indicate the importance of this sort of supervision. Chiericati had been a Venetian *vice-collaterale* for many years during the period in which control over the whole army organization was entrusted to Belpetro Manelmi, a legendary figure in the annals of Venetian military history. Chiericati moved to Rome in the 1460s at the request of Paul II and took over the supervision of the papal army for the remainder of Paul's pontificate. A similar role was exercised by Orfeo da Ricavo in the Milanese army in the 1460s and 1470s.

Inevitably the relations between the soldiers and such civilian officials were full of tension, but at the same time there was room for, and evidence of, cooperation and mutual respect. In a system in which the captains depended increasingly on regular pay, rewards, and favors from the employing state rather than on pillage, booty, and ransom, the agents of that state became important intermediaries and allies as well as watchdogs.

The rewarding of condottieri was always a delicate business. The jealousies and rivalries among them were proverbial and not always lessened by habits of long service in the same army. The problems were alleviated by the tendency in the fifteenth century both to increase the number and extend the range of rewards. Surreptitious cash payments and secret agreements to vary contract regulations in favor of particular condottieri were always possibilities, albeit increasingly exceptional ones. The preferred way of rewarding a senior captain was with an estate or even a formal fief. The enfeoffment of a condottiere who was not a native subject of the state gave the title, privileges, and secure base that he was seeking, while at the same time implied responsibilities and commitments on the part of the grantee. Condottieri were not the only beneficiaries of a "new feudalism" in the fifteenth century, and indeed the term itself is somewhat misleading, as the grant of a fief did not carry with it an automatic obligation to render military service, nor necessarily any extensive local judicial or administrative rights. However, the practice—particularly common in Milan and Venice—conferred a new status on the condottiere; it both ennobled and naturalized men whose noble origins were probably already clear, but whose natural allegiance was far less discernible.

In addition to estates, a system of largely honorary rewards was devised for condottieri. In the principates of Italy honorary membership in the ruling family was conferred—indeed, in some cases, actual membership, by marriage to a daughter, usually illegitimate, of the princely house. In the republics honorary citizenship was given or, in the case of Venice, membership in the Great Council, which was a further way of conferring nobility. Chivalric orders were created with provision at the lower levels of the new hierarchies for the knighting of lesser captains and infantry constables. In the cities, palaces were offered to condottieri for their occasional residence, but there was no great expectation or desire that the soldiers should come permanently to inhabit the cities. The periodic visits of great captains to the capitals of their employers for the conferring of an army command or new rewards, for consultation before a war, or for celebration of victory were marked by elaborate ceremonies, jousting, and feasting. By the mid-fifteenth century these were great state occasions, but while the condottiere might appear decked in triumph and lauded like the heroes of classical antiquity, he came as an employee of the state, to be flattered and cajoled, but not to be detained too long.

The condottiere also often returned for his funeral. The state funeral was one of the last rewards that could be offered to a captain and his family. While the occasion might not be untinged with relief, particularly in the earlier years, it was primarily a way of proving to soldiers that their services and sacrifices were valued and that it was part of the bargain struck between state and captain that his name should be perpetuated and his fame enshrined. Similarly, the effigies that were subsequently created served both to honor the condottiere and to instill a respect for martial virtues in the subjects of the state.

There was, of course, another side to the relations between condottieri and their employers. No system of rewards could be complete without a parallel system of punishment and disgrace. There was, in fact, nothing particularly systematic about the ultimate sanction used against dangerous or difficult condottieri: execution. The decision to execute or murder a captain was not one to be taken lightly, and it usually was a reprisal for desertion or a means of preventing desertion. The execution of Carmagnola by Venice in 1432 was one of the most famous of these episodes. Carmagnola had abandoned Milanese service to join Venice in 1426; it was the one great infidelity of his life, and had undoubtedly been provoked by the jealousy, suspicion, and treachery

towards him of Filippo Maria Visconti. Partly as a result of his change of
sides, Venice began to make dramatic territorial gains at the expense of Milan,
but the fear that he might revert to this former Milanese allegiance obsessed
the Venetians. His every move was watched and every possible letter inter-
cepted. Relations between condottiere and employers worsened, until in the
end the Venetians really had no alternative but to execute him. It is unlikely
that they had clear proof of any intended treachery, otherwise they would
have published it, but a condottiere under open suspicion was a condottiere
lost, and Venice simply could not afford to allow Carmagnola to join Milan.

The public execution of Carmagnola was an exceptional episode in the
story of the condottieri, however, and most of those few who died at the
hands of their employers were done away with in a less ostentatious way.
Jacopo Piccinino was presumed to have been murdered on the orders of King
Ferrante of Naples in 1465 by being thrown from the window of his prison,
although the story was put about that he had fallen while trying to escape.
Like Carmagnola, he was distrusted but too dangerous to dismiss. Niccolò da
Tolentino and Tiberto Brandolini were done to death by Milan, the one as a
reprisal for past treachery, the other on suspicion of intended treachery. In
the case of Brandolini an elaborate and somewhat overdrawn confession—a
catalogue of minor indiscretions and abortive contacts with other potential
employers extending over ten years of service with Milan—was extracted
from the chancellor, Giovanbattista da Narni, and made public.

The problem was that no valued condottiere could entirely escape such
contacts. The first device of a state when threatened by a successful army was
to seek to establish communications with the commander of that army, or at
least with one of the leading captains. Such a move was not necessarily designed to win over the captain but to deflect the attack and possibly secure a
truce. However, in the eyes of the captain's employer, any contact was suspect
and could be magnified into potential treachery. In the case of the defenestra-
tion of Baldaccio d'Anghiari by the Florentines in 1441, it was not so much
the fact that Baldaccio had secretly agreed to take papal service that offended,
as the pope was currently Florence's ally, but rather evidence that he had
allowed himself to be drawn into political intrigues with the Capponi faction
that was at the time contesting Medicean predominance in that city.

Execution, however, whether public or discreet, was an extreme and comparatively rare solution to the problems that arose between condottieri and
employers. More frequent were the imposition of fines or decisions to dismiss
difficult condottieri. Fines, or the withholding of pay, were the usual way of
dealing with a captain whose troops did not come up to the required standard;
dismissal was the best solution for a disobedient or ill-disciplined captain.

When Sigismondo Malatesta took twenty cartloads of antique statuary from two churches in Ravenna for the building of his *Tempio*, his current employers, the Venetians, had three thousands ducats stopped out of his pay. However, dismissal in particular had to be used with considerable discretion, and its effectiveness (and indeed its possibility) depended on the nature of the organization of the particular army. In a large, relatively permanent army like those of Milan and Venice by 1450, quite substantial condottieri could be weeded out by threatening to attack their companies with other troops. Bartolomeo Colleoni was successfully expelled in this way by Venice in 1452, and Roberto da Sanseverino by Milan in 1482. In both cases, while there may have been some thought of actually arresting the condottiere, expulsion and dismissal were probably the more politically acceptable solution. In less coherent and well-organized armies, however, a dismissed company could cause great problems, and indeed such a solution was rarely attempted. This in turn could lead to an atmosphere of growing tension and suspicion on both sides as the state sought to persuade the condottiere to leave of his own volition by simply not paying him and the condottiere tried to recoup his losses by extortion. Alessandro Sforza, when dismissed by Florence in 1454 as part of the demobilization after the peace of Lodi, sought to recover his back pay by plundering a Florentine merchant caravan in Parma.

Mutual suspicion was undoubtedly one of the main defects of the condottiere system. Employing governments feared that their captains would desert or turn their arms against their employers; condottieri mistrusted the ability of governments to pay them properly or to pursue a coherent war policy in which they would continue to have an effective role to play. On the whole, the soldiers seem to have had better grounds for their suspicions than the state governments, but it would be wrong to see wrangles over pay and discipline as the sole sources of contention between condottieri and their employers. Fundamental issues of war policy and military organization were also much debated: soldiers tended to be arrogant about the capacity of civilians to understand military problems, while humanist administrators, often well-read in classical military writings, had different priorities and different preconceptions than those of the captains. Carmagnola battled fiercely for a number of years with the *provveditori* and the Venetian senate over the issue of when, in practical terms, it was sensible to have the army out in the field and when it should be withdrawn to quarters. This was not just a matter of how early in the spring campaigning could start nor of how late in the autumn it could continue; there was also a tradition in Italian warfare of a midsummer break in campaigning when the heat and a shortage of forage made it difficult to keep an army in the field. Michele Attendolo argued with Florence about the advisability of moving the main army to Lombardy in 1431. The issue of whether or not to risk a particular battle was debated both in the camps, between condottieri and commissaries, and back in the councils of government. Condottieri were rarely in a position to bear all the praise or all the blame for the outcome of a battle, even though they were often made to do so.

What are we to say, then, about the military significance of these soldiers of the Renaissance? The annals of the time are filled with their military prowess, praising Muzio Attendolo Sforza for his gift for haranguing and inspiring his men, Braccio for his uncanny ability to get to know every one of his men and to inspire loyalty in them, Niccolò Piccinino for his fiery pugnacity, and the calm, resolute determination of Francesco Sforza and Bartolomeo Colleoni. We can still wonder at Gattamelata's famous march through the snow around the north end of Lake Garda to escape a Milanese trap and Roberto da Sanseverino's equally famous strike across the marshes of the Tartaro to attack Ferrara in 1482. But were they playing at war, as Machiavelli suggested, too concerned about conserving their limited resources and too interested in easy loot to risk serious battles? Were their companies anachronisms, preserving an outdated cavalry tradition at a time when pike infantry and guns were revolutionizing war across the Alps? There are no simple answers to these questions. To some extent it is true that Italy appeared tired of large-scale warfare in the second half of the fifteenth century, but this was more a political reaction to the costs and damage of war than a loss of nerve or enthusiasm on the part of the military class. Inevitably the reduced scale of warfare after 1454 tended to lead the professional military captains toward more peaceful pursuits, but at the same time it gave some of them opportunities to take service abroad, particularly with the dukes of Burgundy, where their skills were much prized.

More importantly, however, the period of relative calm was not one in which arms were forgotten. Italian states by this time had permanent armies, and considerable resources were devoted to maintaining the efficiency of those armies and improving their fighting capacity. This was a period of active experimentation with and development of artillery, particularly in Venice and Milan. It was a period of innovation in fortress building carried through by a generation of outstanding architects—Baccio Pontelli, Francesco di Giorgio Martini, Giuliano da Sangallo—and to some extent guided and inspired by captains and condottiere princes. It was also a period in which the proportion of professional infantry in Italian armies grew rapidly and in which few condottiere companies did not include an infantry element. At the same time, condottieri had become aware of the value of light cavalry, and their companies usually included squadrons of mounted crossbowmen and other forms of light horse.

There is certainly little justice in a charge of technical backwardness leveled at the condottieri. Even in the early fifteenth century, when Italy lacked a clear infantry tradition like that of the English archers or the Hussites, the leading condottieri were using infantry in their companies. This was in part a response to the widespread use of field fortifications during the wars in Lombardy between 1425 and 1454. But even in the late fourteenth century the practice of dismounting men at arms for battle and using them in conjunction with archers and crossbowmen was learned by Italian condottieri from Hawkwood and his English captains. Pietro da Fontana in 1375 used this tactic with devastating effect when commanding the Venetians against the Paduans.

Given the continuous role of infantry and the steady development of artillery and hand firearms, it is hardly surprising that Italian warfare in the fifteenth century differed little in the degree of seriousness and bloodshed from ultramontane wars. The purposes and aims of the wars fought by the condottieri were dictated as much by the states that employed them as by the whims of the captains themselves. Those states were rarely concerned about destroying the enemy, and they were certainly as anxious as their condottieri not to lose the armies that they had assembled at such cost. Hence the tendency toward strategies of maneuver and the avoidance of pitched battles unless circumstances were overwhelmingly favorable.

These were the characteristics of all late medieval warfare, whether fought by mercenaries or by national troops, but the condottieri were the acknowledged masters of tactical maneuvers. They relied heavily on an intimate knowledge of the countryside and on good information to move their relatively small bodies of mounted troops out of reach of the enemy and do maximum material damage with them. During the course of such maneuvers there was always the chance that the enemy could be surprised or lured in desperation into an incautious attack, and these were the usual incentives for battle. In practice, however, the surprise was rarely as complete or the trap as secure as the planners had hoped, and in the last resort the decision to pursue the advantage and go for a full scale battle depended on judgments about the relative freshness of the troops involved, the stage in the campaigning reason reached, and above all the wishes of the employing states as expressed by the commissaries.

The warfare of maneuver and a cautious approach to battle was, of course, much lauded in classical writings about war, and another question which we must explore when thinking of condottieri as men of the Renaissance is the extent to which they drew inspiration from classical example. Given that a majority of condottieri came from a noble educated class, it is scarcely surprising to discover that both they and their humanist admirers were accustomed to citing classical examples and drawing classical parallels to their actions. This was a habit of mind of the time, and it would be unrealistic to imagine that the men of action par excellence would not be to some extent inspired by an ethic that lauded determined activity. There is plenty of evidence that military men like Federigo da Montefeltro, Giangiacomo Trivulzio, and Antonio da Marsciano had classical military manuscripts in their libraries, just as did many less directly committed bibliophiles. The problem, is, of course, that the lessons taught by Vegetius and Frontinus were deeply embedded in medieval and Renaissance military literature, and it is very difficult to attribute specific stratagems or ideas to a pure classical example. No new relevant classical texts came to light at this time, and it is very difficult to determine the extent to which even a noted patron of letters like Federigo da Montefeltro was influenced on the battlefield by his classical learning. The nature of Renaissance warfare was undoubtedly largely dictated by contemporary socioeconomic and political factors; classical authority was only one rather diluted stream in the experience required by a condottiere to confront the immediate military problems he faced. However, it is probably true that the classical emphasis on discipline could be used to good rhetorical effect to remind the lesser members of the military hierarchy of the new requirements of increasingly permanent service in the fifteenth century.

Much of this essay has been devoted to stressing the fact that the mercenary captains of Renaissance Italy did not live in a world apart to the extent that is often supposed. This theme can be reiterated in a general way as one approaches the subject of cultural patronage. The motifs of war were an integral part of Italian culture. It was a world inhabited by both Venus and Mars, and battle scenes adorned the walls of Lorenzo de' Medici's bedchamber. A soldier (or is he a soldier?) watches the peasant girl in Giorgione's *La tempesta*, and the soldier-scholar became the prototype of the humanist ideal individual. Architects, goldsmiths, and painters participated eagerly in the building of fortresses, the fashioning of firearms, and the design of tournament banners. The tournament was one of the great set-piece entertainments as well as the training ground for soldiers.

There is, of course, some sense in which condottiere patrons can be identified with specifically war-oriented projects. Effigies of soldiers dominated funerary art, though they were not always commissioned by soldiers and their families; military treatises tended to come from the pens of humanists in the entourages of condottieri; armor was on the whole designed and decorated for soldiers. It is also possible to identify ways in which the patronage of soldiers was stimulated by specific factors. A search for status within a more mobile and flexible society is often seen as a prime motive in promoting the patronage of culture. Condottieri were not on the whole lacking in social status, but some of them achieved a standing and reputation through their military careers that outstripped their rank in society and led them to sponsor ostentatious cultural projects.

Bartolomeo Colleoni is a good example of a condottiere who reached the very top of the profession as permanent captain general of the Venetian army. He received an extensive fief at Malpaga, close to the frontier with Milan, where he could base his troops and where he decided to set up a court. In addition to the buildings, frescoes, and decorations associated with Malpaga itself, he exercised a dominant role in nearby Bergamo, where he had his funerary chapel created. Colleoni came from minor noble stock and worked his way up from commander of a modest company—a position commensurate with his social standing—to become one of the most important figures in the Italian political and social scene, courted by kings and princes. That circumstance was clearly a major stimulus to his patronage projects. However, the vast majority of condottieri did not achieve that sort of advancement of status, and one has to look for other factors behind their patronage activities.

To some extent, the life-style of the condottieri, the risk of sudden death, and the opportunities for violence and extortion may have fostered a particular attitude toward the church. We need to guard, however, against exaggerating the extent to which these characteristics were peculiar to the military life, or indeed necessarily a part of it. Nevertheless, condottieri were more frequently confronted with sudden death or maiming than many others in fifteenth-century Italy, and they had greater opportunities for displays of unchristian behavior toward their fellow men. The infinite number of chapels created by condottieri in Italian churches bear witness to the particular need felt by these men both for the church's mediation and for divine forgiveness. There are few condottieri about whom we have significant surviving information who cannot be associated with a religious patronage project. From Sigismondo Malatesta's almost pagan *Tempio* in Rimini to Antonio da Marsciano's very traditional donations in his will to twenty-five small Umbrian churches, the choice open to condottieri in fulfilling their desire to benefit the church, or alternatively to perpetuate the memory of themselves within the portals of a church, were numerous.

Endowments offered to many churches in different parts of Italy were to some extent a characteristic of condottiere patronage. This was particularly true in the late fourteenth and early fifteenth centuries, when the captains were often still relatively free agents, and it reflected the transient quality of military life and the urge to leave some mark on the different communities with which they came into contact. However, by the third decade of the fifteenth century this errant quality was far less marked. Condottieri had settled winter quarters and bases, and their patronage activities adjusted accordingly. In this situation the patronage of most condottieri became indistinguishable from that of the nobility from which many had come and within which many were re-embraced by feudal grants.

In one all-important respect, however, condottieri remained a significantly special group. Despite their complaints, despite retentions on the sums owed to them, despite significant levels of indebtedness of states to their soldiers, they were paid reasonably regularly and in cash. Huge sums of money were earned by the leading condottieri and the coffers of states were drained to meet the payments on military contracts. Contracts for as much as one hundred thousand florins a year were being signed in the mid-fifteenth century, and a significant proportion of this money remained in the hands of the condottiere after paying his troops and providing for their needs. Niccolò da Tolentino left two hundred thousand florins at his death in 1434, and Bartolomeo Colleoni, who died in 1475, left 232,000 ducats in cash alone. Unlike merchants and bankers, who had to be satisfied with irregular settlement of accounts and who were heavily dependent on credit transactions, the leading condottieri could insist on substantial cash advances before taking the field with their troops. This was quite separate from whatever windfalls in the form of booty or ransom might come their way.

As a result, at a time when specie tended to be in short supply, condottieri were in a particularly strong position to act as cultural patrons, and artists and humanists competed to enter their service, particularly once the life-style of their entourages had become more settled. Without the resources earned from their military activities, the patronage of the Gonzaga, the Este, the Malatesta, and the Montefeltro would have been far less significant; the ducal palaces at Mantua, Ferrara, and Urbino could not have been built or decorated but for the fact that these condottiere princes enjoyed incomes far in excess of the revenues from their small states. Without these resources many other distinguished patrons of letters and the arts would have been reduced to cultural impotency. Collectively, Italy spent a great deal of money on its soldiers in the Renaissance, but much of that was returned to Italian posterity in the form of lasting cultural benefits.

Machiavelli's denunciation of the condottieri came in works written in the second and third decades of the sixteenth century, even though in significant respects it echoed accusations heaped on the captains of the late fourteenth century by Florentine humanists, at a time when conditions and their behavior were very different from those that prevailed in Machiavelli's day. By the early sixteenth century the term "condottiere" was itself something of an anachronism. The great captains still served under contract and could still be occasionally induced to change sides, but their life-styles were as different from those of Alberico da Barbiano, Broglio da Chieri, Biordo Michelotti, and Tartaglia as the wars they fought were different. This was not just because some of them now served the French and the Spanish; it was because the states that employed them—Italian or ultramontane—had changed so much and because the armies they commanded had finally come to have a predominance of infantry.

In the circumstances, it was natural for Machiavelli to see the solution as a national army in which a mass of relatively untrained citizens might have a role. In identifying a certain separation between soldiers and the societies they served, he was exaggerating the extent of the separation but nevertheless putting his finger on a real problem as the unity and coherence of the state became more important. The immediate solution, however, was not a militia but a professional army controlled by the state and increasingly composed of volunteers or, eventually, conscripts from the population of the state. The condottieri were already involved in this transition in early modern European warfare as Machiavelli was writing. The extent to which condottieri had been drawn into permanent armies by the end of the fifteenth century was a good deal less obvious to Florentines like Machiavelli because Florence had achieved less continuity and less stability in this respect than the other Italian states. This is one of the reasons why the diatribes of the Florentine secretary have to be treated with some care, and why, indeed, the story of the condottieri has to be rewritten.

BIBLIOGRAPHY

For detailed material on the condottieri it is often still necessary to go back to the classic Ercole Ricotti, *Storia delle compagnie di ventura in Italia* (4 vols., Turin: G. Pomba, 1844–45; 3 vols., Milan: Edizioni Athena, 1929). The best collection of published *condotte* and other military documentation is still Giuseppe Canestrini, ed., "Documenti per servire alla storia della milizia italiana dal secolo XIII al XVI," *Archivio storico italiano* 15 (1851).

More recent reviews of the whole problem have taken their starting point from Piero Pieri, *Il Rinascimento e la crisi militare italiana* (Turin: G. Einaudi, 1952; 2d ed. 1970) and his "L'evoluzione dell'arte militare nei secoli XV, XVI e XVII e la guerra del secolo XVIII," *Nuove questioni di storia moderna* (2 vols.; Milan: Marzorati, 1964), 2:1123–80. Other works include: Clemente Ancona, "Milizie e condottieri," in *Storia d'Italia*, vol. 5, pt. 1 (Turin: G. Einaudi, 1973), 641–65; Michael E. Mallett, *Mercenaries and Their Masters: Warfare in Renaissance Italy* (London: Bodley Head; Totowa, N.J.: Rowan & Littlefield, 1974); Raffaele Puddu, *Eserciti e monarchie nazionali nei secoli XV e XVI* (Florence: La Nuova Italia, 1975); and Franco Cardini, *Quell'antica festa crudele. Guerra e cultura della guerra dall'età feudale alla grande rivoluzione* (Florence: Sansoni, 1982). The patronage interests of the condottieri have been well illustrated by Gioacchino Lanza Tomasi, *Il ritratto del condottiero* (Turin: Edizione Radiotelevisione italiana, 1967).

For valuable studies of early aspects of the condottiere system, see Daniel P. Waley, "*Condotte* and *condottieri* in the Thirteenth Century," *Proceedings of the British Academy* 61 (1975): 337–71; and D. M. Bueno de Mesquita, "Some Condottieri of the Trecento and Their Relations with Political Authority," *Proceedings of the British Academy* 32 (1946): 219–41. On the role of the condottieri in the Italian wars, see Frederick Lewis Taylor, *The Art of War in Italy, 1494–1529* (Cambridge: Cambridge University Press; Westport, Conn.: Greenwood Press, 1973). The attitudes of the humanists toward the condottieri are explored in C. C. Bayley, *War and Society in Renaissance Florence: The "De Militia" of Leonardo Bruni* (Toronto: University of Toronto Press, 1961). For a pioneering discussion of company organization, see Mario Del Treppo, "Gli aspetti organizzativi, economici e sociali di una compagnia di ventura italiana," *Rivista storica italiana* 80 (1973): 253–75. For further information on the development of military bureaucracies, see Giangiorgio Zorzi, "Un Vicentino alla corte di Paolo II: Chierighino Chiericati e il suo trattatello della milizia," *Nuovo archivio veneto*, n.s. 30 (1915): 369–434, and, in particular, Michael E. Mallett and John R. Hale, *The Military Organisation of a Renaissance State: Venice, c. 1400 to 1617* (Cambridge and New York: Cambridge University Press, 1984). Professor Hale's recent *War and Society in Renaissance Europe, 1450–1620* (London and New York: St. Martin's Press, 1985) provides a valuable comparison.

T H R E E
The Cardinal
Massimo Firpo

*J*N 1510, the year in which the Portuguese took faraway Goa, Botticelli and Giorgione died, and in Italy Julius II hired Swiss mercenaries, overwhelmed Modena, declared war on Ferrara, and fought the king of France, a work of typical humanistic composure dedicated to the reigning pope was published under the title *De cardinalatu*. The author of this work, Paolo Cortesi, had died shortly before. He had pondered his topic and written his book in the tranquillity of his villa near San Gimignano (where he had retired in 1503, at the death of Alexander VI), calling on his vivid memory of men and events and his twenty years of experience, first as *scriptor* (writer, draftsman) and then as apostolic secretary to the curia.

Space limitations preclude adequate description here of the ideal prince of the church as Cortesi describes him in the three volumes of his work (*Ethicus et contemplativus, Oeconomicus,* and *Politicus*). He depicts the full range of the cardinal's life: his religious rectitude, moral rigor, and duties of governance; the cardinal as a public figure and in private; and his high dignity and many and arduous duties, summed up in the scarlet vestments symbolizing his determination to defend the faith *usque ad effusionem sanguinis*. It is interesting to note, however, that this work, published the same year as the *Institutio christiani principis* of Erasmus of Rotterdam and not long before Machiavelli wrote his own great work on the subject, was originally entitled *De principe* and was intended to treat the topic of the ruler. Cortesi abandoned this aim in the press of the tumultuous, rapidly changing age in which he lived. It was not the fragile states and principalities, shaken by profound crises, guided only by diplomacy and the "benefit of time," vacillating from one side to the other in conflicts between the great European monarchies played out on Italian soil, but the Church of Rome that lay at the center of political and cultural life in Italy. The church, under the guidance of popes just as apt to dispatch their infantry and their horsemen as to hurl interdicts and excommunications, confirmed the universal validity of Guicciardini's rule that "states cannot be ruled according to conscience."

The church was capable of attracting energetic men, offering careers and scope for action, and providing channels for social promotion to talent and ambition. Guicciardini himself, a thoroughgoing layman who spared no invective and no biting sarcasm when it came to the *scelerati preti* that his best interests—his *particolare*—had led him to serve, even Guicciardini, in his youth, had thought of becoming a priest, "not to take my ease with an ample income," he later wrote, "like most of the other priests, but because it seemed to me, being young and with some learning, that it was a start toward achieving greatness in the church and toward the hope of becoming a cardinal some day." This was exactly why Paolo Cortesi's work was entitled *De cardinalatu* and not *De principe*, as Carlo Dionisotti has so cogently pointed out.

We need to examine first how many members of the sacred *Senatus* (as Cortesi calls it) there were and who they were when he was writing his stately model of the ideal cardinal. Far as his model was from reality, Cortesi outlines how a cardinal should comport himself; he stresses his grave responsibilities should the papal throne fall vacant; he describes his duties in governing the universal church along with the pope; and he emphasizes the prestige of the cardinal's position at the summit of contemporary society, as a peer to princes of the blood.

Some statistics first. In Cortesi's day there were thirty-four cardinals. Twelve had been nominated by Julius II, the Della Rovere pope, and twenty-two had been inherited from his predecessors. One of these had received his cardinal's hat from Paul II, another from Sixtus IV, two from Innocent VIII, and eighteen from Alexander VI. They formed an extremely limited elite, but their number was destined to increase during the course of the century, reaching sixty, seventy, and more in the post-Tridentine era. They were also destined to undergo prompt and continual turnover. One hundred and seventy-one cardinals were created in the fifteenth century from Martin V to Alexander VI, the Borgia pope, nearly half of them by Alexander VI and Sixtus IV. In the next fifty years, from Julius II to Paul III, 175 cardinals came to fill their places. A final statistic: the mean duration of the cardinalate for the twenty-seven princes of the church created by the Della Rovere pope was under ten years; it rose to more than thirteen years for the cardinals created by Clement VII and to roughly fifteen years for those named by Paul III.

With this as a base, we can turn to the sacred college as it was when *De cardinalatu* appeared to observe the cardinals as they met in consistory to advise the pope, receive embassies, and assign dioceses and benefices. Five cardinals were the nephews or close kin of popes, and fourteen were not Italian, six of them Spanish and seven French. Thus Italians formed a clear majority in the sacred college. Many of them bore the names of great patrician and princely families: there were a Grimani and a Cornaro from Venice, an Este from Ferrara, a Gonzaga from Mantua, a Medici and a Soderini from Florence, a Fieschi from Genoa and a Del Carretto from Finale, a Carafa, and even a nephew of King Ferrante of Naples. There were also some men of action, like the energetic but unscrupulous Francesco Alidosi, a long-time personal friend of Julius II, who was accused of every evil deed by Paolo Giovio and who died by an assassin's hand on a street in Ravenna at the instigation of the pope's nephew, the duke of Urbino, almost in full view of the pope. Other men of action were Federico Sanseverino, who boasted close connections with the Sforza of Milan, and an extraordinary personage who had made his way up from nothing, Adriano Castellesi.

A man of notable culture capable of composing refined hexameters, writing works with such titles as *De vera philosophia* and *De sermone latino*, and reading Greek and Hebrew, Castellesi (once he had freed himself, somewhat unscrupulously, from an improvident marriage) carved out an extraordinary ecclesiastical career thanks to his experience in the management of curial affairs, his talent for diplomacy, his skill in accumulating benefices and prebends, and the support of Pope Alexander VI. In 1498 he offered Alexander 20,000 ducats from the immense patrimony he had accumulated by systematic sack of the English church and was rewarded with the cardinalate five years later. Castellesi offers a truly three-dimensional portrait of the Renaissance cardinal in all his contradictions, even in his myth. He was judged "a hard and sinister man" and even "terrible," but was also acknowledged to possess *singulare ingenium* and to be *rerum omnium vicarius* of the Borgia pope. He was also suspected of attempting (with Cesare Borgia) to poison the pope to avoid being killed himself. When Julius II became pope, Castellesi was obliged to flee under the most hazardous conditions, and he was deeply involved in Alfonso Petrucci's conspiracy against Leo X. Stripped of his cardinalate in 1518, he disappeared from sight (it was whispered that he had "gone over to the Turk") and was killed by a servant three years later.

Alexander VI—*uomo carnalesco*, according to one contemporary—granted the purple to one of his many illegitimate sons, Cesare Borgia, the ill-famed "duca Valentino," and to five other nephews, cousins, and great-nephews. He filled the sacred college with men who bought their cardinal's hat with cash and with men of action willing to further his boundless ambitions for family advancement and his vast designs (despite his claim in August 1493 that he was satisfied with "enjoying the papacy in peace and quiet"). Alexander VI named forty-three cardinals—a hitherto unheard-of number. In theory, the college was limited to twenty-four or twenty-five cardinals (although not long after Cortesi held that a *plenum* of forty members was appropriate). Some of them merit particular mention. Alessandro Farnese, for example, was universally respected, but there is little doubt that the Spanish pope's relationship with Farnese's sister Giulia had something to do with his election. Their liaison was so blantant that the populace blasphemously called her *sponsa Christi* and the curial records refer to her as *concubina papae*.

There were other cardinals who stood out from the crowd. Ippolito d'Este, who became a cardinal in 1493 at the age of fourteen, was a man capable of having his half-brother's eyes gouged out when a woman to whom he had taken a fancy preferred Don Giulio. Luigi d'Aragona, raised to the purple in 1494 at twenty years of age when he was already a widower (since his wife, a niece of Innocent VIII's, had died two years earlier), was a prince of refined tastes who loved music and the hunt, fine food and beautiful women, horses, and Carnival, which he took as an opportunity to go about masked (disguised as a Moslem) and amuse himself by playing practical jokes on friars. Giuliano Cesarini, a descendant of a long line of prelates that had recently allied itself by marriage to the Borgia family, is remembered by Marin Sanudo as a *zovane di pocha reputation*. Amanieu d'Albret, the brother of the king of Navarre, counted among his merits becoming duca Valentino's brother-in-law a year before his elevation to the cardinalate, an event that did not induce him to change his rowdy way of life. The energetic Francisco Remolins, "a clever man, of the tribe [*razza*] of pope Alexander," as the Venetian ambassador called him in 1517, was apparently married to a lady who was opportunely shut up in a convent on his designation. He had been Savonarola's inquisitor, and rightly or wrongly was reputed to be one "of the worst, cruelest, and most unprincipled men that lived near His Holiness." He was obliged to flee to Naples after the fall of the Borgias. Giovan Battista Ferrari was rumored in Rome in 1502 to have been poisoned by the pope because Alexander wanted to get his hands on the great fortune that Ferrari had accumulated, "most rapaciously," as cardinal datary. Finally, there was Cesare Borgia himself, who promptly renounced the cardinalate in 1498 when his ambitions called him elsewhere and when the pope, as one Venetian wrote in February of the same year, was intent on "giving states to his children."

The names of many of the cardinals designated by Alexander VI reflect the swings of the political pendulum between France and Spain, or deposits to the pontifical treasury needed to finance duca Valentino's enterprises in Romagna. For instance, Charles VIII's arrival in Rome was accompanied by the nomination of two French cardinals in January 1495; barely more than a year later, when the winds of papal diplomacy blew from another quarter, four Spanish cardinals were named. By all accounts, nearly 130,000 ducats were taken in on the occasion of the mass promotion in September 1500 decreed by a pope who, as Sigismondo de Conti wrote of him, "pecuniae omnes vias norit."

It would of course be all too easy to borrow the vivid colors of the great frescoes of the Renaissance painted by Jacob Burckhardt and Ferdinand Gregorovius to evoke the morbid climate of violence, dissolution, greed, and universal corruption that seemed to imbue the entire summit of the church with its commercial logic. It would also be easy to show the wealth of the church being handed over to relatives and friends or sold to the highest bidder, and the cardinals seemingly exclusively occupied with defending the interests of their sovereigns or their own families and grabbing the fattest benefices and the most lucrative positions, sharing between them cities and castles, dioceses and abbacies, offices and legations.

Contemporaries complained that Rome had "become a den of thieves" dominated by charlatans of every sort and a veritable "slaughterhouse"— "every night four or five people (that is, bishops, prelates, and other clergy) are found murdered" was the rumor in Venice in 1500—and the chroniclers of the time declared that "monasteria quasi omnia facta erant lupanaria" and exclaimed "how many friars are whores!" In this context, it is understandable that Savonarola too should have lashed out at the "evil life of prelates and clergy" and at the church. The church was a whore—*ribalda Chiesa* and *meretrice Chiesa*—a Babylon soon to be struck down by an avenging sword. "Go look at the curia today, which sells benefices and even the blood of Christ or the Virgin for a penny," Savonarola thundered from the pulpit. For him, the ecclesiastical hierarchy was incapable of even the most elementary decency: "Before, you were ashamed at arrogance, at lust; now you no longer have any shame. . . . Your stench reaches heaven." "Nihil ius nihil fas: aurum, vis et Venus imperabat" was the harsh judgment of the curia of Alexander VI by the learned Augustinian reformer (and future cardinal) Egidio da Viterbo. Agostino Vespucci, writing to Machiavelli from Rome in a letter dated 16 July 1501, called the pope an *uomo tristo*. Vespucci states:

In plain sight of everyone, [the pope] strips one of his goods, another of his life; he sends one into exile and another to forced labor; he expropriates another's house in order to install some scoundrel in it, and all this for the most superficial of reasons or for no reason at all. Here benefices are for sale like melons, doughnuts, or drinking water at home. The court of the Rota does nothing because all power is in the hands of these rascals, to the point that it seems we need the Turk, given that Christians do not all rise up to uproot this carrion from human society. This is what every right-thinking person is saying. . . . Every night between vespers and one in the morning, twenty-five or more women are brought to the papal palace, not to mention the pope, who keeps his own permanent illicit troop, so that it is obvious that the entire palace has been turned into a brothel for every sort of filthy act.

Pope Julius II, that man "of great, perhaps vast soul, impatient, precipitous, open, and free" who followed Alexander VI, had criteria for the selection of cardinals that were not notably different. A pugnacious prince, quick to anger, he was for Guicciardini a priest in dress and name only. He was also a man determined to reestablish the power of the pope over the church and the power of the church over the Italian peninsula, and the creator of the grandeur of the Rome of Bramante, Raphael, and Michelangelo.

Julius was as skilled as his predecessor at refurbishing the papal strong-boxes and bending consistorial opposition to his will. His nominations to the cardinalate so obviously furthered his own anti-French politics that they pro-voked a genuine split in the sacred college. Four kinsmen were elevated to cardinal at various moments during Julius's papacy, and among the nine car-dinals designated in March 1511 there were such men as Matthäus Schinner, a Swiss who could be counted on to bring his compatriots' invincible infantry to the aid of the papacy; and Matthäus Lang, the "audacious, proud, and severe" imperial counselor, "low of birth and sovereign in courage [*virtù*]" (also known as a great "prebend gobbler") whom Giovio considered "more worthy to be listed among the best captains of war than among the cardinals."

The sacred college also included cultivated men like Oliviero Carafa, a man universally admired by his contemporaries and, according to Sanudo, an "exemplary light of the cardinalate," or like the *iuriconsultorum princeps*, Giovanni Antonio Sangiorgo, or Domenico Grimani. Other cardinals' only claim to fame was a powerful aristocratic family. Few among them—very few—were particularly well versed in religion. One exception was Francisco Jiménez de Cisneros, regent of Castile in the absence of Charles I but also a major theologian and mystic and a rigorous reformer of the Franciscan order, the founder of the humanistic university of Alcalá de Henares, and the pro-motor of that monument of Renaissance philology, the Complutensian Poly-glot Bible.

I should add that corruption and worldly behavior among high prelates prompted no particular scandal. The clear separation between clergy and laity and the austere image of contrition in religious life that gripped the age of the Counter-Reformation was not yet part of the collective consciousness. The later age would consider untenable behavior that was thought close to normal at the beginning of the century—behavior like a cardinal's participa-tion in Carnival festivities and masked balls, in gambling, and in all manner of social pastimes. The same is true of the sexual mores of a good many cardinals of these decades, who, to say the least, failed to practice chastity. They often lived surrounded by offspring, whom they almost always took care to legitimize and endow with a good ecclesiastical income from one source or another.

We need only think of the many and ubiquitous offspring of Cardinal Rodrigo Borgia and the famous Vannozza Catanei, who later had such an influence on papal politics. The policies of Innocent VIII Cibo were conditioned by the need to marry his son Franceschetto in a manner appropriate and adequate to his station (to the point that when his father died Franceschetto is reported to have prayed that "Christ and Holy Mary and all the court of heaven be brought to ruin, now that I am ruined"). Another future pope, Alessandro Farnese, raised to the cardinalate in 1493 at twenty-five, was to father at least four sons, one of whom later became the first duke of Parma and Piacenza. Cardinal Innocenzo Cibo, whom the Venetian ambassador in 1533 called "addicted to worldly and lascivious pleasures," also had four sons, as did the authoritative Ercole Gonzaga, who died in Trent in March 1563, where he presided at the last session of the Council. It was said of Marco Vigeri, a trusted collaborator of Julius II, who elevated him to the purple in 1515, that he was "a man so given to sensuality and the flesh that, publicly keeping a woman in his house, he left a number of children by her when he died." One papal diarist calmly noted in July 1506 that the death of another member of the sacred college could doubtless be attributed to erotic intemperance: "ex nimio, ut dicunt, coitu." Garimberti said the same of a nephew of Leo X's, Cardinal Luigi de' Rossi, who in Garimberti's opinion was brought to an early death by his "filthy . . . infamous, and licentious life." Even Cardinal Benedetto Accolti, a thoroughgoing scoundrel, was thought by his doctors to have passed to a better life in 1549 because of a stroke caused by the "continual and extraordinary drinking that he has done for many years" and by his "great debauchery, particularly with women, and the night he died he had one with him."

Experience and proven ability in the management of curial affairs; personal or family relations with the popes; wealth, in a few cases; outstanding service at the head of the religious orders; the protection of foreign rulers; and a prominent role in papal diplomacy were thus proven paths to the summit of the church in the fifteenth and sixteenth centuries, though cash contributions never did any harm. Even in the past, of course, the political demands of the Holy See had been decisive in the designation of cardinals. There had always been energetic men of action like Giovanni Vitelleschi (named in 1437), a true soldier capable of guiding his men in battle to put down the intractable Roman nobility, to reconquer the Campagna Romana, or to bend rebel cities and petty princelings to his will. He died a violent death and left behind him a reputation for being "extremely cruel, not particularly religious, and restless . . . hard-working, vigilant, avid for a following and for glory, prone to risk-taking, bloodthirsty, [and] insatiable." Another man of action was Ludovico Trevisan (1440; known also as Scarampo), Vitelleschi's successor at the head of the pontifical army in campaigns to recuperate church lands and return the pope to the Vatican. Trevisan began as a simple physician and rose to be cardinal camerlengo thanks to Eugenius IV's trust in him and to his own unscrupulous managerial skills. Calixtus III called him "un savio signore in agibilibus mundi," and he accumulated a princely fortune in a short span of time. His religious zeal can be judged by his contemporaries' nickname for him, "Cardinal Lucullus," and a fellow cardinal said of him, "utinam tam religiosi animi quam ad saecularia vigilis."

Some cardinals were closely linked to foreign courts. There were Guillaume d'Estouteville (1439), who lived with pomp and was of royal blood; the powerful Jean Jouffroy (1461); the unscrupulous Jean Balue (1467); and the imperial counselor Georg Hessler (1477), whose nomination was proudly rejected by the sacred college because he was "humilibus parentibus ortus" and an "animi inquieti vir existimatus et novarum rerum cupidus." There were also men like Joan Margarit i Pau (1483), chancellor to John II of Aragon; the Milanese Giovanni Arcimboldi (1473); and Ascanio Maria Sforza (1484), the brother of Ludovico Il Moro, a man who loved intrigue and, as Guicciardini said, was "corrupted by his boundless appetite for riches" (*History of Italy*, trans. Alexander, 126). There were also representatives of Roman noble families like the Colonna, the Orsini, and the Savelli, as well as swarms of papal nephews and kin.

It was also true, however, that after the long Avignon episode and the crisis of the schisms and the synods of Constance and Basel, an energetic revival offered sporadic opportunities to reach the top of the ecclesiastical hierarchy to men distinguished for their intelligence or their culture. The return of the Papal See to Italy, the intellectual and diplomatic experience of conciliarism, the encounter with Oriental culture that reunion with the Greek church brought to the council at Ferrara and Florence, the papacy's role in Italian politics, and the development of the curial bureaucracy had forced even popes with little sympathy for the new humanistic sensibility to surround themselves with people equal to the demands of the times. Inaugurating a tradition destined to last for over a century, figures like Pier Paolo Vergerio and Poggio Bracciolini, Leonardo Bruni and Antonio Loschi, Flavio Biondo and Manuele Crisolora were called to the papal chancery, as was Giacomo

Ammannati, who was named a cardinal by Pius II in 1461. In 1439, Isidor of Kiev, Bessarion, and Torquemada were elevated to the purple, as was Tommaso Parentucelli of Sarzana (1446). When Parentucelli was elected pope several months later under the name of Nicholas V, he launched the construction of Renaissance Rome, starting with the basilica of St. Peter's. He offered commissions and an opportunity to build to the greatest artists of his time, and he called to the papal court "all the learned men in the world," from Bracciolini to Valla, from Manetti to Decembrio, from Aurispa to Vespasiano da Bisticci (who later praised the pope's generosity, "divine genius," and "universal knowledge of everything"). It was Nicholas V who brought Nicholas of Cusa to the sacred college. Nicholas V's successor, Calixtus III, a man of a very different nature, immersed in dreams of crusades and wild nepotistic ambitions, elevated Enea Silvio Piccolomini to the cardinalate. Less than two years later, in August 1458, Piccolomini took the papal tiara and the name Pius II.

Piccolomini had an extraordinary, perhaps a unique career. He succeeded in making his way, in spite of his family's poverty, with the aid of his intelligence, with study, with the sure competence of a jurist who had learned his law from Mariano Sozzini, and with the prestige of the humanist trained in classical Latin. He was capable of writing erotic verse, political orations, comedies in the style of Boccaccio, pedagogical and doctrinal treatises, and historical and geographical works, and he put his knowledge and his eloquence at the service of an uncommon diplomatic talent. Ambition and intelligence, broadmindedness, culture, and ability, but also good luck and a vast experience of men and things were his weapons in his struggle to become secretary to bishops and cardinals, to win a poet's crown (for some time, he signed his name as "Aeneas Sylvius Poeta"), and to rise from the chancery of the Council of Basel to the staffs of the antipope Felix V, the emperor of Germany, and the pope. Even when he was named bishop, first of Trieste then of Siena, and when he was made a cardinal, he managed to make people forget both his notorious receptivity to feminine charms and his practical and theoretical support of conciliarism. He blandly repudiated the theses of his own *De generalis concilii authoritate* in his later *De gestis Basiliensis concilii*. When as pope he devoted all his energies to the grandiose dream of a European crusade against the spread of Ottoman power, he was fond of declaring, "Aeneam reiicite, Pium recipite."

It was Pius who called to the cardinalate the learned Giacomo Ammannati and fra Alessandro Oliva of Sassoferrato, a man who had become general of the Augustinians by virtue of his talent and his knowledge. Pius said of Ammannati in his *Commentarii*, "pauperem monachum, angustae cellae cultorem," recording with sincere sorrow the death of this "ingens sacri collegii decus."

Francesco Della Rovere, Bessarion's confessor and general of the Franciscans, who was made a cardinal in 1467 and elected pope in 1471 with the name Sixtus IV, rose above his modest family origins to pursue a meteoric ecclesiastical career, thanks to his fame as a preacher, his talents as a scholastic theologian and a widely acclaimed professor who held the most prestigious chairs on the Italian peninsula, and his reputation as an austere and efficient organizer. Once he reached the pinnacles of power, Sixtus displayed incorrigible nepotism in his attempt to transmit power to his family through a flood of prebends and benefices. "The ruin of the Church of God nearly resulted from that election," Vespasiano da Bisticci wrote later. Shortly after, the Della Rovere family replaced the Montefeltro in the duchy of Urbino, and Sixtus IV called to the sacred college no fewer than four relatives who bore his family name (one of whom later became pope Julius II) and two nephews—Raffaele Riario-Sansoni, who was barely eighteen at the time, and Pietro Riario, also an extremely young man.

Sixtus granted thirty-four cardinal's hats—more than all his three predecessors together. It was under his pontificate that the sacred college shifted direction toward an increased interest in the temporal world and a clear intention to strive to involve the papacy in Italian politics, with all its tortuous, labyrinthine complexities and its convulsive precariousness. The courts of France and Castile, Burgundy and Portugal, Naples and Milan had their cardinals, as did the Roman aristocracy and the patriciates of Genoa and Venice. The curia was increasingly infected with simony, urged on by ever more spectacular luxury and an almost barbaric fondness for the display of power and wealth. "The treasures of the *Ecclesia* have to be used for something," one Roman diarist noted among his scathing comments and accusations of atrocities as he reported on the death of Sixtus. Although Sixtus was an indefatigable builder and a generous patron (he founded the Vatican Library, which he decreed must be open to the public), he cannot be said to have opened the doors of an ecclesiastical career to learning, nor to have chosen men of culture for posts at the summit of the church.

An Italian prince in all ways, Sixtus IV prepared the sacred college that elected first Innocent VIII, a tepid person whom Guicciardini labeled "useless so far as public welfare was concerned" (*History*, trans. Alexander, 9), a man who was totally devoted to finding appropriate niches for his progeny and a docile tool in the hands of Cardinal Giuliano Della Rovere. Next, they elected Alexander VI. In the latter conclave tens of abbacies, bishoprics, benefices, lucrative positions, and revenues of all sorts that had been Rodrigo Borgia's were the price he paid for his colleagues' votes—among them Ascanio Sforza, who, "corrupted with very abundant gifts," as Giovio later wrote, "was the principal leader and prime mover [who saw to it] that the man wicked above all other men in the world . . . was made pope."

Some of the men who elbowed their way to the summit of the church hierarchy with little show of compunction merit a closer look. One of these is Jean Balue, about whose origins (beginning with his date and place of birth) little or nothing is known. Sigismondo de Conti called him "vir magni animi et consilii," adding, "qui ex humili Pictavorum pago ortus sua industria ad cardinalatum pervenit." From a start as an obscure cleric who entered the service of the bishop of Angers toward the end of the 1450s, Balue managed to gain the trust of the bishop, who granted him benefices and chose him as his vicar. When the bishop went to Rome on an embassy in 1462, Balue recognized that the opportunity to accompany him was his big chance. He immediately plunged into the rough and tumble of the Roman curia, and when he left some months later he took with him valuable experience and precious contacts, the title of apostolic protonotary, and the conviction that the road to the satisfaction of his ambitions passed through Paris, not Angers.

Euphemistically described as "non abunde litteris ac scientia eruditus," it was surely not his knowledge but his boundless energy and dexterity that helped Balue find a place at the French court. In only the few years between 1464 and 1467 his lightning-swift career, political and ecclesiastical, made him one of the most highly accredited counselors of Louis XI, a position he used to his advantage to accumulate responsibilities, offices, pensions, abbacies, and priorates. After contributing to the intrigues that led to the destitution of his former protector, the bishop of Angers, Balue was made bishop of Evreux in 1464 and bishop of Angers in 1467. In September 1467 Balue was elevated to the purple as a reward for his good offices in persuading the Most Christian king to abrogate the Pragmatic Sanction and for the many political services he had rendered the crown in missions, maneuvers, negotiations, and charges of all sorts. At times he risked his own skin, but he never failed to turn such occasions to a profit and use them to fill his purse. His extraordinary rise was followed two years later by a sudden fall brought on by grave accusations of embezzlement in the collection of tithes and, worse, of lèse-majesté and treason. He was arrested on the order of the king and spent eleven long years in harsh imprisonment before he was liberated, thanks to the pope's intervention, in 1480.

Transferred to Rome in 1482, Balue obtained absolution and was restored to all his dignities, privileges, revenues, and benefices, and he found in the

Vatican court a new arena for action and renewed power. Sent to France as a papal legate on the succession of Charles VIII in 1483, he returned to Rome two years later, laden with honors, riches, and favors, as French ambassador to the Holy See. He continued to play a prominent political role in the curia until his death in October 1491, "finally cleansing the College," wrote Garimberti, who never refused a chance to denounce Balue's "execrable and fraudulent . . . nature," punning on his name to call him *veramente belua* (a true beast). Balue's life is of course an exceptional case, but it is also an exemplary one: through him we can grasp the mechanics of a career that Balue owed to his political astuteness and to his faith in his sovereign, and in which the ecclesiastical framework seems largely extrinsic.

Other ministers of the king of France (who lacked Balue's harsh personality) were blessed by fortune. There was Jean Jouffroy, called from Burgundy to the sacred college in 1461 by Pius II (against his better judgment) because he seemed to represent the entire "auctoritas Gallicae nationis." Pius passed harsh judgment on Jouffroy: he was clever and cultured, but Pius scathingly reproved his ambition, his greed, "et in omne vitium prolapsi mores." A Benedictine monk, abbot of Luxeuil and then bishop of Arras and provided with a number of rich ecclesiastical benefices, Jouffroy advanced largely because of his juridical learning, his subtle diplomatic skills, and the backing of Louis XI. Although he preferred the monk's robe to the scarlet robes of a cardinal, and although Pius II and Cardinal Ammannati detested him and gave posterity a totally negative portrait of him, he spoke up for the cardinalate. In a public oration in Paris in 1468 he stated that the cardinalate was the highest "fontem . . . gloriae" and "segetem honoris," and that it obliged anyone chosen for that function to seek to be worthy of it, not fleeing hard work or danger "pro fide atque sede Romana."

Jean de Bilhères-Lagraulas, finally, had a career in some ways similar. A younger son in a family of minor Gascon nobility and, as such, destined to an ecclesiastical career, Bilhères-Lagraulas became the right-hand man first of Louis XI and later of Charles VIII and was entrusted with delicate tasks and missions. He was made bishop of Lombez in 1473; in 1474 he succeeded Jouffroy as abbot of the wealthy abbey of Saint-Denis; he was ambassador of the Most Christian king in Spain, Germany, and Rome, where in 1493 Alexander VI named him a cardinal. Provided with an impressive series of ecclesiastical benefices, the spiritual care of which never entered his mind, he died in Rome seven years later, not long after he had commissioned Michelangelo to sculpt the famous Pietà.

We might also do well to look at the two Venetian cardinals created by the

Borgia pope, Domenico Grimani (1493) and Marco Cornaro (1500), men who differed enormously and were further divided by open antipathy. Cornaro was a mediocrity, even small-minded; Grimani was extremely cultured and reputed to be "the most learned [man] in Italy in all [sorts of] writing; sober-minded; of upright life and respectable," as the ambassador of the Serenissima wrote in 1517. He was a great collector of books, pictures, antiques, and ancient and precious objects of all sorts; he was an admirer and correspondent of Erasmus, who dedicated his paraphrase of the Letter of St. Paul to the Romans to him; he was frequently suggested as a candidate for the papacy. Nonetheless, both men were granted the purple only because of the thousands of scudi paid by their wealthy families (in Cornaro's case, when he was barely eighteen), and both men accumulated incredible quantities of prebends and ecclesiastical benefices that they later transmitted to their relatives and heirs, inaugurating veritable dynasties of prelates. Four other members of the Cornaro family were made cardinal during the cinquecento, and a number of family members succeeded one another on the episcopal thrones of Padua, Brescia, and Treviso, while Grimani passed on to his nephew Marino the diocese of Ceneda, the patriarchate of Aquileia, and a cardinal's hat—after a new and conspicuous expenditure, of course. Marino failed to pass on membership in the sacred college to another Grimani nephew, Giovanni, only because Giovanni was, counter to all expectations, accused of heresy.

These are far from being isolated instances. Examples of similar careers proliferate in the sixteenth century, and not only in papal families (Farnese, Del Monte, Carafa, Medici) or princely families (Gonzaga, Este, Colonna), or in the higher aristocracy in France (Amboise, Bourbon, and Guise families). The dioceses of Ivrea and Vercelli, for example (the first from 1497 to 1617 and the second from 1503 to 1572 and again from 1599 to 1611), remained the feud of the powerful Ferreri family, whose presence in the senate of the church was assured by Giovanni Stefano (1500–1510), Bonifacio (1527–43), Filiberto (1548–49), Pietro Francesco (1561–66), and Guido Luca Ferreri (1565–85). The same could be said of the diocese of Como, controlled by the Trivulzio family, which had three Trivulzio cardinals during the sixteenth century, or the diocese of Feltre, for nearly seventy years under the control of the Campeggi of Bologna, a great curial dynasty represented in the sacred college first by Lorenzo and later by Alessandro Campeggi. Finally, the diocese of Saint-Papoul, in France, was transmitted from one of the three cardinals of the Salviati family to the next from 1537 to 1568, not without protest from the clergy and the faithful of the diocese, whose Florentine pastors (who had better things to do elsewhere) were paid, in all, no less than 100,000 scudi during the years of their tenure there.

The opportunity to accumulate great wealth, thanks to favors granted by sovereigns and popes and to the practice, by then customary, of dissociating ecclesiastical revenues from the religious functions to which they had originally been connected, was essential to the power of Renaissance cardinals. Paul II chose to assign an interminable number of benefices to the relatives he raised to the purple—Marco Barbo, Giovan Battista Zeno, and Giovanni Michiel (rumored to have been poisoned by Cesare Borgia, who greedily eyed Michiel's immense fortune and the tens of thousands of shining ducats that flowed into his strongboxes). In 1491 Cardinal Balue's estate was valued at 100,000 ducats; in 1465 the pope's camerlengo, Ludovico Trevisan, left an estate valued at from 200,000 to 300,000 ducats, prompting Cortesi to write of him, "nemo affluentior in senatoria dignitate fuit." The wealth of Guillaume d'Estouteville was no less legendary, as was the fortune of Rodrigo Borgia during his thirty-six years as a cardinal (a fortune that enabled him to buy his election to the papal throne). The bishoprics, abbacies, archdeaconates, priorates, canonates, prepositures, cantorships, pensions, and ecclesiastical offices of all sorts with which he later endowed his son Cesare were scattered all over Europe, from Valencia to Nantes, from Poitiers to Milan, from Paris to Arezzo, from Rennes to Geneva, from Liège to Como, from Limoges to Grosseto. Each of these preferments guaranteed annual revenues ranging from a handful of ducats to many thousands. The patriarchate of Aquileia alone, for instance, brought in ten thousand ducats a year, and some wealthy dioceses outside Italy—Valencia, for example—brought in even more. Valencia was bequeathed by Calixtus III to his nephew, later his successor, Alexander VI, and by him to his son Cesare, who, when he renounced his cardinalate in 1498, transmitted it to another Borgia cardinal, Giovanni, at whose death only a few months later it passed to Giovanni's brother Pier Luigi, who was hurriedly made a cardinal in 1500.

Nor was the situation notably different in the sixteenth century: even Tridentine reforms seemed to pass like a light, caressing breeze, hardly touching the accumulation of benefices and the traffic in ecclesiastical revenues. The combined annual income of the members of the sacred college in fact rose, reaching more than a million scudi in 1571. It is also true, however, that the numbers of the cardinals also increased conspicuously, and that there was increasing disparity in their fortunes.

At one time or another between 1530 and 1562, the powerful Cardinal de Tournon held more than twenty-five abbeys in commendam, and in 1524 Agostino Trivulzio simultaneously administered the dioceses of Le Puy, Alessano, Toulon, and Reggio Calabria; in 1532 Giovanni Salviati was simultaneously bishop of Ferrara, Bitetto, Volterra, Teano, and Santa Severina; in

1534 Domenico de Cupis was bishop of Trani, Macerata, Recanati, Montepeloso, Adria, and Nardò; and, until as late as 1548, after the Tridentine and papal decrees forbidding the accumulation of bishoprics, Ippolito d'Este headed the dioceses of Autun, Tréguier, Lyons, and Milan. These examples are only a few among many.

The same was true of other preferments such as pensions taken out of diocesan revenues and minor benefices, often held by the dozen, that could be alienated, exchanged, or ceded to relatives and friends with rights of access and regress. This led to a total confusion between private property and ecclesiastical property and to the right (with the appropriate papal authorization) to bequeath such property by testament. The accumulation of benefices goes far toward explaining the gradual decline of the episcopacy between the quattrocento and the cinquecento, a decline that pushed the anonymous voice of satire in Rome, Pasquino, to call the cardinal "de offizi e benefizi un arsenale."

If we think that at the end of the fifteenth century the annual income of an artisan in Rome amounted to a few dozen ducats and that the Venetian ambassador needed at least 2,000 ducats to live with decorum in a manner appropriate to his rank, it is hardly surprising that the electoral capitulars for the conclaves of 1471 and 1484 fixed the minimum revenue of a cardinal at the considerable sum of 4,000 ducats. The actual income of many members of the sacred college often surpassed that sum to reach the 20,000 ducats and more of Giuliano Della Rovere and Marco Cornaro or the 30,000 ducats a year of Ascanio Sforza under Alexander VI. Even these figures may fall short of reality, perhaps by considerable amounts, thus justifying such reactions as the duke of Milan's angry outburst in 1465 at the greed of "clerical leaders of insatiable gluttony" and Ariosto's biting satire:

> Ho sempre inteso e sempre chiaro fummi
> Ch'argento che lor basti non han mai
> Vescovi, cardinali e pastor summi

(I have always clearly understood that prelates never have enough money to satisfy themselves, whether they be bishops, cardinals, or popes [*Satires*, trans. Wiggins, 43])

Some years later (even after the currency devaluation of the sixteenth century), a list of the annual revenues of the cardinals in 1571 shows sums as high as 130,000 scudi (for Charles de Guise) and varying between 60,000 and 80,000 scudi for Cardinals Charles de Bourbon, Henry of Portugal, Ippolito d'Este, and Alessandro Farnese. Farnese (Paul III's homonymous nephew)—"praepotens divitiis et clientelis," as one colleague called him in 1565—was said to dispose of an annual income of 120,000 scudi at his death in 1589.

The estates of over 200,000 scudi that his cousin Guido Ascanio Sforza di Santa Fiora and the cardinal of Trent, Cristoforo Madruzzo, left at their deaths pale in comparison. Alessandro Farnese was fabulously wealthy (his wardrobe alone was later evaluated at 100,000 scudi): he could afford to build the villa on the Palatine, the grandiose Palace of Caprarola, and the majestic Church of the Gesù, still lend 40,000 scudi to the king of France in 1576, and, five years later, pay 100,000 scudi as a one-third down payment on the dowry for a niece who married the duke of Mantua. Not even the most aristocratic families of Rome, the Colonna or the Orsini, could compete with levels of expenditure that henceforth were accessible only to papal families, and it was indeed from families like the Buoncompagni, the Aldobrandini, the Borghese, the Ludovisi, the Barberini, and the Pamphili that the new Roman aristocracy emerged.

Wealth on this scale was the privilege of only a few powerful cardinals, men whose revenues from innumerable ecclesiastical benefices were supplemented by private fortunes and exceptional political and familial ties. At the beginning of the sixteenth century, for example, one-third of the cardinals had revenues on the order of 2,000 to 3,000 ducats, and immediately after the Council of Trent there were many who had to be satisfied with only a few hundred ducats of revenue from benefices—520 ducats annually, for example, for Cardinal Giulio Antonio Santoro; 850 ducats for the Franciscan Felice Peretti (the future Sixtus V). As a "poor cardinal," Peretti was assigned a supplementary pension, but Gregory XIII, who was hostile to him, attempted to withdraw it when he discovered that Peretti could afford to build a grandiose villa on the Esquiline. That a few cardinals were, as someone wrote in 1531, "so poor that they are dying of hunger" should thus be taken in the context of their princely rank and the life-style deemed appropriate for them in a strongly hierarchical, aristocratic society that clung to symbolic values. Massive expenditures accompanied their high incomes. Many members of the sacred college (often the richest and most powerful) repeatedly sought credit from the bankers to fulfill their needs; they often left sizable debts at their death; and some even requested the pope's permission to retire to their dioceses to hide, far from Rome, their inability to keep up the high level of ineluctable expenditure that accompanied the dignity of the cardinalate.

Each cardinal's palace was a miniature princely court playing its political role on the Roman and international scenes. These courts were peopled by a throng of friends, collaborators, secretaries, servants, cooks, soldiers, and adventurers, often joined by musicians, painters, buffoons, astrologers, and a swarm of relatives and hangers-on of all sorts. Even from this point of view, there were of course notable differences between cardinals, given that the total wealth of some was less than the annual income of others. On the eve of the sack of Rome in 1527, for example, the twenty-one courts of the cardinals then residing in Rome ranged from a minimum of forty-five members (for Cardinal Cajetan) to a maximum of 306 (Cardinal Farnese), but ten out of the twenty-one courts had 150 persons or more and only four had fewer than one hundred. Pietro Riario and Ippolito de' Medici, the young nephews, respectively, of Sixtus IV and Clement VII, had households of about five hundred, and as many as 350 people accompanied Ippolito d'Este to France in 1561. The following year Cardinal Gonzaga, at the time legate to the Council and thus also away from home, limited himself to a following of 160 (three times more than any of his colleagues at Trent). On average (but with notable variations), cardinals' courts in the fifteenth and sixteenth centuries included about 150 persons, some of whom enjoyed the title of *familaris domesticus et continuus commensalis*, coveted because it brought privileges and legally recognized exemptions.

Be they gentlemen or artists, trusted collaborators or humble servants, all this world fell under the heading of "mouths," as the term went, whose upkeep posed significant problems. Even a *signore grande* like Francesco Gonzaga, made a cardinal at barely seventeen in 1461, found it difficult to find a palace in Rome for himself and a suite that totaled more than eighty persons on his arrival and included a majordomo, an auditor, a secretary, a personal servant, a notary, a physician, a barber, various chaplains and chamberlains, and dozens of servants, grooms, and lackeys. There were also relatives and protégés, who might all have servants of their own.

This throng obviously required large living spaces, stables, storerooms, and serving rooms; household equipment was needed, and regular provisions of grain, oil, wine, firewood, and forage, all of which cost hundreds or thousands of ducats a year. Added to this was a variety of wages and pensions to be paid, and renting or acquiring buildings adequate to the cardinal's social position and the size of his entourage involved enormous sums. Cesare Borgia's court cost a full 1,500 ducats a month, or the equivalent of the revenues from two or three dioceses. Cortesi was simply being realistic in *De cardinalatu* when he stated that a cardinal's court must have at least 140 members and that ongoing expenses could not be less than 12,000 scudi a year. Around 1540 the *familia* of Niccolò Ridolfi did indeed cost him around 6,500 scudi a year, and that of Giovanni Salviati between 10,000 and 11,000 scudi, while Alessandro Farnese's court, a few years later, devoured as much as 30,000 scudi annually (18,000 for provisions alone).

Furthermore, veritable mountains of gold went into building the splendid cardinal's palaces that we still admire today, such as the Palazzo Venezia, which Bramante built for Raffaele Riario, the Palazzo Medici (now Palazzo Madama), and the Palazzo Farnese. Beside city palaces, the cardinals build gardens for summer sojourns in the hills and luxurious suburban villas like the Villa Giulia, the Orti Farnesiani, the Villa Borghese, and the Villa Pamphili. Cardinal Bernardo Salviati, for example, whose annual income from all preferments totaled some 20,000 scudi in the 1560s and who kept a court of about one hundred persons (thus it was not among the most numerous and splendid of his time) that cost him at least 5,000 to 6,000 scudi a year, spent over 40,000 scudi to build his palace on the via della Lungara. This was nothing, however, in comparison to the nearly 250,000 scudi that had been poured into building the Palazzo Farnese by 1549, or to the fortune Ippolito d'Este spent on his magnificent villa at Tivoli and its famous gardens and extraordinary playing fountains. He even acquired some fifty Turkish slaves to construct these wonders.

Not all cardinals could afford to build on this scale, of course; nevertheless, acquiring an appropriate residence cost several thousand ducats at the beginning of the sixteenth century. Added to the construction costs were the expenses for the paintings, frescoes, sculptures, and luxurious tapestries that decorated these palaces, and the cardinals also ordered grandiose tombs to leave posterity a solemn image of themselves and restored ancient churches and constructed new ones that often bore their name as patron writ large on the facade. Pope Paul III's nephew, for instance, had the facade of the Gesù adorned with the legend "Alexander Farnesius Sanctae Romanae Ecclesiae Vicecancellarius." The splendor of Renaissance Rome as a gathering point for the major artists of those decades would have been unthinkable without ecclesiastical patronage, and the social foundation of the city's artistic and cultural magnificence lay in the inexhaustible expenditures of the papal courts and the cardinals.

Cardinals also needed to spend freely on their frequent voyages. The papal legate in Spain in 1529 regularly spent from 3,000 to 4,000 scudi a month, for example, and in 1547 the same principle of *magnificentia* obliged Charles de Guise to surround himself with an entourage of eighty persons and hold 30,000 scudi in his strongboxes for incidental expenses when he came to Rome to receive his cardinal's hat. In 1517–18, the long voyage of the Cardinal d'Aragona to Germany, Flanders, and France cost at least 15,000 ducats, spent in part for the upkeep of his entourage (cut to the bone at forty persons) and in part to acquire objects, musical instruments, greyhounds, dozens of horses, and hundreds of hunting dogs. Such extraordinary expenses to satisfy his taste for what was new or picturesque, for monuments, for works of art, and for culture in general consumed a good part of the 24,000 ducats of income for which he was listed at the time. He never feared catastrophic debt in keeping up a magnificence adequate to his rank as a prince of the church and of this world.

In some cases ecclesiastical tastes for splendor could reach spectacular heights, as in the limitless prodigality of Leo X or, before him, in that of one of Sixtus IV's nephews, the same Pietro Riario who abandoned his Franciscan's robe for a cardinal's cloak in 1471. In the last two years of his life, Riario managed to accumulate annual revenues of more than 50,000 ducats, but he also spent over 300,000 ducats a year on sumptuous festivities and banquets. "If death had not interrupted the violent course of his vast desires," one critic remarked, "he would soon have reached the bottom of the treasures of the church."

We need to look beyond the obsessive spending and the princely pomp of such men to grasp the political significance of their magnificence. The scenario of display at their courts and the power and wealth on parade there were expressions not only of a cardinal nephew's personal aims and family grandeur but also of the dignity of the church and its triumphal exaltation. A princely *train de vie* was an ineluctable social necessity. It included artistic and cultural patronage and the financing of religious and charitable institutions. It might at times involve games of chance in which certain cardinals lost thousands of ducats in an evening. It embraced a taste for accumulating art objects, gems, and precious stuffs and a duty to satisfy an eager following of relatives, courtiers, and clients avid for prebends, favors, and, above all, curial positions and benefices. It even excused the follies of some papal "cardinal nephews" afflicted with megalomania. The princely life-style was also made of emulation of the aristocracy and a desire to publish to the whole world one's influence and reputation, personal and familial. It also meant showing forth the high dignity of the role of the cardinal, with all the symbolism of power and grandeur the post contained. Quite obviously, all this contributed to enormously high expenditures, totally out of proportion to the cardinals' relatively modest consistorial incomes and to their rights to the benefices earmarked for them. Such expenditures were impossible to sustain without private wealth. In some cases the cardinals' revenues were enhanced by pensions given, with strings attached, by Italian princes and foreign sovereigns, and in other cases, by income from the few well-paid posts available to cardinals (vice-chancellor, penitentiary, and camerlengo in particular). Above all, the cardinals' income was enhanced by a ceaseless race to garner ecclesiastical benefices.

One indirect confirmation of this is the many proposed reforms drawn up (though never put into effect) during this period, as in the past. If nothing else, they testify to an awareness of the increasing gravity of an ongoing problem and of the need to remedy it. As early as the Council of Constance, denunciation of a sacred college inadequate to its high functions was prominently listed among the infinite ills of the church and the wounds to its body *in capite* and *in membris*. The project for the reform of the curia worked out by Pius II prescribed, among other things, that the cardinals in office when the reform took effect could have a court of no more than sixty persons, and in the future, new cardinals' courts would be reduced to forty persons and their revenues from benefices would be limited to 4,000 florins. The cardinals were also denied hunting and frequent attendance at social gatherings where secular music was played. Other provisions limited the number of horses they could keep (some cardinals were wont to arrive on solemn occasions followed by dozens of horsemen). Alexander VI himself, in the brief and ephemeral period of religious zeal that followed the bitter blow of the mysterious assassination of his favorite son, the duke of Gandia, in the streets of Rome in 1497, attempted to found a commission to draw up a "holy reform of the church" using a proposed reform discussed under Sixtus IV as a starting place.

Alexander's bull on reform, which of course remained in the stage of good intentions, stipulated severe penalties for an excessively worldly existence of gaming, hunting, tournaments, banquets, theatrical performances, and Carnival festivities. It forbade the accumulation of bishoprics, specified that a cardinal must reside near the curia, and established limits to revenues from benefices (to 6,000 ducats) and expenditures for display. It limited the size of the cardinal's household (fewer than eighty persons), and stated that the cardinal's "family" was to include a high proportion of ecclesiastics and to exclude minstrels, singers, acrobats, and other entertainers.

During the years that followed, urgent exhortations arose for other substantially identical (and just as vain) projects for a reform that was increasingly difficult to postpone. During the Fifth Lateran Council (1512–17), for example, Vincenzo Querini and Tommaso Giustiniani, two severe Venetian patricians, suggested in their *Libellus ad Leonem X* (1513) that all ecclesiastical benefices be prohibited to the cardinals, who were to be maintained instead by a pontifical fund created for that purpose. Or there was a papal bull dated 5 May 1514 that offered a series of specific reforms (all of which remained a dead letter) and recommended that the cardinals live "sober, chaste, and pious" lives and occupy themselves, with pastoral solicitude, with the churches and abbeys entrusted to their care.

This uninterrupted stream of attempted legislation was accompanied by appeals from reformers and by polemics and invective aimed at the corruption of the church, the ignorance, greed, and indolence of the clergy, and the degeneration of the curia. Savonarola was indefatigable in his charges that the wooden chalices and golden prelates of old had come to be replaced by golden chalices and wooden prelates. Machiavelli attributed to the presence of the papacy in Italy not only the failure to effect political unity in the peninsula but also its inhabitants' becoming "irreligious and perverse." Guicciardini, who inherited a solid tradition of lucid anticlericalism, was always ready to predict "the ruin of the ecclesiastical state" and to hope that the "mass of rotters" at its head would be reduced "to their deserved end"—that is, "either without vices or without authority."

There were also growing cries for reform from beyond the Alps. Erasmus of Rotterdam went so far as to denounce (among a host of other complaints) the "madness" of powerful cardinals who remained insensitive to the world around them, luxuriating in their immense wealth and increasingly unaware that they were "only the administrators" and not the owners of spiritual goods. These voices and many others resounded in a climate of anxious tension, prophetic expectation, and attentive scrutiny of premonitory signs of imminent disaster, revolution, and calamity announcing the coming of the Angelic Pope and the Sword of Vengeance that would at last chase the thieves from the temple and cleanse the church of the filth that had invaded it.

It would be misleading, however, to limit this survey to the church hierarchy's increasing worldliness during the fifteenth and sixteenth centuries. The narrow view leads to sterile moralistic judgments, even to holding the church hierarchy responsible for the revival of ancient pagan culture; for the loss of authentically religious values brought on by that revival; and for the momentary eclipse, at the summit of the church, of a Christian message conserved and transmitted by the Middle Ages, which Tridentine Catholicism was to revive after the terrible trauma of the Reformation. If we want to grasp all the contradictions implicit in the church's dual nature as both a political and religious power, the historical process that the church underwent from the end of the Avignon papacy and the conciliar phase to the early sixteenth century needs to be seen in a European framework and before the backdrop of the construction of the great national monarchies and, in Italy, the regional principalities.

The church's long sojourn in France demonstrated that any demand for freedom from national control for the papacy would be in vain unless the church had an effective territorial independence and the guarantee of a solid political and financial autonomy. When the Holy See returned to Italy, however, the church needed to regain control over the city of Rome, over the barony, and over the lands of the Patrimony of St. Peter, now subject to new and differently articulated forms of power. All these required a forceful hand if a state was to be constructed. The task was entrusted to the unrestrained energies of men like Giovanni Vitelleschi and Ludovico Trevisan, men whose cardinal's robes barely concealed armor and a sword. As with the secular states, the Church of Rome's military ventures obliged it to develop financial and bureaucratic structures, both temporal and spiritual, a diplomatic corps, a chancery, and a growing court. It also required the beginnings (still embryonic) of governing structures for a territorial principality that became part of the Italian and European scene just as a period of profound instability struck the Italian peninsula and as France and Spain found that the focus of their tangled international politics and the battleground for their clashing ambitions lay between Milan, Venice, Naples, and Florence. This, briefly, was the basic situation that shaped the character of the popes and the high prelates around them that I have attempted to outline.

Non-Italian cardinals (whose numbers declined steadily in the sacred college) were almost exclusively French or Spanish. They testify to the political rivalry between those two great powers for dominion over Italy; a rivalry that directly involved the papacy and obliged it to oscillate between alliance with the one and with the other. Increasingly, the foreign cardinals lived outside Rome at the courts of their sovereigns, often (in France in particular) as powerful ministers of the crown. We have already met Jean Balue and Jean Jouffroy, but others deserve mention. There was Guillaume Briçonnet, for example, "the pinnacle of the entire government," according to Guicciardini, who was followed by the omnipotent "cardinal of Rouen," Georges d'Amboise, following a tradition that was to last well into the seventeenth century and include Cardinals Richelieu and Mazarin. Others wielded equal power: Thomas Wolsey, for example, lord chancellor to Henry VIII of England; Matthäus Lang at the side of Maximilian I of Habsburg; and Francisco Jiménez de Cisneros and Adrian of Utrecht in Spain.

As fewer cardinals from beyond the Alps sat in the college of cardinals, their function of representing the universal church in its various national forms diminished, as did their participation in conclaves. Nine out of eighteen cardinals were non-Italian in 1458, but only four out of twenty-six were in 1484 and only two out of twenty-three were in 1492. In 1503, following the papacy of Alexander VI, their numbers rose to fourteen out of thirty-six, only to fall again to six out of twenty-five in 1513 and, in the conclave of 1521 that elected Adrian VI, the last non-Italian pope for more than four and a half centuries, to three out of thirty-nine. When they lived in Rome, the foreign cardinals were apt to act as ambassadors of their countries, serving a

logic of state rather than that of the church. Thus to some extent they reflected the dimming of the concept of *christianitas* that accompanied the crisis
of the empire, the development of national monarchies, and the consolidation
of a network of Italian states that included the growing importance of the
Papal States. It was not by chance that the position of cardinal protector of
the foreign "nations" was instituted toward the end of the fifteenth century.

At the same time, the dynasties that had come into power on the Italian
peninsula began to appear in the sacred college, where they long remained.
The first Gonzaga to be elevated to the purple was Francesco (1461), and after
him came Sigismondo (1505), Ercole and Pirro (both in 1527), a second Francesco (1561), Federico (1563), Gianvincenzo (1578), and Scipione (1587). The
first Este, Ippolito (1493), was followed by another Ippolito (1538) and Luigi
(1561). Sixtus IV elevated a Sforza, Ascanio Maria, to the cardinalate, and
Innocent VIII named Giovanni de' Medici, who, when he became Leo X, not
only consolidated his family's dominion over Florence but also initiated the
constant presence in the sacred college of members of the Medici clan with
the nomination of Giulio (1513), who was followed by Ippolito (1529), Giovanni (1560), Ferdinando (1563), and Alessandro (1583).

What the papacy lacked was the continuity provided by a dynasty and a
national monarchy, the key elements in both the internal and the external
logic of state formation in the new centralized powers that were gaining control everywhere. The highest religious authority in the Christian West, the
man who governed Rome and the church, proclaiming himself Peter's successor and the Vicar of Christ, in fact suffered all the precariousness of an elec-
tive power that not only could not be transmitted hereditarily but was also
short-lived because the popes were typically of advanced age. During the
profound crisis in pontifical authority of the age of the schisms, this precariousness reinforced the political role of the cardinals. After the defeat of conciliarism and the consolidation of the papal monarchy, the cardinals' political
role was much diminished, but the sacred college nonetheless reiterated its
intention to limit, control, and, at times, oppose papal power, as seen in the
early sixteenth century in the rebel Council of Pisa or in Alfonso Petrucci's
conspiracy against Leo X.

These events reflected divisions among the cardinals, and when the papal
throne was vacant, veritable factions arose in the sacred college corresponding
to the cardinals' various political loyalties and personal interests. At such
times the college became an arena for confrontations, clashes, and compro-
mises between particular interests, personal ambitions, and the opposing
claims of the foreign courts, who were always willing to come to an understanding with an individual cardinal if this might result in an influence on

papal policies. The sacred college also acted as a body to oppose the pope, attempting to limit his authority, demanding wealth and privileges for its members, seeking to profit from a conclave to impose binding electoral capitulars on the future pope, and countering all moves to increase the number of cardinals and thus decrease the prestige of the senate of the church. Throughout the quattrocento and beyond, the creation of cardinals required painstaking negotiations on the part of the popes, whose criteria ran counter to those of the electoral body out of which they themselves had been selected. The first nominations announced by Pius II in 1460, for example, aroused bitter opposition from the consistory, which succeeded in drastically reducing the number of those who "cibum nobis auferant." The man who spoke those words in his own name and that of his colleagues was the all-powerful Cardinal Trevisan, who protested vociferously (provoking smiles from some "qui hominem norant") the rumored designation of men of modest origins: "quos nolim," he said scornfully, "in coquina mihi aut in stabulo famulari."

A glance at the capitulars approved by later conclaves shows that the same problems continued to be raised. Each time there were appeals for measures for church reform, for the convocation of a council, for the extirpation of heresy, for combating the Turks, and for the reestablishment of peace. They were always accompanied by more practical demands for favors and privileges, in particular, for guaranteed minimum revenues (as late as 1522 still set at 6,000 ducats annually), for a promise not to make new nominations, and for assurances that major benefices would be assigned only with the assent of the consistory and that its opinion would be heard on all important matters. The fact that these electoral capitulars were never followed through and that the number of cardinals increased continually during the entire period that interests us here shows that the sacred college gradually lost its function as a senate, ceding to the reinforced monarchical power of the pope. This loss is confirmed by the definitive defeat of the cardinals who saw the sacred college as *pars corporis papae* and, consequently, who claimed the *ius divinum* that was its due as a divinely instituted collective body coresponsible, with the pope, for the government of the church. As the authority of the consistory as a whole weakened, new opportunities opened up for individual cardinals who gained the trust of the popes. One might even say that the pomp and the wealth of Renaissance cardinals were simply the other side of the coin of—perhaps their compensation for—their loss of political power as a body, and signaled the end of their demands for oligarchical and constitutional power at the helm of the institution of the church.

It was the Renaissance popes' vital need to have counselors and statesmen in whom they could place full trust that explains their nepotism. Nepotism (even embryonic attempts to transmit the papal throne to the pope's descendants) palliated the lack of hereditary power. It was also a way of getting around the opposition of the sacred college. Between 1455 and 1534 two members of the Borgia family sat on the throne of Peter, as did two men from the Piccolomini, the Della Rovere, and the Medici families (a third Medici was pope for a few weeks in 1605), a list to which we might add Eugenius IV Condulmer and Paul II Barbo, who were close kin. The spendthrift Cardinal Pietro Riario, who stated in 1473 that "he was a second pontiff," was rumored to be plotting to take the place of his uncle Sixtus IV on the papal throne. Cesare Borgia's attempt to construct a state of his own in Italy failed, as did the Medici family's attempt to take the duchy of Urbino from the Della Rovere family. Still, the tiaras of Leo X and Clement VII turned out to be decisive for keeping Florence under Medici domination, and while the Council was meeting in Trent, Paul III succeeded in detaching part of the church domains to found the Farnese duchy of Parma and Piacenza (which was destined to play a lasting role in Italian history). In the following decades as well, nephews and kin continued to crowd the sacred college, to acquire crucial political roles, and to accumulate immense wealth. Carlo Borromeo did so under Pius IV, as Carlo Carafa had done under Paul IV.

Aside from Carafa (to whom I shall return), the case of the incorrigible Innocenzo Del Monte shows that as late as the mid-sixteenth century, cardinals who prompted cries of scandal were still being created. Julius III persuaded his brother to adopt Innocenzo as a child, and he elevated the lad to the purple when he was barely seventeen. In all, there were five Del Monte kinsmen among the twenty cardinals Julius created. Innocenzo had to be incarcerated on several occasions (to little avail), and he was put in the care of pious monks who, it was hoped, would set him back on the straight and narrow path. Similarly, before Pope Paul IV elevated his nephew Carlo Carafa, a violent, hard-swearing man of war, to the cardinalate, he had to absolve him with a papal brief "ab excessibus. . . . et quibusvis rapinis, sacrilegiis, furtis, depredationibus, vulnerum illationibus, percussionibus, membrorum mutilationibus, homicidiis et quibuscomque aliis criminibus et delictis, et forsan praemissis maioribus per eum tam solum quam cum aliis complicibus . . . commissis." This same man guided Roman politics throughout Paul IV's papacy, and, in 1561, he was sentenced to death for his many misdeeds. Another young Carafa cardinal, Alfonso, was accused of having forged a papal bull and avoided judgment by renouncing all his offices and paying a fine of 100,000 scudi. Henceforth, however, no Del Monte, no Carafa, and no other cardinal nephew could use the treasury, the armies, the feudal holdings, or the authority of the church to win himself a principality.

Between the fifteenth and the sixteenth centuries, then, the church constructed a state within the wealthy, cultivated, and splendid Italy of the Renaissance, and Rome became one of the peninsula's most brilliant centers and political capitals. The men called upon to head it—popes like Sixtus IV, Alexander VI, Julius II, and the powerful men whom they invested with the dignity of the cardinalate, who met in consistory and in conclave, who ran legations and apportioned out bishoprics and abbacies—responded to the logic of the state and to that logic alone. In a famous page of his *Storia d'Italia*, Guicciardini bitterly criticizes just this state of affairs, speaking of events after the return of the papacy to Rome. He says:

Raised to secular power, little by little forgetting about the salvation of souls and divine precepts, and turning all their thoughts to worldly greatness, and no longer using their spiritual authority except as an instrument and minister of temporal power, they began to appear rather more like secular princes than popes. Their concern and endeavors began to be no longer the sanctity of life or the propagation of religion, no longer zeal and charity toward their neighbors, but armies and wars against Christians, managing their sacrifices with bloody hands and thoughts; they began to accumulate treasures, to make new laws, to invent new tricks, new cunning devices in order to gather money from every side; for this purpose, to use their spiritual arms without respect; for this end, to shamelessly sell sacred and profane things. The great wealth spreading amongst them and throughout their court was followed by pomp, luxury, dishonest customs, lust and abominable pleasures: no concern about their successors, no thought of the perpetual majesty of the pontificate, but instead, an ambitious and pestiferous desire to exalt their children, nephews and kindred, not only to immoderate riches but to principalities, to kingdoms; no longer distributing dignities and emoluments among deserving and virtuous men, but almost always either selling them for the highest price or wasting them on persons opportunistically moved by ambition, avarice, or shameful love of pleasure. And for all these misdeeds, reverence for the papacy has been utterly lost in the hearts of men, and yet their authority is somewhat sustained by the name and majesty, so powerful and effective, of religion; and mightily by the means they have of gratifying great princes and those powerful personages around them, by conferring dignities and other ecclesiastical concessions. Whence . . . pricked on by the greed to raise their families from private conditions to principalities, the popes have been for a long time, and very often, the instruments of stirring up wars and new conflagrations in Italy. (Guicciardini, *History*, trans. Alexander, 149–50)

Guicciardini's moral indignation apart (an indignation shared by later historiography), consolidation of the national monarchies and pacts drawn up during the fifteenth century had in fact already given over control of much of the benefice system to the various European sovereigns, who were quick to reward friends and supporters with them, to draw conspicuous indirect financial resources from them, and to make use of them to impose state control over the church. Far from being able to consider Christian Europe an inexhaustible source of money to be wrung with no afterthought from tithes, crusades, indulgences, and annates, the popes were constrained, for political reasons, to sign away revenues of this sort and to compensate for the decline in income by granting a greater role to the central tribunals of the curia in the settling of ecclesiastical controversies.

Above all, the popes were forced to find the financial resources they needed within the Papal States and by secular fiscal means. It is hardly surprising that only a few years later Luther's protest exploded in Germany—that is, in divided and fragmented imperial lands lacking a solid central power capable of withstanding the Roman church's invasive assaults and more rapacious forms of exploitation of the sacred. "It astonishes me much," Luther wrote in 1520, "that the German nation . . . still possesses one penny, thanks to those unprincipled thieves and knaves from Rome." These clergy were "unnameable, innumerable, and unspeakable," and their lair was the papal court, which in Luther's eyes was more scandalous "than Sodom, Gomorrah, or Babylon ever were."

Many of the cardinals of these decades—Giuliano Della Rovere, Georges d'Amboise, Thomas Wolsey, to mention only a few—were of course persons of remarkable stature. Their chief spiritual qualities may have resided in their titles and their vestments, but then, they did not think that their high positions involved any particular religious engagement. Many of their contemporaries, who were used to seeing cardinals more as princes than as clerics, saw nothing scandalous in their worldliness. There were consequences, however, that were all the more serious because they were not confined to the summit of the church but invaded all its many parts and reached the entire body of the regular and secular clergy. Dioceses were often entrusted to the care of modest vicars in the chronic absence of their bishops; cathedral canonates were reduced to lucrative prerogatives of the most powerful city families; monasteries and convents languished in a sorry state, the victims of corruption, and often lacked any form of control or authority. A glance at the rich documentation from the post-Tridentine period gives a vivid picture (particularly for peripheral and rural areas) of the abyss of ignorance of some priests entrusted with the cure of souls—priests who had obtained their priestly ministry by cash payments and often lacked even the most elementary notions of religion. The churches and the ceremonies that were celebrated in them, the solemn vestments, the ancient symbols, the rings, crosses, miters, and pastoral letters, even the language of religion and all the models and forms of ecclesiastical power nevertheless evoked functions, problems, and collective needs that were all the more acute and worrisome for being neglected by an institution and a hierarchy that had become incapable of offering adequate solutions. This contradiction and the profound tension it set up triggered the greatest crisis the Church of Rome had undergone in all its history, the traumatic rupture of the Protestant Reformation.

There is little doubt that the person least suited to cope with problems of this scope was Giovanni de' Medici, Lorenzo the Magnificent's son and Poliziano's pupil, chosen in infancy for an ecclesiastical career and a preadolescent when he was named a cardinal in 1489, two years after the marriage of his sister Maddalena and Franceschetto Cibo. Giovanni had just turned thirty-seven in 1513 when he assumed the tiara and the name of Leo X, and he reportedly expressed his intentions clearly, writing his brother Giuliano after his splendid coronation ceremony, "Let us enjoy the papacy, since God has given it to us." The election of this mild and pleasure-loving person "che non vorria fatica" ("who doesn't like to put himself out"), who enjoyed poetry and beautiful objects but was also fond of parties and Carnival, gambling and hunting, who was "most devoted to music, to jests, and to buffoons," as Guicciardini wrote, and was "a man of very great liberality, if such be the proper name for excessive and boundless spending" (*History*, trans. Alexander, 361), seemed to usher in a golden age of peace and splendor in which arms and war would give way to arts and letters. The ascension of a Medici to the papal throne also sealed the close relations that for some time had linked the Holy See to Florentine bankers, who took care of the curia's massive need for credit, provided financial services, and brought order into the church's secular and spiritual fiscal policies. The two Medici popes ushered in a veritable Tuscan invasion of Rome in every branch of church administration and all curial offices. One Venetian observer remarked in 1520 that "Florentines are into everything," and the anonymous satires of Pasquino declared that even the Holy Ghost would be a scoundrel if it were Florentine ("se'l fusse fiorentin / sarebbe un tristo").

The influx of Florentines was of course reflected in the sacred college. Aside from his cousin Giulio (later to succeed him on the papal throne), Leo named no fewer than four kinsmen as cardinals—Giovanni Salviati, Innocenzo Cibo, Niccolò Ridolfi, and Luigi de' Rossi—and a throng of fellow Tuscans—Lorenzo Pucci, Bernardo Dovizi da Bibbiena, Giovanni Piccolomini, Raffaele Petrucci, Silvio Passerini, Francesco Ponzetti, and the aging Niccolò Pandolfini. As Ariosto wrote in one of his satires:

I nipoti e i parenti che son tanti
prima hanno a ber, poi quel che l'aiutaro
a vestirsi il più bel di tutti i manti

(The nephews and relatives, who are so many, must drink first, and then those who helped to dress him in the most beautiful of all mantles [*Satires*, trans. Wiggins, 67]).

The Medici pope reserved places among the new cardinals for trusted family friends like Passerini and Bibbiena (who signed himself *humil factura* and *fidelissimo servo* in letters to his powerful patrons), but there were also people like Pucci, men who had come to the summit of the papal administration before the new pope's election and who were primarily responsible for carrying out his financial policies. Leadership of the Sacred Penitentiary, a tribunal and curial agency that required a high degree of banking competence, was passed from one to another of the three Pucci cardinals who served in the sacred college in an unbroken chain from 1513 to 1547.

Pucci was seconded by Francesco Armellini, an able and unscrupulous opportunist of humble origins, whose brilliant ecclesiastical career was assured by his acquisition of curial responsibilities with money he earned from high-interest loans and speculations of doubtful legality. Armellini won the trust and gratitude of the two Medici popes through his close collaboration with the great Florentine bank and his creative solutions to the problem of new sources of revenue adequate to their inexhaustible financial needs. To do so, he subjected the citizens of Rome and of the Papal States to ever increasing taxes, he incurred debts at exorbitant rates of interest, and he encouraged the sale of indulgences and put offices of all sorts up for sale, thus extending venality to all levels of the pontifical administration. In all this traffic, of course "that black Armellino [variant of *ermellino*, "ermine, weasel"], who would give heaven and earth for a penny" took care to "weasel his way" into the immense fortune that enabled him to buy his cardinalate in 1517 and the office of camerlengo later.

During Leo X's papacy one group of cardinals attempted the ultimate form of open challenge to pontifical authority with the so-called conspiracy of Alfonso Petrucci of 1516. Only a few years before, a group of cardinals led by the highly respected Bernardino Carvajal had attempted to provoke a schism in the church by seceding from the college of cardinals, which led to the convocation of the Council of Pisa in 1511–12 under the patronage of France. Behind this move lay not only the complex political events of those convulsive years but also opposition (in part ideological) to the direction in which Julius II's policies were moving, in particular to his increasingly obvious attempt to strip the cardinals of their authority and their powers of decision as a senate.

The 1516 rebellion of a group of so-called "young cardinals" was quite another affair. It totally lacked any semblance of conscious demand for a collective role for the sacred college or defense of its ecclesiastical responsibilities. Thus it had no significance beyond the discontent and personal frustration of its protagonists. Some of these men had been among those most clearly responsible for the election of the Medici pope and had often been his chosen companions at his receptions and pleasure parties, but they believed that their expectations had been betrayed and their interests neglected. The conspiracy was promoted by Alfonso Petrucci, a handsome young man from Siena whom Julius II had elevated to the purple in 1511 when he was barely nineteen. Petrucci was enraged when Leo X backed his cousin Raffaele, whom he hated, for an important governmental post in Siena that Alfonso's brother Borghese had held.

As time went on, other cardinals joined Petrucci: Bandinello Sauli, Francesco Soderini, Adriano Castellesi, and Raffaele Riario, by then of advanced age and a powerful kinsman of Sixtus IV's, who, as Guicciardini put it, "was undoubtedly the leading cardinal of the College as a result of his wealth, the magnificence of his court, and because of the long time he had held that dignity" (*History*, trans. Alexander, 295). Petrucci's personal anxieties, misfortune, and humiliation in Siena thus mingled with the ancient family rivalries that motivated Cardinal Soderini (the brother of Piero Soderini, standard-bearer of the Florentine Republic, who had been exiled from Florence at the return of the Medici); with the greed and perhaps the disappointment of Sauli (a friend of Petrucci's and a "good merchant" who, rumor had it, had paid some 50,000 scudi to "have himself made a cardinal" in 1511); and with the personal ambitions of Castellesi and Riario, whom the conspirators planned to make pope and who was still nursing an old grudge against the Medici that dated from the Pazzi conspiracy as well as more recent wounds from an unsuccessful candidacy as pope and the war of Urbino.

The conspiracy thus clearly shows some of the significant ways in which the cardinals interpreted their role on the eve of the events and the profound changes that were to bring an end to the Renaissance curia. The cardinalate was for them a means to wealth and power; it was a dignity connected with their social and political status and a way to reinforce and maintain the status—the *particulare*—of their own families. Thus it was also a way to represent their personal and private interests at the summit of the church, interests that they saw as the special province and responsibility of the sacred college, as distinguished from papal authority.

Petrucci paid with his life for having plotted against the pope; Castellesi and Soderini fled into exile; Sauli and Riario were forced to perform humiliating ceremonies of repentance and paid heavy fines (150,000 ducats in the case of the wealthy Riario). Soderini, whom Cortesi defined as a "homo rerum usu limatus et magnarum artium scientia dissimulanter doctus" and whom Giovio called a "segnalato versipelle infranciosato" (notorious frenchified turncoat) was later imprisoned for his scheming by Adrian VI.

Leaving personalities aside, however, the discovery of the conspiracy gave the able Pope Leo an opportunity to impose on a reluctant consistory, on 1 July 1517, the largest list of new cardinals ever created. Taking advantage of the profound malaise that the conspiracy had created in the sacred college, emphasizing the need to renew its membership, to put an end to its worldliness, and to get on with reform of the curia (but also stifling all opposition and diminishing the political role of the college of cardinals—not to mention refurbishing the papal treasury, sorely reduced by the ill-fated war of Urbino), the pope announced the concession of thirty-one new scarlet hats, even though the most recent electoral capitular had once again set the limit at twenty-four cardinals and thirty-three were already in place.

Some of the new cardinals were designated, like the few Pope Leo had already named, to please foreign courts. Others were men of humble origins, time-tested supporters of the pope, but who "in no other respect," Guicciardini tells us, "were worthy of such high office" (*History*, trans. Alexander, 297). They were, for instance, the unscrupulous financier Armellini, or the greedy datary Passerini ("the one never so avaricious or rapacious that the other did not rival him in greed," Garimberti wrote). There was also Francesco Ponzetti, whose wealth came from the many curial positions he held, from physician to Innocent VIII to treasurer general to the Medici pope. Still others were expert curial jurisconsults like Paolo Emilio Cesi and Domenico Giacobazzi, or members of powerful Roman families (Orsini, Colonna, Conti, Della Valle, Cesarini), prominent Sienese families (Piccolomini, Petrucci), or the leading families of Florence (Pandolfini), Genoa (Pallavicini), Modena (Rangoni), and Bologna (Campeggi). Two were Lombards and members of the Trivulzio family, and three were the Medici kin we have already met.

A spate of rumors immediately arose about the amounts that this throng of cardinals had contributed to the empty papal treasury. It must have been a considerable sum (nearly a half million ducats, according to Sanudo's calculations), given that it was rumored that most of the cardinals had to pay 20,000 ducats for the honor—30,000 in Ponzetti's case, despite his long and solid career in the curia, and as much as 40,000 ducats for Bonifacio Ferreri and the superwealthy Armellini.

Except for their number, these designations to the cardinalate were perfectly coherent with past criteria, although they cannot be said to have furthered the renewal of the sacred college, even if the election of the generals of three religious orders might seem a step in that direction. Tommaso de Vio (Cardinal Cajetan), general of the Dominicans; Egidio da Viterbo, general of the hermits of St. Augustine; and Cristoforo Numai, general of the Franciscans, were men of solid theological culture and well aware of the need for reform. At the Fifth Lateran Council the same Egidio made his famous declaration that "homines per sacra immutari" were needed, "non sacra per homines."

One result of this mass promotion—contingencies specific to those years aside—was to seal the supremacy of pontifical authority over that of the sacred college. Henceforth forms of opposition like the schismatic council of Pisa and the short-lived Petrucci conspiracy would no longer occur. It was from then on (aided by the lacerating religious rupture set off only a few months later by the publication of the Wittenberg theses) that the college of cardinals slowly became a body of high functionaries in the curial government and administration unanimously devoted to the service of the Holy See and innocent of any trace of opposition to or even desire for political negotiation with the power that held the keys of Peter—a transformation that was ratified seventy years later in the great Sistine reform.

Leo X died in October 1521, leaving a sea of debts behind him (Pasquino insinuated that he would have sold Christ for his pleasures—"Cristo aria venduto per le spese"), but also leaving the reputation, magnified by Giovio, of having "fabricated the Golden Age" with his munificence. The century of Leo X, a world that Voltaire was to judge comparable to the ages of Alexander, Augustus, and Louis XIV for artistic and cultural splendor, had by now reached an end. Several months earlier Luther had publicly burned the bull *Exsurge Domine* in the main square of Wittenberg, together with a number of canonistic texts, and in May of that year, after the Diet of Worms, he was placed under the ban of the empire.

A year before, while Hernán Cortés was conquering Mexico, Süleyman the Magnificent was assuming power in the Ottoman empire, and Lutheran doctrines were spreading and finding powerful allies throughout Germany, Raphael and the omnipotent *alter papa*, Bernardo Dovizi, died in Rome. Cardinal Bibbiena, an intelligent, sharp-witted, versatile man, had been an indefatigable negotiator and the shrewd stage manager of the papal election at the conclave of 1513. He had been a trusted chancellor of Lorenzo the Magnificent's and an able diplomat for the Medici, whose varying fortunes he had followed until he was rewarded with the purple. A gallant, sprightly courtier and the author of the licentious *La Calandria*, Dovizi, with all his contradictions, was perhaps the best expression of what amounted to the inability of the highest leaders of the church to grasp or confront the dramatic new problems—political and diplomatic, but also religious, pastoral, and doctrinal—that the Protestant Reformation brutally imposed on the curia. The cultivated and refined Rome of Leo X (men like Bembo and Sadoleto were among his secretaries) found it difficult to see Luther as more than a troublesome German monk to be reduced to silence. The bland Fifth Lateran Council came to a close in 1517, after ample discussion of the many reforms everyone agreed were necessary but with little or nothing accomplished toward putting them into effect.

The papacy of the austere and pious Adrian of Utrecht was too brief to change matters. The son of a modest Flemish artisan who had become a professor at the University of Louvain, Adrian became the preceptor of Charles of Habsburg, a bishop and a cardinal, and grand inquisitor and Charles's regent in Spain. His unforeseen election to the papacy in 1521 was the work of a sacred college many of whose members, as Guicciardini put it, were men "full of ambition and incredible greed, and almost all dedicated to the most refined, not to say most dishonest, pleasures" (trans. Alexander, 331).

Word of his sudden death less than two years later (he spent only one year in Rome, where the plague was raging) was greeted with a universal sigh of relief and "inestimable pleasure" by a curia nearly unanimously hostile to him, one that had expressed its proud scorn of the ultramontane "barbarian" and its fear that his papacy might bring an end to the abusive practices and privileges enjoyed by all. As Giovio's hunting image so neatly put it somewhat later, he risked spoiling "the tail of the pheasant of this Holy See." One correspondent in Ferrara wrote in March 1523, "Although Leo was a leech for money, at least he spent it, but this one sucks and does not spend, so that all Rome is dismally unhappy and never has there been such melancholy in all memory." Francesco Berni wrote in his scathing *Capitolo di papa Adriano*:

> O poveri infelici cortegiani
> usciti dalle man de' Fiorentini
> e dati in preda a Tedeschi e marrani.

(O, poor unhappy courtiers, who escaped from the clutches of the Florentines to be given in prey to Germans and Spanish renegades.)

Berni goes on to lash out at the "forty poltroons" and "unclerical thieves of no-good cardinals" who had "put the church on the brink of ruin" with the election of "a saintly pope who says his mass every morning," an "enemy of

Italian blood," and a low-born drunkard who claimed to "play the lord over Italy."

A violent pasquinade echoed Berni's opinions, attacking the Italians who had been responsible for "having lost the papacy [to gain] a bastard renegade tyrant." The satire continues:

> O vil canaglia, o asin da bastoni,
> bestie senza saper, senza intelletto,
> nati sol a pacchiar e star in letto
> con puttane, ragazi e bugiaroni.

(O vile rabble, O asses [good only] for beating, beasts without learning, without intellect, born only to stuff your faces and go to bed with whores, boys, and buggerers.)

Pope Adrian created only one cardinal, shortly before he died: his trusted datary, Wilhem van Enckevoirt, who was immediately rechristened "Trinca-forte" (Big Drinker). Adrian's successor, Clement VII, a cousin of Leo X's (thus, after a brief interval, another Medici on the throne of Peter), created thirty-three cardinals.

A prelate of unassailable mores and a serious and intelligent man, "prudent and wise . . . a just man and a man of God," according to the Venetian ambassador; a man with a vast experience of government, according to Guicciardini, who knew him well, Giulio de' Medici was (also in Guicciardini's opinion) "impeded by his timidity of spirit [and] by a strong reluctance to spend, but also by a certain innate irresolution and perplexity" (History, trans. Alexander, 363). In the last analysis, as one Roman noted in his journal, he had been "better as a cardinal than as pope." According to Berni, the papacy of Clement VII was

> Un papato composto di respetti,
>   di considerazioni e di discorsi,
>   di pur, di poi, di ma, di se, di forsi,
>   di pur assai parole senza effetti,
> di pensier, di consigli, di concetti,
>   di conietture magre per apporsi,
>   d'intrattenerti, pur che non si sborsi,
>   con audienze, risposte e bei detti,
> di pie' di piombo e di neutralità,
>   di pazienza, di dimostrazione,
>   di fede, di speranza, e carità.

(A papacy made up of respects, considerations, and discourses; of "provided that," "later" "but," "if," and "perhaps"; of great numbers of words without effects; of thoughts, advice, and ideas; of conjectures [too] thin to lean on; of discoursing with you, provided he doesn't have to pay, in audiences, responses, and fine sayings; of lead feet and neutrality; of patience; of shows of faith, hope, and charity.)

It was in these cruel and caustic terms that Berni stigmatized the thousand doubts, the continuous oscillations, the voluble groping, and the narrow-minded subterfuges of a timorous and ultimately inconclusive policy that led the Holy See into the tragic sack of Rome in 1527, when the city was left the defenseless prey of Frundsberg's imperial *Landsknechten*, who first devastated the city then imposed ruinous taxes on it. The sack of Rome signaled the "exterminio et total ruina" of the city, someone in Mantua said in describing the "cruel spectacle that would move stones to pity" of the innumerable killings, robberies, rapes, tortures, and horrors of all sorts that had taken place. Although the pope and some of the cardinals managed to take refuge in Castel Sant'Angelo, others—Pucci, Piccolomini, Cajetan, Numai, and Ponzetti among them—were roughly treated or tortured and held for ransom. In the meanwhile, swarms of drunken soldiers ran rampant through the city, some dressed in cardinals' robes, taking particular delight in ferocious attacks on churches and convents and combining their thirst for booty with a violent scorn for Rome that they had learned from Protestant invective. The cry of *Vivat Lutherus pontifex* echoed in derision through the streets of Rome during those terrible days. To this day, the name of the Saxon monk can be read, carved into the surface of Raphael's fresco of the Triumph of the Holy Sacrament in the Stanza della Segnatura in the Vatican.

Clement VII's nominations to the cardinalate were strongly influenced by the sack of Rome, in particular by the need for financial resources in the tragic situation in which the pope now found himself: without troops, penniless, a prisoner in a Rome stricken by pestilence, and at the mercy of Charles V. This meant that whether Clement liked it or not, cardinalates were up for sale as usual. Sanudo reports that the price was 40,000 ducats apiece for nearly all the cardinals designated in May, just before Frundsberg's soldiers entered Rome, and the same in November, when the papal court was still confined in Castel Sant'Angelo.

It is hardly surprising, then, that Clement, impelled by urgent credit needs (he had to ask Cellini to melt down the chalices used for mass, the pope's tableware, even his predecessors' tiaras), called men from great banking families to the sacred college. Girolamo Grimaldi and Agostino Spinola came from Genoa (Girolamo Doria, Andrea's nephew, would follow two years later); Niccolò Gaddi came from Florence; Marino Grimani and Francesco Cornaro (both of whom were related to cardinals) came from Venice. Others were the kin of cardinals: Vincenzo Carafa, Ercole and Pirro Gonzaga, and Benedetto Accolti.

A truly cruel and corrupt man despite his humanistic culture, Accolti seemed to put his entire energy into giving the lie to Ariosto's vision of the "glory and splendor of the holy consistory" and into lending credence to Giovio's judgment of him as *furioso e pecunioso* (mad and rich). Accolti had committed crimes and violent acts of all kinds, in particular during his tyrannical leadership of the legation of the Marches, which he bought in 1532 for 19,000 ducats. He continued unabated, amid accusations of homicide and rape, plotting intrigues and committing frauds and thefts of all varieties, until he was arrested in 1535 and sentenced to death (later commuted to a large fine).

Finally, many cardinals called to the sacred college were faithful followers of Emperor Charles V, since by then he called the tune in Italy and in Rome. A number of Neapolitans were among them, including Sigismondo Pappacoda, who permitted himself the luxury of refusing the purple.

Except for Clement VII's ambitious eighteen-year-old cousin, Ippolito de' Medici ("mad as the Devil"), who was to cause him many a worry (beginning with Ippolito's refusal to take holy orders to become a subdeacon), and his fellow Florentine Antonio Pucci, nearly all the cardinals later created by Clement VII were named at the request of foreign courts. By then Clement was a pawn in a complex, changeable, and labyrinthine political game in which he attempted to pick his way between Rome and Florence, Habsburgs and Valois. One cardinal he designated was the learned general of the Franciscans, Francisco de Quiñones Another, named as peace with the emperor was reestablished—an occasion celebrated in the solemn encounter in Bologna in 1530—was the impetuous Garcia de Loaysa, former general of the Dominicans and Charles V's confessor. There were also the imperial chancellor, Mercurino da Gattinara; the bishop of Trent, Bernard von Cles; Louis de Challant of Savoy; and the bishop of Burgos, Iñigo de Zúñiga. Three months later Alfonso Manrique de Lara, archbishop of Seville and grand inquisitor, and Juan Pardo de Tavera, the regent of Spain, were added to the list. Finally, in 1533, Clement named Stefano Gabriele Merino, of whom it was rumored that as a child he had been "seen in Rome in charge of the hounds in the house of Cardinal Ascanio" (Sforza). He had become bishop of Jaén and patriarch of the Indies, and was, in the opinion of the Venetian ambassador, a "sapientissimo cardinale e grandissimo pratico" (very wise cardinal and great expert).

Up to then, the French had to be satisfied with four nominations. The first was that of chancellor Antoine Duprat (1527), who died several years later "of obesity and crapulousness" (according to Garimberti) and with feelings of remorse (according to one seventeenth-century historian) for "having observed no other law than his own interests and the sovereign's passion." Later came the nominations of François de Tournon and Gabriel de Gramont, the French ambassador to Rome, in 1530, and of Jean de Longueville, Louis XI's nephew, in 1553. A better balance was struck between French and imperial cardinals only after the reconciliation between the pope and the Most Christian king, sealed by the marriage of Caterina de' Medici and Henry of Valois, heir to the throne, when four French cardinals were named in Marseilles in November 1533. Among them was Odet de Coligny, who later left the Church of Rome to marry and die a good Calvinist in England in 1571.

After the atrocities of the sack of Rome in 1527—a traumatic experience for contemporaries, who in some cases interpreted it in apocalyptical terms— Rome may not quite have been reduced to the "chicken-yard" that one writer called it, but it was no longer the unprincipled but open-minded Renaissance Rome of Sixtus IV, Alexander VI, and Leo X. One visitor toward the end of 1528 found the city "much ruined and devastated." Depopulated and stripped of its artists and men of letters, the city would never again be the same, while new spiritual anxieties and new religious problems soon penetrated even the papal court in the Vatican and the palaces of the cardinals.

The Reformation had spread throughout Germany and was rampant in Switzerland, England, Scandinavia, and eastern Europe. Heterodox doctrines were proliferating in France and Italy. All this required a decisive change of direction and an end to ecclesiastical politics limited to the Italian interests of one pope or one family. Initiating some sort of confrontation with the Protestants that went beyond hasty and summary condemnation was now unavoidable, as was summoning a general council. Third, plans for the institutional reorganization of the church needed to be drawn up, not only to reestablish the credibility of the curia but also to regain control of the clergy and of its religious formation; to stimulate renewed dedication to pastoral care, charitable works, and assistance to the unfortunate; to discipline the religious life of the laity; and to deal with the many difficult tasks made necessary by disputatious clashes with the Protestant heretics, the repression of internal dissent, the expansion of missionary work, and the evangelization of rural areas that were Christian in name only.

During the years and decades that followed, with the Council of Trent (an Iliad for its length and complexity, as Paolo Sarpi said) and the profound changes of the age of the Counter-Reformation as a background, the Catholic Church gradually became aware of all these issues, and of its ends and the means it would use to reach them. A concerned and embittered Giovio wrote in February 1535:

The opulence of the old popes is annihilated for having attended more to the temporal than the spiritual; and thus, bit by bit losing the reputation and authority of religion, the shop no longer turns a profit and we have been led where we now are, to the need for a great council, from which no good can be hoped unless God puts his right hand to it.

Pope Clement (who, incidentally, feared that a council might raise the issue of his illegitimate birth) was hardly the man to take the first step in that direction, nor to promote the long-awaited reforms. When Berni put his biting wit to rewriting Boiardo's *Orlando innamorato* (Berni's work was completed in 1531, but, for understandable reasons, it was left unpublished), his bitter resentment bore explicit anti-Roman and somewhat Protestant connotations:

> Dicon certi plebei che or ora il papa
> vuol riformarsi, con gli altri prelati.
> Io dico che non ha sangue la rapa,
> né sanità, né forza gli ammalati,
> e de l'aceto non si può far sapa;
> dico che allor saranno riformati,
> quando'l caldo sarà senza tafani,
> il macello senz'ossa e senza cani.

(Some common folk say that soon now the pope intends to reform himself and the other prelates. I say that a turnip has no blood; you cannot expect health or strength from the sick, nor make savory sauce from vinegar; I say they will be reformed when summer's heat brings no gadflies and the butcher has no bones and no dogs.)

The problems of the council and of reform could be met only with the election of a new pontiff. On 13 October 1534, the Cardinal Deacon Alessandro Farnese was chosen, "a man gifted with learning, and to all appearance of good morals," as Guicciardini so aptly put it, "who had exercised his office as cardinal with greater skill than that whereby he had acquired it" (*History*, trans. Alexander, 442). He won everyone's votes because he was aging and was reputed to be ill ("which opinions were spread by him with considerable skill"; ibid.).

Farnese was unanimously respected. In culture and experience he was a figure from another age, since he had completed his studies in the Florence of Lorenzo the Magnificent and had received his cardinal's hat from Alexander VI more than forty years earlier. It could hardly be said that he was tormented by profound religious anxieties (he said his first mass at the age of fifty-one in 1519, when he had been an cardinal for twenty-six years). As the Venetian ambassador said soon after his election, he had "continually attended to delights and pleasures." A shrewd and capable diplomat, however, he was determined to continue the policy of reinforcing pontifical authority over the Papal States and over the barons (as the wars against Perugia, Camerino, and the Colonna family show). He was equally determined in pursuing his nepotistic ambitions, and in 1545 he enfeoffed his hapless son Pier Luigi with the duchy of Parma and Piacenza, which he carved out of the church domains for that purpose.

Nevertheless, he brought renewed energy to the many and grave problems that had too long been put off by the Medici popes and too often subordinated to their Florentine interests. It was, in fact, the Farnese pope who instituted the first purposeful commission *de emendanda ecclesia* and who made concrete proposals for the reform of such financial arms of the papacy as the chancery, the datary, and the penitentiary ("the workshop of skullduggery," Cardinal Gonzaga called it), where the most tenacious forms of curial corruption were rooted. In the final analysis, his efforts bore only modest fruit, even considering the constraint of avoiding threat to vital sources of revenue. Still, some of the provisions he fostered certainly had symbolic value as signs of changing times.

One provision for reform promulgated only a few days after the election of the new pope stipulated that all prelates must "go about dressed appropriately." The writer (from Lucca) who reports this news adds, "something that does not much please the younger cardinals and those like them, accustomed to every license." Another decree promulgated 18 February 1547 extended to members of the sacred college the conciliar disposition limiting bishops to one benefice, with obligatory residence in their diocese. Paul III also approved the institution of St. Ignatius of Loyola's Society of Jesus in September 1540 and backed the other new orders—Barnabites, Theatines, and Capuchins—that were to be pilasters of the Counter-Reformation. It was he who agreed, albeit against his will, to the imperial request to set up colloquia with the Protestants, gathering learned theologians and moderates from both sides around one table in an attempt to reach an improbable agreement on doctrine. Above all, it was Paul III who took on the serious engagement (overcoming notable difficulties and well-founded fears) of calling the council. It was he who brought about the agreement that Trent would be the site of the council and who brought its first and decisive session from 1545 to 1547 to a close with the approval of a number of fundamental theological decrees. It was he who instituted the court of the Inquisition in Rome (in July 1542) and set at its head the first permanent commission of cardinals, an administrative device much imitated in the following decades to respond to specific needs in the various areas of the church's endeavors. The number and the functions of such commissions were later formalized in the bull *Immensa aeterni Dei* of 22 January 1588 and with the great Sistine reforms that signaled the end of both the political authority of the consistory and the sacred college's function as a body for collective governance of the church.

A change of direction of this scope also demanded new energies and abilities from the leadership of the curia, hence it contributed to Paul III's determination to renovate the sacred college. His nominations not only increased the number of members of that body (there were forty-six cardinals at the death of Clement VII; fifteen years later, at the start of the conclave that elected Julius III, there were fifty-four) but also improved the character of its members (in the opinion of the Venetian ambassador in 1535 men "of most excellent qualities"). Naturally the new pope, following the time-honored Renaissance tradition and turning a deaf ear to a *mormorio grande* of disapproval, elevated two very young nephews to the purple, Alessandro Farnese (who was fourteen) and Guido Ascanio Sforza di Santa Fiora (who was sixteen). In 1536 they were joined by their thirteen-year-old cousin Nicola Caetani di Sermoneta, and in 1545 by another papal nephew, Ranuccio Farnese, fifteen at the time. The elevation of several men of modest social status or dubious morality also met with bitter criticism. Durante de' Duranti, for example, was "low-born in Brescia and [had] lived in the Roman court for a good thirty years *alli servitii in minoribus di Nostro Signore*, without learning or other good qualities," according to the diarist of the council, and when he died he left a reputation as a man who had "never been useful for anything in his life." There was Tiberio Crispi, half-brother to the pope's sons, characterized by a fellow cardinal as "vir penitus illiteratus neque ingenio admodum perspicaci."

A number of the seventy-one cardinals designated by Paul III during his papacy were named at the request of foreign courts. These included Cardinals Armagnac, Annebault, and Amboise (all cardinals' kin); later, Cardinals Lenoncourt, Guise, Bourbon, and the learned archbishop of Paris, Jean du Bellay. Others were Alvarez de Toledo, Manrique de Aguilar, Mendoza y Bobadilla, Avalos, de la Cueva, Pacheco, Truchsess von Waldburg, Madruzzo, even a son of the king of Portugal, and two Borgias. Italian interests were represented as well: there were a Contarini and a Cornaro from Venice, an Este from Ferrara, a Fregoso from Genoa, a Carafa from Naples, a Ferreri from Piedmont, a Pucci from Florence, a Guidiccioni from Lucca, a Crescenzi and a Savelli from Rome, a Della Rovere from Urbino (the last two barely more than boys), not to mention other offspring of cardinals' families like Giovanni Maria Del Monte (later Julius III), Federico Cesi, and Cristoforo Giacobazzi. Although these cardinals may have been elevated for traditional reasons, it became increasingly clear during these years that the curia's change of direction was guided by some of these same men, who interpreted their high role in a new manner, giving it a religious impetus and a reforming zeal that would have seemed extraordinary, to say the least, in the recent past.

One of these exceptional cardinals was Gasparo Contarini, a man who underwent a religious crisis that led him to reflection on justification and grace in terms not very different from the ones that Luther would later propose; a man who took on weighty philosophical and theological studies in Padua, who entered into public debate with his master, Pomponazzi, and who wrote a *De officio boni viri ac probi episcopi* in 1517 and, somewhat later, a confutation of the *Confessio Augustana*. Born in 1483, Contarini's human and spiritual development was clarified by an intense debate with two other Venetian patricians, Tommaso Giustiniani and Vincenzo Querini (who was raised to the cardinalate in 1514, not long before his death), men whom we have already seen as the authors of the courageous appeal for reform, the *Libellus ad Leonem X*.

Although their thinking shared basic premises, Contarini had not joined his friends in their decision to retire to the hermitage of Camaldoli. He chose instead active involvement in the world, specifically, in the civic and political life of the Serenissima, and he served Venice in a number of diplomatic and government positions. The high consideration in which he was held, both as a person and as an intellectual, won him the esteem of Charles V and prompted Paul III's call to the sacred college in May 1535. Though universally admired, he was a layman, which prompted one prominent Venetian senator of notorious anti-Roman sentiments to snap, "Those priests have even robbed us of the best gentleman this city had." Soon after, Contarini was entrusted with guiding the first attempts at reform of the curia, a task beset by difficulties.

Gian Pietro Carafa was a man totally different from Contarini in both character and attitudes, but his career is equally useful for understanding the changes that took place during these years. Although his doctrinal and political tendencies were rigoristic and at the opposite pole from Contarini's, Carafa too was moved by a profound desire to renew not only his own personal religious life but also that of the church as an institution. Carafa, a descendant of an illustrious Neapolitan family that had sent many representatives to the sacred college, was born in 1476 and given a solid humanistic education that earned him the admiration of Erasmus. Although he was named bishop of Chieti in 1505 and then papal nuncio to Spain, Carafa appeared to refuse to take full advantage of the splendid ecclesiastical career that these achievements seemingly guaranteed him and became a founding member of the Oratory of Divine Love. He left Rome at the sack of the city and renounced his bishopric, retiring to Venice with Gaetano da Thiene and the first brothers of the Theatine order.

With an overall plan clearly in mind and driven by an intransigent zeal for reform, Carafa gradually concentrated his energies on an implacable struggle against all forms of disobedience and religious dissent. The theoretic foundations of his position were laid out in a memorandum to Clement VII written as early as 1532, in which he stated that "heretics need to be treated as heretics." Called to the sacred college in 1536, Carafa laid down the guiding principles of the Holy Office (the Inquisition) and directed it with obsessive rigor, to the point of becoming "the most hated and feared cardinal . . . who has ever lived in our times," as was said after his death. He made free use of the Holy Office to impose his inflexible scruples of orthodoxy, and he gained increasing influence on papal policies. Between 1555 and 1559, when he occupied the papal throne under the name of Paul IV, he loosed sweeping repression. In widely varying forms, levels of intensity, modes, and times, the religious question that was so central to these years ended up involving even such people as Ercole Gonzaga, the cardinal of Mantua and the powerful son of Isabella d'Este; Cristoforo Madruzzo, the prince-bishop of Trent; Reginald Pole, the cardinal of England and a cousin of Henry VIII; and the great diplomat Giovanni Morone. Another cardinal, Federico Fregoso, was not only a Genoese patrician but a man of letters, a theologian, and the author of works placed on the Index not long after (his name was even put to translations of Luther's works). There was also Cardinal Ippolito d'Este, the son of Lucrezia Borgia. He lived magnificently and collected for his library the principal works of Erasmus—whose *Opera omnia* were condemned soon after in the first Roman Index of 1559, but whose name had been raised as a possible candidate for the purple early in the papacy of Paul III.

The Holy See's renewed diplomatic efforts to bring about peace among the European powers in view of the council guaranteed brilliant ecclesiastical careers, crowned by cardinalates, to many nuncios and legates who had served with distinction in difficult missions in France, Spain, Portugal, and Germany. Among these were Ennio Filonardi, Rodolfo Pio of Carpi, Uberto Gambara, Girolamo Capodiferro, Bonifacio Ferreri, Giovanni Morone, Francesco Sfondrato, Girolamo Verallo, and later, under Julius III, Pietro Bertano (a Dominican), Giovanni Ricci, Fabio Mignanelli, Giovanni Poggio, and Girolamo Dandino. Curial experience and solid juridical preparation, as well as the confidence of the pope, determined the designation of men like Girolamo Ghinucci, Giacomo Simonetta, Pier Paolo Parisio, Bartolomeo Guidiccioni, Federico Cesi, Marcello Crescenzi, and Niccolò Ardinghelli.

Above all, demand for reform and for intellectual and theological combat against Reformed doctrines not only suggested the enrollment of men of solid theological preparation like Dionigi Laurerio, the general of the Servites; the Benedictine Gregorio Cortese; Tommaso Badia, a Dominican and Master of the Sacred Palace; but also of humanists, men of letters, and laymen of great culture and prestige. Contarini has already been mentioned. It was doubtless his influence within the curia that prompted the nominations in 1536 of Jacopo Sadoleto, a learned Latinist who had retired to Carpentras just before the sack of Rome to occupy himself with his diocese and his adored studies; of Reginald Pole, who had already clashed with Henry VIII on the questions of divorce and schism and who had written a work entitled *Pro ecclesiasticae unitatis defensione*; of Girolamo Aleandro, a Greek scholar with a wealth of experience in German lands; and, three years later, of Federico Fregoso and Marcello Cervini, the young Cardinal Farnese's tutor and secretary, who would later become pope as Marcellus II.

It was to these men—Carafa, Sadoleto, Contarini, Pole, Fregoso, Aleandro, Cortese, Badia, and Giberti (who had been datary and a powerful minister of Clement VII but had retired, after the collapse of the papacy's antiimperial policies, to his diocese of Verona, where he offered an early model of the exemplary, post-Tridentine bishop)—that Paul III entrusted the drafting, in 1536, of a *Consilium de emendanda ecclesia*, which was delivered to the pope in March of the following year. "Omnes fere reverendissimi favent reformationi; incipit immutari facies consistorii," Contarini wrote two months later. Soon after, in October 1540, Paolo Giovio, a man who had typified the age of Leo X, declared in a letter addressed to the future cardinal Giovanni Poggio that thanks to these reforms he had given up all ambition "of meriting the red hat, which is the due of sons of good fortune."

The most emblematic designation of all—even in the objections that it prompted—was that of Pietro Bembo in March 1539. Bembo was a Venetian patrician and a highly learned man, the official historian of the Serenissima, the author of *Gli Asolani* (dedicated to Lucrezia Borgia, whom he had loved passionately), of *Prose della volgar lingua*, and of *Rime* that were immediately proposed as a model as long as Petrarchism was in vogue. He was a figure from another age, now in his twilight years, and he had given up all hope of obtaining the honor "that is so sought after and perhaps one ought to shun," as he wrote in 1527. He had lived for some time far from Rome.

In his youth, Bembo had frequented the celebrated Renaissance courts of Ferrara and Urbino; he was a friend of Bibbiena's and, with Sadoleto, had written briefs for Leo X. He was the undisputed master of an entire school of literary civility; he lived surrounded by the children he had had with the beautiful and gentle Morosina (who stood as proof of his less than perfect loyalty to the religious vows he had been obliged to make in order to continue to enjoy his notable ecclesiastical benefices).

Bembo was doubtless one of the most prominent representatives of the high humanistic culture to which the church now turned in its search for the aid, resources, and energy it needed to confront its deepest crisis. As Carlo Dionisotti has written, Bembo was "a man for whom the cardinalate, in a Visible Church that wanted to be in the avant-garde of humanistic and human culture, was worth a mass." He said that first mass, when he was over seventy, in July 1541, on the occasion of the death of Federigo Fregoso, who was not only a friend and a fellow cardinal but a member of the group in Urbino thirty years earlier whose conversations were recorded in Baldassare Castiglione's *Il cortegiano*. When men like these entered the sacred college and when they became actively involved in curial commissions, nunciatures, legations, and conciliar politics, the ideal that Paolo Cortesi had presented in his *De cardinalatu* seemed finally realized. This ideal, in Carlo Dionisotti's words, was "the experience of a culture that in the crisis of the Italian states had taken refuge in the church, and in the crisis of the church now bore its not inconsequential message of persuasion and dialogue, of classical measure and the continuity of thoughts and words through time."

Moral rigor, intellectual integrity, and a common will for reform still do not provide a full definition of the significance of the religious commitment of these men, some of whom were ultimately personally engaged in theological debate in the great religious crisis of their time. Contarini's attempts to bring about peaceful reconciliation, and the willingness to engage in dialogue and to mediate between opposing sides that animated his illusive utopia of religious colloquy, went down to defeat in Regensburg in the spring of 1541—a defeat that signaled the end of his political leadership and what amounted to his exclusion from the curia. By no means do they tell the entire story of the tensions and anxieties that such men experienced, however. Others—Pole, Fregoso, Morone, and, in varying measure, other members of the sacred college—had by then left the current dominated by Contarini to follow doctrinal orientations that were often close to Protestantism but that stopped well short of any desire for institutional rupture. Some of them even reconciled an unconditional and liberating adherence to the doctrine of justification by faith alone with undisputed loyalty to the Church of Rome and even with their rank as cardinals. They did so by emphasizing a refined spirituality of mixed provenance—indeed, they were called "spirituals"—that mediated between contradictions and left ample room for individual conscience, the internal voice of divine inspiration, and a providentialist faith in change over the long term. Christianity was for these men a personal and privileged experience of regeneration, and they treated the outward forms of religious life and the arid erudition of controversialist theologians with caustic disdain.

Space does not permit adequate consideration of the thought and the individual positions of these men, of the specific forms of community and action they inaugurated or of the complex relationships that such initiatives established with the men and the milieu of heterodox dissent during those years. The Council of Trent's approval of the decree on Justification of January 1547 signaled the end of the hopes and perhaps of the ambiguous illusions of this small but highly authoritative group of cardinals. It was not long, in fact, before people like Gian Pietro Carafa, who made it his business to destroy the spreading plague of heresy wherever it appeared, were spreading insinuations and arousing suspicions about them.

As early as 1540–41, the men who not long before had been called to the sacred college to support Contarini seemed not only divided but rallied to opposing sides: those for whom reform of the church obligatorily involved theology (who thus accepted some of the basic premise of the Reformation), and those who believed that the church should concentrate on reinforcing its own institution in order to repel its enemies (who thus held that the church should embark on Counter-Reformation). For the latter, enemies were all the more dangerous when they lurked insidiously within the church, and most dangerous at its summit.

Thus the institution of the Holy Office in July 1542 signaled a clear change of direction in favor of Carafa. It also provided his politico-religious line of thought with an excellent instrument for inquiry not only into heterodox preachers and crypto-reform conventicles but also (and perhaps above all) into the "spiritual" cardinals, their friends, and their collaborators to seek what were soon defined as grave deviations, complicity, and heresy. In August of the same year, while Contarini lay dying in Bologna, court proceedings were instituted in Rome against the great Sienese preacher Bernardino Ochino, general of the Capuchins, a man acclaimed and venerated by all, a friend of Pole's and Vittoria Colonna's, who had been mentioned in 1539 as a probable cardinal and who now, in a clamorous gesture that seemed to confirm the worst suspicions, fled to Calvin's Geneva.

Thus in those years the struggle against heresy became a bitter struggle within the sacred college to determine both the objectives and the specific content of the reaction to the challenge of the Reformation to which the Church of Rome had committed itself. Carafa collected denunciations and secret testimony with tenacious patience, daring even to challenge the authority of the pope. He then used this information ruthlessly in curial politics and in the conclaves of those years, defeating moves to elect Pole to the papacy in 1549 (before the conclave opened, Pole's election was taken for granted) and Morone in 1555.

As has rightly been observed, the conciliar debates and their effect on doctrine need to be evaluated in light of the worsening climate of suspicion and intimidation that grew up in the years before the intransigent camp won a definitive victory in the elections to the papacy first of Cervini (Marcellus II, 1555), then of Carafa himself (Paul IV).

These popes made their victory irreversible with their juridical and theological condemnation of the errors of their adversaries. Formal steps were taken to bring to trial Pole, Morone, and the many prelates and intellectuals who in the past had shared their religious orientation. The recent history of the crisis that the church had undergone was reconstructed *sub specie Inquisitionis* (among other ways, by launching posthumous inquiries into the cases of Savonarola and even Contarini), and the first and extremely harsh Index of prohibited books was published. Pole was deprived of his legation and his charge to restore Catholicism to England, and he died in that land in November 1558. Thanks to the protection of Mary Tudor and Philip of Habsburg, he managed to avoid the humiliation of having to respond to the convocation to Rome to appear with Morone before the Inquisition. Morone was less fortunate: he was imprisoned for more than two years (May 1557 to August 1559) in the Castel Sant'Angelo, where he underwent interrogation. The timely death of the pope, which was greeted by outbursts of popular emotion that quite naturally turned against the affairs, the men, and the symbols of the Holy Office, saved Morone from certain death and granted him a precarious rehabilitation during the papacy of Pius IV.

During the last phases of the Council of Trent the church sought political ways to come to terms with reform movements and with the demands of the various European states. Thus it was obliged to call on the abilities, the prestige, and the personal credit of men like Morone himself, but also like Ercole Gonzaga, Bernardo Navagero, and Girolamo Seripando (the last two elevated to the cardinalate in February 1561), all of whom at one time or another presided over the assembly at Trent.

This was a brief and precarious parenthesis, however, in an evolution that

was by then clear—one that had no viable alternative, ideal or cultural, and
that was sanctioned once and for all by the arrival to the papal throne of
Michele Ghislieri as Pius V. Ghislieri had been the tenacious mastermind
behind the Catholic victory at Lepanto; he had been elevated to the purple by
Paul IV as a reward for his long career as an indefatigable inquisitor; he had
presided over the court charged with trying Morone. He now set to work to
take in hand and reinforce the severe repression inaugurated by the Carafa
pope. Pasquino commented in 1570:

> Quasi che fosse inverno,
> brucia cristiani Pio seccome legna,
> per avvezzarsi al caldo de l'inferno.

(Almost as if it were winter, Pius burns Christians like firewood to accustom himself to the heat of hell.)

In Paul IV's papacy that same source of Roman satire had warned,

> Figli, meno giudizio
> e più fede comanda il Sant'Uffizio.
> E ragionate poco,
> ché contro la ragion esiste il foco.
> E la lingua a suo posto,
> ché a Paolo IV piace assai l'arrosto.

(Lads, the Holy Office orders less judgment and more faith. And reason little,
because against reason there is fire. And [keep] your tongue in its place, because
Paul IV adores roast meat.)

Only a few years earlier, Ghislieri's election would have been simply unthinkable. He was a humble Dominican from Bosco, near Alessandria, who had
become cardinal thanks to his total dedication to safeguarding orthodoxy,
although his choleric patron and predecessor did not hesitate to shout at him
and humiliate him in the consistory by calling him a "barefoot friar." He
serves to measure the full extent of the break between these decades and a
still-recent past.

This shift in orientation also affected the sacred college. His three kinsmen
aside, Paul IV named to the cardinalate men unconditionally loyal to him,
docile instruments of his will, and expert collaborators to whom missions
could be entrusted and responsibilities delegated. Thus, along with some who
bore illustrious names (Gaddi, Trivulzio, Strozzi) and a few non-Italians, the
men who took their places in the consistory were above all *homines novi*.
The overwhelming presence of parvenus among the new cardinals is a clear
indication of the decline of the great prince of the Renaissance church in favor
of a new figure, the high functionary of the curial bureaucracy.

There were among the cardinals men of obscure origins who owed their nomination wholly to their long-standing loyalty and total subordination to the pope (the Venetian ambassador judged them "servitori suoi di bassissima condizione"), men like Scipione Rebiba and Virgilio Rosario, or Theatines like Bernardino Scotti (a man, as it was later said, who "nihil ultra breviarium et aliquas literas sacras noscens") and Giovan Battista Consiglieri, the brother of one of the four founders of the Theatine order. Some cardinals—the Franciscan Clemente Dolera and the Dominican Michele Ghislieri—owed their selection to their personal rigor, their preparation in theology, and their total intransigence in defense of Roman orthodoxy; others, like Giovanni Reumano from France or Giovanni Antonio Capizucchi, to their administrative, juridical, and canonistic competence. Paul IV entrusted the most delicate tasks, in particular the direction of the Holy Office, to these men and to his kinsmen. The commission of the sacred college charged in 1557 with trying Morone, for example, was composed exclusively of new cardinals (Ghislieri, Rebiba, Reumano, and Rosario), almost as if to publicize the pope's mistrust of the men who had elected him. The Venetian ambassador and future cardinal Bernardo Navagero wrote in 1558:

At certain [past] times, [the cardinals] numbered only six, and there was great respect and great consideration in making a cardinal, because they judged that for this dignity one needed nobility of blood combined with virtue and, in particular, with goodness. For this reason not only a house but a city or a province would consider itself honored if by chance it had a cardinal. Now they are sixty-six in number, the greater part of them so obedient to the pontifical nod, either through ignorance or through fear, that they dare not or know not how to contradict anything. (*Relazioni degli ambasciatori veneti al Senato*, ed. Eugenio Albéri, series 2, 15 vols. [Florence: Società editrice fiorentina, 1839–63] 3:112).

Pius V followed the same criteria as his predecessor in his selection of cardinals. He explicitly stated his desire to carry on the heritage of Paul IV, not only by continuing the harsh inquisitorial repression that the Carafa pope had inaugurated but also by leaving ecclesiastical affairs in the hands of the men his predecessor had trusted. Pius also carried on Paul's policies by reopening Morone's trial, by insisting on a review of the sentence against the Carafa kinsmen who had been sentenced in 1561, and by granting a cardinal's scarlet hat to the pious and learned Antonio Carafa. The reign of Pius IV and the conclusion of the Council of Trent, when curial opposition succeeded in stifling any specific decree for reform of the cardinals, represented a parenthesis that had now closed, and the new pope sought ways to encourage measures to bring morality to the sacred college. As late as 1560, the Venetian ambassador still held it to be "neither very sacred nor very saintly," and even Pius V himself said it was "full of ambitious men of little conscience."

The pope raised faithful followers to the cardinalate: his secretary, Girolamo Rusticucci, and generals of their orders like the Cistercian Jérôme Souchier, the Franciscan inquisitor Felice Peretti (later Sixtus V), and the Dominican Vincenzo Giustiniani. There were other Dominicans as well: Arcangelo Bianchi, the pope's confessor, and the cardinal nephew Michele Bonelli. In fact, Dominicans were so well represented that some wag wrote in 1566, "Your Holiness wants all Rome to be a monastery of St. Dominic." There were also jurists with long experience in the direction of curial ministries and legations: Giovanni Aldobrandini, Pier Donato Cesi, Giovanni Paolo Della Chiesa, Marcantonio Maffei, and Carlo Grassi. And there were Giovanni Girolamo Albani, an old friend of the pope, the author of a treatise, De cardinalatu, and a strenuous defender of ecclesiastical jurisdiction, and Giulio Antonio Santoro, a man of vast canonistic and liturgical culture, an inflexible persecutor of heresy, and the intransigent head of the Roman Holy Office until he died in 1602.

Beginning with these years, the cardinalate tended to become the crowning achievement of a career wholly within the institution of the church; the dignity was granted to reward a competence that was for the most part juridical, and it reflected increasingly rigid doctrine and discipline and an increasing clericalization of religious life. No longer could the church bring in simple laymen or great intellectuals like Contarini, Pole, or Bembo to serve at its summit. This meant, among other things, that the curial posts vacated by the newly elected cardinals could be put up for sale, which helped, without doing substantial harm to the papal treasury, to put an end to the long-standing Renaissance practice of requiring conspicuous sums of money in exchange for the beretta. It also meant that the more worldly and secular forms of magnificence practiced by the cardinals disappeared, at least to the superficial eye, and that they adopted a life-style more appropriate to their ecclesiastical dignity and to the pious compunction of Counter-Reformation culture.

Naturally, there were still papal kin in a sacred college whose plenum Sixtus V fixed at seventy members. They bore names like Borromeo, Altemps, Serbelloni (all kin of Pius IV), Bonelli (under Pius V), Buoncompagni (later Gregory XIII), Montalto (under Sixtus V), Aldobrandini (under Clement VIII), Barberini (under Urban VIII). Such men were still rich and powerful, but they were no longer in search of a temporal state to rule. Many of the old abuses in the system of benefices remained, and there were still dynasties of cardinals from the Roman aristocracy, from papal families, and from princely houses: a Piccolomini and a Carafa were made cardinals as late as 1844, a Riario Sforza in 1845, a Borromeo in 1868, and a Chigi in 1873. The consistory lost all authority to function as a senate, however, and became merely consultive, reduced to assigning the benefices under its control and to ratifying decisions made elsewhere.

The dense and often bloodless treatises on the cardinalate written during the Counter-Reformation clearly show this trend. They are works such as Girolamo Manfredi's *De cardinalibus Sanctae Romanae Ecclesiae* (1564); *De perfecto cardinali* (1584); *De maiestate dominorum cardinalium* (1591); *De nominibus serenissimis dominorum cardinalium* (1591); Fabio Albergati's *Del cardinale* (1598); Giovanni Botero's *Dell'uffitio del cardinale* (1599); or Girolamo Piatti's *De cardinalis dignitate et officio* (1602). One work that stands out from these treatises for its courageous but tardy defense of collegiality and the cardinals' prerogatives is Gabriele Paleotti's *De sacri concistorii consultationibus* (1593). The bishop, not the cardinal, was to be the key figure in the organizational and pastoral restructuring of post-Tridentine Catholicism.

Paolo Burali, a famous attorney and an important figure in the government in Naples, a Theatine and a reforming bishop, was called to the cardinalate in 1570, at the same time as Santoro. These two men can to some extent be taken as symbolic of an entire new generation of prelates who rose to the cardinalate under the papacies of Paul IV and Pius V by virtue of their pastoral zeal, their piety, their dedication to charitable works, and their moral integrity, but also for their intransigence in doctrinal matters and their narrow controversialist religious culture. Such men were rigid custodians of fixed certainties, willing administrators for a juridical and clerical ecclesiology, and indefatigable supporters of the "ragion di Chiesa."

Burali was beatified in 1772. By then the structures of the church of the Counter-Reformation had been solidified, its personnel subjected to strict discipline, and it sought new hagiographic certitudes that would reflect its new image and its successes. At last, after centuries, it could once again point to models of Christian life and heroes of the faith at its summit. Pius V, the pope who had elevated Burali to the purple, was also beatified in 1672 and canonized in 1712. A century earlier, in 1610, St. Charles Borromeo, the young cardinal nephew of Pope Pius IV, the exemplary bishop of the diocese of Milan and a devout ascetic assiduous in his penance, was also promoted to his place of honor on the altar. John Fisher, the bishop of Rochester who had opposed Henry VIII and whom Henry sentenced to death (Paul III sought in vain to save him by naming him a cardinal in 1535) was also canonized in 1935. Five years earlier, in 1930, Robert Bellarmine, a Jesuit controversialist elevated to the cardinalate in 1599 who had served as the inquisitor of Giordano Bruno and Galileo Galilei, was also declared a saint and was proclaimed a doctor of the church by Pius XI.

BIBLIOGRAPHY

There is a nearly endless bibliography on the subject of Renaissance cardinals: histories of the popes, among which Pastor's study is still indispensable; studies on Rome and on the Renaissance; and biographies of the various cardinals. There are Roman chronicles, diaries, and pasquinades, diplomatic correspondence, and letters and contemporary writings, beginning with those of Cortesi, Machiavelli, Guicciardini, Giovio, and Garimberto. For more ample information, see the bibliographical references in Paul Maria Baumgarten, *Von den Kardinälen des sechszehnten Jahrhunderts* (Krumbach: F. Aker, 1926). See also:

Alberigo, Giuseppe. *Cardinalato e collegialità. Studi sull'ecclesiologia tra l'XI e il XIV secolo.* Florence: Vallecchi, 1969.

Antonovics, A. V. "Counter-Reformation Cardinals: 1534–90." *European Studies Review* 2 (1972): 301–27.

Baumgarten, Paul Maria. *Von den Kardinälen des sechszehnten Jahrhunderts.* Krumbach: F. Aker, 1926.

Chambers, D. S. "The Economic Predicament of Renaissance Cardinals." *Studies in Medieval and Renaissance History* 2 (1966): 289–313.

————. "The Housing Problems of Cardinal Francesco Gonzaga." *Journal of the Warburg and Courtauld Institutes* 39 (1976): 21–58.

D'Amico, John F. *Renaissance Humanism in Papal Rome: Humanists and Churchmen on the Eve of Reformation.* Baltimore and London: Johns Hopkins University Press, 1983.

Delumeau, Jean. *Vie économique et sociale de Rome dans la seconde moitié du XVIe siècle.* 2 vols. Paris: Boccard, 1957–59.

Dionisotti, Carlo. "Chierici e laici." Now in his *Geografia e storia della letteratura italiana.* Turin: Einaudi, 1967, 47–73.

Gardi, Andrea. "La fiscalità pontificia tra medioevo ed età moderna." *Società e storia* 33 (1986): 509–57.

Hallman, Barbara McClung. *Italian Cardinals, Reform and the Church as Property, 1492–1563.* Berkeley: University of California Press, 1985.

Hay, Denys. *The Church in Italy in the Fifteenth Century.* Cambridge and New York: Cambridge University Press, 1977.

————. "The Renaissance Cardinals: Church, State, Culture." *Synthesis* 3 (1976): 35–46.

Hurtubise, Pierre. "La 'table' d'un cardinal de la Renaissance." *Mélanges de l'Ecole Française de Rome. Moyen age–Temps modernes* 92 (1980): 249–82.

Jedin, Hubert. "Vorschläge und Entwürfe zur Kardinalsreform." In his *Kirche des Glaubens, Kirche der Geschichte; ausgewälte Aufsätze und Vorträge.* 2 vols. Freiburg: Herder, 1966, 2: 118–47.

Mozzarelli, Cesare, ed. *"Familia" del principe e famiglia aristocratica.* Rome: Bulzoni, 1988.

Partner, Peter. "Papal Financial Policy in the Renaissance and the Counter-Reformation." *Past and Present* 80 (1980): 17–62.

Prodi, Paolo. *Il sovrano pontefice. Un corpo e due anime: la monarchia papale nella prima età moderna.* Bologna: Il Mulino, 1982.

Prosperi, Adriano. "'Dominus beneficiorum': il conferimento dei benefici ecclesiastici tra prassi curiale e ragioni politiche negli Stati italiani tra '400 e '500." In Paolo Prodi and Peter Johanek, eds., *Strutture ecclesiastiche in Italia e in Germania prima della Riforma.* Bologna: Il Mulino, 1984.

Reinhard, Wolfgang. "Nepotismus. Der Funktionswandel einer papstgeschichtliche Konstanten." *Zeitschrift für Kirchengeschichte* 86, 2 (1975): 145–85.

———. "Struttura e significato del Sacro Collegio tra la fine del XV e l'inizio del XVI secolo." In *Città italiane del '500 tra Riforma e Controriforma: Atti del Convegno Internazionale di Studi, Lucca 13–15 ottobre 1983.* Lucca: Maria Pacini Fazzi, 1988, 257–65.

Rosa, Mario. "La 'scarsella de Nostro Signore': aspetti della fiscalità spirituale pontificia nell'età moderna." *Società e storia* 38 (1987): 817–45.

Soldi Rondinini, Gigliola. *Per la storia del cardinalato nel secolo XV.* Milan: Istituto lombardo di scienze e lettere, 1973.

Thomson, John A. F. *Popes and Polity in the Late Medieval Church.* London and Boston: Allen & Unwin, 1980.

F O U R
The Courtier

Peter Burke

WHAT IS A COURT?

*T*HANKS largely to Castiglione, the courtier remains, together with the humanist and the prince, one of the most familiar social types of the Renaissance. This is fair enough: Castiglione's dialogue is simply the most famous of a large number of treatises on the courtier written in the fifteenth and sixteenth centuries. Ruth Kelso has listed some fourteen hundred treatises of this period on the gentleman and eight hundred more on the lady, and most of them have a good deal to say about courts.

All the same, it is not easy to say what exactly a courtier was. It is tempting to say, parodying Aristotle, that a courtier is an animal whose natural habitat is a court, but many servants who were not described at the time as courtiers could also be found in this environment.

In any case, the court itself is not easy to define, more or less irrespective of the language employed (*curia* or *aula* in Latin; *cour* in French, "court" in English, *Hof* in German, *dwor* in Polish, and so on). As the twelfth-century churchman and courtier Walter Map once wrote, "What the court is, God knows, I know not," it is so "changeable and various."

The court was most obviously a place, usually a palace with gatehouse, courtyards, hall, and chapel (not unlike an Oxford or Cambridge college), but including a chamber into which the ruler could withdraw and one or more antechambers where suitors waited for audience.

However, the court was also a particular kind of institution, the social milieu in which many of the works of art we call "Renaissance" were produced and consumed. Remote as this institution now is from the experience of most people, the court merits the attention of the anthropologist. In fact there are a number of such studies of courts.

A pioneering anthropological or quasi-anthropological study, relatively little-known, still retains its value, not least in producing what Brecht used to call a *Verfremdung-Effekt*, and forcing the reader to see as strange what he or she usually takes for granted. In the biography of Philip II published in 1938 by the German literary historian Ludwig Pfandl, there is a chapter on court rituals which draws parallels with West Africa and makes use of the ideas of Sir James Frazer and of anthropologists (discussing royal "taboo," for example).

The most famous of these studies, however, is surely *The Court Society* (1969) by Norbert Elias (who prefers to call himself a sociologist). Elias focuses on the court in France in the seventeenth and eighteenth centuries, but he has much of value to say about the workings of the system over the long term, arguing that the court is a distinctive social "figuration" (in the sense of a network of interdependence) with its own rationality, and that facile criticisms of conspicuous consumption or ritualized behavior at court fail to take account of the distinctive features of this social milieu.

Another well-known and influential study, Clifford Geertz's *Negara* (1981), is concerned with nineteenth-century Bali but offers reflections on what the author calls the "theater state" that are of relevance well beyond Bali and indeed beyond Asia. Geertz attacks attempts to dismiss ritual as mystification or to analyze it in a utilitarian way as nothing but a means to an end, the real goal being power. He emphasizes what he calls the "expressive nature" of the Balinese state, the concern of the Balinese with display for its own sake. Geertz, who is well aware of the history of political theory and royal rituals in the West—he discusses the ideas of Ernst Kantorowicz and the court of Queen Elizabeth—argues that the European state too was expressive, or at least that it had an expressive dimension. In Europe as in Bali, the center of power was seen as sacred and "exemplary": a model for others to follow. The court was perceived as the embodiment of political and social order, the microcosm of the order of nature, and the reflection of the supernatural hierarchy. It follows from Geertz's argument (although he does not make this point explicitly) that modern moral criticisms of the "flattery" or "adulation" that surrounded Renaissance monarchs and the "servility" of their courtiers are misplaced, ethnocentric, and anachronistic.

The court was, by definition, wherever the prince happened to be, and Renaissance princes did not normally remain very long in any one location. Duke Guidobaldo da Montefeltro may have spent most of his time in his palace in Urbino, but he was an invalid and his territories were small. Most European rulers of the fifteenth and sixteenth centuries spent a good deal of their time on the road, visiting their principal cities or simply moving from one palace to another. Charles the Bold, when he was not on campaign, moved between Dijon, Bruges, Lille, The Hague, and his castle of Hesdin in Artois, with its fine park, where the dukes of Burgundy went to relax and enjoy themselves. Francis I circulated between Amboise, Blois, Chambord, Fontainebleau, the Louvre, and Saint-Germain. Ferdinand and Isabella spent their time in Burgos, Seville, Toledo, and Valladolid. In a reign of forty-three years, as the emperor Charles V reminded his listeners in his abdication speech, he had visited the Holy Roman Empire nine times, Spain and Italy seven times each, France four times, and England and North Africa twice each. Philip II was relatively unusual in wanting to govern his kingdom from the Escorial, and even he made regular visits to Madrid, Toledo, and Aranjuez.

From the ruler's point of view, frequent travel had the advantage of allowing him to be seen by his subjects and to get to know his kingdom. In 1564–66, for example, the young Charles IX went on a two-year tour of France precisely for these purposes. Emperor Charles V traveled constantly in order to hold his empire together. In the Middle Ages, courts had been nomadic because it was easier to take the king to his estates than to transport the produce of those estates to him, and in some countries (such as Sweden) where much of the royal revenue was still paid in kind, this practice still made good economic sense. Some Renaissance rulers moved about incessantly in pursuit of pleasure, like Francis I hunting in the forest of Fontainebleau or James I going to the races at Newmarket.

To other eyes, however, the disadvantages of an itinerant court were obvious. When Rubens traveled to Spain in 1603 on a diplomatic mission, he arrived in Madrid to find that the court had gone to Valladolid, and by the time he had reached Valladolid, the court had moved on to Burgos. The size of royal households posed increasing problems of lodging and supply, especially when a court was midway between two towns. When Benvenuto Cellini followed the court of Francis I in the 1540s, he complained of the conditions in which he was expected to work: "So there we were, following the court through places where sometimes there were scarcely two houses to be seen. We pitched canvas tents like the gipsies; and more than once we had to suffer great discomfort" (*Autobiography*, trans. Bull, 252).

STRUCTURE OF THE COURT

It may be simpler to describe the court as a group of people rather than as a place, and if there were no need to be precise, it might be sufficient to say that a court is the household of a ruler or other important person— Guidobaldo da Montefeltro, duke of Urbino, let us say.

Such a household often numbered hundreds of people—occasionally thousands—meticulously listed in the financial records. In Castiglione's day, the court of Urbino was about 350 strong. The court of Milan, however, was already about 600 in the early fifteenth century; the court of Mantua about 800 in the 1520s; and the court of Rome about 2,000 in the reign of Pope

Leo X. These courts were large compared with their counterparts outside Italy, but the households of other rulers expanded rapidly in the course of the sixteenth century. In 1480, the court of France was about 270, considerably smaller than that of Urbino. In the 1520s, when Francis I was young, it was between 500 and 600, a little behind Mantua; but in the later sixteenth century it fluctuated between 1,500 and 2,000, more or less catching up with Rome. When Emperor Charles V went into retirement at the monastery of Yuste, 762 people were selected to accompany him before he reduced their number to 150. By the later sixteenth century the growth of courts was causing severe financial problems. Henry III of France and Elizabeth of England are among the rulers who tried to save money by reducing the number of their courtiers.

To complicate matters, we find that in the England of Henry VIII, for example, the court was larger in the winter, when it settled down in or near London (in Richmond, Greenwich, Hampton Court, Whitehall, or the lost palace of Nonsuch) than in the summer, when the king went on his travels. The court of Rome went on "vacation" in the summer, when the pope retreated to a villa in the hills. People with the right to meals and lodgings at court did not necessarily exercise these rights all year. Groups of knights often served by rota for three or six months at a time. Individuals might be granted leave for family reasons, after asking the permission of the chamberlain. Before he went to Italy in 1530, for example, Charles V granted his Spanish courtiers release from household service. On occasion the court might be disbanded to save money: Philip the Good disbanded the court of Burgundy in 1454, on the eve of his departure for Regensburg.

As a result of this flexibility, it is not possible to say exactly which people were courtiers and which were not. Should we describe Titian as one of Charles V's courtiers? He was in the service of the emperor and enjoyed his favor, but he did not accompany Charles on his travels. It would have been as difficult for him to paint as for Cellini to sculpt if he had been constantly on the move.

More difficulties arise when we try to describe the household a little more exactly. A royal or noble household was generally divided into two parts, which the "Black Book," the official description of the household of King Edward IV of England, labeled the "house of magnificence" (domus magnificencie) and the "house of provision" (domus providencie). Like any other noble household, a court needed the services provided by cooks, carvers, cupbearers, scullions, laundresses, barbers, gardeners, guards, porters, chaplains, physicians, singers, secretaries, falconers, and so on. However, there was also a need for noblemen and noblewomen, who added to the court's magnificence and for whom the service of the prince was an honor. Passing over the low-status servants in a manner quite normal for the period, the Renaissance iconographer Cesare Ripa defined a court as "a gathering of men of quality for the service of an important and principal person."

This latter group was itself subdivided. It would be wrong to think of courtiers as a uniform group, and it may be useful to offer a typology or to arrange them in a hierarchy. At the summit of this hierarchy one would find the aristocratic holders of a number of traditional offices of high status: the chamberlain, the steward, the marshal, and so on. These offices were domestic in origin. The chamberlain, for example, was supposed to look after the prince's chamber and his clothes, the steward after his food, and the marshal after his horses. However, these domestic functions were exercised in person by the noble officeholder only on special, ritualized occasions. For the rest of the time, the duties were performed by deputies. Robert Dudley Earl of Leicester was Queen Elizabeth's Master of the Horse, but one must not imagine him spending his time in the stables.

The ruler liked to be surrounded by his or her leading nobles, whether to ask their advice, as had been traditional in the Middle Ages, or to keep them under control by cutting them off from their local power bases in the country, keeping the royal eye on them, and encouraging them to ruin themselves by competitive conspicuous consumption. This technique of control may usefully be described as the "Versailles syndrome," as long as we remember that it was not invented by Louis XIV or Colbert. The technique was as well known to the king of Spain's viceroy of Naples in the mid-sixteenth century, Pedro de Toledo, as it was to Henry III of France (when the Guises left his court in 1584, their departure was perceived as an act of protest or even rebellion). In any case, rulers generally wanted to mix with their upper nobility, whose tastes they shared, and to enhance their reputations by entertaining those nobles with "magnificence," a quality for which princes were often praised. The Renaissance discussions of magnificence fit the theories of Clifford Geertz about the "expressive state" as closely as a courtier's hand fitted his expensive velvet glove.

As for the nobility, their motives for coming to court were various: to have the ruler's "ear," as the traditional phrase went, to receive his favor, indeed his favors (*mercedes*, "graces," as the Spanish say—in other words, gifts). One of the reasons for the revolt of the Catalans in 1640 was the absence of the king from Madrid, which cut the local nobility off from the expected flow of pensions, dowries, and other donations. Another reason for coming to court was to see that superhuman, charismatic figure, the prince, and of course to be seen by him. The magnificent, glittering setting exerted its own attractions. The court was imagined as Olympus, the home of the gods, a comparison made by Ronsard in his poems and illustrated by contemporary paintings in which Jupiter appears with the features of Henry II of France, Juno looks like Catherine de' Medici, and so on, a concrete example of the general view of courts as reflections of the supernatural order.

Exile from the court was a punishment, inflicted, for example, on the poet Garcilaso de la Vega by Charles V and on the duke of Alba by Philip II (in both cases for arranging family marriages without first consulting the king). Another Renaissance poet, the Earl of Surrey, was sent to Windsor in disgrace by Henry VIII after striking a companion in a quarrel within the precincts of the royal palace of Hampton Court.

Lesser men went to court hoping to rise socially, for in between the great aristocrats and the humble servants, the court included a substantial middle group.

In the first place, there was what Hugh Trevor-Roper has called "the bureaucratic machine of government"—in other words, administrators, judges, and politicians, increasingly professional in their outlook and their training (generally by the study of law at university). As in the Middle Ages, this group included a number of clerics, such as Cardinal Wolsey in England, Cardinal d'Amboise in France, and Cardinal Bakócz in Hungary (to name only three famous examples, all from the early sixteenth century). The papal court was of course full of clerics. Among the lay courtier-bureaucrats there were men of the calibre of Mercurino da Gattinara at the court of Charles V, William Cecil at the court of Queen Elizabeth, or Sully at the court of Henry IV of France, and also—despite the protests of the nobility—men of low birth such as Antonio Pérez at the court of Philip II and Jöran Persson, a parson's son, at the court of Erik XIV of Sweden. In theory, these men were there to give the sovereign advice and to carry out his commands, but they might in practice collaborate closely with the ruler (as Cecil did with Elizabeth, or Richelieu with Louis XIII) or even make the key decisions themselves, as Wolsey did at the court of the young Henry VIII. In the fifteenth and sixteenth centuries, different departments of government, such as justice and finance, were "going out of court" in the sense that they were settling down rather than following the ruler on his travels, but the high-levels decisions were still made at a small council where the ruler was usually present.

In the second place, there was an important place at court for the so-called "favorites," young noblemen for the most part, the ruler's companions during his leisure as the councilors were during his working hours. In Olivier de La Marche's description of the household of Charles the Bold, duke of Burgundy, he mentions the sixteen "squires of the chamber" and adds that "when the duke has attended to his affairs all day and given audience to everyone, he withdraws to his chamber, and these squires go with him to keep him company. Some sing, others read romances, others converse about love and war." The place of the favorites was in the "chamber," the ruler's private apartments, as that of the great officers of state was in the "hall," or the public rooms (hence the name *privati* in twelfth-century Latin, and the term *privado* in sixteenth-century Spanish).

The high status of these favorites was similar to that of royal mistresses, in the sense that it conflicted with the official or formal social hierarchy and depended on the affection of the ruler. The companions of Francis I were known as his "darlings" (*mignons*). As in the case of mistresses, the personal attractions of male favorites often assisted their success. In the fifteenth-century romance *Jehan de Saintré*, the hero is a page who acquired the king's favor by his charm of manner (*par sa débonnaireté vint en grace au roy*). On occasion, these charms were sexual, as in the cases of Sir Christopher Hatton and Sir Walter Raleigh at the court of Elizabeth, or the Duke of Buckingham at the court of James I (addressed by his master as "sweet child and wife"). To attract royal attention, it was advisable to be well or indeed magnificently dressed. Sir Walter Raleigh, for example, spent a fortune on clothes when he was captain of the bodyguard to Queen Elizabeth, wearing rings in his ears and covering his shoes with jewels.

These royal companions have acquired an unsavory reputation in traditional history, in which good kings have "ministers" while bad kings have "favorites." Some of these favorites may have deserved their bad reputations, particularly when the prince was a young man. In 1514 the Estates of Bavaria complained to their duke, Wilhelm IV (who was twenty-one at the time), that he surrounded himself with low-status companions: "They draw him into disreputable escapades; at night they roam the streets, and when they return, the drinking goes on till daybreak." It is important, however, to take account of the fact that rulers, like other people, needed friends with whom to abandon formality and to relax.

This need for royal relaxation was recognized at the time, as a fourteenth-century example may demonstrate. King Edward II of England had a favorite, "a most intimate companion in his chamber of whom he was very fond" (*camerarius familiarissimus et valde dilectus*), a certain Piers Gaveston. The chronicle that describes Gaveston's fall goes out of its way to explain that the barons hated him for his arrogant behavior, but did not object to his special relationship in itself, since "in almost all the households of great nobles today it happens that a particular individual enjoys the lord's particular affection." Gaveston was remembered as the archetypical evil favorite, however. In the

France of Henry III, for example, a pamphlet entitled *Histoire de Pierre de Gaveston* was published in 1588 as an indirect attack on one of the king's *mignons*, the duke of Epernon. All the same, Henry needed favorites like Epernon and Joyeuse (both of whom he made dukes) for political reasons, as a counterpoise to the power of the duke of Guise.

In other words, the position we now describe as "favorite" with overtones of disapproval was in fact a social role with a positive political function, at least from the ruler's point of view. It allowed a certain measure of flexibility and informality in a milieu in which social behavior was in danger of freezing into ritual (ritual had its advantages for the prince, as we shall see, but these advantages had their price). The role of the favorite was indispensable in the courts of Renaissance Europe, as it had been in those of the Middle Ages and would still be in the age of Goethe (who was the drinking companion of Duke Karl August at Weimar in the 1770s) and indeed in the time of Kaiser Wilhelm II and his *mignon* Eulenburg.

To sum up, the court was an institution with a number of different functions. It was not only the household of the ruler but also an instrument of government. The need of the ruler and his companions to amuse themselves in the evenings with poetry and music as well as by playing chess or gambling, inventing anagrams and *imprese*, asking riddles, or flirting with the ladies helped to make the court a cultural center. So did the common assumption that literature was of practical value, an assumption that underlies Machiavelli's *Prince*, Erasmus's *Education of a Christian Prince* (written for Charles V), or Budé's *Education of the Prince* (written for Francis I). Indeed, the importance of novelty and fashion in this setting made the court one of the main centers of cultural innovation in medieval and early modern Europe.

Some courts in particular fostered poetry and other arts. In the twelfth century the courts of Languedoc and Provence were the milieu in which the poetry of the troubadours developed, until this courtly culture came to an abrupt end at the time of the Albigensian Crusade. In the thirteenth century, Henry III of England spent heavily on architecture. In the mid-fourteenth century, when Robert of Anjou gave his patronage to Simone Martini, Petrarch, and Boccaccio, the court of Naples was an important center of innovation. Historians have spoken of the rise of an international court culture in the late fourteenth century, as visible in Charles IV's Prague as in the London of Richard II.

In the middle to late fifteenth century, the court of Burgundy was at the height of its magnificence. So were the small courts of Italy such as Urbino, Ferrara, and Mantua (the latter was especially important for artistic events after Isabella d'Este married Francesco II Gonzaga in 1490). King Matthias of

Hungary was another munificent patron of architects and scholars alike, and he built up a library of some three thousand books with an Italian humanist, Galeotto Marzio, as the librarian. The early sixteenth century was a great age for the patronage of literature, learning, and the arts, first under popes Julius II and Leo X, and then under the emperor Charles V and his rivals, Francis I and Henry VIII. Erasmus went so far as to call the court of Henry VIII "the seat and citadel of humane studies." The king himself tried to learn Greek, while queens Catherine of Aragon and Anne Boleyn were both patrons of scholars. In the later sixteenth century, Henry III of France and the emperor Rudolph II were intellectuals themselves and good patrons of men who shared their interests.

The recurrent image (best known from fifteenth-century manuscripts) of a writer on his knees offering his book to the prince not infrequently corresponded to reality. In 1515, for example, Erasmus presented his *Education of a Christian Prince* to the young Charles V at his court in Brussels. Machiavelli is said to have presented his *Prince* in person to the younger Lorenzo de' Medici, and the book itself suggests the political value to a ruler of patronage of this kind. One way of building a reputation, he writes, is for a prince to "show that he is an admirer of talent by giving recognition to talented men, and honoring those who excel in a particular art" (*The Prince*, trans. Musa, 191). The application of this generalization is made abundantly clear in the dedication, in which Machiavelli courts his prince: "If Your Magnificence from the summit of his high position will at some time move his eyes toward these lowlands, he will know to what extent I unjustly endure a great and continuous maleficence of fortune" (ibid., 3). It does not seem to have done him any good.

Individual rulers often encouraged artistic and literary activities that could have taken place elsewhere. However, the court was also a milieu in which specific art forms were created, more especially that mixture of music, poetry, and choreography known in Italy as the *intermedio* (because it grew out of interludes between the acts of a play), in France as the *ballet de cour* (because of the importance of dancing), and in Britain as the *masque* (because the actors frequently wore masks). Noblemen and noblewomen took part and, on occasion, so did the rulers themselves. Indeed, a distinctive characteristic of the genre was its transgression of the normal boundary between spectators and performers. Another feature of this type of court festival was its allegorical structure. Themes from classical mythology were more or less transparent disguises for topical meanings.

Among the most famous examples of the genre are the *Ballet comique de la Royne*, presented in Paris in 1581 for the wedding of Henry III's *mignon*, the duc de Joyeuse, to the queen's half-sister, Marie de Lorraine; the *intermedio* presented in Florence in 1589 for the wedding of Ferdinando de' Medici to Cristina of Lorraine; and the *Masque of Queens* presented in London in 1609. In the *Ballet comique*, for example, the gods rescued Ulysses and his companions from the enchantments of Circe, who was brought as a prisoner before the king of France. Music was used, appropriately enough, in support of Catherine de' Medici's attempts to achieve political and religious harmony in France in an age of civil war.

If we look at the structure of the court over the long term, we are likely to find the continuities more impressive than the changes. But changes there were. The most obvious of these was the increase in the size and importance of a few courts at the expense of the rest, the outward sign of the increasing centralization of power. In any one region—France, let us say—phases of centralization and decentralization seem to alternate from the thirteenth century to the eighteenth, but looking at Europe as a whole it is easier to see the shift towards the center associated with the rise of "absolute monarchy."

Changes in the organization and in the culture of the court did not simply reflect changes in the political world outside but also helped to bring them about. An obvious example to take is that of ritual. The spread of an increasingly elaborate and formal ritual of service to secular princes (waiting on them at table, handing them their clothes when they rose in the morning, and so on) can be documented from the late fourteenth century onwards at the court of the emperor Charles IV; in England under Richard II (the emperor's son-in-law); at the court of Burgundy in the fifteenth century; at the Spanish court in the sixteenth century (introduced by the emperor Charles V, who had been brought up in the Netherlands); and at the court of Henry III of France, who created the post of grand master of ceremonies in 1585. These rituals, which reminded some contemporaries of the cult of the ancient Roman emperors, encouraged participants and beholders alike to keep their distance and to treat the ruler as a superhuman being. Whether consciously devised for this purpose or not, they aided the process of centralization by turning great nobles, who had formerly been princes on a small scale, into subordinates—into courtiers.

THE COURTIER AS ARTIST

Like Machiavelli's prince, Castiglione's courtier has become an essential figure in our image of the Renaissance. *Il cortegiano* presents the courtier as a "universal" man, equally skilled in arms and letters, able to sing, dance, paint and write poetry, and to flirt with ladies (or to "court" them) in the fashionable language of neoplatonic love. This ideal figure seems to embody the whole Renaissance movement; the courtier as a performance artist, producing himself, as Jacob Burckhardt would say, as a "work of art." Yet the continuities with the Middle Ages are so strong, both in the theory and the practice of "courtiership" (*cortegiania*), that it is impossible to say exactly when one age ends and another begins.

These continuities are perhaps most obvious in the language we use to describe the kind of behavior expected in courts, most obviously, "courtesy." Courtesy has been described as a medieval "invention." There were no courts in the Athens of Plato or the Rome of Cicero, and if something like a court came into existence under the Roman empire, the new practice continued to lack a theory.

From the tenth century onwards, however, we can see medieval writers adapting the Ciceronian vocabulary of good manners (*urbanitas, decorum,* and so on) to the milieu of the court. First it was the courtier bishops who were praised for their graceful manners (*gratia morum*), and then the knights. The term *cortese* and its equivalents (*cortes* in Provençal, *courtois* in French, "courteous" in English, *hövesch* in German, etc.) are medieval words that carry the implication that the right way to behave is to follow the example of the court. Adjectives of this kind frequently recur in the poetry of the troubadours, in the romances centered on the court of King Arthur, and also in the manuals of good manners known in English as "courtesy-books"—books that were already numerous in the late Middle Ages, although the most famous example, the *Galateo,* was composed in Renaissance Italy.

In the poems of the troubadour Marcabru, for example, composed at the courts of Poitiers, Toulouse, Barcelona, and elsewhere during the twelfth century, we learn of the importance of "courtesy" and "measure" (*mesura,* perhaps not too far from Cicero's *decorum*):

> De Cortesia is pot vanar
> Qui ben sap Mesur' esgardar. . . .
> Mesura es de gen parlar
> E cortesia es d'amar.

(That man can boast of courtesy who knows well how to observe measure. . . . Measure is shown through speech that is fitting, and courtesy through the way one loves.)

The troubadours also taught the importance of *conoissensa*—discrimination— and in particular of distinguishing true courtesy from the mere semblance of it ("courtly show," *cortez' ufana*). Guilhem IX, who ruled Aquitaine in the early twelfth century, was himself a troubadour and was described by a contemporary (in terms not unlike Charles V's encomium on Castiglione four hundred years later) as "one of the most courtly men in the world" (*uns dels majors cortes del mon*).

From the romances, too, the reader or listener receives a clear and vivid image of ideal noble behavior, generally in a court setting. Indeed, real courts might be viewed by contemporaries through spectacles tinted by romance: an English gentleman on a visit to the court of Charles the Bold wrote home comparing it to the court of King Arthur.

In thirteenth-century Germany, the hero of Gottfried von Strassburg's romance *Tristan und Isolde* is a success at the court of King Mark of Cornwall because of his "courtly accomplishments" (*höfsche lere*)—in other words, his knowledge and skill in hunting, music, and languages. What is more, Tristan shows a kind of nonchalance in the quiet manner with which he allows these accomplishments to become known. Again, the hero of the fifteenth-century romance already mentioned, Jehan de Saintré, showed his "skill, sweetness, courtesy, and grace" (*habiletez, doulceurs, courtoisies et debonnairetez*) in the manner in which he sang, danced, rode, played tennis, and served at table. In the prologue to his *Canterbury Tales*, Geoffrey Chaucer describes his squire in language even closer to that of Castiglione, commenting on his ability at riding and jousting, singing and dancing, writing and painting.

As for the courtesy-books, they complement the imaginative literature by filling in the details of everyday life, explaining, for example, how to lay the table in the hall of a great lord, and drawing up a long list of things to avoid (don't talk loudly, take the best morsel from the common dish, smack your lips, drink with your mouth full, pick your teeth at meals, wipe your mouth on the tablecloth, break wind loudly, and so on). If we may be permitted to assume that actual behavior sometimes fell short of the ideal, a vivid if not altogether pleasing picture of meals at court will emerge from these treatises. On the other hand, if these treatises are studied in chronological order, they reveal the long-term trend toward increasing self-control on which Norbert Elias commented in his famous study *The Process of Civilization*. It was through the court that that aid to delicate eating, the fork (an Italian invention, apparently), began to spread through Europe in the late sixteenth century. However, table manners are only part of the story. The Renaissance court was also the carrier of such novelties as soap and toothpaste. The elaboration of ritual was another means of self-control (better described, perhaps, as an acceptance of control over the individual by the system). The courtier was or should have been recognizable by his deportment—his body language, which was revealed in the way he rode, walked, gestured, and (above all, perhaps) danced. Treatises on the dance show how seriously this activity was taken from the time of Domenico da Piacenza's *De arte saltandi* (1416), if not before, and Italian dancing-masters (such as Cesare Negri of Milan) were much in demand in the courts of Europe. Dancing formed an important part of court festivals, and some courtiers seem indeed to have danced their way into royal favor. This was, according to one contemporary, how Sir Christopher Hatton, Captain of the Guard to Queen Elizabeth and later lord chancellor, first attracted the notice of his sovereign.

In the process by which the knight was domesticated, civilized, or at any rate transformed into the courtier, it is clear that women played a crucial role. The court of Urbino, transformed into a salon by the presence of the duchess and her ladies and the absence of the duke, may be taken as a symbol of this development. However, the process goes back at least as far as the court of Eleanor of Aquitaine, who as queen of both France and England occupied a key position in the transmission of the values and the poetry of the troubadours. In the fifteenth century two Italian princesses, Beatrice d'Aragona, who married Matthias, king of Hungary, and Bona of Milan, who married Sigismund, king of Poland, used their positions to disseminate the values of the Renaissance abroad. In the sixteenth century, the court of Margaret of Navarre at Nérac attracted writers and scholars such as Marot, Des Périers, and Jacques Lefèvre d'Etaples, while Queen Elizabeth, although a niggardly patron of the arts, knew how to use the role of "a weak and feeble woman" to domesticate the English nobility.

In their task of polishing and smoothing rough noblemen, these princesses were of course helped by the ladies of the court. In the age of Richard II of England, the presence of large numbers of ladies was unusual enough to attract attention. At the court of Charles the Bold, it was noted that the presence of the ladies in his household cost the duke 40,000 livres a year. In France at the beginning of the fifteenth century, the writer Christine de Pisan held the post of chamberwoman to the queen, but it was only at the end of the century that Louis XII's queen, Anne of Brittany (according to the testimony of Brantôme), "commença la grande cour des dames" (began the great court of ladies). Gradually the idea spread that, as Cesare Gonzaga puts it in Castiglione's *Cortegiano*:

No court, however great, . . . can possess adornment or splendour or gaity without the presence of women, no courtier, no matter how graceful, pleasing or bold, . . . can ever perform gallant deeds of chivalry unless inspired by the loving and delightful company of women. (*The Book of the Courtier*, trans. Bull, 210)

In 1576, the French Estates-General, attempting to reduce royal expenses, asked for the ladies of the court to be sent home. By this time, however, a court was virtually unimaginable without them.

The court was, then, among other things, an educational institution, the "great schoole mistress of all curtesy," as Spenser wrote in the *Faerie Queene*, teaching its members how to speak, how to laugh, how to be silent, how to walk, and (as contemporary critics pointed out) how to deceive. Small boys would be sent to courts (whether royal courts or the households of aristocrats) as pages and remain there as squires and knights. In this milieu they learned not only good manners and the martial arts but also something of music and poetry. Exactly how literature and learning were acquired at court—whether formally or informally—we do not know in most cases (the school of Vittorino da Feltre at the court of Mantua is a well-documented exception). However, the fact that these tastes and skills could be acquired at court becomes clear if we examine the careers of some noble authors. Some of them are better known as noblemen than as writers, like two fifteenth-century English peers, Richard Beauchamp Earl of Warwick and John Tiptoft Earl of Worcester. Tiptoft, who has been described as "the English nobleman of his age who came closest to the Italian prince of the Renaissance," studied at the University of Padua and at the school of Guarino da Verona, but he is better known as a patron than for his own literary work. Duke Charles of Orléans, on the other hand, who wrote verse to pass the time when he was a prisoner of war for twenty-five years in England, is now best known as a poet.

Indeed, some of the most famous poets of the Renaissance were noblemen, courtiers, and soldiers who would probably be shocked if they knew that it was their verses, rather than their other achievements, that had made them immortal. Balassi Bálint, for example, a Hungarian Protestant baron, much of whose short life (1554–95) was taken up by combat with the Turks, spent some time at the court of Vienna in his youth and became a prominent figure at the court of Stefan Báthory, prince of Transylvania before he was elected king of Poland. Balassi knew eight or nine languages and is now most famous as a poet who celebrated his love for Anna Losonczi and Anna Szárkándy in verses that owe something to Italian and something to Turkish tradition.

Again, Garcilaso de la Vega, the son of a courtier, went to court himself on the accession of Charles V (Charles I of Spain), and he served his sovereign as a diplomat in France and as a soldier in North Africa and in Navarre (where he met his death). He played the harp well, and his manners as well as his verses made him a favorite with the ladies. His poems in honor of Isabel Freyre, a lady in the service of the Infanta Isabel of Portugal, followed the traditions of courtly love. He was a distinguished performer in arms as well as in letters, and in Latin verse as well as Castilian. It was thus extremely appropriate that this "most courtly gentleman" (*caballero muy cortesano*), as a contemporary called him, should have been instrumental in the introduction of Castiglione's book to Spain. Garcilaso sent a copy of the treatise to his friend Boscán, who translated it and wrote a letter as prologue to the translation in which he described *Il cortegiano* as a "wise" book (*este libro tan sabio*).

The Florentine nobleman Giovanni de' Bardi, count of Vernio, is best known today for his role in the creation of the *intermedi* at the court of the Medici. He was, however, equally prominent in his own day as a soldier, taking part in the war against Siena and the defense of Malta against the Turks. Castiglione would surely have approved of the count, who found time in the intervals between campaigns to write poetry and plays and compose music.

In the case of England, one thinks of Wyatt and Surrey, the courtly poets of Henry VIII's reign, and of Sidney and Raleigh in the age of Elizabeth. Sir Thomas Wyatt, "esquire of the body" to King Henry, followed a mainly diplomatic career, while Henry Howard Earl of Surrey followed a mainly military one. For both of them making verses was a pastime; Surrey turned to poetry when he was exiled from the court. Renaissance noblemen were generally ashamed to publish books, and the poems of Wyatt and Surrey, like those of Sidney and Raleigh, were not published until after their deaths. Incidentally, Wyatt and Surrey were both familiar with *Il cortegiano*. Surrey's copy of the book, with annotations in his own hand, still survives, while Wyatt's satire on the court seems to allude to Castiglione's ideas.

As for Sir Philip Sidney and Sir Walter Raleigh, their careers read like translations into practice of the ideals discussed in Castiglione's dialogue. After an education at three universities (Oxford, Cambridge, and Padua) as well as the riding-school at the imperial court in Vienna, Sidney embarked on a military career, and he met his death at Zutphen, fighting for the Dutch rebels against Philip of Spain (after whom the strongly Protestant Sidney had, ironically enough, been named). His friend Greville tells two stories about Sidney's death that, whether literally true or not, reveal something of the values of the man and indeed of his class. His mortal wound in the thigh was the result of his failure to wear armor that day. He had refused to put on his cuisses after discovering that one of his companions was going into battle without this equipment: he did not want anyone else to take more risks than he did. When he was mortally wounded, Sidney refused to drink until a dying soldier drank first, saying "thy necessity is greater than mine." Greville described Sidney as "a man fit for . . . what action soever is greatest and hardest among men." This man of action was also a generous patron of the arts and a major writer of poetry and prose. He was the author of a famous sequence of Petrarchan sonnets, of a pastoral romance (which was called, following the example of Sannazaro, the *Arcadia*), and of a defense of poetry. The defense of poetry was also a defense of "learned courtiers," whose style he considered more natural and thus "more sound" than that of scholars. "The courtier, following that which by practice he findeth fittest to nature, therein (though he know it not) doth according to art, though not by art."

It is of course impossible to distinguish Sidney's life from Greville's account of it, in which he is shown to best advantage. One may suspect that his life as well as his poetry was created as a conscious work of art. Suspicion becomes certainty in the case of Sir Walter Raleigh, whose propensity for self-dramatization is revealed in his elaborate courtship of the aging Queen Elizabeth and his acceptance of the public roles of the courtly lover of the remote goddess "Cynthia" and her faithful dog (the queen nicknamed him her "pug"). Behind the scenes, Sir Walter was in hot pursuit of a different quarry, one of the queen's ladies-in-waiting, Elizabeth Throckmorton. When the queen learned that Sir Walter had secretly married Throckmorton (who was pregnant), she was furious, and the pair were imprisoned in the Tower of London. Sir Walter's career was ruined. On Elizabeth's side at least, the game (or ritual) of love had been serious or semi-serious (it is hard to find the exact words to describe courtly performances on the border between fact and fiction). The Renaissance court was the scene of an extremely stylized example of what the American sociologist Erving Goffman has called "the presentation of self in everyday life." Or, as Queen Elizabeth herself put it, "We princes I tell you are set on stages."

The Artist as Courtier

Some courtiers, like Garcilaso de la Vega and Walter Raleigh, were or became artists—in both the literal and the metaphorical senses of that term. Conversely, some artists (painters, sculptors, architects, musicians, poets, and so on) became courtiers—that is, they were summoned to court on account of their artistic gifts by rulers who had a taste for these arts or wished to show themselves to be magnificent and munificent patrons.

Music, for example, had an important place in court life. Princes wanted singers for their chapel, trumpeters to accompany processions, and harpers and lutenists to entertain them in their chambers. The dukes of Burgundy seem to have been particularly fond of music. Philip the Good took two distinguished composers into his household, Gilles Binchois and Guillaume Dufay, the former as his chaplain and the latter as music tutor to his son Charles the Bold. Charles learned to sing, play the harp, and compose music. He took his musicians with him even on campaign, to the siege of Neuss, for example. Ercole d'Este, duke of Ferrara, was also a patron of musicians, and a famous letter shows him hesitating between two candidates for employment, Heinrich Isaak and Josquin des Près.

The advantages of court patronage are shown by such musical success stories as the careers of Orlando di Lasso at the court of dukes Albrecht V and Wilhelm V of Bavaria and of Valentin Bakfark at the court of Sigismund Augustus, king of Poland. Lasso, a Fleming who had lived for some years in Italy at the court of Mantua and elsewhere, spent nearly four decades at the court of Bavaria, where he was *Kappelmeister*, married into the duke's household, and was raised to the nobility by the emperor Maximilian II. His letters reveal his close relationship to Duke Wilhelm; one of them ends with the "signature" *Orlandissimo lassissimo amorevolissimo*. Bakfark, a lutenist from Transylvania, spent nearly twenty years at the Polish court and received many gifts from the king.

Examples of the favor shown by princes to musicians can easily be multiplied. The English lutenist John Dowland, who failed to obtain the court post he wanted at home, was honored and well rewarded at the courts of the landgrave of Hesse and the king of Denmark, the young Christian IV. The musician Luis de Milán owed his position at the court of Valencia, which he describes in his charming dialogue *El Cortesano*, to his skill in playing and composing for the *vihuela de mano*.

Some artists also achieved high status at court, where their services were in demand not only to decorate apartments but also to paint portraits and to design costumes and settings for festivals. Jan van Eyck was *valet de chambre* as well as painter to Philip the Good, duke of Burgundy, and he accompanied the embassy to Portugal in 1429 in order to paint the portrait of the future duchess. As a court painter he was freed from guild restrictions. Thirteen artists (eleven of whom were Italians) were ennobled in the course of the fifteenth century, and fifty-nine artists (twenty-nine of whom were Italians) in the sixteenth century, eleven of them by the emperor Rudolph II alone. Titian, who was a nobleman by birth, is an obvious example of an artist who knew how to behave in the court milieu. So was Raphael. He was not a friend of Castiglione's for nothing, and Vasari praises not only his art but also his *costumi*:

He was endowed by nature with all that modesty and goodness which are seen at times in those who, beyond other men, have added to their natural sweetness and gentleness the beautiful adornment of courtesy and grace, by reason of which they always show themselves agreeable and pleasant to every sort of person and in all their actions." (*Lives*, trans. De Vere, 4:209)

Bartholomeus Spranger was apparently on intimate terms with the emperor Rudolph, who would spend whole days talking to the painter and watching him work.

Yet the status of the artist at court remained somewhat ambiguous, as Cellini's famous autobiography reveals. He tells stories of Francis I calling him *mon ami* and of Grand Duke Cosimo de' Medici giving him *infinite carezze* and promising him great rewards, but he also describes how he was kept waiting all day outside the door of the king's mistress, Madame d'E-tampes, how difficult it was to get the treasurer to pay the money Francis had promised, and how Cosimo withdrew his favor and called Benvenuto *mal venuto* (unwelcome).

Those artists who did manage to acquire and enjoy a permanent and prominent position at court tended to turn into administrators of the arts. Velázquez, for example, spent much of his time in royal service performing his duties as keeper of Philip IV's art collection, in charge of acquisitions, hanging, and so on. At the court of Rudolph II in Prague, Hans von Aachen not only painted portraits but also copied pictures the emperor liked and bought paintings for the imperial collection. Other artists took responsibility for organizing court festivals: Bernardo Buontalenti in Florence, Baldassare Belgioioso (Balthazar de Beaujoyeulx) in Paris, Michael Sustris in Munich, and Giuseppe Arcimboldo at the imperial court in Prague. It is possible that Gil Vicente, best known for his plays but employed at the court of King Manuel of Portugal as a goldsmith, performed a similar function. At all events, Manuel spent large sums of money on court festivals.

Rather more secure in their status were the writers and intellectuals (or, to use a word of the period, *litterati*). Indeed, at this point the contrast between the courtier as artist and the artist as courtier breaks down, although it remains possible to distinguish more or less full-time courtiers of more or less high status. Sir Philip Sidney, for example, was more courtier than poet, while Edmund Spenser was more poet than courtier.

Some rulers enjoyed the company and conversation of humanists, like

Alfonso of Aragon, king of Naples, whose court included Lorenzo Valla, Bartolomeo Fazio, and Antonio Beccadelli. In any case, every court had some posts available for *litterati*. One such post was that of court preacher: the friar-humanist Antonio de Guevara, for example, was preacher to Charles V, and although he was soon elevated to a bishopric and resided in it, he did spend years at court, mainly in Valladolid, acquiring the experience that underlies his *Aviso de Privados*, not to mention his *Menosprecio de Corte*. Another post for intellectuals at court was that of royal physician. It was on occasion held by a humanist, like Thomas Linacre, physician to Henry VIII, or Guillaume Cop, who served Francis I. Tutor to the prince's children was another such post, occupied by such Renaissance humanists as Roger Ascham (tutor to the future Queen Elizabeth); Johannes Aventinus (tutor to the sons of the duke of Bavaria); George Buchanan (tutor to Mary Queen of Scots); and Jerónimo Osorio (tutor to the nephew of King John III of Portugal).

Posts for intellectuals multiplied in the course of the fifteenth and sixteenth centuries. After the invention of printing, libraries grew rapidly and required the services of a scholar-librarian such as Galeotto Marzio (librarian to King Matthias of Hungary) or Guillaume Budé (librarian to Francis I). Francis also appointed the writer Jacques Colin as *lecteur du roi*, charged with reading aloud to him. The emperor Ferdinand I appointed the art dealer Jacopo Strada his court antiquary, while his successor Maximilian II called Carolus Clusius to Vienna to be his court herbalist. Maximilian's successor, Rudolph II, called the Danish scholar Tycho Brahe to Prague to be "imperial mathematician" (in other words, astronomer or astrologer), and Tycho brought with him his young assistant, Johannes Kepler, who followed him in that post.

It was becoming increasingly common for rulers to appoint writers as secretaries or as court historians. Henry VIII employed the Italian humanist Ammonio as his secretary, presumably because he could write letters in good classical Latin. Budé served Francis I in a similar capacity, while the poet Jan Kochanowski was secretary to Sigismund Augustus of Poland and spent over ten years at his court. Georges Chastellain was appointed chronicler to Philip the Good of Burgundy, and Hernando del Pulgar to Ferdinand and Isabella.

Humanists not infrequently held the post of official historian: Paolo Emilio at the court of Louis XII of France, Johannes Aventinus at the court of Bavaria, Benedetto Varchi and Gianbattista Adriani at the court of Grand Duke Cosimo de' Medici, and so on. They were of course expected to present the actions of the prince or his ancestors in a favorable light, but they were also sometimes given privileged access to archives. The duke of Bavaria wrote to the abbots of his duchy asking for Aventinus to be given access to medieval documents preserved in their monasteries, while Cosimo had inventories made of the contents of the state archives for the benefit of Adriani.

Poets too were expected to praise. Some of them became poets laureate, literally crowned with laurel by the emperor. Petrarch claimed to have been crowned by the emperor Charles IV, Sigismund crowned Panormita, Frederick III crowned Enea Silvio Piccolomini, Ermolao Barbaro, and (apparently) Conradus Celtis, while Maximilian crowned Glareanus, Dantiscus, Vadianus, and Hutten. In return for such honors, or in expectation of them, the poets flattered their patrons. Celtis, for example, was lavish in his praises of Frederick's successor Maximilian, dedicating books to him and writing plays in his honor.

Epics in Vergilian style presented lesser rulers as so many Augustuses. The Sforza had their *Sforziad* (written by Filelfo), Federico da Montefeltro, duke of Urbino, his *Feltria*, and Borso d'Este his *Borsias*. Humphrey Duke of Gloucester, younger brother of Henry V of England, had his *Humfroidas* (the work of an Italian humanist in his household, Tito Livio de' Frulovisi). The kings of France had their *Franciade*, written by no less a poet than Ronsard, which included a prophecy of the future greatness of Charles IX. The first part of the epic was published in the year of the Massacre of St. Bartholomew, 1572. It is no wonder that Ronsard left it unfinished. The kings of Portugal had their *Lusiads*, published by the great poet Luíz de Camões in the same year as Ronsard's epic, 1572, and addressed to King Sebastian, comparing his deeds to those of Rodomonte, Ruggiero, and Orlando, and inviting him to win still more glory. Sebastian seems to have taken this advice all too literally; he died fighting in North Africa in 1578, thus allowing his kingdom to be incorporated into the empire of Philip II.

Ronsard also contributed verses to court festivals such as the fêtes at Bayonne in 1565 when Catherine de' Medici was reunited with her daughter, the queen of Spain; the reception of the Polish ambassador in 1572; and the marriage of the duc de Joyeuse in 1581 (on the last occasion he received 2,000 ecus for his contribution). Ronsard is a good example of a courtier-poet in the sense that he grew up in this milieu, having been page to the dauphin François, the short-lived eldest son of Francis I. Clément Marot's career followed similar lines. The son of a courtier, Marot was a page to the secretary of Francis I and *valet de chambre* to the king's sister, Margaret of Navarre. He wrote neither epics nor verses for festivals, but much of his poetry has the stamp of the court on it—letters to the king or to members of his entourage, epigrams on royal dogs, and so on. The protection of the king and his sister (and, on Marot's visit to Italy, the protection of Renée, the wife of Ercole d'Este of Ferrara) was as necessary to the poet's safety as to his economic survival, since he was suspected of heresy.

THE CRITIQUE OF THE COURT

This list of success stories, to which it would be easy to add more names, risks giving too favorable an impression of the court as a milieu for artists, writers, and scholars. Some of them failed to get positions at court; others obtained such positions but came to regret it. If some people saw the court as heaven—"ung paradis terrestre," as Claude Chappuys put it—others saw the court as hell (a comparison that goes back to Walter Map in the twelfth century).

Take the case of Edmund Spenser, for example. Spenser was a minor courtier (a client of a more important courtier, Sir Philip Sidney), and his epic, *The Faerie Queene*, was both a glorification of Queen Elizabeth and a kind of courtesy-book (especially the story of the courteous Sir Calidore in book six). However, Spenser was not well rewarded. He received a small pension from the queen and the post of secretary to the Lord Deputy (that is, the viceroy) of Ireland, and that was all. His reference in the poem to "shadowes vaine / Of courtly favour" may well express his own bitterness and frustration. Another disappointed writer at the court of Queen Elizabeth was John Lyly. Although he was the author of the fashionable romance *Euphues* (1579) as well as of some plays, he failed to get the post of master of the revels, or indeed any other office at the court.

For various reasons a number of writers left court for country retirement, like Jan Kochanowski, who deserted Kraków for his beloved estate of Czarnolas, or indeed Ronsard, who in later life spent more and more time in Maine. Sir Walter Raleigh, the author of a bitter but vivid description of the milieu he was leaving ("Say to the court it glows / And shines like rotten wood") retired to Sherborne in Dorset, an estate that Queen Elizabeth had given him when he was still in favor. Ariosto did not leave Ferrara, but his satires make it clear that he preferred independence to service and his own home to his room in the ducal palace.

Artists too were sometimes ambivalent towards courts. Baldassare Peruzzi left the papal court and went back to his native city of Siena, "loving the liberty of his former country more than the favour of the Pope," Vasari tells us (*Lives*, trans. De Vere, 5:70). Mantegna hesitated a long time before accepting an invitation to the court of Mantua, reflecting on what he called "the many persuasions of others to the contrary." We have already heard Cellini's complaints of his treatment at the courts of Francis I and Cosimo de' Medici.

Some people who remained at court nevertheless wished, or claimed to wish, that they were far away. The critique of the court was a literary and moral topos that originated in late antiquity (as the satires of Juvenal and Lucian bear witness), was revived in the Middle Ages, and continued throughout the Renaissance.

Typical examples of this traditional critique are the statements that "The court is like a sea whose waves are pride and envy," that it is "constant only in its inconstancy," and that it is a place of deceit (from flattery to slander). Whatever may have been the case in nineteenth-century Bali, it is clear that in Europe the "theater state" did not appeal to everyone. Modern criticisms of the servility of the court society of the preindustrial world are in fact little more than reiterations of comments made at the time.

During the Renaissance the critique of the court was voiced by many leading writers, among them Enea Silvio Piccolomini, Ariosto, the French poet Alain Chartier (at one time secretary to the dauphin, later Charles VII), the German humanist Ulrich von Hutten, and the Spanish preacher Antonio de Guevara. Chartier went so far as to define the court as "a group of men who meet to deceive one another." Guevara devoted a treatise to the binary opposition between court and country, stressing the noise and servitude of the court and the peace and liberty of life in the country (for nobles residing on their own estates).

It may be useful to make a distinction between the critique of the court and that of the courtier. The court was often criticized from the point of view of the courtier and described as a place where life was uncomfortable and hopes were disappointed. For a good example of this kind of critique we may turn to Piccolomini's treatise, *On the Miseries of Courtiers*, which takes the form of a letter addressed to his friend Johannes de Eich and is dated 1444. It combines traditional commonplaces with vivid illustrations, doubtless drawn from his experiences at the court of the emperor Frederick III (despite the author's claim that the imperial court is a happy exception to the rule). The commonplaces include the misery of seeing the unworthy rewarded while the worthy languish, the instability of everyday life ("who was in favor yesterday is in disgrace today"), and the loss of liberty (one had "to laugh and weep with the prince, to praise whomever he praises and insult whomever he insults"). The illustrations of the misery of life at court deal in particular with the problems of eating and sleeping. The servants are dilatory in serving the food but extremely quick to take it away; the conditions in which it is served are not very clean. "The bedclothes are dirty and stinking" (like Richard II of England and Henry III of France, the future Pope Pius II seems to have been a pioneer in his concern for hygiene), and it is sometimes necessary to sleep in the stables or to share one's bed with a stranger. There is no privacy in court.

The common description of the court as the scene of envy, slander, flattery, and every kind of deceit already tells one something about the way in which Renaissance courtiers were perceived by other people, but the list of the vices attributed to them is almost endless. Courtiers were frequently described as ignorant, idle, frivolous, pretentious, and obsessed with their appearance; the men effeminate, the women shameless. It is not necessary to take all these criticisms literally. They reflect, among other things, the envy of the unsuccessful for those who have been more fortunate, the soldier's contempt for civilians, and the provincial's hostility to the metropolis. Time has not been kind to these moralists, and it is difficult today to suppress a smile when reading *L'Isle des hermaphrodites*, a pamphlet that attacked the court of Henry III for its use of forks, toothpaste, and perfume (all signs of effeminacy, according to the anonymous critic).

One recurrent theme in the anti-court literature of the period is what might be called Italophobia, a reaction or backlash against the culture of the Renaissance, or at least certain aspects of it, on the grounds that it was foreign. Like "Americanization" today, "Italianization" was denounced by ethnocentric moralists. The term *italianisation*, like *italianisé* and *italianisateur* can be found in two dialogues by the French Protestant printer Henri Estienne published in 1578. Like critics of "Franglais" in more recent times, Estienne was concerned with the corruption of the noble French language by alien modes of speech. He associated *italianisation* with *courtisanisme*: it was in court circles, he thought, that people considered it chic to say, for example, "à bastanse" (*abbastanza*) instead of "assez."

The critique of Italian manners was not confined to language. Ironically enough, given the rejection of linguistic faults in the *Cortegiano*, that book and its author became a symbol of affectation, at least in some circles, in England, France, and elsewhere. The empty-headed courtier, obsessed with clothes and the rituals of politeness, figures in a number of English comedies in Shakespeare's day, and he is not infrequently named "Balthasar" or even "Castilio" to make the message even clearer. In many foreign eyes, Italians were associated with flattery, deceit, cunning, and (needless to say) with Machiavelli. These xenophobic reactions were especially violent in France, where Italians were particularly visible in court circles from the time of Francis I onwards (and still more so, for obvious reasons, in the age of Catherine de' Medici), but similar attitudes were to be found elsewhere from England to Poland.

By the early seventeenth century, criticism of the court, once individual and moral, had become collective and political. "Court" and "country," which had long been names for alternative noble life-styles, now became labels for political parties, or at any rate factions. Lucy Hutchinson, in her biography of her husband, Colonel Hutchinson, described the court of James I in her youth as "a nursery of lust and intemperance. . . . The generality of the gentry of the land soon learned the court fashion and every great house in the land became a sty of uncleanness." Those who denounced the immorality of the court, she continues, were called "puritans."

Lucy Hutchinson's apocalyptic vision of a society divided between "the children of light" and "the children of darkness" (the latter dominated by the court) is more extreme than any criticism of the court we have considered so far. It was not her vision alone, and it had important political consequences. The conflict between the children of light and the children of darkness is better known as the English Civil War, in which Colonel Hutchinson fought on the side of the Parliament. This notable change in the political climate, which affected central Europe as well as England, makes the early seventeenth century an appropriate point at which to end an essay on the Renaissance courtier.

BIBLIOGRAPHY

Barberis, Walter. "Uomini di corte nel '500." In *Storia d'Italia, Annali*. Turin: Einaudi, 1981, 857–94.

Boucher, Jacqueline. *La cour de Henri III*. Rennes: Ouest France, 1986.

Buck, August, ed. *Europäische Hofkultur im 16. und 17. Jahrhundert*. Wolfenbütteler Arbeiten zur Barockforschung, Bd 8–10, 3 vols. Hamburg: Hauswedell, 1981.

Cartellieri, Otto. *Am Hofe der Herzöge von Burgund*. Basel: B. Schwabe, 1926.

Dickens, A. G., ed. *The Courts of Europe: Politics, Patronage and Royalty 1400–1800*. London: Thames & Hudson; New York: McGraw-Hill, 1977.

Elias, Norbert. *Der höfische Gesellschaft: Untersuchungen zur Soziologie des Königtums und der höfischen Aristocratie*. Neuwied: Luchterhand, 1969. *The Court Society*. Trans. Edmund Jephcott. Oxford: Blackwell, 1983.

Evans, Robert John Weston. *Rudolph II and his World: A Study in Intellectual History, 1576–1612*. Oxford: Clarendon Press, 1973.

Geertz, Clifford. *Negara: The Theatre State in Nineteenth-Century Bali*. Princeton: Princeton University Press, 1980.

Green, Richard Firth. *Poets and Princepleasers: Literature and the English Court in the Late Middle Ages*. Toronto and Buffalo: University of Toronto Press, 1980.

Greenblatt, Stephen Jay. *Renaissance Self-Fashioning: From More to Shakespeare*. Chicago: University of Chicago Press, 1980.

———. *Sir Walter Raleigh: The Renaissance Man and his Roles*. New Haven: Yale University Press, 1973.

Gundersheimer, Werner L. *Ferrara: The Style of a Renaissance Despotism*. Princeton: Princeton University Press, 1973.

Hanning, Robert W. and David Rosand, eds. *Castiglione: The Ideal and the Real in Renaissance Culture.* New Haven: Yale University Press, 1983.

Huizinga, Johan. *Herfsttij der Middeleeuwen.* Haarlem, 1919. (*The Waning of the Middle Ages.* Trans. F. Hopman. Garden City: Doubleday Anchor Books,. 1954.)

Jaeger, C. Stephen. *The Origins of Courtliness: Civilizing Trends and the Formation of Courtly Ideals, 929–1210.* Philadelphia: University of Pennsylvania Press, 1985.

Javitch, Daniel. *Poetry and Courtliness in Renaissance England.* Princeton: Princeton University Press, 1978.

Kelso, Ruth. *Doctrine for the Lady of the Renaissance.* Urbana: University of Illinois Press, 1956.

————. *The Doctrine of the English Gentleman in the Sixteenth Century.* Urbana: University of Illinois Press, 1929.

Kiesel, Helmuth. *"Bei Hof, bei Höll": Unters. zur literar. Hofkritik von Sebastian Brant bis Friedrich Schiller.* Tübingen: Niemeyer, 1979.

Kipling, Gordon. *The Triumph of Honour: Burgundian Origins of the Elizabethan Renaissance.* The Hague: published for the Sir Thomas Browne Institute by Leiden University Press, 1977.

Knecht, R. J. *Francis I.* Cambridge and New York: Cambridge University Press, 1982.

Levey, Michael. *Painting at Court.* New York: New York University Press, 1971.

Lewalski, Kenneth F. *"Sigismund I of Poland: Renaissance King and Patron."* *Studies in the Renaissance* 14 (1967): 49–72.

Loades, D. M. *The Tudor Court.* London: Batsford, 1986.

Lytle, Guy Fitch, and Stephen Orgel, eds. *Patronage in the Renaissance.* Princeton: Princeton University Press, 1981.

Ossola, Carlo and Adriano Prosperi, eds. *La Corte e il "Cortegiano."* 2 vols in 1. Rome: Bulzone, 1980.

Pfandl, Ludwig. *Philipp II., gemälde eines Lebens und einer Zeit.* Munich: G. D. W. Callway, 1938.

Rebhorn, Wayne A. *Courtly Performances: Masking and Festivity in Castiglione's Book of the Courtier.* Detroit: Wayne State University Press, 1978.

Romani, Marzio A. and Amedeo Quondam, eds. *Le corti farnesiane di Parma e Piacenza, 1545–1622.* 2 vols. Rome: Bulzoni, 1978.

Smith, Pauline M. *The Anti-Courtier Trend in Sixteenth Century French Literature.* Geneva: Droz, 1966.

Solnon, Jean François. *La cour de France.* Paris: Fayard, 1987.

Starkey, David, et al. *The English Court: From the War of the Roses to the Civil War.* London and New York: Longman, 1987.

Stevens, John. *Music and Poetry in the Early Tudor Court.* London: Methuen, 1961.

Tenenti, Alberto. *"La corte nella storia dell'Europa moderna (1300–1700)."* In Marzio A. Romani and Amedeo Quondam, eds. *Le corti farnesiane di Parma e Piacenza, 1545–1622.* 2 vols. Rome: Bulzoni, 1978, 1:ix–xix.

Uhlig, Claus. *Hofkritik im England des Mittelalters und der Renaissance: Studien zu einem Moralistik.* Berlin and New York: DeGruyter, 1973.

Vasoli, Cesare. *La cultura delle corti.* Bologna: Cappelli, 1980.

Warnke, Martin. *Hofkünstler: zur Vorgeschichte des modernem Künstlers.* Cologne: Dumont, 1985.

F I V E
The Philosopher and the Magus
Eugenio Garin

J T may seem strange to see the philosopher—but a philosopher who is also a magician, an astrologer, and even a man of science—as a human type characteristic of the Renaissance, indeed, as "reborn" precisely in the Renaissance. Yet Jacques Le Goff was right, in 1957, to refuse the term "philosopher" in his presentation of the "intellectuals" of the Middle Ages. Furthermore, the chapter in the companion volume to the present work, *Medieval Callings* (Chicago: University of Chicago Press, 1990), which he edited, includes a chapter on "intellectuals" rather than "philosophers." Le Goff has correctly observed that compared to men like Bonaventura of Bagnoregio, Thomas Aquinas, and other theologians and saints, "the philosopher is another personage." The philosopher was, as Le Goff rightly states, explicitly or implicitly, the philosopher of the Greek city states and, more generally, of the ancient world: philosophers were teachers of life and men of science, physicians of the soul and the body, radical reformers and critics ready to attest to the truth even unto death—men like Pythagoras and Empedocles, Socrates and Plato, Democritus and Epicurus, Pyrrho and, later, Plotinus, without forgetting Cicero and Seneca.

The return of the ancient philosophers in the Renaissance, however, not only opened the gates to a flood of rhetoric but also changed the face of studies and refurbished the image of the philosopher and of philosophy. Now no longer, or not necessarily, a schoolteacher, the philosopher was no longer bound by any orthodoxy; he was impatient with all claims to hegemony; he was critical by vocation and often rebellious. He was a restless seeker experimenting in all realms of experience like Leon Battista Alberti and Leonardo da Vinci; he denied consecrated truth like Pomponazzi; he yearned for arcane truths and mysterious revelations like Ficino. He was a magician like Cornelius Agrippa, a prophet of universal peace like Erasmus, a physician for a body in harmony with the forces of nature like Paracelsus, or a witness to the truth like Giordano Bruno.

Just as philosophy broke sharply with the past, recognizing no "book" or

123

"author" as its spokesman, and blazed new trails and forged new alliances, so too the philosopher refused barriers or predetermined paths and was open to the active life and intensely involved in the moral and political world, in man, and in man's existence. At base, it was the philosopher who was the "universal man" of the Renaissance to whom so much rhetoric has been (and still is) devoted. He launched a new mode of investigation, of living, and of forging a culture. Unlike the eighteenth-century *philosophe* (with whom he nevertheless has a distant kinship), he was not mass-produced: although many dabbled in philosophy, true philosophers were few. Nonetheless, those few inaugurated a human category that is among those most characteristic of the epoch. More than *maîtres à penser*, they were teachers of life.

No wonder this was the moment of Diogenes Laertius's greatest popularity. Translated into both Latin and Italian (Venice 1545), his works had their widest circulation in curious vernacular compendia and adaptations, some of medieval origin. Generously illustrated and clearly designed for a "popular" audience, at times they included maxims, moral teachings, and consoling dialogues inspired by classical culture. Toward the end of the century, to pick just one example, we find printed works like the *Vite degli antichi Filosofi moralissime, e delle loro elegantissime sentenze, cavate da Diogene Laerzio, e da altri antichi autori*, sold, with graceful engravings, *In Firenze, Appresso all'Archivescovado* in 1593.

In 1621, *The Anatomy of Melancholy*, one of the most singular books of the century, was published in Oxford. Extremely popular throughout the seventeenth century, it was the work of the enigmatic "Democritus Junior," Robert Burton, who was born in 1577 and later (in 1626) became librarian of Christ Church College. When Burton's book was published, Shakespeare had died fairly recently and Francis Bacon was still alive and working. In his massive and bizarre book Burton, who was a competent astrologer, condensed and passed on to learned circles in England a large part of the philosophical and scientific thought on humanity of roughly two centuries—precisely, of the Renaissance. He treats Italian thought in particularly great detail, and in fact this work was one of its principal channels of diffusion in England.

Although Burton does not say so explicitly, both his choice of topic— melancholy and the melancholic person—and the fact that he cites Ficino continuously show that Marsilio Ficino was one of his major sources. The melancholy man, born under the sign of Saturn, is the intellectual—the philosopher, and in particular the new type of philosopher who had recently appeared in Europe and of whom Ficino himself was an example. He is both moralist and physician, magician and astrologer; like the ancient sages, he laughs and weeps over worldly things. For him, melancholy resembles Plato's divine *mania*. The very idea of concealing his identity behind the mask of Democritus Junior may have been suggested to Burton by Ficino, who is recorded as having had one of the walls of his "academy" decorated with the terrestrial globe, with Democritus on one side laughing at men's follies and, on the other, Heraclitus weeping over their misfortunes.

In the meandering introduction to his work, Burton explains who Democritus was, and although his portrait may not be very faithful, it proves him to have been Burton's model. It was of course a classical model, constructed on the Pseudo-Hippocratic letters, which Burton much admired. I might add that in the fifteenth century Leon Battista Alberti had used the same source to particularly good effect in his *Momus*, an extraordinary work published during the sixteenth century in two Latin editions, a widely circulated Italian translation, and a Spanish translation. "Among the philosophers," Alberti writes, "I have found only two whose discourse is profound and rational: Democritus and Socrates." He dwells on Democritus at some length, presenting him as the ideal natural philosopher intent on grasping the deeper structure of beings. For Burton as well, Democritus seeks hidden truth. He is justly admired in the city of Abdera, but "the citizens of Abdera" did not consider his "ironical passion" for laughing at "their whole life" as wisdom, but "took him to be mad" (*Anatomy*, 1:48). Burton—Democritus Junior—knows he is not the equal of the ancient sage: he lacks his predecessor's knowledge of the physical world and of mathematics, and unlike Democritus, he has no responsibilities in the community. Nonetheless, the new Democritus sought to write his namesake's lost book about men and their "melancholy" in order to minister to them and cure them of it, just like the Democritus of the Pseudo-Hippocratic letters.

This is not the place to pursue the image of the "philosopher," of Democritus, or of Democritus Junior that Burton projects. Anyone interested in doing so would trace the gradual emergence of the philosopher out of the gallery of figures mentioned in Burton's interminable and often apparently random quotations—which are in reality chosen with subtle care and are highly representative. This image is that of the "new" philosopher, which Burton contrasts with the spurious philosophers he had mocked in a youthful comedy, *Philosophasters*, performed 16 February 1617 at Christ Church College, in which he portrayed the "asses" who filled the schools and whose only aim was to produce still other asses. The asses were university professors; the schools, even the oldest and most famous universities: *Accipiamus pecuniam, demittamus asinum, et apud Patavinos Itali.*

Burton's theme (or Democritus Junior's) was already nearly a commonplace. His originality lay in his emphasis on two characteristics of the new philosopher that differed from the old university "master": the new philosopher was a "sage," respected and consulted by the entire community. In short, he was a "civic" philosopher. He was also a "natural" philosopher—a physician, "magician," and astrologer—who sought to know things by operating on them. Here Burton's reference to Democritus as a model for a new type of philosopher (which he shared, over the century and a half that separated them, with Alberti) takes on special importance. According to Alberti, when Democritus could not investigate human anatomy he dissected animals ("It seemed to me impious to cut up human beings with knives"). He did so with a specific therapeutic aim in mind:

To discover the seat of the principal evil of living beings, wrath [iracundia], and thus to understand the origin of the fits, the fervor, and the fire that turn the human mind upside down and destroy all forms of rationality.

Still, the figure of the philosopher, whose image was fixed according to classical ideals and who was proposed as a model for people to imitate, was either the teacher of morality, the most frequent example of which was Socrates; or a detached investigator of the physical world like Democritus. Both models offered an expectation of practical results ranging from prediction of the future to the healing of illness. Later—and to a certain extent this was true of Marsilio Ficino—the two models and their aims came to be joined indissolubly in a medicine for both body and soul.

A great work of art, Giorgione's Three Philosophers, documents the changed image of the "philosopher" with singular effect. In it three enigmatic figures are absorbed in thought. The youngest of them, seated, looks with mixed astonishment and expectation toward the entrance to what Leonardo da Vinci called "the menacing and dark cavern"—perhaps Plato's cave. Who these three philosophers were (and conjectures have been numerous and widely varied) may not be important. They may indeed have been intended, as some scholars have suggested, as symbolic figures; three generic "philosophers" like the men encountered in a princely court or a Studio: one a young scholar curious about nature, another a venerable older man, and the third an Oriental. They are of course philosophers according to the image that gradually developed during the fifteenth century, a figure thus very different figure from the magister of the medieval university. What makes the painting particularly valuable for our purposes is that its evolution is inscribed on the canvas in a series of cancellations and corrections that permit us to "read" transformations in the "figure" of the philosopher.

As Salvatore Settis recalled some years ago, an X-ray made of the *Three Philosophers* in the early 1930s revealed that the philosophers were originally intended as the Three Magi, with the "Oriental" of the final version clearly figured as black. Moreover—and here Settis's interpretation is of particular interest to our purposes—the Magi, their calculations spread out before them, are observing the star that announced Christ's birth and showed the way to the manger to those who knew how to interpret it. The Magi were not only Wise Men but astrologers. As is known, there had been particularly lively debate in the fifteenth century between the supporters and the critics of judicial astrology on the question of the star. Marsilio Ficino devoted one of his *praedicationes* to the problem *de Stella Magorum*, and Pico treated the topic as well. In the final version of his painting, Giorgione transformed his astrologers into philosophers; nonetheless they investigate the mysteries of nature (or the youngest of their number does so) using calculations and measures, thus reflecting Ficino's often reiterated position on the succession through time of various types of intellectual investigation. In other words, what the philosopher did was to take the questions to which magicians and astrologers sought an answer and bring them up to the level of rational investigation. Inversely, the philosopher's investigation had thinly veiled roots in magic.

Furthermore, the new philosophers, like the Magi and the astrologers, continued to ponder the cave. On the one hand, the cave refers to Plato, but on the other, it ineluctably recalls a famous passage of Leonardo's in the Arundel Codex:

Wishing to see the great abundance of varied and strange forms made by the art of nature, . . . I arrived at the entrance to a great cavern, before which . . . bent double and steadying my weary hand on my knee, with my right hand I shaded my lowered and half-closed eyes, frequently leaning to one side and the other to see whether anything could be discerned inside, which was prohibited me by the great darkness there. And [when I had] been [there] a while, there suddenly arose in me both fear and desire: fear for the menacing and obscure cavern; desire to see whether something miraculous might lie inside.

Seeing into the cavern—that is, probing deeply into the natural world—meant interrogating the stars, analyzing the structure of living things, dictating laws to the city (indeed, in a more literal sense, constructing it), finding therapies for melancholy and madness. These are some of the tasks taken on by those who were considered philosophers from the fifteenth to the sixteenth century, as the term gradually shifted meaning under the pressure of profound cultural change and the new diffusion of the ancient philosophers. In 1554, when Johannes Herold presented his new Basel edition of the complete works of Petrarch in four folio-sized volumes (*per Henricum Petri*, reprinted in 1581), his most evident concern was to show Petrarch as a philosopher of the new age. From the outset, the title page presents Petrarch as a philosopher, orator, and poet: "Defender and restorer of the reborn literature and of the Latin language, polluted and nearly destroyed by centuries of horrid barbarity." His works combined natural and moral philosophy; they were the new encyclopedia of all the liberal arts (*liberalium quoque artium Encyclopediam*). Herold drove his point home in the dedicatory epistle, where he cites Erasmus's and Cardano's praise of Petrarch. Petrarch took his love of philosophy from nature; he would never have been the master of style that he was if he had not been a philosopher; his work was a reconstruction of the encyclopedia of the arts, and so forth.

Two things are clear in Herold's presentation of Petrarch: first, the sharpening image of the great intellectual exponent of *reflorescentis literaturae* was linked to a renewal taking place outside the schools (Petrarch refused a university chair) but recognized as valuable by Cardano, Erasmus, and Vives; and second, the conviction that this cultural phenomenon was the *one* philosophy, that whoever possessed it was a true philosopher, and that any well-administered civic society should take a philosopher of the sort as its guide and civic model. "Who will ever deny that this Petrarch, and other men like him, are rightly venerated in well-ordered states?" ("Quis igitur negat, vel hunc Petrarcham, vel etiam alios viros huic similes, a rebus publicis bene institutis, merito coli?")

Petrarch's name and personality come up for a more profound reason. Although he lived in the trecento, on the cultural level he and the polemic he launched brought an epoch to an end. His famous dialogue ironically entitled "On His Own Ignorance and That of Many" (*De sui ipsius et multorum ignorantia liber*), completed and transcribed by the end of 1367 but circulated only in 1371 (and still all too often misinterpreted), represents something like a manifesto against the way the schools conceived and taught philosophy, to which he opposes attitudes that gained increasing strength in centuries to follow. The work is not anti-Averroistic, nor, in the last analysis, anti-Aristotelian. It contrasts the image of philosophy that was proper to classical antiquity with the image that dominated the schools of his time: philosophy as a free and rational search for truth and philosophy as commentary on a "book" and an "author"—indeed, on *the* book and *the* author, Aristotle. For Petrarch, Aristotle was great, even outstanding, but he was not unique. There was also Plato, many of whose works Petrarch had at arm's reach ("Platonis libros domi habeo"); there were Pythagoras and Anaxogoras, Democritus and Diogenes; there was Socrates; there were Plotinus and Porphyry, Cicero and

Seneca. And each philosopher had his own philosophy, his own position, in an intense dialogue with the others, which could not be ignored.

Even though his position was not proclaimed amid fanfares from a professorial chair, Petrarch and his many emulators shook the intellectual world profoundly. To a vision of philosophy as "reading" and "comment" on a truth, the substance of which had already been established and which merely required clarification and development of detail, he opposed a vision of philosophy as multiform investigation, discussion, and analysis of process; as a plurality of conceptions of the physical world and of life; as multiplicity and variety. The return to the past of classical antiquity was not a renunciation of religion, but of Christian, Arabian, and Hebrew philosophies as philosophies linked to a religion. It was a return to philosophy as man's rational interrogation concerning man, the physical world, and things. Above all, it was an investigation of man's action in the world and of his destiny. Montaigne opened his essays on "ce premier de Mars mille cinq cens quatre ving" with the confession, "Ainsi, lecteur, je suis moy-mesmes la matiere de mon livre" (Thus, reader, I am myself the matter of my book). Some two centuries earlier, Petrarch might have written as much in preface not to one book but to all his writings, his poetry, and his letters. The only problem (and this is true of Montaigne as well) is that Petrarch's restless, tormented, and contradictory human experience reflects all human society, all men's experience, and all men's sentiments, filtered and analyzed through and discussed in terms of human history and the documents of human history: books, works, beliefs, illusions, and dreams. This was his philosophy. Petrarch pursues the point both in his treatises and his letters, where the polemic stance of the *De Ignorantia* broadens to attack logic (the "barbaric" logic of the English) and physics (the "physics" of insensate particles), to return insistently to man.

Although Petrarch exalted solitude, he was no hermit. He traveled ceaselessly throughout Europe; he loved, or at least he had loved, with passion; he wept for his dead; he worried about the future of his homeland; he dealt with lords and sovereigns and, in his fashion, was their peer. Above all, he "remembered" the remote centuries of classical antiquity, calling them back to mind and emulating their values and their wisdom. His philosophy was not the "required reading" of academic courses; it was the wisdom of Socrates and Seneca. But this was exactly why the new philosophy—the high philosophy that was being rediscovered in the ancient Greek and Latin philosophers—arose outside the schools and *against* the schools.

There is a free translation of *De remediis* and other works of Petrarch by Monsieur de Grenaille, a state prisoner in the Bastille (entitled *Le sage résolu contre la fortune*, also published as *Les entretiens de Pétrarque* and reprinted several times during the eighteenth century) that is difficult to read without emotion. Petrarch, Grenaille tells us, had helped him face the most terrible trials; he had "revived the Stoics" and even "taken the place of the Stoics."

Both Petrarch's sensitivity and his ideal of the wise man contributed much to the definition of an image of philosophy that persisted until the seventeenth century. That image stressed the priority of a philosophy of man that was at once moral, political, and aesthetic over logic and physics; the struggle against the dogmatism of the Scholastics; and a philosophical pluralism—that is, the notion, increasingly clear as the fifteenth century progressed, of a multiplicity of voices, possibly convergent, but which nonetheless must be compared without dogmatic claims. In part with his discussions on physicians and medicine, Petrarch launched a debate on the relationship between intellectual disciplines (the "dispute of the arts"), a debate that was to become fundamental and was to prompt a crisis in the very structure of the encyclopedia of knowledge and, in the long run, in the relationship between knowledge and action and the active and the contemplative life.

Discussion of the Renaissance (and, more precisely, of the philosophy of the Renaissance) has for some time focused on the influence of *studia humanitatis* on philosophy to ask whether undisputed "humanists" such as Leonardo Bruni and Lorenzo Valla, Erasmus, and Vives can appropriately be considered "philosophers" and whether they contributed to the progress of philosophy and the sciences. Conversely, it asks whether undisputed philosophers like Marsilio Ficino who were also expert in classical studies (and the poets were the first among these) should be considered "humanists." Lexicons and university records have been scrutinized to see what the humanists meant when they called themselves "humanists," what they taught, and what titles the chairs of famous professors bore. In dealing with a cultural crisis that was at first limited to small avant-garde groups but that eventually shook to its foundation not only the entire structure of knowledge (beginning with language) but all civil society, with profound repercussions in the domain of religion, some have attempted to deny the very existence of the crisis or to place it back within the very institutions that it challenged and into the cultural contexts that it rejected.

The most serious limitation of this sort of interpretation has been to take the structure of the university "schools" as a starting point, without recognizing that it was precisely the medieval university that had fallen into disrepute and was being challenged, and that culture and intellectual investigation were seeking other locales or beginning to form other structures. Through a revolt against the barbarity of Scholastic Latin, the sterility of terminological logic, and the oppressive dictatorship of Aristotle (in extremely poor and misleading translations, what is more), it was the methods and the instruments of attaining knowledge that came under attack. The challenge was even more severe in a more strictly philosophical domain, where it was the very distinctions between the various disciplines, their order and their rank, that were challenged. The debate on poetry and myths, which passed from Boccaccio, an artist, to Coluccio Salutati, a jurist, moralist, and philosopher, before enlivening the philosophical works of Cristoforo Landino and Marsilio Ficino, had a profound resonance. Above all, however, it had the great merit of throwing into crisis the rigid boundaries not only between philosophy and poetry but also between the arts and philosophical reflection, thus opening the way to the vogue for poetic expressions of theology.

When the philosophy of the Renaissance is approached using inadequate intellectual categories and inoperative distinctions, it makes it difficult, if not impossible, to grasp what was most brilliant and original in men like Marsilio Ficino and Giordano Bruno: their theory of the imagination to begin with. Not to mention the extensive use of Plato and the Platonic tradition, which implies openness to a different means of access to and way of conceiving of reality; to a different manner of practicing and conceiving of philosophy, from the dialogue as the heuristic instrument par excellence to the theory of memory (memory proper and its significance); from the ambiguous relation between poetry and philosophy to a concept of mathematics. Linguistic problems and questions of translation and of the relation of words to things were always of decisive importance. They led to highly significant use of the image of the book of nature or the physical world as a book, a book written in languages that remained to be discovered and which could only be deciphered with the aid of new techniques.

Beyond the metaphors, it was in this direction that the new philosophy tended, working consciously to counter the philosophy of the schools and launching a provocative appeal for revolt to the "grammarians." In Paris in 1509, the printer-publisher Josse Bade was perfectly aware of the "revolutionary" nature of Valla's works in general and the *Dialecticae disputationes* in particular when he published that work, claiming that it contained "the fundamentals of universal philosophy" and refuted not only Aristotle, Boethius, and Porphyry but "modern philosophers" (*recentiores philosophi*) as well. This was what Valla himself had proudly proclaimed more than a half century earlier in a 1444 *Defensio* against a number of accusations. He presents his *Dialectics* as a sort of "Discourse on Method" covering all intellectual knowledge precisely because it challenged all its categories. Valla was perfectly aware of this. Still, Josse Bade's challenge, in Paris in 1509, to the Sorbonne, the greatest medieval university, is easier to understand when we recall that he had also published Valla's commentary on the New Testament (*Adnotationes*, or *De Collatione Novi Testamenti libri duo*), a manuscript copy of which Erasmus had found in the Abbey of Parc near Louvain.

Erasmus's admiration for Valla and for his *De Elegantiae* (of which he wrote a "Paraphrasis, seu potius Epitome") is well known. The *Adnotationes* were quite another affair, however. Collation of the Latin and Greek texts of Holy Writ put the word of God to the test linguistically and with "scientific" rigor. The "grammarian" became a theologian, and he posed as preliminary to further discussion the problem of language, of the text, and of translation, with all the historical implications inherent in such matters. Erasmus immediately recognized not only the exceptional importance of Valla's work but also its many implications for traditional knowledge. His fine preface in the form of a letter to Christoph Fischer, written in Paris in 1505, stresses "grammar" in its relation to philosophy and theology, and it proclaims that no "great men" (that is, true and competent scholars) had ever hesitated to include Valla "among the philosophers and the theologians" (*Laurentium . . . inter philosophos quoque ad theologos*). Erasmus states that he is well aware that Valla's adversaries were many and that they could not tolerate seeing a "grammarian" take up philosophy and theology. Erasmus nonetheless insists that grammar is "indeed concerned with extremely small matters, but without which none can become great; it raises small questions, but they have extremely serious consequences." Without a profound and solid knowledge of language and of the structure of discourse, any serious grasp of its meanings is impossible.

In short, Erasmus understood that grammar was not a discipline intent on usurping the functions of philosophy and theology but rather a method of reading and interpreting texts that had every intention of supplanting other methods. Without knowing the language of a text, without some familiarity with its structures and without a firm grasp of the historical and cultural context in which it arose, any attempt to approach the text was impossible. If, moreover, the text in question was a translation, perhaps a translation of a translation, the entire issue of translation arose—that is, of the delicate operation of transferring a discourse from one linguistic and cultural context to another. When Erasmus published his Greek and Latin New Testament (Froben, 1516), he was conscious of performing a profoundly revolutionary act in which philological exegesis was in reality a sweeping operation to renew "Christian philosophy" that was closely connected with the *Enchiridion militis christiani* (the *Manual of the Christian Knight*; 1503; 1515), the *Institutio principis christiani* (1516), and the *Querela Pacis* (1517)—that is, with the Christian humanism for which he had become the spokesman throughout Europe.

Valla and Erasmus: in different ways and in varying measure, these two men were true philosophers and great intellectuals typical of the age of the Renaissance. They were humanists who, with thorough philological grounding, turned their learning to active reform and to an original conception of life and reality. Critics of the temporal power of the church, enemies of the Peripatetic Christianity of the Scholastics, and profoundly marked by classical authors, they were the interlocutors of sovereigns and popes, for whom they wrote works of vast resonance. In his *Elegantiae*, Valla moves from linguistic analysis of the term "persona" to a discussion of the Trinity, where he disagrees with Boethius; in *De voluptate* (published in 1512, again by Josse Bade), he outlines a daring and original rethinking of Epicurus in Christian terms (attenuated in later editions), which circulated throughout Europe in the early sixteenth century in the wake of his *Còllatio* and his *Dialectica*. Erasmus, so often and so erroneously compared to Voltaire, was a sincere champion of a rigorous Christian humanism. Like Valla with his *Elegantiae*, with his *Adagia* and the *Colloquia* Erasmus gave Europe not a new pedantic version of classicism but its highest inheritance from the ancient world. His critical awareness quite possibly reached its fullest (and most tragic) development in his *Moriae encomium* (*In Praise of Folly*). It is by reflecting on Valla and Erasmus, on their presence and the diversity of their influence, that we can best grasp the connection between humanism and the philosophy—the "new" philosophy, no longer "Scholastic"—that characterized the age of the Renaissance.

We need the courage to say once and for all that these men were not *new* philosophers but simply philosophers, because it was in the Renaissance and only in the Renaissance that the "philosopher" (and the scientist), a previously nonexistent figure, was born. Furthermore, he was born because the ancient philosopher (and the ancient man of science) was *reborn*. The relation of the new philosopher to his classical counterpart was complex: the older philosopher was a model and a point of departure, but the new philosopher needed to part company with this model to conquer his own autonomy and respond to the demands of new times. Truth, in short—or philosophy, or science—was not something found in a book on which one commented *ex cathedra*, a process that invited comments on those comments (as Averroës and St. Thomas commented on Aristotle, John of Jandun and Tommaso de Vio commented on Averroës and St. Thomas, and so on). Neither was the search for truth conditioned by its relation to "revelation," Hebrew, Christian, or Moslem. Truth was an answer to be sought in experience of things and in human history. It was of course also to be compared with what books said, but only inasmuch as they documented similar attempts to seek truth and thus were open to evaluation by reason. The Renaissance closed a cycle; as Machiavelli said, it was a return to origins.

Nicholas of Cusa, who was probably the greatest philosopher of the fifteenth century, wrote of the return to classical antiquity in 1433, in a highly significant text: "We see that all minds today, even the greatest scholars in all the liberal and mechanical arts, seek out ancient things, and with great eagerness, as if one could hope that an entire cycle was about to come to a close (*ac si totius revolutionis circulus proximo compleri speraretur*)."

A cycle was indeed closing: the "tree of knowledge" was changing, thus bringing a change in the relationship between intellectual disciplines. The old sacred precincts of scholarship and teaching—the medieval universities—were finding life difficult, while new forms of encounter and collaboration were coming into being, and new institutions for the pursuit and transmission of knowledge, often with ambiguous connections to the university, were taking form. In addition, accepted "authors" and "authorities" were shifting rapidly, thanks to the renewed study of antiquity, to an increasingly widespread knowledge of Greek, and to a massive revival of Latin authors. Particularly in the fields of science and philosophy, a new library emerged of texts that were to revolutionize a number of disciplines. Plato and Plotinus became accessible, but so did Archimedes and Pappus, Proclus and Iamblichus, Hero and Ptolemy.

Furthermore, while the philosophical library was being transformed, the old structure of knowledge was overturned. Coluccio Salutati had already pondered the connection between poetry and theology (at least concerning the pagan nations). How were astronomy, astrology, and philosophy related? Where should moral or political philosophy be placed? The universal man of the Renaissance was above all someone who lost track of the boundaries between the various fields of knowledge and action, someone who wrote an essay on political thought in a painting or, like Raphael, portrayed Diogenes Laertius and the lives of the philosophers; someone who included an essay on morality in a lyric poem, who wrote a treatise on architecture that included a chapter on the state, or who fit a condensed dissertation on philosophy or the basic principles of a treatise on perspective into a work on painting. Anyone who wanted to translate Proclus needed to be a philosopher, but also a mathematician. But above all, he needed an excellent command of Greek, and much more, if he hoped to understand his author in depth and comment on his work. Possession of ancient languages coupled with a thorough grounding in the scientific and philosophical disciplines was all but indispensable, at least at the start, although later there were collaborative efforts between philosophers, philologists, and scientists. When the Greek text of Ptolemy's *Geographia* became available in the early 1400s, both Jacobus Angeli of Scarperia (between 1406 and 1410) and Leonardo Bruni, a philosopher, translated it into Latin. The text had come down without its maps, so geographers redrew them on the basis of Ptolemy's descriptions. Rather than philologists becoming philosophers and men of science, now a variety of specialists could be called on for collaboration and aid. The edition of Ptolemy's *Geographia* (or *Cosmographia*) that was published in Bologna in 1477 (dated 1462, however) was based on Angeli's Latin version of the work and was edited by a veritable "team" of scholars: Girolamo Manfredi, Pietrobuono Avogadro, Galeotto Marzio, Cola Montanus, and Filippo Beroaldo.

Where the rising tide of the new humanistic culture was strongest (even within the Studios), the equilibrium between the various disciplines and within teaching methods began to shift. In Florence in 1473, one of the officials who supervised the Studio expressed the hope that there would be no talk of hiring friars to teach philosophy, given that the students had lost patience with *fratesca ingenia, ac fratescas et crassissimas doctrinas*.

The Florentine Studio may have been a special case. It was famous throughout Europe, according to Philip Melanchthon, for having called highly acclaimed Byzantine scholars to teach the ancient Greek philosophers—men like John Argyropoulos, who read Aristotle in the original, touched on all of Greek thought in his commentaries, and, in private, compared Aristotle to Plato. Argyropoulos taught philosophy officially, but the Studio also included Angelo Poliziano, a philologist, who made broad use of Aristotle's *Poetics* (for the first time in Europe) in a course on Latin comic drama, and who launched a course on logic with an extraordinary inaugural lecture on "The Witch" (*Lamia*). Interestingly, on 25 October 1499, the officers of the Studio ruled that the professors of philosophy must read Aristotle in the authentic text alone, on which they were to comment, rather than teaching simply by giving a literal exposition of its contents (*debeant legere et interpretari textum librorum Aristotelis, not autem commentaria super libris predictis ad verbum exponere, . . . prout faciunt*).

The split between the *fratesca ingenia* with their *crassissimae doctrinae* (which were the disputations on physics, metaphysics, and theology of an enervated thirteenth-century late Scholasticism) and the new "philosophy" of revived classical philosophy was thus reflected in institutions like the Florentine Studio in the new philology and its claims. The same split burst through in the cities and the courts, where a totally different sort of intellectual discipline and "master" gained ground. In the Studios, where Aristotle was required reading, a new Aristotle in Greek appeared, following the great Greek commentators (Alexander of Aphrodisias, for example), and he was not easily reconciled with the dominant orthodoxies.

Above all, new questions were put to the ancient philosophers, first (as early as Valla) concerning the relationship between poetry and history—the *Poetics* was to be at the center of intellectual debate throughout Europe in the sixteenth century—and next, concerning moral and political philosophy. The "experts" who responded to the challenge were men active in their various fields: poets and writers, the magistrates and the chancellors of the free cities, courtiers and men in government. They were scholars like Leonardo Bruni, the "humanist" most widely read throughout Europe in the first half of the fifteenth century, a historian and an eminent statesman, who translated Aristotle's moral and political works and whose translations and commentaries became essential to all theoretical discussion. They were, in short, politicians and historians who reflected on politics and history and thus practiced philosophy—that is, they applied critical thought to the problems and experiences they knew intimately, making use of the traditional "authors"— whom they continued to venerate—for comparison and reinforcement, but not as a source of theory. They were soon followed by men with no connection to the schools, men like Niccolò Machiavelli, who troubled the sleep of Scholastic philosophers for centuries to come.

The effects of the changes brought by the "cultural revolution" that had accompanied the return in force of the ancient philosophers went beyond the relative prestige of the various intellectual disciplines and beyond institutions. This cultural revolution brought a new image of the theoretician—of the "philosopher"—who was henceforth one who subjects his own experience to critical reflection and who acts as well as theorizes.

Marsilio Ficino, whose figure loomed large in European culture in the fifteenth and sixteenth centuries, is the classic example of the new philosopher. Although we know that like his father before him (the personal physician of Cosimo "Il Vecchio" de' Medici), he was a physician, we do not know where he studied medicine or even whether he completed his studies. We do know that he practiced medicine, and that he wrote abundantly. In the 1460s he inundated the world of philosophy with an entire library of Platonic and Neoplatonic works translated from the Greek, up to and including Psellus and the Byzantine Middle Ages but centering on Plato and on Plotinus, whose works he translated and commented on in their entirety. Ficino included among his philosophers (as early as 1463, but the printed edition is dated 1471) hermetic writers whom he thought to be theologians of great antiquity, perhaps contemporary to Moses and certainly no later than Moses. According to Ficino, these writers had formulated the unifying bases of human religious beliefs; thus they lent support to all those in the contemporary world who worked for a return to the ideal of concord in religious belief to which Nicholas of Cusa had devoted a splendid dialogue in September 1453, immediately after Constantinople had fallen into the hands of the Turkish troops of Mohammed II. *De pace fidei* is a great work and Nicholas of Cusa a great philosopher, sensitive to scientific problems, but not a university professor and remote from the problematics of late Scholasticism. He was a cardinal of the Holy Roman Church, a man of action and a statesman, who moved in a world of councils and schisms.

Marsilio Ficino was also a prominent personality who moved among princes and lords, far from the universities. He was a born teacher, however, and he had his own circle of "fellow philosophers" at the Villa of Careggi, which the aging Cosimo had dreamed would be the seat of the new Platonic academy. Hermeticism—a singular and fascinating mix that Ficino concocted of non-Christian Gnosticism, magic, and astrology in an atmosphere of Neoplatonism—aroused extraordinary interest from 1471 on and infiltrated all aspects of culture, poetry and the figurative arts, religious thought, and customs. We soon find it in Paris in the intellectually advanced circle of Lefèvre d'Étaples, who claimed to love Ficino like a father ("amore Marsilii Ficini, quem tamquam patrem") and who published an edition of Nicholas of Cusa's works in 1514. In 1515 Cornelius Agrippa, with all the fumes of brimstone connected with his philosophy, opened his course on Hermes Trismegistus in Pavia with a lecture that was in great part a simple transcription of Ficino.

Thus Hermes invaded the sixteenth century, riding the wave of popularity of Ficino's translations and propaganda. First and foremost, hermeticism meant exaltation of man—a man who was the hermetic god Anthropos in human form and "a great miracle," as Giovanni Pico della Mirandola stated in his famous discourse. Hermeticism was a vision of reality as universal life and universal love; as universal light (and intelligibility). Ficino stresses the theme of the life of the universe in his *Three Books on Life* (*De vita libri tres*), a work much admired, widely circulated, and often reprinted during the sixteenth century. This life was cosmic, raining down from the heavens to fertilize the earth in the wedding of all things; it was universal light and love understood as the substance and the motor force of all physical phenomena.

In an *Apologia* written to defend his work from an accusation of magic (promoted by ecclesiastical circles in spite of Lorenzo de' Medici's protection of him), Ficino writes:

Heaven, the husband of earth, does not touch the earth, as is the common opinion. It does not have intercourse with its wife; but by the rays of its stars alone as if with the rays of its eyes, it illuminates her on all sides; it fertilizes her by its illumination and procreates living things. If, therefore, it bestows life even by its glance, does heaven have no life proper to itself? (*Three Books on Life*, trans. Kaske and Clark, 401)

Ficino's name was known throughout Europe. His reputation was based not only on his major translations and commentaries but also on his own works, *De vita libri tres*, *El libro dell'amore*, *De voluptate*, and *De sole et lumine*, to which we might add translations, compendia, and commentaries with such suggestive titles as "The Mysteries of Iamblichus," "The Fantasy of Priscian," "The Demons of Psellus," and "The Dreams of Synesius." His work investigated less-frequented territories (the world of fantasy); it was filled with fascination for the occult and the seduction of magic; in it Lucretius met Plotinus in a suggestive blend of poetry and philosophy. In a century of great art, Ficino's thought constantly operated at the boundaries of poetry and the figurative arts. This, much more than the systematic *Theologia platonica*, was the secret of Ficino's lasting success throughout the sixteenth century. One eye-witness recalls that in the summer of 1583, when Giordano Bruno was presenting a series of lectures at Oxford, one learned listener (probably the physician Martin Culpepper) accused him of plagiarizing the third book of *De vita* (the famous *De vita coelitus comparanda*), and forced him to interrupt his lecture. It would be difficult to decide whether this anecdote is more telling as proof of Bruno's reliance on Ficino or as evidence of the learned Englishman's familiarity with Ficino's works.

Ficino championed Platonism at a time when Aristotle's authority was in crisis, but he was respectful of Aristotle, as of all the great classical thinkers, Epicurus included. He defended the one common source of religions in a *prisca theologia*, and he was so persuaded of the religious significance of the Platonic tradition that he gave a "reading" of Plotinus in the Church of the Angioli in 1487, to the great scandal of the general of the Camaldolese order, Pietro Delfin. In 1489, Ficino made a striking impression by insisting that the philosopher is a magician insofar as he deals with the sciences of nature and operates on the plane of nature—thus reiterating Pico's thesis (by then condemned) that "natural magic" was the practical aspect of the science of nature. Ficino also clearly rehabilitates astrology (within certain limits) as the study and use of the natural forces residing in heavenly bodies. As the farmer "prepares the field and the seeds for celestial gifts," he states, "so the doctor, the natural philosopher, and the surgeon achieve similar effects in our bodies in order both to strenghten our own nature and to obtain more productively the nature of the universe." Ficino adds that much the same occurs with "the philosopher who knows about natural objects and stars, whom we rightly are accustomed to call a Magus" (*Three Books on Life*, trans. Kaske and Clark, 387).

This is not the appropriate place to discuss magic in Ficino. He made broad use of magical texts and discussed talismans in detail, not denying their effects. During the sixteenth century an elegant pocket-sized volume, often reprinted, was in circulation that united the better part of Ficino's translations of not only a hermetic but also a more strictly "magical" nature.

Giovanni Pico, count of Mirandola, lord of Concordia, and one of the most complex and significant figures of the Italian quattrocento, was without doubt a "philosopher," even a "new philosopher" of the same stamp as Marsilio Ficino. Born into a wealthy and powerful family, Pico was not a university professor, even though he had ties to many famous professors and he welcomed followers. Like Ficino, he was impressed by hermeticism, and his best-known work, the discourse on man, begins with a hermetic saying, "What a great miracle is man, O Asclepius." Unlike Ficino, however, Pico added to hermeticism the mysticism of the Hebrew cabala, which he studied early in his life and with great enthusiasm, precisely because he thought it held the key to a religious reunification of Jews and Christians. His formation was Aristotelian, but he soon discovered Plato and Plotinus and he wrote on the Platonic theory of love in "friendly disagreement" with Ficino. He nevertheless continued to admire Aristotle, and he dreamed of harmony among philosophers, who seemed to him equally seeking truth, which they viewed from different but ultimately reconcilable points of view. He knew Greek and loved classical antiquity, but he did not condemn all Scholastics, and in fact granted the importance of many of them.

Pico was firm, however, in his support of the rights of reason, and for that reason he combatted divinatory astrology, which, by use of the horoscope, claimed to link particular events—accidental occurrences in the lives of individual people—to universal causes such as light or heat. However, he defended mathematical astrology, or the study of the laws regulating celestial motion. He rejected necromantic magic, but defended natural magic, which occurred, according to him, in the moment when science operated on nature. Pico often repeated that the magician "marries the world," by which he meant that he exploits the natural relations between physical forces in order to obtain new results. Ficino writes eloquently on the marriage of heaven and earth, picking up from Lucretius the theme of the love and the life immanent throughout a universe full of beings. Pico was more interested in defining the precise line of demarcation between real, ascertainable processes and arbitrary and fantastic connections. Perhaps precisely what divided the two philosophers (who were friends, even if Pico attacked some of Ficino's positions) was that Pico showed less indulgence toward the world of the imagination and toward the power of fancy that were so strong in Ficino.

A similar lack of interest in the realm of the imagination probably lay behind Pico's eloquent defense of the technical language of the philosophers, where he fails to grasp the deeper values in the humanists' linguistic positions. Ermolao Barbaro wrote to him, on 5 April 1485, to express his pleasure that Pico had added a knowledge of Plato to his background in Aristotle ("because anyone who separates Aristotle from Plato cannot [properly] speak of him"). Above all, Barbaro congratulated Pico for having abandoned the barbaric style of the Scholastics, who were under the illusion that they were still alive but in reality were dead ("these Germans and Teutons who were not truly alive even when they were living . . . sordid, rough, uncultivated barbarians").

Barbaro was a typical example of the "new" philosopher. Of a noble and cultivated family and expert in Greek, he had a strong interest in the natural sciences and was a superlative scholar of the writings of Pliny and Dioscorides. He was persuaded that anyone unable to comprehend the terms of a scientific work with some exactitude would understand little of the science itself. In 1485 he confided to a friend that he had lectured in Padua on Aristotle's moral philosophy and had held important magistracies, adding that he proposed to teach the original Greek text of Aristotle's physics, theology, poetics, and rhetoric, using the Greek commentaries. All that the Latin and Arab Scholastics had done, he was fond of repeating, was plagiarize the Greeks, and to demonstrate the truth of this claim he "amused himself" translating Themistius.

Pico responded to Barbaro on 3 June 1485, in a famous letter that came close to being a defense of the Scholastics (something that Leibnitz was later to deny). Pico states:

We were famous while we lived, O Ermolao, and so will we live in the future, not in the grammarians' schools, not where children are taught, but in the assemblies of the philosophers and the circles of the wise, where it is not the mother of Andromache, the sons of Niobe, and frivolities of the sort that are treated and discussed, but the principles of human and divine things.

Pico's letter prompted long discussions for both its content and its stylistic qualities. Barbaro answered him immediately, shrewdly observing that Pico himself gave particular attention to appropriate language and to precision and elegance of expression. Barbaro understood that beyond their debate about form, it was philosophy—the *new* philosophy—that they were debating; it was clarity of ideas and clarity of expression. He admitted that philosophy was made of things (*philosophiam rebus constare*), not of words; but for that very reason, he said, words must render things with precision rather than polluting them with inappropriate terminology (*sordidis verbis et ignobilibus inquinari, contaminari, pollui non debere*). Barbaro knew that the issue was not ornamentation but clarity and precision—in other words, rigor.

By the time Pico wrote his letter in 1485, Ficino, Pico himself, and others like Gianozzo Manetti had begun to write philosophical works in the vernacular as well as in Latin. This was a far cry indeed from Scholastic jargon. Furthermore, the new philosophy now tended to produce a different sort of work directed at a new public—readable, brief, pleasant works with a broad appeal. Even Pomponazzi, who was a professor (albeit a somewhat scandalous and highly provocative one), not only reduced the immortality of the soul to an amiable perfume but did so in a lively little book, just as he put his theory on the connection between miracles, enchantments, and "fantasies" into a pleasing little work full of themes taken from Ficino.

Moreover, the new philosophers now circulated their ideas more rapidly, not in boring and incomprehensible lecture courses in great part copied from one another, but in an exchange of letters that were in general elegantly written and often, even during the fifteenth century, written in the vernacular. They replaced Scholastic Latin, a dreadful initiates' jargon ridiculed in macaronic verse, with a clear and accessible Latin and soon, in a good number of works, with the vernacular. In other words, science and philosophy—the "new" science and the "new" philosophy—sought a new public to whom new things could be said in new ways. Some sixteenth-century writers (in Italy, Alessandro Piccolomini and Sperone Speroni, for instance) pointed out that there were even women who wanted to read and to learn, as did men in business and in government and others who had neither the time nor the inclination to study Latin and Greek. Such concerns clearly imply that philosophy was, or was also, logic, moral and political philosophy, poetics, the science of nature, and psychology. In other words, it was something truly new.

This was why the debate that Barbaro and Pico had stirred up in their exchange of letters persisted. During the sixteenth century, Philip Melanchthon went back to it on several occasions, not only in 1523 in his *Encomium eloquentiae* but also in 1558 in his "Response to Pico in Defense of Ermolao."

In 1670, Leibnitz returned to the charge, although with altogether too much indulgence toward Pico ("He sought to diminish and conceal the faults of the Scholastics rather than to defend them"). By the mid-seventeenth century, however, Descartes had recalled that the sciences were founded "not on obscure and grand things, but on the easiest and most obvious ones" and had written his famous *Discourse on Method* in French. Even earlier, in 1555, Ramus published his *Dialectique* in French.

Ficino, Pico, and Ermolao Barbaro are all undeniable exemplars of great intellectuals of the new type. Such men operated outside the university Studios or had ambiguous connections with some of their representatives; they dealt directly with princes and cardinals; they participated in what today would be called the political culture of their country. Whether they were wealthy in their own right, were maintained by great lords, or lived on ecclesiastical benefices, they moved within an infinite network of relations. They also tended—like Ficino, with the backing of the Medici—to found new cultural institutions such as the academy at Careggi. It was they who launched the new modes of investigation that show the profound revolution that was at work not only in the specific field of philosophy but also in all the various approaches to reality and in all disciplines—all the *arti*.

Anyone who reads works of as broad a scope and as great beauty as Marsilio Ficino's *El libro dell'amore* will reach a better understanding of the new relationship established between the fine arts and the new philosophy: the theory of beauty and of love and the theory of life and light are indeed connected with Platonic thought, Platonic thought visualized in the manner of the quattrocento masters. This often makes it extremely difficult to draw a clear distinction between the artist (or the scientist), the moralist, and the philosopher. This was characteristic of intellectuals of many callings—men of letters, painters, technological experts like architects and engineers, and scientists (astrologer/astronomers and mathematicians). Where does Poliziano the poet end and Poliziano the philologist begin? Or the "grammarian" and the "logician," the rhetorician and the dialectician?

A historiography unfortunately still current falsifies Ficino, forcing him into schemata and problems that were not his, but this historiography is at a loss to know where to place figures like Alberti and Leonardo, ultimately hastily categorizing them under the ambiguous label "universal men"—a term as resounding as it is meaningless. It was precisely these men and their restless and insatiable search for knowledge (a search given concrete substance by precise questioning of experience and continual practical contact with reality) that brought into being the new function of philosophizing, seen as an overall vision of man and the world.

For a number of his highly authoritative contemporaries, Leon Battista Alberti was a thinker somehow connected with Ficino's renewal of philosophy. Cristoforo Landino, *maestro* in the Florentine Studio, cast him as the protagonist of a debate on the relative value of the active life or the contemplative life, placing him (wrongly, however) with the Platonists. More accurately, Alberti was an exponent of the new cultural orientation and a technician, but also a student of mathematics and of optics, a great theorist of painting, sculpture, and architecture, and a man deeply involved in the problems of contemporary society, the city, and the family. A disheartened vision of things emerges from some of his works in Italian and many of those in Latin, where Stoic influences take on singularly dark colors, almost as if Alberti were aware of the profound crisis of his age. He combines a disenchanted view of the world with a singular sensitivity to the needs of his times, to which he offers straightforward responses in an extraordinarily precise, carefully focused use of both Latin and Italian and in a dialogue format that gives full rein to opposing ideas.

Some scholars have attempted to impose unity on Alberti's works under the sign of aesthetics, harmony, beauty, and even mathematical rationality. In reality, he gives the impression of being open to all contradictions and of having a vision of philosophical thought as an awareness of the dramatic nature of the human condition. We cannot easily forget his praise, already mentioned, of the two true philosophers he considered worthy of the name, Socrates and Democritus, nor his accusation that all the "other" philosophers were changeable and vague, each offering a different model of the universe. This resulted in an infinite number of possible worlds (and an infinite number of madmen) because each philosopher pursued a world of his own devising.

As his works clearly show, Alberti was well grounded in philosophical theory, but his various studies were aimed at a specific theoretical problem or precise technical question, be it perspective, mathematical games, an astronomical question, or a problem in optics. Furthermore, although his strongest interest and his most prolific research were in the field of the moral sciences, from the architectonic structure of cities and houses to the meaning of life, his ambition was encyclopedic, aiming at a global conception of reality—in short, at a philosophy. The bitter ironies of the *Momus* say as much. We should keep in mind, however, that this was an aspiration common to many artists. Since painting (but the other arts as well) took as its subject the world in its entirety, it required universal knowledge, hence a philosophy. Lorenzo

Ghiberti's *Commentari* (the third commentary in particular) is typical in this respect, whatever opinion one might have of the work's mode of composition.

The most extreme example, however, is undoubtedly Leonardo da Vinci. The many inappropriate questions that have been raised concerning his contribution to the rise of modern science, his inventions, and his anticipation of modern technology are quite beside the point, but his explicit attempts to construct a great encyclopedia of vibrant cultural experience are of enormous interest for an understanding of his age. Similarly, out of the mass of his many works there emerges both a constant search for innovative techniques and an effort to define a unifying point of reference for experience, which he ultimately finds in philosophy, the only discipline capable of being placed at the root of appearances.

Leonardo makes the striking statement (in *Madrid II*, fol. 107r), "benché ttutte infine le matematiche sieno speculation filosofiche" (although in the last analysis all mathematics is philosophical speculation). His discourse on painting is even more striking, however, especially when we recall his own painting and its power to render "the surfaces, colors, and forms of anything created by nature" (*Treatise on Painting*, trans. McMahon, 1:6). He states that "painting is proved to be a philosophy because it treats of the motion of bodies and the rapidity of their actions," although, he adds, "philosophy penetrates those same bodies, considering their properties" (ibid., 1:5). This implies a relationship between the mind and the eye and between light and beauty that Leonardo goes on to state explicitly: "He who disparages painting loves neither philosophy nor nature" because "if you disparage painting, which alone can portray faithfully all the visible works of nature, you certainly disparage a discovery which considers all manner of forms with subtle and philosophical attention" (ibid.). Elsewhere he states a favorite maxim: *Prima nella mente, e poi nelle mani* (first in the mind, then in the hands).

Before 1474, Ficino wrote in his *Libro dell'amore* that beauty is "resplendent in the body by the *influxus* [astral influence] of its idea." Reading Leonardo's various texts on painting brings to mind Ficino's fine vernacular prose; inversely, one inevitably thinks of works of the painters of the age (Botticelli heading the list) on reading Ficino's and Pico's commentaries in the vernacular on Plato's *Symposium*. There is a constant tension in Leonardo—which is what is fascinating about him—as he attempts to connect the human mind and its works with reality, or works of art with the truth of nature: Leonardo tells us, "I have seen flying swallows light on painted iron bars before the windows of buildings" (ibid., 1:21). Leonardo came, of course, from the *bottega* of Verrocchio. He was the illegitimate son of ser Piero, a notary, and, according to Vasari, "in learning and in the rudiments of letters he would have made great proficience, if he had not been so variable and unstable" (*Lives*, trans. De Vere, 4:89). He was nevertheless a great engineer, architect, and constructor of machines of all sorts; he was curious about physics and an expert in hydraulics; his knowledge of human anatomy was extraordinary and his anatomical sketches included every part of the body. He dealt with a sovereign like Francis I as his peer, and he took advantage of the king's hospitality to set to work organizing a gigantic and admirably illustrated encyclopedia (truly *de omnibus rebus et de quibusdam aliis*) with a view to publication. At least, this is how Canon Antonio de Beatis describes him in a famous passage of the canon's *Itinerario*, a description of a voyage through Europe of Cardinal Luigi d'Aragona. André Chastel, writing on Cellini, notes that Francis I thought Leonardo "a true philosopher; a prodigious magician." This was literally true: Leonardo embodied the full ambiguity of the magician with his vision of the world as a corporeal mass living by the perennial circulation of waters, just as humankind lived by the circulation of the blood ("the same cause moves the waters . . . as moves the blood in the human species"), in a perpetual round of machine and organism, mechanism and spontaneity. He was engrossed by an insatiable search for the "profound magic" (to use the words of Giordano Bruno) that consists of "knowing how to draw out the contrary after having found the point of union."

The philosopher's eye was no longer satisfied with a gloss of a written page: it returned to looking at the contradictions inherent in reality and to the enigmas and the dramas of life itself. We need only recall Pietro Pomponazzi, who was a physician as well as a professor of philosophy and whose much-discussed essays on immortality, fate, and enchantments (*De immortalitate animae, De fato*, and *De incantationibus*) exploited all the possibilities of Alexander of Aphrodisias's commentary on Aristotle in the interests of a lucid and totally terrestrial and "material" vision of human destiny. It was a vision that later not only seduced the erudite libertines of seventeenth-century France but, on the eve of the eighteenth century, spread to England (blended with the impiety of Giulio Cesare Vanini), thanks to Burton's *Anatomy of Melancholy*. Pomponazzi's contemporaries—the Augustinian Ambrogio Flandino for one—presented him as a prototypical libertine; as an atheist and a materialist; as intemperate and immoral, a man given to vices and of less than laudable mores; as one who praised the Stoics but imitated the Epicurians (*Zenonem laudo et Epicurum vivo*).

There is little reticence or pretense in Pomponazzi's essays. Immortality is merely a "perfume" of immortality; fate is the order of nature, which constrains the becoming of all things by its necessity *per infinita saecula, et in infinitum*. Pomponazzi turns Augustine's observation that the shadow of evil provides a framework that makes the light of goodness more resplendent into a mocking witticism: "It is by no means a cruelty that some are crushed by others, that some command and others serve: this is something quite natural, like the wolf who eats the lamb or the serpent who kills other animals." Except that, Pomponazzi warns, we want to remain on the natural level and within the limits of reason (*stando in puris naturalibus, et quantum dat ratio humana*). Given fate, and given the mortality of the soul (*si anima est mortalis*), there is no liberty, virtue, justice, or religion (*nulla libertas, nulla virtus, nulla religio*). As for enchantments and seemingly miraculous occurrences, Pomponazzi, like Ficino, explains them as figments of the imagination.

Although Pomponazzi's polemics, his invective, and his books, which were burned publicly (*De immortalitate* in Venice, for example) aroused the wrath of the friars of half of Europe without his undergoing the fate—as he said jokingly—of roast chestnuts; although for nearly two centuries his daring thought had an enormous influence on others (such as Vanini, who borrowed copiously from him), he was not alone. Heinrich Cornelius Agrippa von Nettesheim, physician and magician, was equally famous. Agrippa was lecturing on the *Pimander* of Hermes Trismegistus in Pavia before 1520, at a time when Peretto was working on his *Immortalità dell'anima* in Bologna, and he was read by Jean-Jacques Rousseau two hundred years later.

Of a restless and adventurous temperament, Agrippa traveled throughout Europe meeting learned men and organizing more or less secret "sodalities." He took Pico's magic and Ficino's hermeticism (a great influence on his thought) and added some of the cabala from Reuchlin's *De verbo mirifico*. The result was one of the great books of magic of the Renaissance, the *De occulta philosophia*, on which Agrippa worked all his life, completing the first draft in 1510 and finishing the definitive version in 1533. Nearly simultaneously, in 1531, he published *De incertitudine et vanitate scientiarum atque artium*, a *declamatio* in 103 chapters vibrating with polemic force and repeating some of the themes on which Gian Francesco Pico had touched in his *Examen vanitatis doctrinae gentium*.

In reality, Agrippa contrasted the "pestilential" Aristotle's philosophy of nature with his own view of magic (the magic of Ficino and Pico) as the culmination of a movement to constitute an active science of nature and an operative knowledge (*naturalium scientiarum summa potestas, absolutissima consummatio, activa portio philosophandi naturalis*). The *De vanitate* questioned the foundations and the methods of all knowledge, not as a form of skepticism but as a radical and critical attempt to refound science on an authentic basis. Agrippa was quite consciously attempting to do what Giovanni Pico had done for astrology: to distinguish rigorous science from a mixture of superstition and fraud in the disciplines involving knowledge of the heavens. Agrippa's aim was to extend Pico's critique to a definition of all forms of rational knowledge. Thus he showed that he had understood that the problem born of the new crisis in medieval knowledge could be the foundation of a rigorous science that might nevertheless make use of the active, operative possibilities of the natural sciences.

In short, Agrippa wanted to save Ficino's medicine and Pico's astronomy. At the same time, he intended to combat the "theologasters" and the "sophists" who stood ready to condemn magic and cabala when they as much as heard them mentioned. As he said in an open letter written in 1535 to the city fathers of Cologne: "Those squeamish asses are offended, not by the name of philosophy but by those of cabbala and magic, which if merely spoken generate suspicion." In this instance, the chief of the "squeamish asses" and the "untamed beasts"—the enemies of *bonae litterae*—who accused and condemned "all that they do not understand" was the Dominican Konrad Köllin of Ulm, but Agrippa's invective was aimed at an entire category of university professors and officially recognized theologians:

These pigs, these filthy hogs, are in the habit, when something fails to please them or they do not understand it, of going about grunting about heresy, scandal, spells, superstition, and evil influences, condemning as pagan perfidy all classical philosophy except their pestilential Aristotle. . . . With me, they have the presumption to accuse and judge Giovanni Pico of Mirandola, Marsilio Ficino, Florentine, Johannes Reuchlin of Pforzheim, and Francesco Zorzi, Venetian.

By now Agrippa felt himself alone. He wrote to Erasmus on 20 December 1531: "I am yours, I swear by your words, I am your loyal soldier, I consign myself and I entrust myself to you." He had been censured by the theologians of Louvain and Paris; in Cologne the theologians accused him of having inveighed *in totam Universitatem*. Banished from imperial territory and sought by the justice of Francis I, he died a miserable death in Grenoble. His black dog, rumored to be the Devil in disguise, threw himself into the Isère. In reality, however, even if Agrippa was isolated and persecuted, he was no less a typical representative of "philosophy"—of the "new philosophy," that is, of the philosopher-magician, who was by this time conscious of the epistemological problems brought on by the crisis in medieval knowledge. Repercussions of these problems were to be fatal to the schools and the university Studios, the traditional institutions of teaching and scholarship.

Another man was traveling throughout Europe at the same time and in much the same manner as Agrippa: the yet more restless and bizarre Paracelsus, or, as he presented himself on occasion, Philippus Aureolus Theophrastus

Bombast von Hohenheim, physician and alchemist ("I am Theophrastus, and I am of greater worth than those with whom you compare me. I am I, and I am the *monarcha medicorum*, and it is permitted to me to demonstrate to you what you are unable to demonstrate"). His most learned biographer, Walter Pagel, notes that Paracelsus found inspiration in the *De vita* of Marsilio Ficino and called him "the best of the Italian doctors" (*Italorum medicorum optimus*). Ficino wrote (and later regretted it), "We are used to calling 'Magus' the philosopher expert in things natural and celestial." This was a statement that Paracelsus could make his own.

It is difficult to speak briefly about Paracelsus. The strange congeries of his work used the new medicine as a base for a blending of the concept of nature as universal life, living force, and "magic"; the relation between the macrocosm and the microcosm; a reinterpretation of astrology; and a conception of the creative power of the imagination that recalls both Ficino and Pomponazzi. All this was written in dialectical German, not in the Latin of either the old or the new erudition, even though Paracelsus had corresponded with Erasmus, the prince of humanists, who had suggested the publisher, Froben, to him. "I do not come from their schools, nor do I write in conformity with them," Paracelsus insisted. "I am a philosopher who did not go to school with you." He inveighed against Galen and Avicenna at every opportunity, although he stopped short of publicly burning their books. He likens Aristotle to a moss, a fungus growth, and a boil. Like astronomy and alchemy, medicine is founded in philosophy, he states, because it is founded in nature. "The physician must proceed from nature; what else is nature if not philosophy, and what is philosophy if not invisible nature?" He could speak more harshly:

Do not trust the foolish words, "Our fathers are Galen and Avicenna." The stones will crush them. Heaven will make different physicians who will know the four elements, and in addition magic and cabbala which are a cataract before your eyes. They will be dowsers, they will be adepts, they will be Archei, they will be spagyri, they will have Quintum Esse, they will have arcana, they will have mysteria, they will have tinctura: What will become of your soup-kitchens in this revolution? Who will dye the thin lips of your women-folk and clean their pinched faces? The devil, with the cloth of hunger. (Pagel, *Paracelsus*, 110–11).

Alexandre Koyré, great historian though he was, mistakenly denies that Paracelsus was well informed about contemporary thought, but he was correct in finding him both highly effective and fascinating. His was "a curious doctrine," Koyré writes, "and certainly confused—a mixture of mysticism, magic, and alchemy. Extremely beautiful, however, because it represents a sincere attempt to see the world in God, God in the world, and man participating in both and 'comprehending' both." It was a doctrine open to the future, even if Paracelsus's "experience" and his "experiments" bore little resemblance to the experimental techniques of modern science and if his faith in fantasy, imagination, and even in dreams and visions outweighed his faith in reason. We must grant him the positive value of a radically unconventional attitude in a moment of revolt against tradition and authority.

We find more magic and astrology, more imagination and dreams (many dreams!), more anxieties, and another troubled life filled with inquisitorial trials and unbelief in Girolamo Cardano (1501–1576), physician and mathematician, who carted about the world both his misfortunes and his genius along with his philosophy and his astrology—which he used to draw up a detailed horoscope for Christ (to the scandal of many) and for his own long life.

Cardano quarreled with Niccolò Tartaglia over who had first discovered the solution to cubic equations, but he was undeniably a respected mathematician. One of his mathematical works was published by a friend, the theologian Andrea Osiander, who wrote a letter (Ramus called it a *fabula absurdissima*) in preface to an edition of Copernicus's *De revolutionibus orbium caelestium* in which he stated, "Therefore alongside the ancient hypotheses, which are no more probable, let us permit these new hypotheses also to be known" (*On the Revolutions*, ed. Dobrzycki, trans. Rosen, xvi). The publication of this mathematical work assured Cardano a vast audience: "This was the start of our glory," he wrote in 1562.

All the philosophical themes that had been debated for more than a century return in Cardano: nature, life, occultism, unbelief, the power of man, magic. He was to call himself *magus, incantor,* and *religionis contemptor* and to admit himself possessed by *cupiditas omnium occultarum artium*. He found it difficult to decide which of his many achievements was worthy of greatest acclaim:

In arithmetic I advanced almost the whole field of the science including the sections treating, as they call it, of algebra. . . . In geometry I dealt with . . . infinity with finite numbers and through finite, although it was first discovered by Archimedes. In music I discovered new tones and new intervals, or rather brought back into practice and use such tones and intervals as were already found according to the treatises of Ptolemy and Aristoxenus (*The Book of My Life*, trans. Stoner, 216).

Cardano realized that the old encyclopedia was no longer serviceable, and he set to work on a new one. In 1547 he published his highly successful *De subtilitate rerum* and, in 1557, "with material left unused" to which he had not managed to give "order and completion," his *De rerum varietate*. The

De subtilitate, which went through several editions, was translated into French by Richard Le Blanc in 1556. Immediately reprinted, it was debated at length and in pedantic detail by Giulio Cesare Scaliger, thus giving wide publicity to Cardano's ideas and fantasies.

Cardano was fond of boasting of his own singularity, so it is natural that his most successful (at least his best-known) work, his autobiography, a rough portrait of his misadventures and his greatness, should be full of it. He presents himself as a scientist, a magician, an occultist, and an unbeliever. In reality, he was simply one of the small but growing number of thinkers who had originally opposed Hermes Trismegistus and Plato to Aristotle and who now, independent of Plato (though not of Hermes) sought "nature" with the aid of the senses.

Bernardino Telesio was also one of these. He lashed out at people who invented worlds and took their fantasies for reality. "They fabricate a world according to their own will and wishes," Telesio states, adding that he and his fellows, "lovers and observers of all human knowledge," had "chosen to consider *this* world and each of its parts, together with the passions and the actions and the operations of the things contained in it," heeding only "the things that sense makes manifest."

Francis Bacon, who refers more than once to Telesio, saw him simply as instrumental to the revival of the pre-Socratic philosophy of Parmenides. Bacon accused Telesio (as he had Patrizi, Bruno, Campanella, and many others) of having confused their fables with science without even liberating their thought from the errors of the peripatetics (*Peripateticis scilicet notionibus depravatus*). Still, if it was true that the "nature" appealed to by the dialectics of primordial physical forces (heat and cold) was also a "fable" and that it bore little resemblance to the physics of Galileo or the "fable" of Descartes, it was nonetheless by that road that the new science and the new philosophy made its way. Certainly, even Telesio was recounting a fable—*his* fable—but he was also moving on a new plane and seeking new paths.

The old universities closed their doors to Telesio. He had to be satisfied giving vent to his "dreams" in an academy in his native Cosenza. A loyal student of Telesio, his chief propagandist, and his publisher, Antonio Persio, was elected (not without limitations, since he was a *linceo postumo*) to the Accademia dei Lincei along with Galileo, and he prompted Federico Cesi's interest in Telesio's works. Nonetheless, Telesio's works were listed on the Index, as were Patrizi's; Pierre de la Ramée was assassinated during the St. Bartholomew's Day massacre; Bruno and Vanini were burned at the stake; Campanella was imprisoned for life; Copernicus and Galileo were condemned; and Descartes did not publish his *Le monde* for fear of the possible consequences.

These men were still a suspect and often persecuted minority, even though in the sixteenth century they were not a merely bizarre minority. It is true that the "schools" continued to teach Aristotle and his commentators, old and new, and that men like Petrus Tartaretus in Paris, Chrysostomus Javellus Canapicio in Italy, and many others of their ilk continued unperturbed to embalm an outdated peripatetic philosophy in widely circulated manuals. They wrote, of course, in frightful Latin, whereas by the mid-sixteenth century the philosophical works of Pierre de la Ramée and Alessandro Piccolomini were published in French and in Italian for readers who included gentlewomen and men in commerce and government. Piccolomini and Ramus were different men, however, who belonged to a different world, on the other side of a divide that had been deepening since the early fifteenth century. They were rebels against Scholastic tradition who had learned from the ancient writers that books were many, not just one, and that beyond the books of men there was the great book of nature, comprehension of which required reason, not authority. They were men who sought knowledge, but for action; men who were ready for anything, even for seeking out the secrets of "natural" magic to gain dominion over the physical world, but who were also determined to liberate "science" from "magic." They now lived in another world irreconcilable with the old; in a universe without confines, in which infinite numbers of other systems were in motion and the earth revolved around the sun. In this new world man sought a dependable measure not only by searching within himself, like Montaigne, but by seeking (also like Montaigne) better acquaintance with the inhabitants of hitherto-unknown lands, who were difficult to reconcile with traditional theology. (From what Adam were the Americans descended? What Redeemer had saved them?)

The church condemned these men without exception, precisely because they were destroying its world. Thus the church condemned the philology and the theology of Valla and Erasmus as well as the astronomy of Copernicus and Galileo, the politics of Machiavelli, the psychology of Pomponazzi, and the natural philosophy of Telesio, Palingenius Stellatus, and Giordano Bruno. Excluded from or regarded with mistrust by the time-honored sanctuaries of knowledge—the universities—the new philosophers made use of the occult and the esoteric and found other places in which to meet and study under the protection of princes and sovereigns. There, in academies and societies of various sorts, they toiled to find a secure foundation (or at least a basis open to critical debate) for a new encyclopedia of knowledge and a new science to usher in the reign of man. Thus the paths of reason would be freed from the insidious dangers of the occult, astronomy freed from divinatory astrology, and physics from ceremonial magic.

For two centuries, this was the task of a small number of men compelled to fight on more than one front, with no group identity, who lacked a clear sense of what they were and what they sought. The crisis of the medieval encyclopedia had swept away ancient distinctions along with the barriers between disciplines. The artist had become a man of science; the philologist, a theologian; the historian, a moralist; the physicist, a philosopher. They were "new philosophers," restless and rebellious men, knights errant of knowledge, who moved among dreams and magic, among utopias and illusions of universal and perpetual concord; men capable of critical reflections, profound inner investigation, and mystical vagabondage amid the souls of the stars coupled with mathematical formulas for translating the motion, finally proved not to be circular, of celestial bodies.

After two centuries of polemics and doubts, Descartes provides an almost symbolic close to a long chapter of extraordinary adventures. He had encountered the Rosicrucians and had read all the books he could find on "the sciences esteemed to be the most curious and rare," but he had closed such books once and for all. He had dreamed three extraordinary dreams—more than Cardano's—and had described them in detail, but he spoke of them no longer. He had learned that all the sciences are connected in the unity of "universal mathematics" and that they form the encyclopedia of knowledge ("quippe sunt concatenatae omnes scientiae . . . et tota simul encyclopedia"). To this unity he dedicated the remainder of his life.

BIBLIOGRAPHY

Cassirer, Ernst. *Individuum und Kosmos in der Philosophie der Renaissance*. Leipzig and Berlin: B. G. Teubner, 1927. (*The Individual and the Cosmos in Renaissance Philosophy*. Trans. Mario Domandi. Philadelphia: University of Pennsylvania Press, 1972.)

De Gandillac, Maurice. "La philosophie de la 'Renaissance.'" In *Encyclopédie de la Pléiade*, vol. 2, *Histoire de la Philosophie*. Paris: Gallimard, 1973, 3–356.

Gadol, Joan. *Leon Battista Alberti: Universal Man of the Early Renaissance*. Chicago and London: University of Chicago Press, 1969.

———. "Universal Man." In Philip P. Wiener, ed., *Dictionary of the History of Ideas*. 5 vols. New York: Scribner, 1973, 4:437–43.

Heller, Ágnes. *A Reneszánsz Ember*. Budapest: Akadémiai Kaido, 1967. (*Renaissance Man*. Trans. Richard E. Allen. London and Boston: Routledge & Kegan Paul, 1978; reprint New York: Schocken Books, 1981.)

Koyré, Alexandre. *Mystiques, spirituels, alchimistes du XVI siècle allemand.* Paris: Gallimard, 1971.

Kristeller, Paul Oskar. *Die Philosophie des Marsilio Ficino.* Frankfurt am Main: Klostermann, 1972. (*The Philosophy of Marsilio Ficino.* Trans. Virginia Conant. New York: Columbia University Press, 1943.)

Nauert, Charles G., Jr. *Agrippa and the Crisis of Renaissance Thought.* Urbana: University of Illinois Press, 1965.

Pagel, Walter. *Paracelsus: An Introduction to Philosophical Medicine in the Era of the Renaissance.* 2d rev. ed. Basel and New York: Karger, 1982.

Rossi, Paolo. *Francesco Bacone. Dalla magia alla scienza.* New ed. Turin: Einaudi, 1978. (*Francis Bacon: From Magic to Science.* Trans. Sacha Rabinovitch. Chicago: University of Chicago Press, 1968.)

Shumaker, Wayne. *The Occult Sciences in the Renaissance: A Study in Intellectual Patterns.* Berkeley: University of California Press, 1972.

Suchodolski, Bogdan. *Anthropologie philosophique de la Renaissance.* Trans. Irena Wojnar and Benoît Zawisza. Wrocław: Zakład Norodowy Imiena Ossolińskich, Wydawnictwo Polskiej Akademii Nauk, 1976.

Wind, Edgar. *Pagan Mysteries in the Renaissance.* 3d ed. Oxford: Oxford University Press, 1980.

Yates, Frances A. *Giordano Bruno and the Hermetic Tradition.* Chicago and London: University of Chicago Press, 1964.

S I X

The Merchant and the Banker

Alberto Tenenti

*J*F certain conditions are respected, it is at least theoretically possible to describe a social type in a particular epoch. Perhaps it would be better to speak of a social level instead of a social type, but that term is even more fleeting and ambiguous, hence more difficult to circumscribe. The notion of type is not only more ambitious but even debatable on the historical plane, which always presents enough variety and complexity to make it resist simplification or reduction to categories. Such reservations may not apply here, since my objective is to ascertain to what extent we can identify and characterize the human type of the merchant and the banker in the period of the Renaissance in Europe. Our subject is not a preconceived assumption that we can take for granted but only a perspective to be explored and a path to be taken. Historical investigation is fond of stressing changes, differences, and nuances, and justly so. This does not mean, however, that it must never explore constants or single out profiles to trace.

An operation of this sort, however, is subject to both general and specific constraints on the historical plane. Thus a characterization of the medieval merchant does not respond to the same demands—or offer the same difficulties—as one of the Renaissance merchant. This is primarily because we still think of the Middle Ages as a thousand-year span, during the course of which human and social types necessarily changed. We speak of the Middle Ages well before the rise of feudalism (thus the two are not coterminous), but we continue to use the term when some distinguishing characteristics of the age had changed profoundly or by and large had disappeared. If it is an unenviable task to circumscribe types throughout the entire span of the so-called medieval period, it is quite another affair to do so for the Renaissance, a much more clearly defined phase that only lasted roughly as many decades as there were centuries in the Middle Ages. In spite of notable differences that persisted among the various countries of Europe, they were in many ways more fully integrated than during the preceding millennium, thus providing a degree of homogeneity that facilitates description.

Admittedly, chronology within the abnormally long time-span of the Middle Ages requires definition. The medievalists' appetites for absorbing centuries aside, mercantile circles in Western Europe before the thirteenth century had little in common with their later counterparts. Naturally, certain innovations took hold slowly and discontinuously, but between the thirteenth century and the fourteenth century a number of procedures typical of later centuries—the use of Arabic numbers, double entry bookkeeping, insurance, the letter of exchange, and so forth—were introduced into commerce. Thus it seems meaningless to continue to speak of the medieval merchant as a figure seemingly still struggling with certain religious beliefs or theological prohibitions. Would it not make more sense to describe the mercantile world internally, on the basis of its new and unique properties, rather than externally?

These observations seem to me opportune, even mandatory, as a means to defining, albeit approximately, our present field of investigation. In the commercial realm, the thirteenth and fourteenth centuries appear to have been above all (though not exclusively) a time of both a great beginning and a change of direction. Placing the start of the Renaissance phase at roughly the first decades of the fifteenth century stresses that even on the practical level—that is, on the level of techniques that were by that time in increasingly common use—the mercantile world clearly differed from its medieval counterpart. What needs to be shown next is how the merchants' and the bankers' use of such procedures was closely and consistently linked to their social and political attitudes and their attitudes toward art and culture.

Although the beginning of the fifteenth century should not be taken as an absolute line of demarcation uniformly valid from all points of view, it nonetheless seems reasonably trustworthy. Defining the end point of the period in the mercantile field may prove a good deal harder. Many of the dominant traits of the mercantile world of the Renaissance persisted at least through the seventeenth century. Nonetheless, it seems reasonable to choose 1570 as an end point. Where long-term trends are concerned, any overly precise date is contestable or inadequate. Still, although a number of mercantile techniques did not change much after the mid-sixteenth century, on nearly every level the historical context changed a good deal more in those years than it had between the late fourteenth century and the early fifteenth century. The thrust of the Renaissance changed notably, evolving rapidly (though not in the same fashion in all lands) in the direction of new religious, cultural, and politico-social forms. Thus, although I prefer to avoid direct reference to either the Council of Trent or the build-up of Catholic and Protestant powers in two great opposing camps, that moment seems to me an opportune end point for our discussion.

Precisely because the evolution of European history is complex, however, any approach limited strictly to chronological periods may prove inadequate. From the first centuries after the fall of the Roman Empire, society settled into relatively well-defined orders that corresponded roughly to roles that were considered fundamental: those of the clergy, noble warriors or knights, and the peasantry. Merchants and bankers did not play a sufficiently autonomous or essential role to be recognized as a category; in fact contemporary economic relations left them out of consideration. In southern Europe and north-central Europe the situation slowly changed, especially from the eleventh and the twelfth centuries.

Around the mid-thirteenth century a Franciscan, Berthold von Regensburg, devised a more articulated division of the body social into nine orders, one of which he reserved for merchants. There theoretical and ideological classifications only roughly corresponded to reality, as they failed to note the more original aspects of mercantile activity. Because the theorists sought relatively immutable social types in an attempt to fix the structure of human society as rigidly as possible, they did not perceive the dynamic and precedent-breaking nature of commerce. In fact, they even regarded commerce with increased mistrust and partial condemnation, as if they sensed that it alone offered a threat to the hierarchy they had elaborated.

For centuries the dominant culture hindered or sought to discredit this social group and its operations. The problem involves the Renaissance directly, but it existed beyond the time bounds of that period, permeating nearly the whole of European civilization. The culture of the ecclesiastical and noble matrix of society long regarded the merchant with hostility, which meant that a number of prejudices were deeply rooted in the shared mentality of the various countries of Europe. It also meant that this collective aversion and unfavorable atmosphere had indirect but lasting repercussions on the merchants themselves, perhaps even when they dedicated themselves to commerce with ardor and conviction. Gradually and at different times and places, clerics and nobles, shepherds, peasants, and workers all had their myths. Merchants practically never did so.

This is hardly the place to attempt to explain the attitudes of an entire civilization and its high culture. Undoubtedly it is because they are irremediably individualistic that even in more recent times the merchant and the businessman have failed to arouse the same transports of admiration that seem the due of those who have worked for the common good, from the missionary to the physician, from the soldier to the union worker or the politician. One need only glance at the most recent biographical dictionaries to see a reflection of these ancient prejudices and this unspoken ostracism. If a merchant was also a traveler, a man of letters, or a printer, the biographer will devote much more space to his achievements in geography, literature, or publishing, passing over his economic activities or presenting them as clearly secondary.

The merchant has a certain stature for his highly indirect and posthumous merits as a predecessor or a first incarnation of the capitalist. As a social type who furnished at least part of the soul of the middle class, he has generated one decidedly negative phantasm: that of the "trahison de la bourgeoisie." Thus an analysis of the figure and image of the merchant throughout the entire span of Western civilization would offer something like a psychoanalysis or an X-ray of the middle class. On this scale, the Renaissance was altogether too brief to furnish an adequate response to the larger question; nonetheless, it was a highly significant moment. We need to keep in mind, however, that the Renaissance was not a brilliant isolated episode but rather an outstanding moment in a process that took centuries. In short, the social and human type I hope to evoke here can be considered from two basic points of view: one sees the merchant in some respects as a point of arrival in a long previous development; the other shows him, on other levels, as a luminous point of departure.

In my opinion, altogether too much importance has been accorded to what the churchmen wrote on the subject of certain mercantile activities. It would have been much more appropriate and pertinent to interrogate the merchants themselves and to observe their behavior and attempt to deduce something concrete from it. Even today, rather than investigating the historical conditions and the specific procedures of economic operators, some writers are satisfied simply with citing the image the theologians presented of them. When they do so they fall into a genuine historiographical trap, because they are forced into the position that all merchants were radically and permanently torn between a yearning for riches and an anguished fear of punishment after death for the accumulation of wealth. This is, arguably, in good part an ecclesiastical vision, and its validity in every individual case is far from being proven. We may presume that the merchant, like others, doubtless took into account what the priests, monks, and friars were preaching. The actual influence of their sermons is extremely difficult to measure, however, and, in any event, any valid measurement would have to be internal, not external. It remains to be proven that the merchant—even the medieval merchant—was truly the victim of a split personality.

Historians have not reacted very coherently to this problem, and even today a good many of them are still influenced by the ways in which church-men posed the problem in centuries past. The result is a highly contradictory portrait of the merchant of both the Middle Ages and the Renaissance. According to some historians, even in the sixteenth century the merchant was imbued with a powerful attachment to traditional religion; according to others, as early as the Crusades the Venetians unscrupulously trampled all religious considerations to further their flourishing economic interests. Naturally, collective behavior differed, even notably, from one region to another. Still, even the historians who stress the strong attachment to the faith of sixteenth-century merchants and their great piety recognize that no spiritual obstacle halted their expanding enterprises. If the merchants had felt constrained, the church's prohibitions would have had an enormous resonance in their consciences, even at the height of the Renaissance, and, at the same time, the same individuals would soon have found ways to get around the prohibitions and pursue their operations.

Debatable historiographical positions such as these present insoluble logical difficulties, particularly when the question has practically never been examined systematically and internally. The basic evidence is indirect and external (as in the theological texts, for example), or it is sporadic and often less than persuasive. Some historians, for instance, have recorded the number—at times large—of masses or the generous sums that merchants at death's door left as pious bequests. What they fail to take sufficiently into account is that such practices had entered into common practice, and that when they had the means, churchmen and nobles did the same for the sake of their own souls' salvation. Acts of devotion like bequests and other forms of piety had become manifestations of prestige—"status symbols"—and it was natural that wealthy merchants should no more neglect them than other members of the social elite.

In any event, it has not yet been proven that, as a group, economic operators (at least from the thirteenth century on) were truly tormented by ecclesiastical prohibitions as they conducted their affairs, or that they were inordinately preoccupied, on a day-to-day basis, with an irreconcilable struggle between God and Mammon. They were certainly no more anguish-stricken than other Christians, who in one way or another pursued worldly goods just as enthusiastically. When the merchant heeded the injunctions of the church, he always did so—as did most of the faithful, each in his own sphere—so as to reconcile its demands with the requirements of his own occupation. In general, he compromised to the advantage, not the disadvantage, of his commercial affairs by making some fairly marginal concessions to ecclesiastical injunctions regarding the pursuit of gain.

One source of misunderstanding on this issue has been to confuse religion or morality with the dictates of the church. It is true that the church set forth a number of obligatory beliefs and claimed a monopoly of both the cult and the criteria of good and evil. For one thing, however, it has never been ascertained how far ecclesiastical demands were actually accepted and satisfied. In fact, it has been stressed that only after the Council of Trent could the Catholic Church exert a broad and effective influence, and one might add that the same was true of the Protestant churches in lands in which they were dominant. For another, it has been aptly shown that in the later Middle Ages and the Renaissance, the church adopted and developed pious practices—even beliefs—that were strongly influenced by the mercantile spirit of lay society. The first of these was indulgences, the object of a true commerce that of course involved economic operators as well as the clergy. The classic and best-known example is the Fuggers, who lent money to Albert of Brandenburg to enable him to acquire the archbishopric of Mainz, in return for which they obtained a right to half of his revenues from the sale of indulgences. Indulgences were not the only financial operation in which the clergy was involved, however; the curia demanded generous fees for confirming many benefices, and collected tithes, annates, and so forth.

Adequate analysis of the merchant's behavior patterns thus requires more than simply ranging certain theological positions on one side and their presumed effects on the merchant's conscience on the other. Just as much if not more, it requires consideration of the mercantilization of the church. If economic operators could come to an understanding with the church with such great (and increasing) ease, it was because in many sectors the church's positions were becoming consonant with the merchants' mentality and their methods of attaining wealth. What else, for example, was the promotion of belief in the expiation of faults in Purgatory, if not a double-pronged economic speculation and a veritable business deal? The Christian acquired merit by paying for the relief of souls in Purgatory, and the church granted the worshiper a somewhat imaginary credit in the books of divine grace while its strongboxes grew heavy. Thus it is not too paradoxical to state that mercantile behavior patterns, at least from the fourteenth century on, invaded the church to a greater degree than that body proved itself able to attract the faithful to pure observance of its more austere precepts concerning profits.

At this point, we can formulate some notions about the period of the Renaissance in particular. First, the merchant did not stand out—as did certain humanist intellectuals—by virtue of any particular independence from the precepts of the church; even less did he express any misgivings on the subject. He participated in collective piety and was sensitive to the religious tensions of his times. Significantly, merchants played an important role in the diffusion of the Protestant Reformation, although they cannot be said to have rallied in mass to Protestantism, even in northern lands. Many of them differed from the majority of the population in that they were less confined to their own town or area. They traveled often; they had repeated contacts and exchanges of opinion in other lands, particularly in the urban centers in which they congregated. They could read and write, so they had access to an important network of both oral and written information. Their culture and even their religious faith was thus more open, more critical, more refined, and more flexible than that of the peasant majority or the humbler townspeople. Their piety was not the ancestral, habit-ridden, superstitious, obtuse piety of most of the population. It has rightly been observed that the merchant and the banker considered the church—at all levels—to be a power whose good will it was useful and necessary to cultivate. Furthermore, a good many members of mercantile families devoted their lives to ecclesiastical careers.

The merchants were first and foremost burghers: men to whom business dealings and family prosperity were of the highest importance. Thus by and large they maintained good relations with an institution as revered and influential as the Church of Rome, as they later did with the various Protestant churches. This was of course not the whole extent of their religion. They participated in the legacy of beliefs common to the entire continent, but with a good dose of autonomy and self-sufficiency that derived from their relatively high rank in society and their participation in the most evolved urban circles. During the Renaissance there were few remaining traces—even in the highly partial ecclesiastical sources—of the aversion and animosity that the same mercantile activities had prompted in the past and that had led to condemnation and bitter censure. For his part, the merchant (particularly if he were Catholic) might still feel some scruples concerning the propriety of certain of his operations, but in no way did he hold well-being and wealth in this world irreconcilable with salvation of the soul. Nor did the theologians refuse him those satisfactions (with certain reservations and subject to certain precautions, however). On the merchant's side, the conviction that success in commerce could not be displeasing to God and might even attest to his favor was shared by Catholic and Protestant merchants; on the church's side, by this time it was the various churches that felt some embarrassment before the enormous rise in economic profits and the world-wide increase in trade.

The time has come for a closer look at the collective psychology of the merchant and the banker of the Renaissance. His religious concerns, although not exactly secondary, represented only one aspect of a world that was mentally and ethically rich, that had matured and that boasted a solid and well-articulated professional structure. Merchants and bankers were Christians, and as Christians they had substantially the same moral problems common to all the faithful. During the Middle Ages, the clergy had targeted certain of their activities for blame (credit manipulations in particular) and had treated merchants as if they were engaged in particularly reprehensible operations. By the fifteenth and sixteenth centuries, however, times had changed; ecclesiastical phobias had lessened and the church's prohibitions had become notably more flexible, tolerant, or increasingly innocuous. Furthermore, in the psychological universe and the set of mental attitudes that the merchant had forged for himself, these hindrances represented only one quite specific problem of limited weight. The merchant had elaborated his own vision of life and of his daily activities, a vision that was perhaps less striking that those of the clergy or the nobility, but that existed alongside their visions and had been created without their aid.

On the conceptual and theoretical planes, economics in Western Europe was slow to free itself from politics and even from religion, not to mention philosophy and science. Europe had to wait until the late eighteenth century for its Quesnays, Smiths, and Ricardos, and in the sixteenth century it produced no economist comparable to Machiavelli or Copernicus. The autonomous vision of which the merchants were the capable and undeniable carriers cannot be called truly modern, but rather represents an intermediate phase between what historians call "medieval" and "modern." To repeat, mercantile procedures emerged and the merchants' psychological horizons were defined as early as the thirteenth and fourteenth centuries, and their broad-scale implantation began with the Renaissance. We should note, however, that economic operators were only dimly aware of this process; ideological statements take muffled forms showing some awareness but little urgency. Nor is it surprising that the most striking portraits of the merchant and his activities during the period were not written by true merchants. Leon Battista Alberti was certainly not one, and even Benedetto Cotrugli was one only in small part.

The Renaissance merchant, conscious that his function had more than a personal utility and persuaded that it was essentially legitimate and ethically suitable, felt increasingly at ease in his sphere of activities. Still, he operated pragmatically, as if he were unable (which was probably the case) to state his demands or his ideal goals explicitly. He acted as though he had no intention of asserting his originality or his novelty, which existed in fact but were never stated theoretically or formulated as demands. He limited his efforts to forging his self-sufficiency tenaciously, while he enjoyed a growing measure of prestige in a society in which he had long-standing and deep-set roots. Furthermore, with variations of place and circumstance, he became one of the determining factors in the evolution of European society. His cultural and professional formation, strong as they were, were structured not to seek (and in fact to avoid) intellectual controversy or taking a theoretical stance.

Two further elements enter indirectly but noticeably into the apparently modest picture of mercantile demands. The first, already mentioned, is the long-standing lack of recognition—or inadequate or grudging recognition after the fact—of economic activities, commercial and financial activities in particular. Second, during the fifteenth century, before the outbreak of the wars that filled the sixteenth century, there was a widespread atmosphere of stagnation. It was a period of simmering tensions still dominated by a search for compromise, a trend toward some sort of harmony, and a desire for peaceful coexistence. Was not an attitude analogous to that of the merchants also true of contemporary generations of humanists? They, however, had in hand or were fast regaining a mental *outillage* that was at least potentially more aggressive.

And yet, if the humanists needed to regain the patrimony of classical ethics to become forceful enough to assert civil society's emergent autonomy from ecclesiastical ideals, the merchants created their own self-sufficiency, albeit in less resounding terms and more modest style. It is a recurrent theme that lay culture gained ground gradually, emphasizing the values of the active life over those of the contemplative life devoted to religion. The merchants very soon brought a significant, though ideologically less defined, contribution to this process. It has become a common historiographical theme to contrast the "merchant's time" and "the church's time." As far as the actual measurement of the passing hours is concerned, this opposition is much less valid than is thought, however. The earliest portable personal clocks were manufactured only in the late fifteenth century, and their diffusion was obviously extremely slow and limited to the elite. Furthermore, until the fifteenth century, even public clocks were rare, and the few that existed were restricted to urban centers. It was still the church that signaled the passing hours, and its hold on the rhythms of daily life was far from a thing of the past during the fourteenth, fifteenth, and sixteenth centuries, even in the urban centers that had public clocks.

Where awareness of time is concerned, the most vigorous contribution of the mercantile vision lies elsewhere and has a deeper significance. During the fourteenth and fifteenth centuries, when the clergy were still insisting that human life was unsubstantial and transient, the merchants not only believed every instant to be precious but used that belief to found their fortunes and regulate their lives. Echoing the Gospel parable of the pounds or the talents entrusted to servants in order that they be multiplied, Berthold von Regensburg stated that the time God granted man was to be spent both in earthly toil and in working for eternal salvation.

One humanist born in the early quattrocento and raised in a family of great merchants presented the question in a quite different light from the German friar. When he describes the life of a father and head of family occupied in commerce, Leon Battista Alberti makes not the slightest mention of the fate of his soul, nor does he speak of the use of time as something for which the merchant must respond in the Great Beyond. The merchant's time, like that of any active man, is presented as consubstantial with his own deepest being. We are both soul and body, Alberti states, but our substance is also inseparably time because it is on the scale of time that we are measured. In Alberti's dialogue, the whole of the merchant burgher's activity is presented as a continuous self-programming in view of both a calculated and an intensive utilization of the unfolding existence that everyone thus forges for himself. The more completely and intensively we use time, the more we realize our potential and give the most and the best of ourselves.

We can find this dynamic vision of duration, which Alberti borrowed from the mercantile world, in the correspondence and the records of the men who engaged in commerce. In the first place, it seemed to them unpardonable to draw up accounts without noting the exact date of each operation, first because it was of prime importance to have an immediate grasp of the relationship between the passing months and the profits realized. One merchant remarked sarcastically that there should be no years of eighteen months. Another relationship that merchants strove to grasp better was the movement of goods and ships from place to place and the time it took them to arrive. Profit was strictly connected with elapsed time, as was the reinvestment of capital. Failure to exploit the time appropriate for a new business transaction was the equivalent of leaving the sum invested to stagnate, as any eventual lost time generated a halt in earnings, thus a net loss. One of the maxims governing Italian Renaissance commerce (and not only during the Renaissance) warned against *i denari morti*—dead money—an elliptical and highly expressive term.

The merchant's mentality was regulated by images like this, which provide illuminating glimpses of their daily, incessant quest for earnings. It was absolutely impermissible to waste time or let an opportunity go by: "Solicitude is the mother of wealth." A delayed transaction was unproductive, an error, and a "bestial" act contrary to all mercantile reason and deserving of scorn. The merchant had a clear perception of the inexorable law of time; time was a dimension of both the gain he hoped for and the loss he feared. Its relentless passage devoured profits when a transaction took too long to reach a positive conclusion. Consequently, the longer a credit was extended, the less it was worth. Similarly, the more business stagnated, the shakier the merchant's position was: "We are as dead," Andrea Berengo wrote from Aleppo in the autumn of 1555, for instance, when it turned out that he was waiting in vain for some silk he had intended to trade.

Although we know that the profits to be earned from trade were often high in the era of the Renaissance, it would be naive to conclude that earnings were anything like regular, let alone automatic. The economic operator's life was a dramatic one, and his faith in his own energy and his daring use of capital far from guaranteed his success. A deeply felt, multifaceted awareness of the value of time was coupled with constant tension as the merchant did his best to cope with distances, to make a profit from the fluctuating availability of goods, and to avoid any number of unforeseeable dangers. Fortune was not a purely allegorical figuration for the merchant: it was a confused mass of perils he knew lay beyond his control and that he could no longer confront simply by calling on God's aid, even if he had no doubts as to God's sovereign power. Andrea Berengo, for example, advised recourse to the Holy Ghost, but he also recommended drawing up an insurance contract.

The insurance policy was an important aid that the merchant created practically ex nihilo as early as the thirteenth century, but that really took hold during the Renaissance. Not all merchants insured all their goods, and they seldom insured them for their full worth. Furthermore, *sicurtà* were not equally available in all markets. Nevertheless, along with a more professionalized concept of time drawn from practical experience, insurance contracts constituted a second and essential part of the vision and the practice of commerce in the Renaissance. Insurance was a mechanism used to redress the balance between taking too high a risk and putting too great a reliance on faith in God. Merchants were of course aware that their own abilities and those of their associates were one of the best guarantees for success; moreover, the trade they had usually learned from childhood was being practiced increasingly well. Still, by inventing insurance and utilizing it more and more, the merchant showed he had truly come of age, since he used the logic of insured profits to create a solid guarantee against loss of earnings.

A dynamic view of passing time, the intensive use of time, and the use of the new instrument of insurance brought the economic operator of the Renaissance a security that enabled him to seek out new ways to confront the dimensions of time and risk. Another technique, launched earlier but by now skillfully organized and widely practiced, offered a rational solution to the problem of distance. An intensive network of correspondence backed ongoing transactions and permitted their continual verification. In varying measure, both letters of exchange (which may logically be included under the heading of commercial correspondence) and business letters in general were instruments that the merchants invented and skillfully exploited to further their affairs. Although the merchant still traveled extensively, by now he could not do without correspondence, an invaluable aid to which he devoted a large part of his energies. No one in this period devoted himself to the intensive and systematic exchange of news more assiduously than the economic operator, to the point that it eventually became a true information network.

The gradual and organized control of time, space, and risk were not the only foundations of the mercantile world of the Renaissance, but they are a first indication of its solidity and its special autonomy. Other, more obviously traditional supports were the structure of the family and the image of themselves that the economic operators proposed to and imposed on society—an image, as we have already seen, that was split between reality and representation. The merchant and the banker by this time occupied an undisputed and preponderant place in society, but they still encountered resistance to the expression and affirmation of themselves as a type eliciting positive connotations. The long-standing ecclesiastical condemnation of certain of their activities, which had to some extent entered into common opinion, was coupled with traces of the equally ancient, outdated three-part division of society into warriors, priests, and peasants. The merchant was never able to formulate an intellectual challenge to the theologians' prejudices in his regard, nor could he prove how little truth was left in the archaic tripartite division of society. He won his place gradually thanks to the real importance of his activities and services and to his ability to construct his own range of existential values and operational techniques. Instead of becoming aggressive because of these acquisitions, and instead of demanding prerogatives over the other strata of society, the merchant was content to take his place in the accepted hierarchy and accept its vertical structure. In other words, during the Renaissance the merchant hardly ever contested the superiority of the aristocracy and the clergy. He even thought he could rise in society by entering the ranks of the clergy and, even more, of the nobility.

This general process assumed a variety of forms in the different parts of Europe. Thus one might cite the case of the Verkinchusen brothers, originally from Westphalia and international traders in the area of the Hanseatic League. The older brother, Hildebrand, who died in 1426, was the more adventuresome but less successful of the two. Although he was made a citizen of Lübeck, he traded for the most part in Bruges. His first wife was the daughter of the burghermaster of Dortmund, his second wife the daughter of a rich merchant in Riga. His fortunes fluctuated. When he turned to trade with Venice, Peter Karbow, his partner, managed his affairs there so badly that he suffered serious losses. He then imprudently lent 3,000 crowns to Emperor Sigismund, who was so slow in paying them back that Verkinchusen was arrested for insolvency and never recovered. His brother Sievert, on the other hand, first left Lübeck for Cologne, then returned to his native city to become particularly prominent in the amber trade, prospering to the point that in 1431 he was admitted to the patriciate of that city.

The careers of another set of brothers, Kunz, Hans, Paul, and Mattias Mulich, is even more significant. Born in Nuremberg, they established themselves in Lübeck, where they became citizens. In the waning decades of the fifteenth century and after the turn of the century, they were active in trade with Livonia and Scandinavia to the north and southern Germany to the south. The youngest of the brothers, Mattias, was the most successful socially: he became a patrician of Lübeck in 1515 and contracted marriage alliances between his family and lineages of higher birth, the Castorp and the Kerckring families. He had connections with the dukes of Schleswig and Mecklenburg and even with the king of Denmark, who endowed him with a fief in Oldesloe.

Juan di Torralba, active during the first half of the fifteenth century, provides a similar example from the Spanish world. Torralba was already trading prominently in the Barcelona market in 1425. From 1428 to 1435 he headed an international trading company, and from 1437 he became a shipowner as well. He acquired a large Genoese ship capable of carrying a cargo of 1,200 barrels and put it in the command of his son-in-law, Juan Sabastida, who came from a noble landowner family. The network of Torralba's commercial operations grew along with that of his social relations. Without abandoning commerce completely, he took on high posts in the royal administration in Barcelona and intensified his relations with the court of Aragon. Back in 1431 Torralba had taken a part in a loan made to King Alfonso V, the future Alfonso I of Naples. Soon after, he invested in bonds funding the public debt and acquired rights to revenues from public and ecclesiastical holdings, but he also engaged in banking activities. Finally, after 1440, a series of real estate operations made him the owner of at least five buildings in Barcelona. His success did not outlast his lifetime, however. Under Torralba's guidance, his son-in-law used the ship entrusted to his care for profitable trade and equally profitable corsair activities, but at Torralba's death in 1458 Sabastida abandoned commerce and retired to his ancestral lands.

Other examples could be cited in lands from Poland to France. Pietro Bicarani, a Venetian active in Wrocław at the beginning of the fifteenth century, established profitable contacts in governmental circles in Kraków. After becoming mint master for the Polish monarchy he lent the city of Kraków a large sum of money. Soon after, he and a nephew were granted a lease for over a decade on the salt mines in Wieliczka and Bochnia. Thanks to his contacts at the Polish court, Bicarani served the Republic of Venice as ambassador until his death in 1414.

A Florentine, Antonio Ricci, had a similar career in the same circles. He first took a lease on the two salt mines of Kraków, then, with his brothers, rented other mines near Leopolis. He later moved to Wrocław, where he became a member of the city council. Another Florentine, Nicolò Serafini, succeeded Ricci as director of the same saltworks, where he accumulated notable wealth until he retired. He ultimately took Polish citizenship, thanks to which he became a member of the patriciate of Kraków. Aghinolfo Tebaldi had a similar career: in the latter part of the fifteenth century he controlled not only a number of sizable saltworks but also a good part of the revenues of the Polish crown. By the time he died in Kraków in 1495 his responsibilities had enabled him to become feudal proprietor of a large number of villages.

Other Italians fared well in Marseilles. The Remesan family, for example, transferred operations from Savona to that busy port city, where they became naturalized as French. From Marseilles they traded to the west with Spain, to the east with Italy, and into the hinterland as far as Lyons. Toward the end of the fifteenth century, one of their number, Giacomo, became a member of the mercantile aristocracy of the city. Members of the Vento family from Genoa rose similarly and were ennobled after being suppliers for the French army in Italy. The careers of other prominent local merchants—Jean de Villages, for example, a Marseilles city councilman, a shipowner, and a corsair—followed a similar pattern. A wealthy entrepreneur, de Villages was particularly active between 1462 and 1477. He was commander of the fleet assembled by Jacques Coeur, of one squadron of ships sent against Savona in 1461, and of another sent against Catalonia in 1466. As well as owning a number of houses in Marseilles, Jean de Villages acquired the title to the castle of La Salle in Valbonnette. Jacques Forbin, who was active in the late fifteenth century, acquired the lordship of Gardanne in 1482 thanks to his prosperous trade activities. Jean Forbin, a successful merchant and shipowner, acquired the lordship of La Barben from René of Anjou in 1474. There was even a woman, the daring Madeleine Lartissat (1480–ca. 1545), who followed this same path. A slave trader and shipowner established in Marseilles, she became commercial director for the admiral and corsair Bertrand d'Ornezan, baron of Saint-Blancard, and she shared ownership of the island of Pomègues with Luisa di Remesan.

Last in this brief survey of the mercantile world is the Spannocchi family of Siena. The first notable member of this family, Giacomo (d. 1420), the son of a retail merchant, had an unremarkable but successful career. He left Siena for Ferrara for political reasons, and in Ferrara he opened a bank and ran a woolens warehouse. Obviously an enterprising man, he acquired three houses between 1411 and 1415 and transformed them into two inns. The figure of Ambrogio Spannocchi (1420–ca. 1478) is somewhat more out of the ordinary. Ambrogio moved to Rome, where he managed to gain entry into the inner circle of Pope Calixtus III. Thanks to Calixtus, Spannocchi became provisioner general for the papal army against the Turks. He also lent the pope money to assemble a fleet and opened a bank in Valencia, the Borgia pope's city of origin. His fortune continued to wax under Pius II, who named him depository of the apostolic chamber and granted him permission to quarter his arms (grain stalks, or *pannocchie*) with the Piccolomini crescent moons. He also opened a bank in Rome under the name Spannocchi-Miraballi. Ambrogio Spannocchi soon opened another bank in Naples, where he became a counselor to King Ferrante. He also owned ships and traded in grains and alum. Later, after being named papal treasurer by Sixtus IV, Spannocchi turned to acquiring lands in and around Siena, and he commissioned Benedetto and Giuliano da Maiano to build him a palace in that city between 1472 and 1474. At his death he was buried in the Spannocchi family chapel in the church of San Domenico in Siena.

Ambrogio Spannocchi gave the family's rise in society a strong start, and it continued in the late fifteenth and early sixteenth centuries. The family fortunes reached their highest point in two brothers, Antonio (1474–ca. 1530) and Giulio (1475–ca. 1535) Spannocchi. By 1495 Antonio, who was barely twenty-one, was already an ambassador for Pope Alexander VI, while Giulio was already a member of the Siena city government. The two brothers continued to carry on their mercantile activities, notably in alum production and the grain and cloth trades. In Siena, their bank functioned as the state treasury, and in Rome, on the accession of Alexander VI, the Spannocchi family replaced the Medicis as depositories of the apostolic chamber. Their fortunes soon took a turn for the worse, however. The bank in Siena failed in 1503 and the Naples bank in 1504, obliging them to sell a good deal of the real estate around Siena that they had acquired in the late 1400s. They retained their villa at Campriano, however, along with its castle, awarded to their family by the Sienese. The two brothers retired from business after their financial reverses but their fortunes had not completely declined. Antonio was for nine years treasurer of the March of Ancona, Giulio was named captain of the people in Siena in 1528, and together they collected the excise tax on wine in their city from 1505 to 1524.

I have deliberately chosen to concentrate on economic operators who were active during the fifteenth century and have neglected other, more important and better-known figures. One cannot claim that the men I have presented were any more significant for being relatively more ordinary, but at least they can provide a framework for the careers of the more famous families and figures to whom I shall soon turn. They also permit us a certain number of indispensable observations on the merchant and the banker of the Renaissance.

First, it is truer in this field than in many others that our knowledge too exclusively regards those on whom fortune smiled or who distinguished themselves in other realms as well as commerce. To date, scholars have paid less attention to the mercantile world in and of itself—that is, to economic operators of the second rank or of mediocre intellectual gifts—than their specific weight in the life of European society would merit. The Medicis, the Fuggers, the Affaitatis, and their like stood at the peak of a pyramid that had an extremely broad base. There were a great many merchants whom we could even call rural, and whose sphere of action was limited, never reaching beyond their own village or town. One such unknown was Pierre Garet, a wholesale merchant and tanner in Saint-Loup, near Poitiers. It cannot be said that Garet lived in provincial retirement, however. His resources were sizable enough to enable him to buy bonds of the Hôtel de Ville in Paris. Still, information on the components and characteristics of this category of merchants is not abundant, nor is it much greater concerning economic operators in urban areas. Every city had its pool of local and foreign merchants, however, all of whom were engaged in the production and distribution of goods as well as in middle- and long-range trade. Nonetheless, our information is still so scanty that we can talk in practical terms only about merchants engaged in international trade.

This fact obviously influences our image of the Renaissance merchant. To what extent was the merchant henceforth anchored to his company headquarters or his shop rather than voyaging to distant lands? A number of factors besides the lack of systematic research make it difficult to respond. It is fairly evident that larger enterprises were directed from a central office, where the head remained on a more or less permanent basis and from which he oversaw and coordinated their various operations. The very large companies were the least numerous, however, even though they were of great and perhaps determinant importance. On a lesser scale, a broad range of economic operators fell into roughly two categories. The first sort stayed put, tied to their shops or to the centers that produced the goods they traded (whether sugar or books, soap or textiles). The second sort moved about fairly frequently, though for a variety of reasons. Some restricted their movements to frequenting the fairs in their own regions or the urban centers around which their activities gravitated. Others were itinerant merchants. Another category of merchant, however, contributed more, in the current state of our knowledge, to shaping our image of the economic operator of the age. Usually with one or more partners, this sort of merchant operated in a different market from his native town, subsequently moving on to trade in still other markets and to pursue the interests of the other companies in which he invested.

This was the international merchant, whether he traded only between Genoa and Marseilles or Ancona and Split or between England and the Guinea coast or Seville and the New World. Even if it captures our attention more than perhaps it should, this mid-range, long-range, and on occasion extremely long-range trade was busy and intense. It was to learn this sort of trade that the young merchant traveled and, when a sizable or delicate transaction required personal supervision, the older merchant as well. Voyages often involved not months but years of residence abroad, which means that, except for the soldier and perhaps the pilgrim, the merchant of this epoch was the person who traveled the greatest distances, the most frequently, and by the greatest variety of routes. It is hard to judge whether land or sea travel was of greater importance, though sea voyages are easier to document and were certainly more adventurous. Land transport companies might enable the merchant to avoid having to accompany his merchandise himself, whereas he might have felt more obliged to trade personally in the seaports and when ship transport was involved. Moreover, during the fifteenth and sixteenth centuries, maritime trade in Europe is known to have increased immeasurably.

Several further remarks need to be made that also apply before and after the period of the Renaissance, the first of them about the range of articles traded and types of economic activity. The merchant of the time tended not to specialize but to seek earnings from any source. Some, of course, traded almost exclusively in one sort of goods (booksellers and printers, for example), but they were clearly in the minority. Generally, a trader was more interested in an opportunity to turn a profit than in the nature of the merchandise, buying and selling whatever was available where he happened to find himself for the greatest and surest gain. Bartolomé de Avila, for example, who worked out of Valladolid during the first half of the sixteenth century, by and large specialized in textiles, silks in particular, but he sold cloth of all sorts from a number of places of origin. His contemporary, Sansin de Villanueva, who operated in the same market, traded indiscriminately in all sorts of articles from clocks to playing cards, from jewels to textiles, from mirrors and books to scissors, knives, and candlesticks. Roughly 250 different products are listed in the postmortem inventory of one Rostock merchant in 1566. It is not surprising that this multiformity was reflected in other aspects of the merchant's activities than trade. He might be involved in manufacturing: even though they were primarily printer-publishers, the Giunta family in Venice owned a sugar works and a soap factory. Or he might have investments, acquire land and real estate, own and operate ships, buy shares in the public debt funds, or deal in insurance policies.

This is why I have made no attempt to distinguish between the merchant and the banker. Naturally, most merchants limited themselves to occasional monetary or credit ventures and did not manage actual banks. Conversely, very few people concentrated all their energies on running a bank. The Venetians Andrea (1444–93) and Antonio Cappello (1461–1541) can serve as an example of men who were predominantly bankers. Andrea had studied law, and in his youth had traded between Flanders and England. In 1480 he and the Lippomano brothers founded a private bank, which soon became one of the biggest in Venice. He lent large sums to the state in exchange for a share in the fiscal revenues of Venice, and he soon became a senator of the Republic. He died in Rome, where he had been sent as ambassador. Antonio also got his start trading in the London market, along with his brothers Silvano and Vittore. Later (1507) the three brothers and Luca Vendramin opened a *banco di scritta* on the Rialto. Although he kept up these many enterprises for more than twenty years, he took on a number of civic responsibilities as well: he was Provveditore di Comune (supervisor of the commune) in 1509 and Savio alle Decime (a director of the tax board) in 1521. He also held a large number of shares in the public debt fund. He acquired a number of apartment houses and shops in the center of Venice, built at least eight houses on a piece of land he had bought in Murano, and, together with his brother Silvano, built a lead foundry. Again with Silvano, he owned a palace on the Grand Canal and a vast estate in Méolo on the Terraferma, and he owned a handsome house in Murano, where he was fond of going to get away from it all.

Other examples would have offered similar careers. Not every merchant managed a bank, but banking often complemented the direction of large companies and the making of large family fortunes. In short, rather than being an activity in and of itself, banking was exercised on the side, along with other prosperous activities carried on with partners, by contractual arrangement, and for a predetermined period. In several instances, the founding or the closing of a bank were events that affected the public good, thus involving the entire community and the city government. Banks were almost always private, however. Moreover, much like other ventures, they were usually run by family members and with the family's other business interests in mind.

The merchants and bankers of the Renaissance differed from those of the preceding period in that they were more apt to invest their capital in landed property, either city real estate or country residences. The question of whether men of mercantile circles in the fifteenth and sixteenth centuries drew greater satisfaction out of landownership than their predecessors is fairly easy to answer. Not only did a Norwegian work, the *Speculum regale* (*King's Mirror*), explicitly advise merchants to put two-thirds of their earnings from particularly successful commercial operations into land as early as the thirteenth century, but by the later thirteenth and the fourteenth century burghers in the major urban centers had acquired sizable amounts of land in the nearby countryside. In the Renaissance this process simply intensified, not so much because increased profits could be gained as because the elite as a whole adopted a life-style stressing greater comfort and greater social gratification.

The merchant was particularly receptive to anything that promised him a greater prestige or satisfactions of a more aristocratic nature. (This applies, of course, to the wealthier merchants.) When Leon Battista Alberti portrayed the economic operator of the early quattrocento, he took it for granted that the family would own at least one holding outside the city with a tenant farm and a house for the proprietors. In Ragusa, thirty years or so later, Benedetto Cotrugli preferred having two properties outside town, one nearby to furnish produce for the town house, and another in a locality particularly propitious to recreation and relaxation. Unlike Alberti, who celebrated the "villa" as a veritable terrestrial paradise, Cotrugli expressed reservations about rural delights. Precisely because they were such a temptation, he feared that the merchant might be led to abandon himself to them and neglect more vexatious tasks. Although it has not been proven that Cotrugli's fears were well founded, at least in this period, it is known that Renaissance merchants enjoyed relaxing in their rural residences. Alberti's *De architectura* speaks at some length about building a villa, now something within the reach of city-dwellers and men in commerce and no longer considered a luxury reserved for nobles or high clergy. Doubtless the proprietors of these houses managed to strike a balance between their commercial concerns, the pleasures of country living, and the air of nobility that land ownership conferred.

Italian merchants of the Renaissance tended to imitate or openly practiced an aristocratic life-style, but they seldom took the trouble to join the aristocracy. They were already members of a prestigious urban patriciate, and their values tended to remain republican and anti-feudal. When they had contacts with foreign rulers, however, they did not disdain the titles they were granted. Aside from the merchant nobles who have already been mentioned, one might cite Gaspare Ducci of Pistoia (1492–ca. 1577), who made a fortune in Flanders and France. First an agent, then branch manager in Antwerp for the Arnolfini-Nobili firm, based in Lucca, he soon became an expert in financial operations in the exchange. He made a good deal of money, enough to lend large sums to Francis I of France, who charged him with putting his system of public loans into order, and to Charles V, who named him an imperial counselor. He was ennobled, made lord of Kruibeke, bought a sumptuous villa in Hoboken, and lived surrounded by a small troop of armed servants, whom he loosed on his adversaries.

Other merchants rose to the nobility outside the Italian peninsula. The Najac family, for example, rose rapidly in Toulouse during the first half of the fifteenth century. By 1462 they had been ennobled by Charles VII and invested with seigneury over two villages. Huc Najac held several prestigious posts, investing his earnings in land and buildings, but the family declined rapidly after him, perhaps thanks to excessive expenditure on conspicuous consumption. Jean Amic (d. ca. 1460), also from Toulouse, had a quite different career. Both a retail merchant and an international trader, Amic also operated as a money-changer and a money-lender. He owned a palace in Toulouse and at least half a dozen other buildings, and he was fond of acquiring seigneuries, whose titles he bore, but he remained a businessman as well as a loyal supporter of royal power.

In England, Richard Gresham (1485–ca. 1549), who began his career in commerce at a very early age, was soon wealthy enough to become a shipowner and to lend money to King Henry VII. His relations with the court and the leading ministers strengthened on the accession of Henry VIII, and he was ennobled in 1537, one year before he became Governor of the Merchant Adventurers' Company.

In Flanders Erasmus Schetz (1495–ca. 1550), born in Maastricht, rapidly rose to wealth in Antwerp. In 1539 he built a palace, where he was host to Charles V in 1545 and acquired the seigneury of Grobbendonk in exchange for an annual payment of one thousand florins. As banker to the emperor, Schetz lent Charles the sum he needed to go from London to Spain with his suite in 1523. Bartholomew Welser specialized in trade with Spanish America and invested in copper mines in Haiti. When his family was elevated to the nobility in 1531, Welser held a monopoly on the importation of slaves. Finally, there was the banker and jeweler Joris de Vezelaere (1493–1570), for twenty-five years supervisor of the imperial mint in Antwerp. Between 1533 and 1535 he built a castle at Deurne, but he continued to be active in both retail commerce and money-lending.

Although the merchants and the bankers of this period undeniably had professional and cultural values of their own, they also shared in some of the more striking characteristics of the world in which they lived. We have seen this in a few merchants who rose to the nobility, but it is even more evident in the merchants' relations with rulers, in their artistic tastes, and in the book trade.

In a certain sense, the merchant and the banker of the Renaissance had an identity problem. In medieval society, when the merchant was less likely to be part of the patriciate (and even less of the nobility), he tended to have only sporadic contacts with rulers and remained, by and large, within his own occupational sphere, thus presenting a more consistent figure. Again, if this was true before the year one thousand and still held true in the eleventh and twelfth centuries, it was less so in the thirteenth and fourteenth centuries. By the Renaissance, in any event, it was clear that the merchant felt at ease not only in the city council but also in princely entourages. Furthermore, he now supported artistic and cultural ventures as a private person rather than exclusively as a member of a religious confraternity or an occupational corporation.

In the fourth book of his *Della Famiglia*, Leon Battista Alberti states that a merchant of a certain status needs to know how to win the good graces of lay rulers and high clerics and explains at some length how to do so. This humanist had no intention of turning the economic operator into a courtier, strictly speaking, but rather into a person capable of moving in court circles. From the thirteenth and fourteenth centuries, merchants had been well aware of the tangible advantages that the favor of sovereigns could bring them, and for that reason they often lent rulers enormous sums of money, even when the loan involved high risk and was given without security. By the fifteenth and sixteenth centuries princes and monarchs had notably consolidated their power, but they had not developed adequate financial mechanisms to turn their power to best advantage or, above all, to confront extraordinary expenses, either for war or peace. Thus a number of opportunities were open to economic operators, ranging from exemption from customs duties to monopolies, from investment in mines to collecting personal and excise taxes in repayment of cash loans. There was perhaps no ruler in this period who did not take advantage of the bankers' loans, and by this time a greater number and variety of sources of income had made merchants less exposed to the insolvency of sovereigns.

Perhaps the best illustration of this self-interested exchange of favors is Jakob Fugger (1460–1525). At first destined for a career in the church, the young Fugger was instead sent from Augsburg to Venice, where he was trained in the techniques of commerce. During his stay in Venice he acquired broader cultural and artistic interests, and he returned to Augsburg aware of his rising status. Fugger remained a merchant, faithful to the profit principle, to the end of his life, but he was expert at satisfying the needs of a number of rulers while pursuing this end. In 1487, Archduke Sigismund of Habsburg turned over to Fugger his share of the earnings from the archducal silver mines in the Tirol as security for a loan. Trade in silver (later, in copper from other mines), foundries, then the Fugger bank, founded his fortunes. For a time Fugger even held the monopoly on the curia's remittances from the sale of indulgences and benefices in the better part of the lands north of the Alps.

Thanks to these monopolies and to similar operations in the Spanish kingdoms, Jakob Fugger amassed the enormous fortune that earned him the nickname "the Rich." After his marriage in 1498, he began to live on a vast scale, and he acquired from Emperor Maximilian the county of Kirchberg and the lordship of Weissenhorn, which made him the lord of a large number of vassals. Jakob continued to live as a merchant, however, as did his heir, nephew, and successor, Anton Fugger, and he furnished more than a half million florins to the young Charles of Burgundy to finance his election to the imperial throne in 1519. He funded a large housing development for the Catholic poor in Augsburg (the *Fuggerei*) composed of 106 independent lodgings whose tenants paid a purely symbolic rent and were obliged to recite a *Pater*, an *Ave*, and a *Credo* daily for the souls of the founders and their family. Two years after Jakob's death, the Fuggers' holdings are calculated to have been worth nearly two million gold florins.

Although on a much smaller scale, Italian merchants and bankers ranging from the Chigis to the Affaitatis often show analogous successes and behavior patterns. Italy was different, however, in that its economic operators did not limit their activities to making money but in many cases converted their mercantile power into political power. Municipal statutes in the great commercial preindustrial cities of Venice, Florence, and Genoa permitted the wealthiest citizens to turn their supremacy into more or less direct control of their respective governments. The situation of course varied greatly from one republic to another, but the city in which patrimonial wealth was most explicitly turned into political dominion was undoubtedly Florence. Here, to some extent following the model of other great families like the Albertis and the Albizzis, the Medicis succeeded in becoming not only the wealthiest citizens of their city but for all practical purposes heads of the Florentine government for over sixty years (1434–94). Their lordship was unofficial and not even openly spoken of, but it was so effective that once their family wealth had assured them the support of the communal government, the Medicis retained their dominion even when their economic fortunes declined. The Medici family's greatest commercial coup was to make Florence itself—its finances, its political power, and its statehood—something like family property. This merchant lineage weathered the vicissitudes of the end of the quattrocento and the beginning of the sixteenth century and used the cardinalate and the papal throne (granted to two members of the family) to become, in 1530, a house of dukes and later grand dukes that would continue to reign until the eighteenth century.

The Grimani and the Gritti families in Venice, the Buonvisis in Lucca, and some of the major houses of Genoa had similar careers, differences in form and measure aside. On both sides of the Alps, the intermingling of commerce and power, monarchical or republican, was one of the most striking characteristics of great mercantile families during the Renaissance, even though the great majority of economic operators stayed within their own occupational sphere.

Analogous remarks could be made concerning the merchants' and the bankers' relations with art and culture. As with the link between politics and commerce, the development and the general characteristics of the new society offered the wealthiest merchants an opportunity to sponsor art and promote culture. The period of the Renaissance may have been no less cruel than others in European history, but it was nevertheless a time of a highly composite, interconnected, and intercommunicating elite. Humanists and men of letters, painters and architects, were the familiars of princes and leaders of government, and merchants, money-lenders, and financiers soon were at home among them, perhaps standing apart from the others. Still, on occasion during the relatively brief course of about a century, they lived in such close contact with those of other social strata that they give the impression of at least partly sharing their identity.

As we have seen, between the fourteenth and fifteenth centuries the merchant developed a nucleus of new techniques that provided him with the basic tools of his trade and that were his unique intellectual patrimony. Even his writing hand often differed from the one used by copyists and other cultivated circles. His instruction, aside from reading and writing, normally included the rudiments of mathematics, geography, and law. It has been observed that he incessantly noted his growing acquisitions as if inspired by a taste for continuing education. During the Renaissance, the merchant's needs and his accumulated experience brought notable contributions to accounting, cartography, and geography, even to astronomy and navigation, as well as to economics and finance.

His contribution to culture in general needs to be viewed as openly and flexibly as possible. What influence, for example, did the indirect pressure of expanding mercantile circles have on the promotion of the use of vernacular languages? Was it not thanks to the merchant's exactitude, always translated into numbers, that a society that until then had been satisfied with approximations increasingly demanded precision? The merchant's daily manipulation of measures and calculations must necessarily have influenced collective attitudes, though it is not easy to demonstrate any direct influence on a mathematical vision of the world. As is known, numbers were an active tool in the service of commercial interests before they came to enhance scientific understanding. When an increasingly rational mode of thought came to replace anthropomorphic or semi-magic concepts, it was at least in part owing to the imposition of the mercantile vision in its largest sense.

The problem of merchants' and bankers' relations with artistic and cultural spheres during the Renaissance is equally complex. Their real receptivity to culture is difficult to define, all the more so since our analysis is necessarily based on examples and rarely on systematic observation. What seems indisputable is the merchant's attachment to his dwelling and his fondness for having a prestigious residence. Architecture was in many ways the most utilitarian art form and the one that provided the most immediate social benefits. The economic operator gave it priority, and when he had his country villa he often built an impressive town house, often on the scale of the *palazzo* so lovingly described by theorists of Renaissance architecture from Leon Battista Alberti on. The language of building was the most eloquent and the most appropriate for celebrating and crowning the success and prestige of a family of merchants in an urban setting. The historic centers of a number of European cities attest to the importance of the merchant family palace. It was often an imposing and massive construction, sometimes but not always directly inspired by the new Renaissance style, but always magniloquent and severe. Its owner had little reason to envy the noble and the prelate on this score.

The merchants' connections with other forms of art are less consistent and indeed quite varied. If merchants cannot be said to have been insensitive to beauty, it is hard to state with what intensity they sought it or what objective they had in mind. Even with varying intentions, however, merchants were by this time commissioning works on their own account rather than simply financing collectively commissioned works. It is for this reason that the artistic genres of the portrait and the funeral monument prospered increasingly during this period. That does not mean that the merchants necessarily chose the best artists; even less, that they commissioned works for predominantly aesthetic reasons. Undeniably, they liked to have both the outside and the inside walls of their houses adorned with frescoes and they hung a large number of paintings in the rooms of their palaces, but it is risky to speculate whether they were more inspired by current taste or personal preference. They had the means to rival, if not to equal, the noble and ecclesiastical patrons of the age. Furthermore, their greater curiosity concerning foreign lands and their frequent voyages contributed to making them large-scale collectors, particularly of coins and medals.

Merchants with truly personal artistic tastes or a humanistic and literary background seem to have been rare, but it would be a mistake to neglect one rather special but typically Renaissance category among them—the printer–publishers. The printed book was undeniably a vehicle of culture, but it was also a new product. Furthermore, from its inception it was a mass-produced product that required sales distribution and involved commercial competition. Although today's bibliophiles inventory incunabula with passion and laud the handsomest works, the historian needs to stress that printing was a new and profitable economic activity. As in other areas of production and commerce, the merchant publishers of the age included a full range of operators whose commercial activities—once again—we know best through their most prominent representatives.

William Caxton (1420–ca. 1491), for instance, started out in London as a draper's helper and later, in 1465, became governor of the Mercers' Company in Bruges. He passed into the service of the duchess of Burgundy and began to translate literary works, but after 1471 he devoted his energies to printing. He perfected his art in Cologne, where he produced the first books printed in English (1474). During the next fourteen years, when he was established in Westminster and was a favorite at the courts of Edward IV and Richard III, he set more than eighty thousand pages of type and translated twenty-one books.

Caxton's colleagues on the continent were many. In Paris, between the bridge of Notre-Dame, the church of Saint-Séverin, and the rue Saint-Jacques, Antoine Verard (d. 1512) published and sold more than two hundred works in French. In Lyons, the German Sebastian Greyff (known as Grifo) was active from 1528 until his death in 1556, and, thanks to his broad cultural grounding, he produced works in Latin, French, Greek, and Hebrew. Christophe Plantin (1520–ca. 1589), born in Touraine, learned his trade with a typographer in Caen. He prospered in Antwerp, where he became the city's leading printer. The Florentine Filippo Giunta (1450–1517) came from a family of wool merchants. He had a solid classical education, and from 1497 he specialized in printing works in both Latin and Italian in an italic cursive typeface. His books were inexpensive, of a convenient size, and elegant, rivaling those of Aldo Manuzio, his opponent in a spirited commercial quarrel that Giunta won. We owe more than a hundred titles to Filippo Giunta, but Luc'Antonio Giunta the Elder (1457–1538) produced even more. A better businessman than Manuzio, Luc'Antonio Giunta also distinguished himself for his technical skill in the printing of classical texts, medical works, and liturgical books.

The many-sided figure of the merchant and the banker put an indelible stamp on the life of Renaissance society. Such men added substance to its middle strata, where they formed an irreplaceable connective tissue in a renewal of the structure of society, and they brought a dynamic ferment and a conscious spirit of initiative that were widely recognized at the time. Even the most lasting forms of civilization, from the arts to science and from technology to culture, owe much to the merchants and the bankers.

S E V E N
The Artist
André Chastel

*T*HE term *artista* did not exist during the Renaissance. Leonardo does not use it in the mass of writings he left, the largest literary legacy ever left by a painter. When it came time to praise the new times, Giorgio Vasari collected the lives of *artefici del disegno*, "practitioners of the visual arts." It would be a mistake to overlook the professional orientation of this work in favor of its treasury of anecdotes, for Vasari's originality lies, in part, in his striking insistence on the requirements, even the burdens, of the artists' calling and on the concrete problems—one might even say the "physics"—of artistic activities. The novel aspect of Italy's cultural leadership for two centuries was not only its celebration of personalities but, even more, an interest in the work of practitioners and in techniques. After all, contemporary men of letters—the *letterati*—were developing the study of the alphabet, of paleography, and of lexicology as well as the theory of eloquence.

It was not by denying the material, concrete reality of the "arts of design" or their normal and obligatory place in the domain of the *artes mechanicae* that those who produced these works were to be raised to a new status. Quite the contrary, it was by exalting the resources of their calling and by deeper investigation of the "operational" nature of their activities. This is clearly one aspect (and not the least) of the new emphasis on the *vita activa* that led both humanists and merchants to be favorable to the exploration, conquest, and possession of positive contents of the physical world. The quattrocento was one of the great centuries of technology, understood as a precise utilization of instruments and their full exploitation, both in introducing order into space and in the domain of representation.

For the Renaissance, the *artifex* was someone who used his individual skills to participate in a general enterprise aiming, according to the time-honored formula, at the beautiful and the useful. If we can avoid the flattering, favorable, and somewhat mysterious connotations of the term that we owe to Romanticism and Symbolism, we can perhaps observe a phenomenon characteristic of the "humanity" of the Renaissance.

THE ARTIFEX

A Place in Society: The *bottega* occupied a considerable and easily perceived place in the streets of cities and towns. People went to *botteghe* for all useful objects: for furniture, clothing, and arms just as much as for knick-knacks, pious images, and luxury items. The cityscapes in the backgrounds of altarpieces and miniatures show their stalls and often, behind them, people at work. There were a great many such workshops in cities like Florence, Venice, and Milan, where, except for periods of stagnation linked to economic cycles, an abundant production responded to a regular demand. Around 1460 Benedetto Dei mentions forty *botteghe di maestri di prospettiva* (marquetry-workers who produced inlaid coffers, chair backs and headboards, and benches) in Florence and a number of other woodworkers who made frames for altarpieces, chairs, and beds. We need only open Cellini's memoirs at random for a notion of the importance of the goldsmith's role: gold and precious stones, which were among the major forms of wealth, passed through their hands.

We need to resist our first impulse and keep in mind these concrete images of those in the arts as tradespeople before passing on to a definition of their moral status as "creative artists." Above all, it would be a mistake to start, as has on occasion been done, with the notion that the situation of the *artifex*, like that of the poet, changed decisively after Dante and Petrarch had proclaimed sovereignty in their domain.[1] This stance confuses sporadic aspiration with true condition, and a claim exclusive to some milieus with a generalized trend. Dante's mention of Giotto and Petrarch's of Simone Martini of course indicate affinities between exceptional people, but their problem was not that of the common lot. It is not inaccurate to say that the condition of the *artifices* remained modest and without particular dignity. They were producers of useful objects. Moreover, they were tied to their guilds, and these corporations had precise statutes: one could not set up shop at will, and contracts were governed by rules. The ledgers of a well-stocked workshop like Neri di Bicci's clearly show that above all he was at the service of a clientele of confraternities, patricians, and donors who all had specific demands. The isolated artist working to please himself alone in the solitude of his garret did not exist. The way to mastery was not through a school but through a *studio*—a

---

1. "All became liberal artists, divinely inspired like the poet, while their crafts appeared no less 'philosophical' or even 'prophetical' than poetry itself." Ernst Hartwig Kantorowicz, "The Soverignty of the Artist," in Millard Meiss, ed., *De artibus opuscula XL: Essays in Honor of Erwin Panofsky,* 2 vols. (New York: New York University Press, 1961), 1:267–79, referring to Karl Borinski, *Die Antike in Poetik und Kunsttheorie* . . . , 2 vols. (Leipzig: Dieterich, 1914) 1:183.

workshop organized as a place to apprentice and win one's stripes in good time. Artists learned by observing masters, which is why we find so many formulas like *fu discepolo di Piero* (Piero della Francesca) or *. . . di Piero da Castel del Pieve* (Perugino). What we know of Tuscany, where the documentation is enormous, is doubtless true of the smaller towns elsewhere as well.

All painters began that way: Giotto and Duccio with Cimabue; Benozzo Gozzoli with Fra Angelico; Leonardo with Verrocchio; Andrea del Sarto with Fra Bartolommeo; Bronzino with Pontormo, and so on. There was a continuous chain from one artisan to another, and without it we can understand neither the solidarity of their common calling nor the acts of emancipation that were the rule. Luca della Robbia, for instance, had a large family who kept the papers of the family firm until the mid-sixteenth century, and we know as much about the founder as we do about his successors. He was born around 1400, and, Vasari tells us:

He was placed by his father to learn the art of the goldsmith with Leonardo di Ser Giovanni, who was then held the best master of that art in Florence. Now, having learnt under this man to make designs and to work in wax, Luca grew in courage and applied himself to certain things in marble and bronze, which, seeing that he succeeded in them all . . . (Vasari, Life of Luca della Robbia, *Lives of the Most Eminent Painters, Sculptors and Architects*, trans. De Vere, 2:119)

This developmental pattern was constantly repeated: long specialized training, then, *cresciutogli l'animo*, individual initiative, at times the forward leap of a genius—who does not, however, lose contact with his craft.

In nearly all remarkable careers the same phenomenon of growing ambition appears, and we see the artisan *salire di basso in alto*, as the master biographer, Vasari, so often says. This did not necessarily mean achieving a higher social status, but rather a high degree of responsibility and renown within the artisan category. Cellini is a perfect example. He relates his technical tours de force and the feverish casting of the *Perseus* with relish because his age—as Cellini well knew—enthusiastically admired those works. Throughout his autobiography, however, Benvenuto is obsessed by his ambition to rise from the rank of goldsmith to that of sculptor, which would assure him greater consideration.

When he achieved success, an artist might be tempted to exploit a winning formula indefinitely, as did Perugino, a master of advantageous publicity, and many others. Doing so earned them the scathing reproaches of the moralists, however: the promise of true glory, which always required further effort and greater care—*studium et diligentia*—should never be sacrificed to money. The professions were kept on their toes by competition and by the shining example of great achievements. The "dynamics" of the artistic trades, based on masterpieces, is worthy of note. Donatello, who may have been short in physical stature but whose energy was boundless, was determined to show the Florentines, the Romans, and the Paduans extraordinary things in sculpture. To do so, he flouted custom now and then. He astonished, and he succeeded.

Contracts: Juridical forms were extremely important, and an enormous quantity of contracts for commissions in Italy from the thirteenth to the seventeenth century has been found, published, and commented on (rarely exhaustively, however) in the years since Johann Wilhelm Gaye published his memorable survey (1839–40). Examination of these documents shows, above all, a cautious formalism, material and financial specifications, and protective clauses regarding delays or poor workmanship. The painter's or the sculptor's activities were simply a particular instance of craftsmanship. As has been shown, these contracts were drawn up on the model of the *locatio operarum* involving *merces*, not *pretium*—*merces* that included payment in kind of various sorts and specific details concerning the furnishing of raw materials when their high price posed a problem (gold and ultramarine blue, for instance).

None of all this seems to point to new times. The painter was often required to follow a model; the commissioner often reserved the right to refuse the work.[2] A small sum was promised *pro manu sua*, not, as has been thought, as an appreciation of the quality of the work (where the amount would be ridiculously small) but rather as compensation for the artist's time. These clauses applied to major and minor artists alike, as they were to some extent automatic, which means that the artist's condition can be judged by these documents only if they are interpreted with great care.

The strictness of the contracts indicates that they were observed loosely. They also required periodic renewal, as with Piero della Francesca, who long delayed completion of the Perugia altarpiece, and with Leonardo, who contracted in 1483 to paint a *pala* for the confraternity of the Immaculate Conception in Milan that was finally delivered in 1508, after a number of

2. This is clearly shown in the contract for the Ruccellai Madonna of 12 April 1285: "quod si dicta tabula non erit pulcra et laborata ad voluntatem et placibilitatem eorundem locatorum quod ad dictum pretium me aliquam partem ei persolvendum nallatenus teneantur" (Archivio di State, Florence). This document is interesting to historians as it proves that this Madonna was not the work of Cimabue, as was thought in Vasari's day, but of Duccio. The refusal clause was retained in contracts, but with a progressive laxity. But if in 1515, as Vasari recounts, the administrator of Santa Maria Nuova in Florence refused Rosso Fiorentino's altarpiece because the figures in it seemed to him "diabolical," the contract surely must have permitted refusal.

negotiations and a large amount of paperwork. The work, moreover, was simply a copy of a previous painting, the *Virgin of the Rocks* (now in the Louvre, done with the collaboration of Ambrogio de Predis). On occasion, there are surprising differences between the laboriously detailed specifications for a work and the finished painting. In May 1515, Andrea del Sarto signed a contract with the nuns of a Florentine convent for a Madonna and Child between St. Bonaventura and St. John the Evangelist, with two angels crowning the Infant Jesus. This *pala* was to be completed within the year, and the painter's advance was to be returned if he failed to respect the deadline. The panel was completed in 1517 (according to the date on the base), and St. Francis had replaced St. Bonaventura, the angels are supporting Mary, and there is no crown.

Generalizations should be avoided, however. A great many *botteghe* for which account books survive (Neri di Bicci's, the Vivarinis') kept their promises and delivered their works without discussion. It was mostly the "stars" of an art who quarrelled with their patrons. Considerable sums sometimes changed hands, and if the tomb of Julius II became a "tragedy" for Michelangelo when later revisions reduced its scale and its parts, it was because the Della Rovere heirs were aware of the exceptionally large advance that the pope had paid the artist.

In December 1502, the Signoria of Florence wrote to the Maréchal de Rohan, who was growing impatient waiting for the bronze *David* that he had ordered from Michelangelo, "In what concerns the works of painters and sculptors, as you know, it is difficult to promise anything with certainty" (Wackernagel, *World of the Florentine Renaissance*, trans. Luchs, 361). Piero Soderini, who was standard-bearer of justice at the moment, was to repeat the message several times to the French authorities, who were not very understanding. North of the Alps, such shows of independence from civil power were not acceptable.

One famous example may shed some light on the question. Lorenzo Ghiberti, a goldsmith, was a member of the Arte della Seta, the silk-workers' guild, because gold and silver thread were required for luxury fabrics. He enjoyed an exceptionally favorable situation. Still, the 1407 agreement for the first door he made for the Baptistery in Florence stipulates, first, that the commissioner, the Arte di Calimala, was to furnish the bronze required; second, that the master "must on every day when work is done, work with his [own] hands the entire day, like any wage worker and, refraining from work, the lost time must be entered on his account."[3] Similar regulations

3. "Deve ogni giorno che si lavora lavorare di sua mano tutto il dì, come fa chi sta a provi-

regarding the "employee" appear in innumerable contracts. It is here that we can grasp the juridical constraints put on the artist. How binding these constraints were is another question.

The clause requiring daily work on Ghiberti's part should not be interpreted to mean that the entire project had to be realized *di mano sua*. This would have been impossible, given the size of the project as a whole and the number of other jobs on which Ghiberti was working at the same time as the two major commissions for doors to the Baptistery. Jobs were *always* carried out by a team under the direction of the master artist. Ghiberti was required to execute personally only "quelle parti che sono di più perfezione come capelli, ignudi, e simili" (those parts that require more perfection, such as hair, nudes, and the like). The division of labor within the *bottega* was of capital importance, but more often than not it is difficult to ascertain. No fresco was made without assistants, no altarpiece without collaborators, no monumental sculpture without helpers.

This practice was universal; it applies to the Tuscan-Umbrian team that worked on the Sistine Chapel in 1481 as it does to Raphael working in the *Stanze* in the Vatican. When the *bottega* met with success, it grew, and the role of the collaborators who executed the master's sketches increased. In a great many cases, the "artist" was the firm, and ingenuity and a spirit of adventure are required to distinguish who did what portions of the finished work. The attributions of modern criticism (and of the market) too often forget this fact. What counted was the "label" authenticating the work's origin or provenance, which means that the master's signature began to appear, particularly when the work was destined for another city or another land. Very often a work thus "authenticated" involved a good deal of collaboration from the master's assistants.

Contracts often stipulated payments in kind: sacks of grain, barrels of wine. If the *artifex* was paid in cash, it would be in silver coins (*lire*) or gold coins (*fiorini*). Differences in pay could be considerable, and favor and reputation counted for much. Examination of the modalities of payment show that "the moment that signals the [artist's] arrival at a social position comparable to that of a merchant in the major guilds is . . . when payment is stipulated in gold coins" (Alessandro Conti). This was true in Rome concerning the team working on the Sistine Chapel under Sixtus IV; of Giovanni

---

sione, e scioperandosi lo sciopero gli debba essere messo a conto." Richard Krautheimer in collaboration with Trude Krautheimer-Hess, *Lorenzo Ghiberti* (Princeton: Princeton University Press, 1956), 369.

Bellini in Venice; and of Michelangelo in Florence for the bronze *David*. It sheds light on an anecdote Vasari tells about Leonardo:

It is said that, going to the bank for the allowance that he used to draw every month from Piero Soderini, the cashier wanted to give him certain paper-packets of pence; but he would not take them, saying in answer, "I am no penny-painter." Having been blamed for cheating Piero Soderini, there began to be murmurings against him; wherefore Leonardo so wrought upon his friends, that he got the money together and took it to Piero to repay him; but he would not accept it. (Vasari, Life of Leonardo da Vinci, *Lives*, trans. De Vere, 4:103)

Leonardo was offended because he felt himself above the level of the artisan. Why, then, was he paid in *quattrini*? And why did Leonardo take up a collection from his friends to reimburse Soderini? Are we to suppose that Soderini, unhappy because Leonardo was delaying work on his painting for the Great Hall of the Signoria, was attempting to teach the painter a lesson by paying him like someone of a lower category? Everything that concerns Leonardo is singular.

Artifex Polytechnes: The "dynamics" of the trades created new phenomena. To take one example: Giuliano da Sangallo was a woodworker; he made coffers and church pews. From making models in wood he passed on to architectural design and from there to construction, at the urging of his patrons, Lorenzo de' Medici and Cardinal Giuliano della Rovere (the future Julius II), who encouraged him to invent and accomplish new things. This was true of many less brilliant careers. After 1500 all eyes were turned on Michelangelo, whose *cursus* was rapid and spectacular. The principle was the same, however: Michelangelo entered young into the workshop of a painter (to the consternation of the Buonarroti family); soon he outshone all. His driving force was the pursuit of a masterpiece. He arrived at his goal at the age of thirty with the *Pietà* in St. Peter's and the *David* commissioned by the Signoria of Florence, judged the most polished and accomplished works ever seen.

When an artist had made his name in one artistic specialty it was rare that he did not turn his hand to another with equal success. One of the most frequent and most interesting traits of the age was an invitation to talent to work in several and even in all domains. In 1334 Giotto was given the official charge of directing all the city's building projects: the painter had become an engineer. Two centuries later, no one was astonished when the Republic put Michelangelo in charge of the fortifications of Florence. There are many examples of extended competence: Francesco di Giorgio, a painter and sculptor, built churches and wrote a treatise on architecture. Painters produced theat-

ricals with "machines" (technologically advanced special effects), and prepared
floats with decorative plaster edifices for city festivities. Raphael and Giulio
Romano were painters, decorators, and architects. Verrocchio was perhaps the
most typical of the multi-talented heads of a Florentine *bottega* until his
discepolo, Leonardo, became the hyperbolic demonstration of the type. Leonardo's letter to Lodovico Sforza in 1482 is disconcerting in its enumeration
of the skills this thirty-year-old *artifex* claimed to possess. It is a tendency
typical of the great artistic workshops of the last third of the quattrocento,
however. The problem of the *artifex* was intensifying.

There were, as always, specialized *botteghe*, like those of Neri di Bicci,
who modestly limited his production to altarpieces; the Della Robbias' glazed
ceramics industry; the workshop of the Vivarini family in Venice; or the
studios of the goldsmiths who worked for the curia in Rome making pontifical ornaments. A new phenomenon expressing the unity of artistic activity
arose, however, to coexist with the *artifex polytechnes*. The idea of the team
head responsible for the whole job was extended to a broad range of social
practices that included ornament, theatrical decor, interior decoration, and
more. What was needed was a sort of "artistic director," which is what Leonardo was in Milan, Vasari was in Florence in the following century, and
Bernini was in Rome a century later. There was an increasing demand for
urban spectacle, and a growing number of works in both churches and private
dwellings was only one facet of that demand.

One illustration of this phenomenon is an instance of what one might call
astrological anthropology: the tradition of figuring the *artifices* as the children of Mercury. A plate depicting Mercury in a famous series of copper
engravings (ca. 1460) shows the activities under the protection of that god—
the goldsmith's art, sculpture, and painting, but also astronomy and music—
all arts that relied on calculation and technology. This image reflects the
common vision of the practical nature of the technological world. Sixty years
later, the formula was still valid in northern Europe, where the engraver Hans
Sebald Beham gave it a vigorous interpretation. Roughly the same definition
of the "Mercurians" can be found among the philosophers. Marsilio Ficino
lists among them inventors, technicians, and *ingenieri*—all those who rely
on measurement and on *ratio*—along with messengers and thieves. The
mention of music is interesting in that it reminds us that there was music in
nearly all the *studii*, the masters—Leonardo, Giorgione, Sebastiano Luciani,
and others—setting the example. In short, the unity of the arts was a practical reality.

It is hardly surprising, then, that the unity of the practitioners' world was
usually designated by the simple but appropriate term, *arti del disegno*.

Many of the implications of this term escape us today. It was to crystallize around the institution of the academy during the age of Duke Cosimo de' Medici. Its meaning was broader, however. On one occasion Michelangelo praised the *arti del disegno* in the manner of the dialecticians. For him, *disegno* was involved whenever intelligence was used: in war, in navigation, in studying the heavens, in the adornment of houses and the ornamentation of cities, and more. Within a century or two, the idea had reached maturity.

A Brief Sociology of the Milieu: Artistic circles did not have a very good press. Quarrels about money, rivalries that reached the point of defamation or crime, wine, scandals, and libertine living provided a wealth of material for gossip and for police reports in which not everything is necessarily legend. The restless *artifices* made up a miniature society within society, and their mores and their vagaries were the delight of the chroniclers.

At the time of the Council of Florence (1438–39), when the authority of the Medici family was finally well established, painters deluged Piero de' Medici (who passed for a competent connoisseur) with letters. Domenico Veneziano wrote in April 1438 to request a commission for a retable that, he claimed, would be a masterwork. Fifteen or sixteen months later, in August 1439, a whining plea arrived from Fra Filippo Lippi: "I am clearly one of the poorest friars in Florence and I am left with six young nieces to be married off [who are] not well and good for little . . . " First Cosimo, then the pope, needed to summon a good deal of indulgence for this Carmelite who was as fond of women as he was of money. He was one of the first of a long list of artist-*débauchés*. Cosimo's word on these insufferable men who must nonetheless be tolerated—"non sono asini vetturini" (they are not carters' donkeys)—in fact opened a new chapter in art history.

The *bottega* provided a focus for the life of the group, but on occasion the group became a coterie. Sacchetti's novella 136 (written around 1390) reports a conversation in San Miniato of a group of artists who gathered around Taddeo Gaddi to deplore the fact that painting had sorely declined since Giotto. Anecdotes abound: friends gathered around Botticelli in the evening to talk about everything under the sun, including politics (Savonarola found favorable terrain among them) and art. Somewhat later, in the early 1500s, the same thing occurred around Baccio d'Agnolo, one of the many woodworkers who turned architect. Vasari tells us:

But for all this he never gave up his workshop, where there were often gathered round him, in addition to many citizens, the best and most eminent masters of our arts, so that most beautiful conversations and discussions of importance took place there, particularly in winter.

Vasari goes on to list those who attended these evenings:

The first of these masters was Raffaello da Urbino, then a young man, and next came Andrea Sansovino, Filippino, Maiano, Cronaca, Antonio da San Gallo and Giuliano da San Gallo, Granaccio, and sometimes, but not often, Michelagnolo, with many young Florentines and strangers. (Vasari, Life of Baccio d'Agnolo, Lives, trans. De Vere, 6:66)

This is valuable information. We have the right to extend it back in time: artists' conclaves were a long-established custom. The story-writers tell us about them. How can we deny that Ghiberti, for example, owed his authority to gatherings of this sort? It is clear that as the generations passed, these discussions in which art obviously figured prominently led to the establishment of the academies and to organized *disputationes*.

This was not the direction taken by the nonconformist, anarchistic individualism of some groups. To give one example, Giovan Francesco Rustici was an eccentric. Annoyed by what he perceived to be the shortcomings of the jury that established the fee for his group sculpture of St. John the Baptist preaching (over the north door of the Baptistery), he kept to himself, which did not prevent him from participating in curious "confraternities" in which a good time was had by all. Their "parties" for the most part consisted in dinners organized with an extraordinary fantasy, at which joking titles were given to the dishes and *intermedi* (dramatic and musical interludes) were offered.

These parodic and somewhat Rabelaisian *solidatates* flourished in the cinquecento. For a meeting of the Compagnia del Paiuolo (the Company of the Cauldron) in 1512, Andrea del Sarto created an octagonal temple resembling the Baptistery out of jellies, parmesan cheese, and marzipan, with columns made of sausages. When the Company of the Cauldron proved insufficient, there was the Company of the Trowel (La Compagnia della Cazzuola), placed under the patronage of St. Andrew. This private club brought together men of the world, artists, musicians, poets, and others determined to amuse themselves with parodic theatricals involving disguises, one of the most remarkable of which was a fantasy on Freemasons. They also put on complete spectacles such as Pluto's descent into hell. Activities of the sort led quite naturally to the public performance of comedies, as with *La Calandria* and *La Mandragola*.

Analogous activities took place in Venice. Around 1500, private receptions, dances, and musicales—*radunate*—proliferated under the leadership of "star" painter-musicians like Giorgione. The gilded youth of the city also banded together in somewhat frivolous clubs that were accused of nocturnal disturbance of the peace. The best known of these, the Compagni della Calza, was famous for its handsome costumes (which can be seen in Carpaccio's crowd scenes) and its organized festivities, evening receptions, and dramatic performances. Artists were of course connected with such circles for amusement and pleasure. They also existed in Rome, where Cellini edifies his reader with tales about some quite unrestrainedly festive evenings. Thus artists tended to form small independent groups within society, quite aside from the corporations and confraternities in which, by definition, they had a place.

"Serious" artists did not have a high opinion of these little bands, especially when they included idlers and gossip-mongers, as in Florence. Vasari got off a salvo against them in an anecdote that must have occurred around 1550:

> For in those days the art of design in Florence had fallen into the hands of a company of persons who paid more attention to playing jokes and to enjoyment than to working, and whose occupation was to assemble in shops and other places, and there to spend their time in criticizing maliciously, in their own jargon, the works of others who were persons of excellence and lived decently and like men of honor. (Vasari, Life of Aristotile da Sangallo, *Lives*, trans. De Vere, 8:18)

One day as Vasari was returning home on horseback with a servant, the band confronted him near the Medici palace, and one of them asked him sarcastically for news of "His Lordship." Messer Giorgio, infuriated by the man's mocking tone, responded brutally that instead of being a miserable wretch like them, he had become rich. They pronounced him *goffo* (ill-mannered), but he earned the esteem of the clergy. He added that instead of "the clothes that beggarly painters wear" he now dressed in velvet: "vestivo di que' panni che vestono i dipintori che son poveri ed ora sono vestito de velluto." All these marks of status stood as proof of his success, and this was how the true artist could be distinguished from the untalented rabble of his envious rivals. The practice of affixing satirical comments to public presentations of works tells us that the insults of these small bands of mockers were feared. This was particularly true of artistic life in Florence, a city famous for its sharp retorts. Donatello said there was nothing more stimulating.

The question of clothing is not trivial. Leonardo, in a famous passage, supports the superiority of painting over sculpture by the fact that the sculptor seems a horse-fly "dusted over with marble powder like a baker with flour" while the painter sits comfortably at his easel, well dressed like a gentleman (C.U. fol. 20). Leonardo contrasts the style of the fashionable painter who frequents a court with the sculptor, who is nothing but a worker, but he did not intend this to apply to all painters or all sculptors. The social level of a painter or a sculptor depended to some extent on behavior and his degree of financial success. This had been true for some time. In his *Life* of Cosimo (Il Vecchio) de' Medici, Vespasiano da Bisticci has this to say of Cosimo:

And because Donatello was wont to go clad in a fashion not to Cosimo's taste, Cosimo gave him a red mantle and a cowl, with a cloak to go under the mantle. . . . After a day or two of wear [Donatello] put them aside, saying that he would not wear them again as they were too fine for him. (Vespasiano, *Renaissance Princes, Popes, and Prelates*, trans. George and Waters, 224)

This time, an artist refused social promotion by means of dress. A caustic remark of Vasari's about Alfonso Lombardi helps us to understand why Donatello feared being *dilegiato*: Alfonso, who was a "very handsome in person and youthful in appearance" and something of a dandy,

used always to wear on his arms, on his neck, and in his clothing ornaments of gold and suchlike fripperies, which showed him to be rather a courtier, vain and wanton, than a craftsman [*artifice*] desirous of glory. (Vasari, Life of Alfonso Lombardi, *Lives*, trans. De Vere, 5:132)

The institutional framework of the artistic professions changed only later, with the appearance of the "academies." It was in custom that patterns of behavior expanded and diversified. When society opened its doors to *artifices*, all types of artists could be seen, from the docile artisan to the insolent man of talent demanding attention; from the agreeable and inventive purveyor to the introverted *malinconico e solitario* painter; from the devoutly religious artist to the unscrupulous cynic. In a century or a century and a half, the productive capacity of the *artifices* had expanded in all directions, and by the force of things original types began to appear in this milieu. The artist had become a "cultural" figure.

Incidents in Venice: The most unexpected and, in the last analysis, most revealing aspect of this evolution occurred when the artist set a distance between himself and his patron. Isabella d'Este sent message after message to Leonardo to urge him to paint the portrait of her that he had promised (the famous drawing of Isabella, now in the Louvre, was a study made in Mantua for that purpose). Leonardo's habitual procrastination was not the only reason for this. Isabella's quarrelsome exchanges with Giovanni Bellini, in which Pietro Bembo acted as intermediary, are among the best examples of difficult relations between patron and artist. In one letter (to which I shall return) Bembo gives an explanation as illuminating as it is rare. Recounting his fruitless attempts to persuade Bellini to do an allegorical painting, Bembo explains that "he does not like to be given many written details which cramp his style; his way of working, as he says, is always to wander at will in his pictures" (Gaye, 2:76; quoted from Chambers, *Patrons and Artists*, 131).

The artist always worked on commission: we are not yet in the nineteenth century, when the painter worked on his own and then sold his works. Even in this earlier age, however, once a project had been agreed upon and a contract drawn up, the artist had every intention of operating as he wished and without further direction. Moreover, he found a way to get out of certain engagements.

These are admittedly exceptional cases. All *artifices* did not behave this way: far from it. Perugino, who accepted too many commissions and at times fell several months behind, could nonetheless be counted on to deliver his work, albeit somewhat hastily completed. Mantegna executed his orders quite dependably. When Dürer spent some time in Venice in 1506 (where, incidentally, Bellini was the only artist to show him kindness), it took him only five months to finish the *Madonna of the Rosary*, ordered for the German church of San Bartolomeo. He was conscientious and exact, like any good northern European artisan. But many Italian *artifices* whom we know also signed, dated, and delivered their retables with admirable punctuality. Not all artists had the independent and nonchalant attitude toward their responsibilities of some great masters of art.

Dürer's letters give a good idea of what the artist's life was like. When he left Nuremberg for Venice, on the invitation of the merchants of the Fondaco, guild protectionism assured him a cool reception from his colleagues. His attractive personality won him friends, however. They gave him good advice; he managed to extend the deadline for his work and he began to enjoy himself. He did a little business on the side, trading in precious stones in particular, as, it seems, did most artists who traveled. He wrote his friend Pirckheimer in February that people were most agreeable: "Gentlemen wish me well, but painters not so much." He was happy; the "cultural" climate agreed with him. In his last letter, written in October 1506, when his return home was in his thoughts, he made the much-quoted comment: "Hier bin ich ein Herr, daheim ein Schmarotzer" (here I am a gentleman, at home a parasite). We should keep in mind, however, that with his masterpiece, the *Madonna of the Rosary*, a painting in the Venetian style, and with his engravings, which were sold and plagiarized everywhere, Dürer passed into the upper class, so to speak. In short, he achieved social promotion by becoming the sort of "gentleman" that a recognized artist was in Italy. This 1506 episode puts the problem that concerns us here in a nutshell.

DOCTRINE

A Place in Culture: The church reached a decisive turning point with Nicholas V and Pius II: modern art became the art of the church. After the episodes of spectacular spending under Julius II and Leo X, however, came the brief but significant reign of Adrian VI, who was determined to put an end to all that. The Medicis made a point of supporting the arts, but the interlude of Savonarola counted for much. Although Castiglione, who was Raphael's friend, thought it necessary to recommend that the courtier be an enlightened patron of the arts, he admitted that not everyone agreed with him. In other words, the general trend toward increased artistic production—even overproduction— did not occur without some resistance and even opposition.

Throughout the Renaissance, there was something like a pitched battle between those who, for religious, moral, or intellectual reasons, considered with suspicion the growing emancipation of artists and the favor they enjoyed, and those who had an instinctive confidence in a new organization of the intellectual disciplines and tended to favor manifestations of art.

The argument of the latter group always invoked the spiritual, scientific, or poetic dimensions of art. Leonardo's maxim, *pittura è cosa mentale*, was put to question. Michelangelo, refusing to enter into the debate, stated simply that the artist deserved to be considered an intellectual: "Si dipinge non colle mani ma col cervello" (you paint not with your hands but with your brain). We are also told, however, that Botticelli was mocked because, *essendo persona sofisticata* (roughly, being too clever for his own good), he thought himself up to illustrating Dante.

The Problem of the Architect: A key text in this regard is the preface to a contract drawn up between Luciano da Laurana and Federigo of Montefeltro in 1468:

We deem as worthy of honour and commendation men gifted with ingenuity and remarkable skills, particularly those which have always been prized by both Ancients and Moderns, as has been the skill [*virtù*] of architecture, founded upon the arts of arithmetic and geometry, which are the foremost of the seven liberal arts because they depend upon exact certainty. It is an art of great science and ingenuity, and much esteemed and praised by us. (Gaye, 1:214–25, quoted from Chambers, *Patrons and Artists*, 165)

This remarkable and remarkably complete declaration contains all we need to know. First, it is a discourse in the form of a manifesto announcing the duke of Urbino's "cultural" intentions. Architecture is first among the arts and should not be seen as dependent upon practice. Its reason for being, its *virtù,* was its mathematical grounding, by which it achieved the dignity of the *artes liberales*. The reference to classical antiquity, which is to some extent a stylistic flourish, backs up a declaration of intent to favor a rational, learned, approach. This is a somewhat unusual way of justifying the choice of an architect for a castle. The praises of the artist that customarily accompanied contracts have become a manifesto and a program. We sense a will to break down the barriers between the disciplines: the university *quadrivium* no longer held a monopoly on learning. Now it resided in certain persons gifted with the *ingegno* and the *virtù* needed for modern times.

Rather than simply giving expression to an existing state of affairs, this text opens a door to the future. It implies that much would be required of those who claimed to apply such propositions; it called for a new type of architect who would represent art as science.

In all the cities of Italy, civic power defined its public image through architectural enterprises. The authority of the Florentine *comune* found expression in the Palazzo della Signoria; that of the various religious orders and the great prelates, in churches and other building projects. Civil and religious projects shared a concern for the management of space, with all that it required: loggias, statues, places appropriate for ceremonies and liturgy. If architecture was seen as chief among the arts, it required well-prepared and aware architects. The extraordinary success of men like Brunelleschi, Bramante, and Antonio da Sangallo, for example, would be incomprehensible without this more general orientation. People turned to the learned architect for suburban villas in Florence or Naples as well as for reorganization of the urban setting of the chief monuments of Rome or Venice. If need be, they were summoned. Thus Francesco di Giorgio, Giuliano da Sangallo, Bramante, and, eventually, Leonardo da Vinci were invited to Milan and Pavia to give their expert opinions. The architect was the privileged interlocutor of power. Even the Venetian Senate, which did not like exclusive positions, ended up accepting Jacopo Sansovino's. Science was required, not just practice.

The condemnation of construction not backed by rules—which by simplification was called "Gothic"—signified that the maximum was expected of the high science of a mathematics that was incontestible and, in principle, accessible to all. There is an amusing text that relates the enthusiasm of the citizens of Florence for a proposed facade for Santa Maria del Fiore in 1490 that proves, at the least, that a taste for construction, in the form of building projects, interested everybody. The hour had come, however, for theory, for reflection, for treatises outlining the best methods. Luca Pacioli owed a good part of his success as a lecturer to the fact that he offered the general public "scientific" recipes from which all could profit. His *De divina proporzione* is doubtless the most extreme (and, to modern eyes, the least convincing) expression of this desire to define the mathematical structure inherent in all technical operations.

"Architectural study" thus was part of the intellectual domain. Recourse to ancient texts created a sort of hindrance to knowledge, however, as it hesitated between problems of construction and of archaeology. Leon Battista Alberti's treatise, De re aedificatoria, which was honored with official publication and endowed with a preface of capital importance by Cristoforo Landino (1482), was an effort to promote a new architectural reasoning. Vitruvius and the assimilation of classical antiquity formed an intelligence that became aware of the logic of construction and the implications of that logic, and it learned how to draw the consequences. In principle, the shift from theory to practice presented no problems, since the patron was sufficiently well informed that he could act as an architect. The chroniclers praised Federigo da Montefeltro for his talents as a builder, as they did Sigismondo Malatesta and Lorenzo de' Medici. Something like an exchange of responsibilities took place. Because there was a fairly well developed common store of doctrine (as the reference to mathematical order indicates), the authorities could make use of it and a great lord could play the architect. The term took on a quasi-symbolic meaning, designating an aptitude of the human mind rather than a profession.

One result was an effervescent ferment of speculation and imagination that filled the half century from 1470 to 1520 with projects, both realized and on paper (rarely published, however). There must have been a moment when a degree of specialization began to be required, although writers continued to assert that the ars aedificandi was a science.

The case of an "average" architect like Baccio d'Agnolo (1462–1543) illustrates this development, which peaked in a polemic aimed at poorly trained builders who came to architecture from other occupations and laid claim to that great profession, "a science," Vasari tells us, "which has not been practised for several years past save by carvers and cunning impostors who profess to understand perspective without knowing even its terms or its first principles" (Vasari, Life of Baccio d'Agnolo, Lives, trans. De Vere, 6:65). We are in 1550. Vasari had presented Bramante as an absolute model, but he knew that Bramante's constructions had prompted some disappointment, and now he had to argue for competence. Improvised architects, be they decorators, sculptors, or painters, had been led to work on "columns, cornices, and bases, and all the ornaments" of architecture (ibid.). These, Vasari tells us in a pretty image, are the characters (le figure) that the art of building places on the stage. This was not enough, however, and technique was not simply imagery. Thus Vasari's life of Baccio is a scathing criticism of the architect-decorators who had invaded Florence. Vasari's criticisms echo the well-known dressing-down that Michelangelo inflicted on Baccio regarding the gallery surrounding the base of the cupola of Santa Maria del Fiore:

Michelangelo Buonarroti . . . perceiving that in carrying out this work they were cutting away the toothings that Filippo Brunelleschi, not without a purpose, had left projecting, made such a clamour that the work was stopped; saying that it seemed to him that Baccio had made a cage for crickets, that a pile so vast required something grander and executed with more design, arts, and grace than appeared to him to be displayed by Baccio's design. (Vasari, Life of Baccio d'Agnolo, *Lives*, trans. De Vere, 6:68)

The result, as was often the case in Florence, was to form committees, which left the gallery unfinished, as it is to this day.

Quarrels of this sort show how vital the problem of the architect was. Underlying the manifesto in Laurana's favor was a doctrinal question that persisted for some time. The architect, the paragon of art as science, armed with the potentialities of mathematics, easily took on universal significance. At base, this superior *artifex* was related to Pico della Mirandola's complete man, made to dominate nature. Before him, in Gianozzo Manetti's *De dignitate et excellentia homines*, we read that man's grandeur is manifested by his ability to make things. Now Brunelleschi's cupola had been added to the pyramids, to Archytas's mechanical dove, and to Archimedes' exploits. In their optimistic phase, Ficino and his friends never missed an opportunity to praise the present times, when the works of the architects, engineers, and painters proved the nobility of the human mind. By complete exercise of organizing Reason, man became *deus in terris*. It was tempting for some particularly intelligent and active minds to apply such an encouraging label to themselves. A new idea of the artist could then appear, and "divine" became the supreme praise.

It is easy to see why the architect could serve as a paradigm. In would unfair, however, not to mention the parallel reference to music, in which all the milieus involved in art and represented in the present discussion demonstrated a seemingly well-informed interest. *Musica*, like *architectura*, referred back to the *artes liberales*, since it had a theoretical basis, explained, for example, in Gafurius's *Theorica musicae* (1492). The number of artist-musicians—artists who were sought after because they were also musicians—is so great that we can state that music had won a remarkable place in both the life and the culture of the artists' studios. Since music was harmony and the resolution of dissonance, it was ultimately used as an *analogon* of beauty.

The term "music" is at times used with a highly charged universal sense, somewhat like "poetry" during the nineteenth century. Ficino seems to echo a widespread opinion when he states, "The music of the soul is led by steps to all the limbs of the body. It is this music that orators, poets, painters, sculptors and architects seek to imitate in their work" (letter to Antonio Canigiani in Ficino, *Opere*, ep. L; quoted from *The Letters of Marsilio Ficino*, trans. Language Department, School of Economic Science [London] 1:92). It took a philosopher to reduce to an ideal unity all the activities of the soul aimed at introducing rational order into discourse and images. This was Ficino's way of noting (in a moment of optimism) one aspiration of the new culture.

One mind went as far as was possible on the path of art as science, a path that seemed so clear in theory and proved so hazardous in practice. For forty years, operating in all repertories and trying out all techniques, Leonardo da Vinci took on the task of constructing a new type of knowledge that was to embrace all reality and lay new and secure foundations for the practical operations of the *artifex*. The result was another form of culture, distinct from the culture of letters (Leonardo declared himself an *omo senza lettere*), and which sprang, for the most part, out of questions arising from the normal experiences of the artists' studios where the *artifex polytechnes* was trained. His age was unable to grasp the significance of Leonardo's enterprise, however. The problem of the artist in general (no longer of the architect alone) is distorted by his unique example. His embarrassed contemporaries did not know what to make of him. Even Castiglione deplored the great painter pursuing his chimeras and lost for art. By his fascination with the impossible, Leonardo introduced a new dimension—in any event, a new seduction—of the "universal artist."

Audendi potestas: We need to keep in mind to what extent the texts recovered from classical antiquity, published and commented on with fervor, served as models for artists' actions and, in the long run, influenced their biographies. If an ancient precedent could be produced, it added validity to one's actions. Although Leonardo's contemporaries regretted that he had left paintings unfinished, they still examined them with a close attention that may have been bolstered by a remark of Pliny the Elder's:

The last works of artists and their unfinished pictures . . . are more admired than those which they finished, because in them are seen the preliminary drawings left visible and the artist's actual thoughts, and in the midst of approval's beguilement we feel regret that the artist's hand while engaged in the work was removed by death. (Pliny, *Naturalis Historia*, 35: 145, trans. Rackham)

A number of exemplary situations clustered around the name of Apelles: there was his contest of virtuosity with Protogenes; his besting of an incompetent critic; the maxim of relentless work, *nulla dies, sine linea*; his supreme recompense in the deference shown him by Alexander the Great, who ceded the beautiful Campaspe to him; and so forth. Rapidly and by a sort of osmosis between humanist culture and the culture of the artists' studios, these themes and the striking phrases expressing them entered into artistic folklore. When they did, countless artists—Botticelli, Leonardo, Titian—were compared to Apelles. The publicity-minded praise of artists that began to proliferate was full of references of the sort. The classical encomium helped give a flattering image of the artist and his powers, which was precisely the idea behind the little lists of *artifices* that have already been mentioned.

This new "artistic literature" set off a privileged category within society—or rather, within the common work of civilization. A glance at historical reality should suffice, however, to show how slanted this operation was, and how artificial and publicity-oriented. It might almost lead us to forget that artists, both major and minor, were everywhere in contact with or in the service of ecclesiastical authorities or devotional organizations, as in the past. Lay artistic production—the portrait, the history, the allegory—was still infinitely smaller in comparison. There was a "rigorist" current in the church that worried not only about the artist's immorality but also about the propriety of his works. Censors periodically deplored uncontrolled evolution in art. St. Antoninus, who, operating from Fra Angelico's San Marco, could hardly deny all value to art, expressed reservations about the painters' increasing tendencies to iconographic whims. There was a "pietist" trend, to which little attention was paid, however, that laid the foundations for later efforts at Catholic reform. How, then, can one account for the astonishing liberty that painters and sculptors enjoyed?

This is a difficult question. As Carlo Dionisotti reminds us, the future of an "intellectual" was almost inevitably on the side of the church, either in the services of the curia, like Leon Battista Alberti, or in the religious orders, perhaps with the final reward of the cardinal's hat, as with Pietro Bembo, Paolo Giovio, and others. Legend has it that Bibbiena had Raphael in mind for the same recompense. Clement VII granted Sebastiano Luciani the lucrative office of keeper of the seals, which earned him his surname, del Piombo, and after which he produced little, Vasari tells us. The artists' relations with the church, however, were usually those of purveyors and clients.

The demand for statues, altarpieces, and choir stalls and for the decoration of sacristies had become so great that it surprised no one to see monks and friars as painters and decorators. Fra Angelico is the greatest example of the monk-painter who brought honor to his order. His was an example that was always cited by later reformers and champions of devotional art. There was also a veritable "School of San Marco" that clustered around Fra Bartolommeo when he returned to art, producing significant works, after his momentary abandonment of painting at the call of Savonarola.

The problem lay elsewhere and can be put simply: there was no precise doctrine of art in Western Europe, even in church canons. There was no theology of the image, as in Byzantium, and no general codification. There was only usage or tradition (*consuetudo*). Certain elementary definitions like the famous "quod legentibus scriptura, hoc idiotis cernentibus praebat pictura" of Gregory the Great had taken the place of theory throughout the Middle Ages. Durand of Mende remarked (around 1280) that painters treated the *storiae* of the Bible freely, and Cennino Cennini simply took over this notion at the beginning of his treatise (around 1420).

An adage taken from Horace's Letter to the Pisans (hence its name *Dictum Horatii*)—*quodlibet audendi potestas*—circulated at least as early as the thirteenth century and authorized some more or less fantastic inventions. It would be a mistake to see this infinitely reiterated formula as a sign of a new state of mind, but it does seem to have served as a stimulant for initiative on the part of the *artifices*. In the sketchbook of one member of Benozzo Gozzoli's circle containing studies of faces, hands, and other particulars, we read, with some surprise, the entire formula in Latin, transcribed as a sort of manifesto: *pictori[bu]s atque poetis sempre fuit et erit equa potestas* (Boymans Museum, Rotterdam). This time, the claim to enjoy a "cultural" privilege comparable to the poets' found expression in an artist's studio

What made that *potestas* legitimate was the personal gift—the *ingenium*—that distinguished the artist. This helps us to understand Giovanni Bellini's statement, as reported to Isabella d'Este by Pietro Bembo, in the letter already cited:

The invention, which you tell me I am to find for his drawing, must be adapted to the fantasy of the painter. He does not like to be given many written details which cramp his style; his way of working, as he says, is always to wander at will in his paintings, so that they can give satisfaction to himself as well as to the beholder. (Gaye, 2:71, 73, quoted from Chambers, *Patrons and Artists*, 131)

Bellini was no longer an artisan at the service of a gracious princess; he was already an artist in the modern sense of the word who intended to have his *ingenium* respected.

Not every artist had come to that point, but the idea of a certain distance between the project or command and the later elaboration of the finished work placed the *artifex* halfway between the artisan and the poet. Naturally, Michelangelo made the best of Horace's dictum when the occasion arose. In his famous statement (piously recorded by Francesco da Hollanda in 1532) praising the "irrational" decorative theme of *grotteschi*, Michelangelo quotes it as axiomatic. It was of course also on this point that the censors of his *Last Judgment* made it their duty to attack him. The theologians of the Counter-Reformation later perceived, with some embarrassment, that there had never been a true doctrine of images in the Latin church.

This de facto situation left judgment on such matters to the local authorities, the religious orders, and the confraternities. The indulgence that had been shown to the artists' independent life-style had a parallel in the liberty left to their imaginations. Gozzoli in the Campo Santo in Pisa and Sodoma at Monte Oliveto Maggiore take pleasure in voluble story-telling. For thirty or forty years, altarpieces offered new interpretations of the Madonna. In the Santo (the Basilica of St. Anthony) in Padua, Donatello embroiders on the saint's legend. The painter and the sculptor were far from being held to precise norms by the religious authorities. It was understood that a work must respond to devotional needs when it appeared on a chapel wall or on an altar, but its creator had every intention (and increasingly so) of being appreciated on his own and for his merits as a painter or sculptor. The public had always shown its appreciation of the qualities of artists, even during what we call the Middle Ages, but the Renaissance artist could openly demand a freedom of invention that went somewhat beyond the initial notion of service. This was all the more true when the patron—confraternity, bishop, or great lord—was proud of having a Botticelli, a Mantegna, or a Titian in its chapel or his *Studiolo*.

Thus it is hardly surprising to see the desire to be counted among the leading figures of the culture eventually giving rise to the "artist's house." In treatises on architecture in which everything is calculated according to social hierarchy, the *casa del povero artefice* is little more than an enlarged workshop, as in Francesco di Giorgio, writing around 1500, and in Serlio, around 1540. Donatello, who moved often, had to take what he could get. We know by his tax declaration that Masaccio laid claim only to a small corner of the studio, but Ghiberti, not much later, felt he needed a house with a courtyard and a portico. In Mantua, Mantegna added a room to his *studio*, apparently for displaying his collections, and he placed a statue of Mercury over his front door. The next generation subordinated working space to the construction of a facade like that of a palazzo. This was true of Raphael in Rome and, following his example, of Giulio Romano in Mantua and Federico Zuccaro in Rome and Florence (where he also designed the fantastic decorations covering Andrea del Sarto's house). And then there was Vasari, with his house-museum-spectacle in Arezzo. The curve was complete.

Virtù and Glory

A Place in History: Dum viguit eloquentia, viguit pictura—the power of art responds to that of literature—Enea Silvio (or Aeneas Sylvius, as he preferred to be known in literature) Piccolomini wrote in a letter to Niclas von Wyle in 1456. Was this universally true, or true only of "great figures" (the term "genius" was not yet current)? Piccolomini soon provides the answer: *Post Petrarcham converserunt litterae, post Joctum surrexere pictorum manus.* *Manus* recalls that he is speaking of a manual occupation, but the pairing of Petrarch and Giotto had been accomplished and was to mark the epoch.

We need to return to a famous text with an enormous influence. Dante's mention of Giotto and Cimabue in Canto XI of the *Purgatorio* is not the unconditional glorification of the figurative arts that some have seen in it. In the general context of sins of pride, Dante is illustrating the vanity of re-nown—*fiato di vento*—and he cites the example of Cimabue being replaced by Giotto because these artists were familiar to all. His verses attest to the fame of the two painters—which is by itself remarkable—but that is all. There is no more "cultural" exaltation of two fashionable artists than there is of the two miniaturists, Oderisi of Gubbio and Franco of Bologna, whose art, to tell the truth, does not seem exceptional.

Dante's mention of these two painters had immense consequences, thanks to the influence of commentaries that focused on the personality of Giotto rather than his art. After Dante and following his lead, Giotto was admired as an illustration of how a simple artisan could achieve glory. The commentators were men of letters, and they were shocked to see two *homines ignoti nominis et bassae artis* compared with two poets as famous as Guido Guinizelli and Guido Cavalcanti. They knew Benvenuto da Imola's famous explanation, which gave the early trecento a serious starting point: "Appetitus gloriae ita indifferentes occupat omnes quod etiam parvi artifices sunt solliciti circa illam acquirendam, sicut vidimus quod pictores apponunt nomica operibus."

This was a doubly important observation: if the painters had begun to sign their works—and examination of altarpieces confirms this—the habit was not favorably regarded by all, and particularly not by the clergy; that is, the intellectuals. They saw in this a manifestation of pride that was all the more blameworthy for exposing the artist's name to the public gaze in the sanctuary and giving them a renown that writers attained only exceptionally. What is more, these "people avid for glory" were of humble origin—*parvi artifices*—and lacked the literary culture considered the necessary foundation of true glory.

Benvenuto's commentary enables us to avoid a trap that the enthusiasm of nineteenth-century historians often led them into—the idea that chronologically parallel developments in art and literature necessarily involved a mutual awareness and a sort of complicity between writers and artists. We need to begin the other way around, from the difference in nature—social and mental—between the cleric and the artisan. The two classes knew nothing of one another. It is true that an intelligent head of a studio like Ghiberti knew that he needed to turn to literature to assure his fame and wrote his *Commentari*—a high-sounding title—in which he sketched a totally new view of the artistic professions. After him, however, the great practitioners wrote and published only treatises. After all, Leonardo never managed to write a book.

Thus it was up to the *letterati* to assure artists a place in chronicle. And indeed, in Naples and Florence in the fifteenth century, humanists manifested their interest in the *uomini famosi* of painting and sculpture. In his introduction to the edition of the *Divina Commedia* that included his commentary (1481), Landino speaks briefly about the living masters of his time, and Ugolino Verino also enumerates living artists in chapter 53 of his *De illustratione urbis Florentiae*, written about 1500. *Artifices* appear in local chronicle, then in guidebooks such as Canon Albertini's guides to Rome and to Florence (1510). From the late quattrocento, things worked to favor artists, leading them more and more toward a fame they had never known before.

Descriptions of artistic talents remained approximate and banal, however. This was, as has been shown, for lack of vocabulary. The *letterati* knew well that one had to be an artist to speak about art:

Ars erit, quae disciplina percipi debet. . . . Ea, quae in oratore maxima sunt, imitabilia non sunt, ingenium, inventio, vis, facilitas et quidquid arte non traditur. (The art is that which we should acquire by study. . . . The greatest qualities of the orator are beyond all imitation, by which I mean, talent, invention, force, facility and all the qualities which are independent of art. Quintilian, *Institutio oratoria*, II, XIV, 5; X, II, 12, quoted from Butler trans.)

What Quintilian had to say about eloquence could and must be applied to the figurative arts. Thus the absence of direct criticism, even of works that the writer declares he admires, is hardly surprising. Literary analogies comparing Michelangelo with Dante, for instance, or Titian with Ariosto remained the best available resource. Still, Quintilian had suggested other words— *ingenium, vis*—to indicate aspects of art not strictly connected with its technical side (*ars*), and these were the terms used to describe the motivating force behind artistic activity. As we have seen, in 1468 Laurana was praised for his *ingenio e virtù*, and these two terms were to do constant service to indicate why certain works and certain talents deserved attention. Aretino uses them incessantly, and not only to speak of artists.

The artists whose bizarre behavior attracted the attention of their amused or irritated contemporaries were often seen merely as generous spirits carried away by their excessive *virtù*—in other words, by their passion for art. Paolo Uccello's geometric calculations for combined perspectives in marquetry are of this order, as was the "physiognomic" research of Donatello. Pollaiuolo, Leonardo, and Michelangelo carried on horrifying experiments in anatomical dissection that went far beyond common practice. Vasari thought it worthy of note that one promising young man, Bartolommeo Torri, literally lost his mind around 1550 thanks to the dissections he performed. He kept *le sporcherie della notomia* in his house and even kept "limbs and pieces of men" under his bed. He hid from the world, "neglecting himself and thinking that living like an unwashed philosopher, accepting no rule of life, and avoiding the society of other men, was the way to become great and immortal" (Vasari, Life of Giovanni Antonio Lappoli, *Lives*, trans. De Vere, 6:264). Some energy was wasted.

It is impossible to evaluate the influence of Leonardo's technical research or his methodical and insatiable exploration of the mysteries of the nature and the fecundity of the human organism. We could perhaps speak of a "Leonardo effect" that incited painters to a display of exotic themes and subtle attitudes and to indulge in esoteric speculations. It was rumored of all the eccentrics and solitaries—Beccafumi, Francesco Rustici, Parmiggiano—that they conducted research on the solidification of mercury, which was how the commonality expressed disapproval of secret experiments on disquieting materials. Cellini, for all his volubility, helps us to grasp that for the throng, the artist's aura had to include a bit of the fantastic. He was inordinately pleased with himself for having participated in a necromantic séance in the Colosseum. Moreover, after a crisis of intense piety in Castel Sant'Angelo, Cellini flattered himself that he had acquired a truly singular gift: "There is one thing I must not leave out—perhaps the greatest that ever happened to any man. . . . From the time I had my vision till now, a light—a brilliant splendour—has rested above my head" (Cellini, *Autobiography*, trans. Bull, 231). This aureole could be seen clearly through the morning mist, but also in the evening at twilight. Only initiates saw it. This is a perplexing episode: are we sure we understand? In the Renaissance, pride had no limits.

As commonplaces crystallized into legend around certain artists, it moved them into the realm of folklore. *Virtù*—creative power (which could go astray)—was distinguished by a total, explicit, and passionate aspiration for "glorification," which meant access to the superior order in the memory of men that justifies and excuses everything. But glory had an implacable adversary in the life of man: *Fortuna*. Works that had to be interrupted, works that were contested, accidents, passions, and the death of protectors were all blows of fate. There were few careers without drama or setback. When an artist showed his "divine" capabilities, Heaven's jealousy was blamed for removing him from humankind.

The exaltation of the "genius" of the artist could have surprising results. When Giulio Romano died on All Saints' Day in 1546, the following epitaph was composed:

> Jupiter saw the sculpted and painted forms,
> Gifted with life, and mortals' dwellings fit for heaven,
> by the *virtù* of Giulio Romano. Furious
> He assembled the council of the gods
> And removed him from the earth, unable to bear
> Being outdone or equaled by an inhabitant of earth.[4]

Vasari published this *elogium* in pure pagan style in the 1550 edition of his *Lives*, but he removed it from the 1568 edition.

Benvenuto da Imola was indignant at the claim to fame implied when artists signed their works. Although this practice was not universal, it made many converts during the quattrocento. There was the pretended inscription, the more or less ostentatious *cartellino*, the name inserted onto a stair step, on a vase, or even, as a game, on the shaft of an arrow (Perugino). In many instances, the signature was a commercial trademark. We read *Titianus Cadorinus pinxit* on the Ancona altarpiece (1520), but not on the Pesaro *Madonna*, an altarpiece painted for the Church of the Frari in Venice (1519–26).

As for the self-portrait, its history exactly illustrates the development that interests us here—the passage from duly accepted artisanal status to the ostentation of the virtuoso emerging out of obscurity. In the trecento, the painter of a fresco that included a number of portraits might slip his own face into the composition, but toward the wings—that is, at the edge of the scene, as in Taddeo Gaddi. Masaccio and Filippino Lippi did just that in the Brancacci

---

4. Videbat Juppiter corpora sculpta pictaque
   Spirare et aedes mortalium aequarier caelo
   Julii virtuti Romani. Tunc iratus
   Concilio divorum omnium vocato
   Illum e terris sustulit; quod pati nequiret
   Vinci aut aequari ab homine terrigena.
   (Vasar, *Le vite*, CLUEB 5:295, n. 1)

Chapel. With Perugino, Luca Signorelli, and Pinturicchio, the painter came out of the throng, and his self-portrait stood alone in its frame. Later, all manner of variations became possible, including the artist's distorted image in a mirror. Vasari gathered together a number of these self-portraits of the artist when he understood that the moment had come to give them their due and added illustrations to the second edition of his *Lives of the Artists* in 1568.

In the preface to his *Historiae sui temporis*, Paolo Giovio declares, speaking from the heart, "In hac vita . . . nihil beatius esse potest quam nominis famam . . . ad non incertam spem sempiternae laudis extendisse." He meant that all great men needed literary praise, and thus had an interest in assuring themselves the aid of an eloquent author. The artist was useful too, however, since, as classical doctrine taught, painting and sculpture had been invented to keep alive the memory of faces. Thus the author and the artist both served as instruments of the rhetoric that was indispensable for the proper administration of glory. Giovio's statement provided Vasari with the idea for a fresco series in the Sala della Cancelleria in the Palazzo Farnese *ubi Paulus dispensat praemia* ("The Rewarding of *Virtù*"), in which Giovio himself, Reginald Pole, Jacopo Sadoleto, Pietro Bembo, Michelangelo, and others are depicted around Paul III.

Vasari's *Lives* responded to similar preoccupations. The biographical framework was inevitable: the work combined the traditional review of *uomini famosi* with the literary formula of *elogia*. The idea for the work is supposedly linked to a reception given by Cardinal Alessandro Farnese at which Paolo Giovio was present. Vasari incorporated in his work all the arguments put forth during the previous century to establish the "cultural" dignity of artists, along with whatever seemed to him appropriate to a comprehension of their place in society. If Vasari, an artist turned writer, could, for the first time, introduce artists into history on an equal footing with others, it was because they had already won the battle that he narrated.

In 1540, Paul III officially emancipated Michelangelo and Pierantonio Cecchini from their guild (*ars scalpellinorum*). In 1571, Cosimo de' Medici did the same for all artists. Vasari's arguments on their behalf had borne fruit. In the meantime, the Accademia del Disegno had been created, which assured the non-artisanal status that artists in the "major arts" demanded. A fatal gap had been established between the artist and the artisan. Still, when we visit the Chapel of the Confraternity of St. Luke in the cloister of the church of Santissima Annunziata in Florence, where Vasari's frescoes decorate the walls and where he hoped to be buried, we can still see, behind the figure of St. Luke, the patron saint of painters, the paint grinder, the good artisan, hard at work.

BIBLIOGRAPHY

Anderson, Jaynie. "The 'Casa Longobarda' in Asolo: A Sixteenth-Century Architect's House." *The Burlington Magazine*, June 1974: 296–302, esp. pp. 301–2.

Baxandall, Michael. *Giotto and the Orators, Humanist Observers of Painting in Italy and the Discovery of Pictorial Composition*. Oxford: Clarendon Press, 1971.

Burke, Peter. "L'artista: momenti e aspetti." In *Storia dell'arte italiana*. I. *Materiali e problemi*, vol. 2, *L'artista e il pubblico*. Turin: Einaudi, 1979, 87–116.

Camesasca, Ettore. *Artisti in bottega*. Milan: Feltrinelli, 1966.

Chambers, D. S. *Patrons and Artists in the Italian Renaissance*. London: Macmillan, 1970.

Chastel, André. *Chronique de la peinture italienne à la Renaissance, 1280–1580*. Fribourg (Switzerland): Office du Livre, 1983.

Conti, Alessandro. "L'evoluzione dell'artista." In *Storia dell'arte italiana*. I. *Materiali e problemi*, vol. 2, *L'artista e il pubblico*. Turin: Einaudi, 1979, 117–269.

Gaye, Johann Wilhelm. *Carteggio inedito d'artisti dei secoli XIV, XV, XVI*. 3 vols. Florence: G. Molini, 1839–40.

Gilbert, Creighton. *Italian Art, 1400–1500: Sources and Documents*. Sources and Documents in the History of Art, gen. ed. H. W. Janson. Englewood Cliffs, N.J.: Prentice-Hall, 1980.

Gombrich, E. H. *The Heritage of Apelles: Studies in the Art of the Renaissance*. Ithaca: Cornell University Press, 1976.

Grote, Ludwig. *"Hier bin ich ein Herr." Dürer in Venedig*. Munich: Prestel, 1956.

Klein, Robert, and Henri Zerner. *Italian Art, 1500–1600: Sources and Documents*. Sources and Documents in the History of Art, gen. ed. H. W. Janson. Englewood Cliffs, N.J.: Prentice-Hall, 1966.

Lecoq, Anne-Marie, and Pierre Georgel. *La peinture dans la peinture*. 2d ed., Paris: Biro, 1987.

Wackernagel, Martin. *Der Lebensraum des Künstlers in der florentinischen Renaissance*. Leipzig: Verlag E. A. Seemann, 1938. (*The World of the Florentine Renaissance Artist: Prospects and Patrons, Workshop and Art Market*. Trans. Alison Luchs. Princeton: Princeton University Press, 1981).

E I G H T
The Woman of the Renaissance

Margaret L. King

𝒜T the end of the Middle Ages and the beginning of the Renaissance, in stone and paint and glass, the mother of God smiled at her baby for the first time: the mother nurturing; the baby, playful and unbounded potential. In the embrace of mother and child, projected in gothic sculpture and quattrocento color onto eternal beings, was born the explosive culture of the Renaissance. "Renaissance man" was born of Renaissance woman.

Renaissance man has many well-defined faces: eight of them head the other chapters of this volume. Renaissance woman seems faceless. A man could be prince or warrior, artist or humanist, merchant or cleric, sage or adventurer. Women rarely assumed these roles, and even when they did, it was not these but other roles that defined them. She was mother or daughter or widow, virgin or prostitute, saint or witch, Mary, Eve, or Amazon. These identities (derived from her sexual status alone) engulfed her and extinguished any other selfhood that she claimed. She struggled, during the Renaissance centuries, to define and express that selfhood. She struggled without success, since by the end of the Renaissance the fixity of sexually defined roles for women had been reaffirmed in society and culture and woman's condition had not advanced but declined.

MOTHER AND CHILD

Most Renaissance women became mothers, and motherhood was their profession and their identity. Their adult lives (from their mid-twenties in most social groups; from their adolescence in the elites) were a cycle of childbirth and nursing and childbirth again. Women below the elite classes gave birth every twenty-four to thirty months. The intervals between births were governed by the period of lactation, which limited fertility; when the child was weaned, a new conception could take place. Wealthy women bore even more babies than poor ones. The need to secure an heir, corollary to the need to transmit wealth effectively, compelled them to be fruitful. Since they did not nurse their own children (of which renunciation more later), they could conceive again soon after each birth. Alessandra Macinghi Strozzi, related to the Alberti and Strozzi commercial dynasties of Florence, gave birth to eight children in the decade from 1426 to 1436. Henrietta Maria, the queen of King Charles I of England, was pregnant almost without intermission from 1628 to 1639. Such fertility, which could reach staggering heights, well beyond the average maximum biological fertility of twelve births for the human female, was in the interest of the family, which required at least one surviving male heir for its proper continuity. The women of the Donato family of Venice, for instance, may have achieved this average in each generation from the fourteenth through the seventeenth century. At the turn of the fifteenth century, Magdalucia, the Venetian wife of Francesco Marcello, gave birth to twenty-six children, exceeding this figure.

To bear children was both a woman's privilege and a woman's burden. In Italy and France, the woman who had just borne a child was celebrated and pampered. Canon Pietro Casola of Milan described the chamber of a new mother of the noble Dolfin family in Venice in 1494. The room was hung with ornaments worth at least 2,000 ducats, and the female attendants wore jewels worth at least 100,000 ducats. For a passing moment the woman who gave birth, like a bride at her wedding, occupied a position of unparalleled honor. It was a badge of honor, likewise, to be pregnant. The *Madonna del Parto* of Piero della Francesca, pointing to the belly in which she nurtures the future Christ, was also the figure of the ordinary woman soon to bring forth life. When the Venetian nobleman and ecclesiastic Gregorio Correr spoke to Cecilia Gonzaga, daughter of the ruler of Mantua, of the temptations in her own house that might distract her from her intention to take the veil, he mentioned the swelling bellies of her brothers' wives and the cries of a newborn infant calling to her for nurture. The wife of Francesco di Marco Datini, the renowned merchant of Prato of whose life a bonanza of surviving records fortunately bears witness, longed for a child. Unsuccessful in giving birth herself, she gave equal love to her husband's child by another woman.

Women of the elite classes were expected to love their children, and many did, nurturing and educating them to the age of seven (daughters until marriage), finding in motherhood opportunity for both creativity and expression. Circumstances required Alessandra Macinghi Strozzi, the mother of eight, not only to bear but also to rear her surviving children when her anti-Medicean husband (who soon died) and elder sons were exiled from the city. The seventy-two letters she wrote to her sons between 1447 and 1471 bear witness to her maternal concern for their welfare. To her son Filippo, the eventual restorer of the family's fortunes, she sent medical advice, news of investments, packages of new linens and ripe cheeses, and reports on the progress of younger siblings and cousins.

Of grander stature but equally solicitous was Margaret Beaufort, a descendant of the English Lancastrian line, who spurred her son, the future Henry VII, king of England, to high achievement and strict virtue. This patroness and forerunner of the high-placed learned women of the Tudor age intrigued constantly to place her only child on the throne of England. Mother and son later exchanged letters revealing deep affection. Sending him birthday greetings, she called him her "only desired joy in this world." In recognition of her motherly love, he confessed himself as much bound to her as to any living being. Less than a century later, Beaufort's compatriot, the gentlewoman Elizabeth Grymeston, wrote a full-scale tract to her son, Bernye, offering wisdom on education, marriage, devotions, and death. The force of love is the greatest force there is, she told him, and no love is greater than that of a mother for her child. So common was the practice of a mother's ongoing guidance of her older children, notably her sons, that the epistles, handbooks, and diaries composed for this purpose constitute a major genre of female authorship.

Even mothers who loved their children could dread childbirth. A fearful prospect, it was the particular punishment of God upon Eve for her duplicity in Eden: less than man's punishment, argued the fifteenth-century Veronese humanist Isotta Nogarola; worse than his, responded her male partner in a dialogue on the subject, because she bore the accumulation of both penalties, unending labor as well as the pain of childbirth. The archhumanist Erasmus called it the worst of all human pains. The birth of her first child propelled the English mystic Margery Kempe into a six-month-long depression.

Far worse than depression, the consequence of birth for many women was death. Tended by midwives trained in the school of custom, women could not survive certain complicated births or bacterial infection, a threat to rich and poor until well into the modern era. Gregorio Dati noted the deaths of the first three of his four wives in a litany that could serve as a memorial for women of the past: Bandecca "went to Paradise" in 1390 after a nine-month illness started by a miscarriage; Betta, after the birth of an eighth child (1402), "went to Paradise" as well; Ginevra, who bore Dati eleven children, died in childbirth not long before 1421 after suffering enormously, and "passed to Paradise." The torment of the English Lady Danby was likewise recorded by her sister, writing in 1648: having already borne nine children and miscarried six times, Lady Danby gave birth a sixteenth time and welcomed the death that followed two weeks later. Puerperal fever swept an

Edinburgh infirmary in the winter of 1774, infecting nearly all women within twenty-four hours of giving birth; every woman who fell sick died.

The mothers who survived often lived to face the death of the baby they had yielded forth with such pain (woman's "labor" indeed). Child mortality was ferocious. Children faced a possibility of survival ranging in Western Europe from 20 to 50 percent. They fell prey to plague, diarrhea, flu, catarrh, tuberculosis, starvation. Those who survived babyhood were still particularly vulnerable through the adolescent years. In fifteenth-century Pistoia, nearly 18 percent of infants died between the ages of 1 and 4; nearly 11 percent between age 5 and age 9; another 8 percent between 10 and 14. In Milan in 1470, 5 percent of newborns died within the first day of existence. The Dati who listed his wives past and present tracked the births and deaths of his children: of at least twenty-five legitimate births (plus one illegitimate birth and two miscarriages), at his death in 1435 it seems only nine children still survived. Of the twenty-six children born to Magdalucia Marcello, thirteen survived to a "robust age." Of Alessandra Strozzi's five sons, only two were living after the death of the youngest, Matteo, in 1459. His death grieved her, she wrote, more than anything else ever had, but she took comfort in the knowledge that he had received proper medical and clerical attention and had been welcomed by God in heaven.

The apprehension of child death hovered over birth. The newborn child may have been looked upon by Renaissance mothers as a transitory being in whom only a tentative if powerful affection could be invested. In France, the Chevalier de la Tour-Landry (1371) warned his daughters not to rejoice too much in the birth of a child or to celebrate the event with too much pomp; God might be angered, and the child might die. The English reformer John Wycliffe coldly advised that mothers should be grateful for God's great mercy in taking a child from this world.

Loved or not, the babies who survived were fed by breast, commonly for eighteen to twenty-four months. Little else could be provided, and this, too, was woman's specific task. In villages and towns all over Europe, most adult women must have been nursing one or more babies most of the time—their own and, as we shall see, those of others. Women of the nobility and the patriciate, of the courts and cities of Renaissance Europe, refused to nurse their babies. Their refusal flew in the face of an overwhelming body of advice from humanists and physicians drawing from authorities as old and as honored as Aristotle and Plutarch. San Bernardino trumpeted to women listeners in the piazza that the day they put their babies out to nurse they fell into sin. Francesco Barbaro, the author of the elegant and widely read *De re uxoria* (1415), declared it a mother's natural duty to feed her infant at her breast.

The milk of the mother whose womb carried a child, he said, was the nourishment proper to it. A century later, the Spanish-born Juan Luis Vives made the same arguments in his famous work on female education, the *De institutione foeminae christianae* (1529). Outside of humanism, the same expert advice was repeated routinely in both Catholic and Protestant manuals and sermons.

More than simple reluctance may have accounted for the avoidance of breast feeding by women in elite groups. Their husbands often did not approve of the appearance of a nursing mother. Lactation, moreover, having a contraceptive effect, may have been limited so that more children could be conceived. A higher birth rate was desired in these social strata in order to ensure the transmission of wealth, knowledge, and power, just as among the poor too high a birth rate threatened scarce food resources. Whatever the reasons, the avoidance of breast feeding by elite women was nearly universal. The children of the rich were fed at the breasts of the poor. For babies of the very wealthiest, a nurse was provided who lived with the household. More commonly, from the cities of Italy, France, Germany, and England, babies were sent to the country within days of birth to be wet nursed by peasant women. Some nurses had such an abundance of milk that the demands of caring for additional children were satisfactorily met. Others had recently buried their own babies or had weaned them, or (lured by fees nearly twice as great as those earned by domestic servants) they handed their own babies over to still other nurses. Montaigne reports having seen peasant children whose mothers were nursing other women's babies put to the teats of goats for nourishment. One child died when removed from the goat for which he had formed a deep affection.

Many children died in the hands of country wet nurses—more than those (in England, for example, twice as many) who would have died had they stayed under maternal care. Their deaths came from a variety of causes: poverty, malnutrition, neglect. The Tuscan notary ser Lapo Mazzei put fourteen children out to nurse the day after they were born; five survived. In one town in English Buckinghamshire, between 1578 and 1601, 6 percent of all burials were of children put out to a nurse. Babies were not always wanted, and nurses often obliged by dispatching them. A classic method was "overlaying"—rolling over in bed, in the presumed innocence of sleep, to cause suffocation, a death that had the appearance of an accident. Also effective in the disposition of unwanted children were starvation, exposure, and drugging. Of twenty-three children placed in the care of one Mrs. Poole in England in 1765, eighteen died within one month of birth, two died as older infants, and three remained alive.

Possibly the absence of maternal affection was a factor in infant death at the hands of nurses (as the absence of consistent warmth from a single figure in modern institutions has great negative impact on infants and children today). Stefano Guazzo seems to lament his own abandonment in his *Civile conversazione* (1581), in which a child reproaches his mother for having carried him only nine months in her womb before dispatching him to a nurse for two years. Children were often handed from nurse to nurse, and if the mother died they were kept with nurses for years. The Florentine Giovanni Morelli relates that his father, in the early trecento, was in a nurse's home until the age of ten. Indeed, it would be no surprise to learn that a toll of death and sadness was reaped over several centuries from the custom of exporting the babies of the upper classes to foster mothers for several years.

Wet nurses may have inflicted upon children left in their care the kind of abuse that ended in death, but so did mothers (and fathers). Every century prior to our own has known infanticide. In antiquity a normal and accepted form of population limitation (especially the population of females), infanticide was proscribed and hated in the Christian centuries. But it was practiced nevertheless. The greatest concentration of infant murder was among the poor and unmarried. Within stable peasant communities, illegitimate births were successfully avoided much of the time, if only by the remedy of marriage in the case of premature pregnancy. In city and country, among poor women and prostitutes, illegitimate births nonetheless occurred. The fate of these infants was often miserable; they may have been the largest class of victims of the violence of mothers who were, without doubt, themselves victims. Court judgments of such women bear this out. Often, if the baby had been baptized, they were dealt with lightly for the sin of disposing of an unwanted infant they were unable to rear. When they were condemned, however, the punishment was unequivocal and severe. Infanticide was punished by death, and by a means (drowning, burning) far more painful than that typically used (hanging) in the case of a male criminal. In sixteenth-century Nuremberg, the penalty for maternal infanticide was drowning; in 1580, a year in which the severed heads of three infanticidal mothers were nailed to the scaffold for public contemplation, the penalty was changed to beheading. Many women suffered such a fate: infanticide was the major cause, after witchcraft, for the execution of women during the Renaissance.

Mothers unable to care for infants illegitimate and legitimate could also abandon them in the hope that abandonment was a lesser sin than murder (although the result was often the same) and that some charitable stranger would allow the child to live. Foundling hospitals, which had been established since the eighth century in some Italian cities, spread from the fourteenth to

the sixteenth centuries. The resources of such institutions were gen
insufficient for the task of rearing orphaned children. Newborns could
be cared for by resorting to wet nurses, with the unsatisfactory results already
seen. Those who survived infancy had only dim prospects for adulthood. In
fifteenth-century Florence, death rates ranged from about 25 percent to 60
percent—a wave of child death that seems only mild when compared with
the 90 percent sometimes reached in the foundling homes of eighteenth-
century Paris, London, and St. Petersburg.

If poor women sometimes abandoned their children to the hospital and
wealthy women abandoned them to the wet nurse, where is the happy unit
of mother and child with which this portrait of Renaissance woman opened?
The pain of childbirth, the despair of child death, the stress of poverty, the
insecurity of wealth, and the ferocity of the law engulfed them both.

WIFE AND HUSBAND

Just as the happy dyad of mother and child had a tragic underside, so did the
amiable pair of husband and wife. Marriage was the product of calculation,
for the institution served above all as a mechanism for the production, preservation, and transmission of property. The vehicle of the transfer of property
from old to new family units was the woman.

In many towns of Flanders and in a handful of other locations women
could inherit property (and valued rights such as guild membership) just as
men did. Here the propertied woman was an attraction for the would-be
husband. More commonly, women were excluded, by primogeniture, by entail, or by custom, from the inheritance of property. But a woman had secure
title to her dowry, which enabled her to marry—a high dowry to marry well,
and thus enjoy a certain status (because of her husband's enhanced financial
position) for the duration of her marriage. The granting of the dowry thus
freed the father from further economic obligation for the welfare of his
daughter, a feature particularly attractive to the poor man. Now he could
tend to his sons. For the wealthy, however, the purpose of the dowry was
more to transfer property from man to man than it was to provide security
for the woman who in name possessed it.

A woman given in marriage could secure for her father's line, if her dowry
could attract a wealthy mate, an ample inheritance for his descendants. The
connection purchased by the dowry insured the well-being of grandsons who
would identify, however, with their father's lineage. The same dowry that
benefited a father's descendants provided for the new husband's line a temporary source of income-producing wealth. Husbands, on the whole, were
the chief beneficiaries of the lump sums settled on the daughters of the elite

classes. Fathers of females strove to pay out as little as possible for their daughters' dowries, while fathers of males attempted to attract as much as possible for the marriage of their sons. The fifteenth-century Leon Battista Alberti urged that the dowry should be, even if modest, concrete and immediately payable to the husband. The Donato family in Venice managed over two centuries to net 123,177 ducats, the profitable difference between their dowry income and their dowry outflow.

The woman herself inherited nothing but the title to the wealth that custom obligated her father or his surrogate to provide. Rarely was she able to use it herself. The sum (substantial enough to burden estates and to discourage the marriage of all daughters) was defined immediately prior to marriage, and it passed forthwith into the husband's control. It became unequivocally the woman's again only if both her father and her husband happened to die. It was hers to dispose of at her own death, and it passed, increasingly by testament, to her own children or other relatives (and disproportionately, at least in Italy, to daughters). If a husband's use of dower funds was irresponsible, some women could sue for the restitution of their dowries. But some women lost the capital to which they presumably had rights, due to the improvidence of their husbands. The Florentine Giovanni Morelli described in 1403 the case of his too pliable sister Sandra, who had been persuaded by her husband Jacopo to sign over some farms to him. Jacopo was ruined, and at the time Morelli wrote, Sandra was a young widow with a twelve-year-old son and no dowry, a dependent in her brother's household.

The dowry was, then, the cement of marriage, binding partners who were chosen (often by parents) with material goals in mind. Both parties were expected to comply. Alberti, for whom the need to perpetuate a lineage weighed equally with property considerations in the arrangement of a marriage, urged the use of harsh measures for the child who resisted not merely the father's choice (he was to offer a range of suitable spouses), but marriage altogether. By a certain age—Alberti suggests twenty-five—the father should threaten disinheritance. The logic was compelling: the purpose of the inheritance, after all, was not the amusement of the son, but the continuation of the line. Alberti boasted that his family had been rich for two hundred years, a long history in his volatile city, and indeed his was the only family among the Florentines that succeeded in passing on a great fortune to a third generation.

Some women of the elite classes, particularly in England, also resisted the pattern of calculated parental choice in marriage (as some Italian men apparently did). Margery Paston, the daughter of English gentry, refused her parents' choice of a husband, for which she was confined for months and beaten repeatedly. When she married the steward of her family's property, she was barred forever from the presence of her parents—who nevertheless continued to employ her husband. And Frances Coke (daughter of the famous jurist Sir Edward Coke) fled after being forced into a marriage in 1617 with the wholly incompetent John Villiers, brother of the English royal favorite, George, Duke of Buckingham. Abandoning marriage for adultery, she was ostracized: independent, but at a fierce price. These examples of resistance are, however, unusual. Time after time, dutiful children, impelled by parental force and the economic logic of matrimony, swore to remain faithful to each other.

Marriage was presumably forever in the premodern era, but there remained grounds for separation or annulment in unusual cases. These included consanguinity, adultery (the woman's, not the man's), impotence, leprosy, and apostasy. In rare cases, a husband's extreme brutality could give cause for legal separation. Some Protestant theorists (Luther himself, Martin Bucer, and most vociferously, on the verge of the modern era, the English poet John Milton) argued for greater divorce rights. Still, even in Protestant countries, marriages were more frequently ended by the nonlegal recourse of desertion (a male prerogative). In the English city of Norwich in 1570, more than 8 percent of all women aged 31 to 40 were deserted wives. In the upper classes women could leave an adulterous husband and insist on support: the wife of the Earl of Sussex won her case and was provided with 1,700 pounds per year in the late sixteenth century.

When divorce, separation, or desertion did not end marriages, death did, and more promptly than in our era. Life expectancy was low, and marriages frequently ended before the woman passed beyond the age of childbearing. Rare was the marriage in which the couple found communion together following the maturity of their children. Marriage was a transitory nucleation between the age of economic sufficiency (the late twenties for men, a little sooner for women in most of Europe and in most classes) and early death. Remarriage was common following the death of a spouse, so that the household can be seen as a constantly shifting constellation of children of different fathers or mothers competing for rights and privileges. A remarried woman could be made to renounce claims (beyond her dowry) to her husband's property—and even to her children. But a widow could remain in her deceased husband's house as long as she lived "chastely" and the children were present. In Venice, a bed and a little stove were always kept ready in a noble household for the return of a daughter whose marriage had ended and who was no longer comfortable in her husband's home.

Some marriages, however mercenary their origin, were more like the romantic pairings of our twentieth-century imagination, and were companionate and mature. Those couples who enjoyed friendly relations in marriage were the successful realization of a premodern (as well as modern) ideal among Catholics and Protestants alike. In the confessional manuals of the late Middle Ages, the sermons of the Reformation, and the handbooks of the humanists, the ideal of mutual love and obligation is voiced. Fra Cherubino, in his late fifteenth-century *Regola della vita matrimoniale*, urged genuine affection and insisted that the couple reside together, comfort each other, and guard each other from sin. Cherubino's countryman, the patrician Barbaro, wrote that a wife must love her husband, console him, and inspire him. The conjugal relationship should be a model of "perfect friendship," where intimate concerns are shared and the burdens of both partners lightened. In the service of this ideal, Barbaro minimizes the requirement of beauty in a wife (and wealth, too, but he is speaking about a class of bridegroom of superabundant wealth), stressing good character and good parentage. Alberti, similarly, weighs character and family above all, and notes as a secondary goal of marriage (the first being to perpetuate the man in his children) reliable companionship. The German polymath Heinrich Cornelius Agrippa von Nettesheim went further in his *De nobilitate et praecellentia foeminei sexus declamatio* (1509): if marriages were based on love and companionship rather than money and interest, he claimed, it would put an end to adultery and divorce.

If Catholic and Protestant advisers urged a companionable relationship among spouses, they also urged a patriarchal one. Thus they posed an impossibility: that mutual love prevail, and that masculine authority be absolute. The patriarchal conception of marriage whereby the woman was subject to her husband's authority was a pattern that deepened during the Renaissance centuries. Barbaro advised that a wife must love her husband, but she must also obey him: nothing greater than obedience, in fact, could be demanded of a wife. The Englishmen William Whately's *The Bride Bush* (1617) presents the same recommendation: a woman should tell herself that her husband is her better and her ruler. John Calvin saw the subjection of the wife to the husband as the pattern of their mutual subjection to God himself. Wives whose behavior was felt to be absolutely incorrigible could be beaten. Fra Cherubino urges this remedy only if all kindness and persuasion had failed, when the errant wife should be beaten soundly, not in rage, but in love, for the sake of her soul. Some Protestant leaders warned against such a practice, and in Calvinist Geneva wife beaters were reported to the Consistory. In Protestant England, however, the custom flourished until quite recent times. The English expression "rule of thumb" refers to the traditional rule of law that a wife could be beaten with a stick no greater than a thumb's diameter.

The literature that outlined the ideal marriage also defined, both explicitly and exhaustively, the limited range of sexual behavior proper in marriage—the only sexual activity considered tolerable at all. Its first aim was procreation. The learned chorused: sexual relations in marriage were for the sake of conceiving children—who might be saved and, as Fra Cherubino put it, fill empty seats in heaven. A second purpose of sexual activity in marriage, grudgingly accepted, was to prevent adultery. If the "conjugal debt" were paid promptly on request by male or female, the impassioned spouse would not be tempted to stray. For either purpose, the sexual act itself was to follow certain norms: it was to occur in a proper place, at a proper time, with the proper organs (in debito vase), and in the proper way (in debito modo); at all costs, not bestialiter. All other sexual activity was lewd and prohibited. Even proper marital activity, if too impassioned, was sinful. The Chevalier de la Tour-Landry (1371) urged his daughters, for the sake of marital chastity, to abstain three days a week—at least on Friday, and profitably on Saturday as well out of reverence for the virginal Mary.

If from the confessional, pulpit, and scholar's library male advisers peered at the marriage relations and sexual activities of Renaissance men and women, physicians issued prescriptions about health. Up to the threshold of modernity, most European women were tended to, in obstetrical and gynecological matters, by midwives or female doctors. Modesty required it, and professionalized male physicians stood aside. In Naples in 1321, Francesca, the wife of Matteo di Romana of Salerno, was licensed by the Royal Court to practice medicine (although of course she had not been university-trained) after promising to abide by the traditions of the profession. The permission was granted because it was considered better for women than men to attend women patients. Of the training and effectiveness of this medical personnel we have much to learn. Many were women practicing in the public arena what others practiced at home (and still do today): the application of home remedies, herbs and teas, warmth, and prayer.

The extension of male expertise to women's bodies began in the Renaissance centuries. Laws were promulgated in cities and states to restrict more sharply the practice of medicine by those without proper training—a category that included all women. In 1485, King Charles VIII of France withdrew the right of women to practice as "surgeons" (medical providers trained through practical apprenticeships). In Italy, such fifteenth-century academic physicians as Giovanni Michele Savonarola and Antonio Guainerio began to write authoritatively about gynecological issues. Using midwives as agents, or sometimes even acting himself, Guainerio urged aggressive, often painful and disabling (though generally nonsurgical) treatment of female illnesses. The German physician Eucharius Rösslin published a guide for midwives, the

Rosengarten (1513), which, while assuming that women practitioners would actually attend births, provided the latest male professional guidance.

As subject to the will of others in the management of her own body as she was in her social relations, it is evident that a woman's identity faded to anonymity within the marriage bond. Legally and economically subject to her husband and hemmed in by the strictures of male divines and experts, many a Renaissance woman of the elite classes found, perhaps, a sole area of freedom in her power to dispose of her dowry, a means by which she could help construct a future for her children, the parallel in the economic world of the primary creativity of birth.

WOMEN'S WORK

A twofold punishment devolved upon Eve, cast out of Eden, and all her daughters: the condemnation to ceaseless toil and to painful childbirth. Indeed, in joy or in torment, in all of history it has been woman's lot not only to bear children but also to work.

Wives and daughters in all but the loftiest upper classes worked about the household. In the country, they assisted in all farm tasks. They herded livestock, cared for poultry, and gathered eggs; they milked cows and carted pails; they planted and processed flax and hemp, which they washed, beat, spun, and wove to make shirts and table linens; they sheared sheep and spun and wove wool for cloaks and blankets; they tended the kitchen garden for herbs and vegetables, which they then cooked. Not excused from the heaviest fieldwork, women plowed, mowed, weeded, raked hay, and pitched dung; they sowed, harvested, and gleaned. Even aristocratic women engaged in farm work at the managerial level if their husbands were away at war, as they often were. In France in the spring and summer of 1689, the Countess of Rochefort inspected her crops, repaired the mill, accounted for 178 chickens and turkeys, supervised the carding of wool and the winding of silk, and tasted, stored, and sold wine.

City women, like their country counterparts, performed and supervised household work. In those families sufficiently well endowed to have furniture, linens, tableware, and food supplies to sort and store, women were responsible for such tasks. The seasoned merchant Giannozzo Alberti, for instance, an interlocutor in Leon Battista Alberti's *I libri della famiglia*, introduced the young wife he had recently married to her new role by touring the household. He showed her the proper places for grain, wine, wood, and tableware, which she was to manage; for his silver, tapestries, robes, and jewels, which he was to manage; and for his records and ledgers, which she was not to touch. The role in domestic management prescribed for women by Italian quattrocento authors also appears in Protestant advice books in the sixteenth and seventeenth centuries. A husband's duties were performed in the world beyond the house: to get goods, money, provisions, deal with many men, travel, converse, and dress for such occasions. A woman's duties were confined within the smaller circuit of household walls: to gather and save and arrange and rearrange and account for goods; to spend nothing, say nothing, and dress to be attractive to her husband.

In that same home to which they were confined, some women engaged in the kind of skilled, productive, and high-status work that yielded considerable self-esteem. The wives and widows of men involved in the production or trade of textiles were perhaps the most privileged women workers of the whole Renaissance milieu. In this family manufactory, they often supervised other workers as well—daughters, apprentices, journeymen—and so gained habits of authority. Occupied in the home, they could tend to other household needs and to the rearing of their children. In northern Europe, including France and England but particularly in the German and Flemish cities, they became guild members either by succeeding their deceased husbands or in their own right. Although theoretically barred by law from buying and selling goods or from lending, borrowing, or donating money without the approval of husband or guardian, many women in fact circumvented such regulations.

Tradeswomen with a great variety of skills abounded. In mid-fifteenth-century Strasbourg, women are listed in the following capacities: blacksmith, goldsmith, wagoner, grain dealer, gardener, tailor, cooper. In Paris, female silk spinsters were permitted to supervise apprentices (although the nature and number of these employees was strictly limited). Husband-and-wife teams of cotton and silk lacemakers could hire twice as many apprentices as the husband alone, but widows of glasscutters and gemworkers, themselves allowed to continue working at their husband's trade, were not permitted apprentices because the skill was thought too delicate and dangerous to be taught by a female. To prevent male unemployment, a Bristol (England) law of 1461 barred the hiring of wives, daughters, and other women in the weaving trade, but excepted wives already working alongside their husbands.

As long as the craftsman or trader was an individual whose place of business and place of residence were the same and whose own economic status was assured by his ties to guild structure or the urban patriciate, his wife or widow had access to public economic life. When in the latter two centuries of the Renaissance such conditions shifted in favor of larger economic units organized outside the home, women suffered. New legal restrictions were devised to prevent their owning or transferring property or benefiting from guild association. Middle-class women, moreover, could not leave their homes to go to the workplace. This was the unhappy destiny of poor day-workers. The former had to be content with lower-status work in the home, and the latter had to perform work that sank in prestige as it left the home workshop. Even as they continued working, women of all classes were forced into the condition of dependency and penury that has characterized most working women throughout history.

In Italy, women participated in textile production and guild organization as they did in the north, but only during the earlier years of the Renaissance. For instance, a Sienese statute of about 1300 concerning the wool merchants' guild forbade members to pay a spinster until work was completed, and ordered guild consuls to see that all weavers, "male and female," kept their combs well set. Even where women were admitted to guilds, restrictions abounded. In Florence, women could not gain entry to the greater guilds, such as the Arte di Calimala, but they did have equal access to the less prestigious Linaiuoli. Earlier than in Flanders, Germany, or France, however, women were excluded from those occupations. Restrictions beginning in the fifteenth century resulted in exclusion by the sixteenth. Women excluded from the urban textile crafts found a role in sericulture in the keeping of silkworms, the winding of raw silk thread, and the weaving of finished silk cloth, tasks performed in the farmhouse apart from the city economy. In the sixteenth and seventeenth centuries, these pursuits to some extent replaced the positions lost in the wool crafts of the fifteenth century. They were also pursuits less productive of self-esteem and wealth, however. Poor country women tending to sericulture can scarcely be compared to the substantial female partners and heirs of northern craftsmen in the textile industries.

Women who worked as part of a family unit, whether as household manager or tradeswoman, enjoyed a relatively high economic and social status. Women who worked adrift from their families enjoyed none of these benefits. These were the female day laborers, the dispossessed of Europe, who wandered about in search of work for miserable pay as servants and spinners and carters. In France, where most work was agricultural work, the largest category of working women was that of daughters of smallholders or agricultural day laborers, few of whom could afford to maintain their own families. Poverty's first victims among their children were daughters: boys inherited what there was to inherit; girls were disadvantaged. From early adolescence until the age of marriage, if they did not first fall prey to malnutrition or disease, these young women worked at a variety of jobs. If lucky, they worked on large peasant farms, acquiring the skills that would serve a peasant husband, or as servants in bourgeois and noble households. Otherwise, they streamed to towns to work for shopkeepers or craftsmen or larger textile manufactories. Wherever they worked, their wages were less than men's—perhaps half—because women's pay was never meant to support life, and barely did. This recompense they accounted for in little notebooks, accumulating a dowry with the narrow attention a miser gives to his heaps of gold. They learned a trade and hoarded their wages, hoping that years of underpaid labor would result in a combination of capital and skills that could purchase a husband. In Italy, it seems that poor women were even more restricted. Whereas in the towns of northern Europe women could work at crafts and in shops, as peddlers or market vendors, in Italy they were barred from such public pursuits. In southern Europe, the goal of protecting women's honor—in itself an economic concern, since successful marriage depended upon demonstrated chastity—required their isolation.

Rich or poor, women spun thread and wove cloth, descendants of Andromache, who supervised her handmaidens' work while Hector warred, and Penelope, who wove daily as she waited for the return of Odysseus. At one end of the ladder of social status and economic well-being, they were the guildswomen of Europe. At the other end, in home or shop, they were the uprooted, no longer protected by the family shell: the day laborer; the undowered daughter forced into dependency; the unmarried "spinster," whose English appellation derives from the craft that was her necessary occupation; the widow. Consider the last: the widowed mother of William Stout, an Englishman, lived with first one son then another, spinning until within four months of her death in 1716 at the age of eighty-four. As daughter, as wife, as widow, without thought of retirement, she had spun.

For some poor women, one alternative was prostitution, for this, too, is a form of women's work. Tolerated in the Middle Ages, prostitution was accepted and indeed institutionalized during the Renaissance period. Toulouse operated its own municipal brothel from the late fourteenth century. In Montpellier in southern France, a special section of the city, which they were not to leave and from which they could not be expelled, was designated for prostitutes. By the middle of the fifteenth century, royal protection was extended over such houses. By that date, authorized prostitution was the rule in most sections of Europe, and prostitutes themselves had acquired a certain status. Official indulgence towards prostitution faded in the following century. Protestantism and Counter-Reformation theory alike discouraged what was perceived as sexual immorality, and an upsurge in venereal disease and crime in the vicinity of the brothels reduced enthusiasm for these institutions.

Although institutionalized prostitution declined in much of Europe in the later Renaissance, the phenomenon flourished in the lush cities of Italy. Largely for this reason, the humanist Roger Ascham urged that innocent English boys not be exposed to the immoral customs of Italians, which he excoriated at length in his influential *Schoolmaster* (published posthumously in 1570). Protestants accused Rome of harboring prostitutes, sodomites, and pimps. Consider the accusations made against Pope Julius II by Erasmus (in the person of St. Peter barring the gates of Paradise) in the *Julius exclusus*. There was some substance to these protests. Nearly 12,000 prostitutes made up a robust fraction of the 100,000 residents of Venice in 1500. The common whores lived in the slums off the Rialto bridge. In splendid apartments lived the "honored courtesans," elegantly dressed, skilled poetesses and musicians who entertained gallant travelers and Venetian patricians, many of whom were unmarried out of patrimonial interest and especially reliant upon their presence. The 1570 *Catalogue of all the Principal and Most Honored Courtesans of Venice* (giving addresses, prices, and procurers) listed 215 of them. Two courtesans, Gaspara Stampa and Veronica Franco, were among Italy's leading women poets. Veronica Franco, whose own mother had introduced her to the profession, eventually retired (when nearly sixty) to found an asylum for poor prostitutes.

Curiously, the high-caste courtesan, with her luxurious apparel and apartments, her poetic skill, her literary coterie, her lute, and her lapdog, resembled the patrician's or nobleman's wife, who, increasingly over the Renaissance centuries, was distanced from the world of work. Facing vast hours of leisure, the elite wife engaged in the kind of repetitive and useless tasks (needlework and knitting, parties and visiting, card games and gossip) that could without appearance or taint of industry fill that vacuity. Her job was to reflect her husband's honor, dimmed if the work of her needle was for use or sale, enhanced if for decoration. As women lost their productive role in the European family, some critics would charge (as did the English authors Daniel Defoe and Mary Wollstonecraft) that they became a kind of legal prostitute. Meanwhile, for those of the comfortable classes, the dignity of work rescued women from the shame of concubinage, and for the poor, the burden of work approximated the slavery of which concubinage was but one face.

Daughter, Mother, Widow

The three persons of the female sex—virgin, woman, crone—are known to us from ancient myth. The triple-headed goddess haunts the womanhood of the Renaissance as well. In each stage of life, women posed different models for the men of the Renaissance. The wife-mother was the fruitful and productive guarantor of family wealth and honor. The widow-crone was a

worker, a dependent, a delinquent mother who abandoned the
children, the wealthy prize of a mercenary apprentice, or, worse,
enemy of society, the witch. The daughter-virgin could be a fear
a potential bidding chip in the negotiation of wealth, a creature w
gotten, or an asset in the spiritual quest. Dante wrote of the un
father who receives both a daughter and the burden of a dowry at   ...tn
of a girl (*Paradiso* 15:103–5). Genealogists of noble houses handled daughters cavalierly, informing us of the value they held in Renaissance society by
simply omitting 30 percent of females from the records that more amply
record male births.

Little valued in themselves, daughters were the link between male heads
of families. By them the lineage was preserved. Through them wealth, of
which they could touch not much more than what they could wear as silken
or jeweled ornament, was channeled. One asset was required of them for
these roles: chastity, assuring the legitimacy of heirs. The eighteenth-century
English sage Samuel Johnson, for whom the virginity of the Roman Catholics' Mary had no luster, explained in brief the significance of female chastity:
all the world's property depends upon it. Outside the family, the virginal
daughter was even more prized: as a professional religious, she was no threat
but an asset to the family welfare. In the early fifteenth century, Leonardo
Giustiniani urged Francesco Barbaro not to lament a daughter who had chosen the convent: she would be more productive at prayer than if she had
given bodily birth to heirs. The daughter-virgin chosen to fulfill what has
been seen as her physiologically determined mission—to bear children—was
destined to pass through the character of mother-wife to reach that of widow-
crone. Such was the fate of Eve. The daughter-virgin chosen to pursue a
different course had but one genuine option: to imitate the model of Mary,
virginal even in motherhood, unchanging in substance, immaculate into eter-
nity. The woman of the Renaissance who joined the community of the saints
instead of a husband's lineage was at once deprived of mature womanhood
and released from its confines.

MONACHATION

The men of medieval Christendom availed themselves of an institution for
the control of a surplus female population unknown to antiquity, to Asia, or
to Islam—the convent. Female religious communities spread alongside their
male counterparts from the early centuries of the Christian era. In time, the
population of these convents and the ranks of their superiors came to be
drawn from the upper classes, who could best claim the privilege of a humane
and useful asylum for their superfluous daughters. Patrician and noble

women bearing a dowry like the ones brought to a husband, but smaller, filled the convents of Europe. In Renaissance Italy, a large fraction of all women were nuns. In Florence, Venice, and Milan in the fifteenth century, some 13 percent of women were nuns. In 1552 in Florence, 15 to 16 percent of all women lived in convents (and that figure does not include Florentine women who lived in convents outside the city). Most cloistered women were patricians, and most unmarried patrician women were nuns. Whatever else it may have been, monachation, the process of placing women permanently in religious communities, was a means of controlling the outflow of family wealth. Many women resided unwillingly in convents (as in the moribund nunneries of sixteenth-century France and Germany, the preserve of the excess daughters of noble and bourgeois families), and many parents had left them there to be forgotten. An English father of the Protestant seventeenth century dispatched his unwanted daughters to continental nunneries. When they wrote begging for letters expressing interest and affection, he replied that in the absence of urgent matters he found an annual communication quite sufficient. Even mothers dispatched their offspring to conventual isolation with indifference. When her daughters Ippolita and Paola Gonzaga entered convents, Isabella d'Este expressed satisfaction: Jesus was likely to prove a docile son-in-law.

In Protestant lands after the later sixteenth century, the convent was no longer an option for the father of unwanted daughters. Indeed, the employment of the convent as a prisonhouse for unmarried women was particularly deplored by the founder of that movement, Martin Luther, who wrote that only one woman in thousands had a God-given aptitude for virginity. He himself married a former nun. More women appear to have married in Protestant England than in Italy, for instance. In the seventeenth century, in the classes below the elite, perhaps 10 percent of all mature women were spinsters. In the late sixteenth century, more than 95 percent of peers' daughters who survived to adulthood married, but by 1700 that figure dropped considerably, to 75 percent. Pressures for marriage were severe.

Although some women went willingly to the convent in search of the holy life, some were unwilling and resisted the conventual ideal imposed upon them for economic reasons. Placed at age eleven in the convent of Santa Chiara in Montepulciano by her widowed mother, Caterina di messer Vieri di Donatino d'Arezzo fled both the community and her vocation a few years later, hoping to marry. The humanist Coluccio Salutati, responding in 1399 to a letter from her, rebuked her for forsaking her childhood vow and warned her that the marriage she sought was worse than incest, lower than debauchery, as she was pledged to her true husband, Jesus. She married nonetheless, and in 1403 a papal order annulled her vow and permitted the legitimization of her children. A fortunate outcome, but many women remained in the condition of celibacy others had chosen for them.

Some unwilling nuns left written works to inform us of their views. Nuns made up a great fraction of educated women, and cloistered women were disproportionately literate. It was a commonplace of advice books that young girls should not be taught to read or write *unless* they were destined to be nuns. Finding in the convents the leisure to study and write, women composed works (for the most part outside the Latinate scholarly mainstream) largely in the vernacular, and necessarily devotional in type. Among these were the moral plays written for the many festivals of the church, which constituted a genre that was one of the few in which cloistered women could, however obliquely, express themselves.

One such play, the *Amor di virtù*, constitutes a protest against the conventual imprisonment of women. Written in the mid-sixteenth century by the Florentine nun Beatrice del Sera (1515–86) of the Dominican convent of San Niccolò in Prato, this play abounds with an imagery of rocks, walls, and towers by which women are confined against their wills. Women were not born for happiness, one player complains, but to be made prisoners, slaves, and subjects. The heroine is eventually saved from prison. Its author, in contrast, continuing to grieve for the freedom snatched from her at an early age, had to await an eternal reward for her patience. In the meantime, she could address the microcosmic world of her fellow prisoners, from which whispers reached the larger world of male culture without ever modifying its hostility.

The Venetian nun Arcangela Tarabotti addressed that male world directly, protesting against that city's government for encouraging the monachation of undowered girls. The girls were pawns, claimed her angry diatribe, *La semplicità ingannata* (published just before she died in 1652), in a conscious policy to prevent the impoverishment of noble families who would otherwise have to provide substantial dowries. When she wrote, there were perhaps three thousand women in Venetian convents, a peak for the era. By the next century the practice was in decline. The playwright Carlo Goldoni described in his memoirs the decision made concerning his niece and ward, who was being educated in a convent. When she described herself as being "in chains," he realized that convent life was not for her. She was released, and married instead.

The cases of women enclosed in religious communities unwillingly and hopelessly, poignant though they are, must not blind us to the reality that many women were enthusiastic nuns. The ideal of chastity was uniquely prized in Roman Catholic theology and eloquently championed from pulpits. It appealed to women for whom other socially valued goals were unavailable. They could not normally achieve great wealth or great power in their own right or develop the most esteemed craft or artistic or intellectual skills, but chastity, achieved by negation alone, was a summit for which they could strive. At the end of time, the crown of virginity would become a crown of joy as the 144,000 virgins gathered around the risen Christ. Accordingly, women denied their bodies in every way in order to gain the consummation of union with the divine. Self-denial, self-starvation, self-mutilation, and self-destruction became the paths by which many women hoped to gain an eminence that the secular world would not permit them. In chastity, a triumph of denial, women could find a fulfillment parallel to that of the esteemed wife-and-mother in secular society, and in marriage to Jesus they found a unification without carnal obligation (although with much carnal imagining at times) or risk.

Just as conventual women could perform the role of "bride" apart from the secular world and its dangers, they could engage in productive work without the economic and social threats that encumbered their secular sisters. They could care for the poor, the sick, the insane, the abandoned children. If they did not, who else would? What a rich bounty of self-esteem laboring nuns could harvest from the performance of these vital tasks! They could form schools and teach, transmitting to future generations the culture of their ancestors as surely and richly as biological mothers did when they talked to their babies. If their interests were intellectual (clearly many fell into this category), they could write devotional works or translate saints' lives from Latin into the vernacular for the benefit of less-cultivated companions, or even compose religious verse and drama. From the privileged security of the cloistered community they could write letters to the great and powerful, exhorting them to stricter obedience. A very few ruled over their communities as abbesses or prioresses, attaining the equivalent of male supervisory power as was nowhere else possible for them in their society.

Many women sought peace and dignity in the religious life. As a child, Cecilia Gonzaga, the daughter of the marquis of Mantua and a pupil of the humanist Vittorino da Feltre, yearned for the holy life. Having resisted her pleas at every turn and attempted to force her to marry for family convenience, her father conceded her wish by his testament. When he died in 1444, she entered the convent that her mother and companion had supported. Nearly a century earlier, Sancia, the wife of King Robert the Wise of Naples, had promoted the cause of the Spiritual Franciscans with lavish donations and spirited defiance of the pope. When King Robert died, his widow entered a house of the order of St. Clare in 1344. When she herself died a year later, her holy remains were without blemish or odor. Among the women who flourished in the religious orders of the Renaissance, the fourteenth-century St. Catherine of Siena reigns preeminent. Heroically self-denying and tireless (her published works appear in eleven volumes), she headed a large community (part of the Dominican third order), cared for the poor and the sick, helped plan a crusade against the Turks, campaigned to restore the schismatic papacy to Rome, and harangued political and church leaders to pry them out of the great blindness into which, she contended, they had fallen.

In the pursuit of their holy goals, the cloistered heroines of the Renaissance engaged in behaviors that are suspect in a secular and post-Freudian world. Their emotional lives tended to narcissism, anorexia, hysteria, and a heady Christ-eroticism. Hindsight suggests to us that these disorders (amounting in some cases to chronic mental illness) stemmed from the repression and coercion that typified the sexual and social lives of women in past centuries. Rudolph M. Bell and Donald Weinstein have shown that 42 percent of female saints had conflicts of some kind arising from sexual experience, compared to 19 percent of male saints.

A glance at individual cases confirms the impression given by such data. The fifteenth-century Italian Angela of Foligno stripped naked to offer herself to Christ and drank the water in which she had washed the feet of lepers. In the same country and century, Elena di Udine, who had been married for twenty-seven years to a member of the Cavalcanti family of Florence, resorted after her husband's death to a convent under the Augustinian order. There she engaged in severe penitential rituals, imitating the passion of Jesus by wearing a crown of iron barbs on her head and a thick noose around her neck as well as adopting the more usual practices of the hair shirt and flagellation. Married at age sixteen to a vicious husband, Catherine of Genoa managed to endure his brutalization after a conversion experience that enabled her to smother one kind of bodily pain with another. She engaged in extreme penitential practices within her own home, wearing a hair shirt, sleeping on thorns, fasting, and praying on bare knees for hours on end.

When ordinary women willingly entered the convent and remained in the conventual life, their experience was likely to be different from that of most men who chose a similar path. Women's orders were enclosed even when the corresponding male orders were not, and conventual women were placed under a hierarchy of male supervisors that limited their rights to govern themselves and to pursue their sacred and freely chosen mission. The Poor Clares, the Franciscan companion order founded by the saint of that name—who had hoped to work, like her brethren, within the noisy theater of urban society—were detached from the world soon after their founding. They lived sequestered and enclosed, tending only to those within their walls and teaching only children attached to their convent, even in urban locations.

Three centuries later, St. Angela Merici established a new order for non-cloistered women, an offshoot of the male Confraternity of Divine Love. Her goal was to involve women living in the world with charitable and educative work. The Ursulines were forced to accept the same reduction to enclosure as the Clarisses, however. Pope Paul V ruled in 1612 that the order be cloistered under the Augustinian rule. The English recusant Mary Ward, operating within the Jesuit order (and recognizing no male superior but the pope), attempted and briefly succeeded in establishing (from 1609) a European network of schools for girls, the Institute of the Blessed Virgin Mary, in which five hundred pupils were enrolled by 1631. Like Merici's venture, the women workers in Ward's order were to be unenclosed, but they, like the others, were thwarted by the official church. Ward's opponents appealed to the pope, complaining of her aggressive posture in spiritual matters. She in turn appealed to Pope Urban VIII in 1624. The order was suppressed in 1629, and when Ward resisted she herself was declared a heretic and schismatic.

OUTSIDE THE CLOISTER: PIETY, WITCHCRAFT, AND PROTESTANTISM

Women who for one reason or another were not in nunneries—because they were wives and mothers, because they were poor and could not afford to pay a conventual dowry, because they yearned for a different kind of religious experience—found opportunities to express religious faith outside the cloister. They joined the crowds that knelt for hours in the *piazze* to listen to such preachers as San Bernardino; they thronged behind Savonarola. They marched in the many processions launched to discourage plague or famine or to celebrate holy days. Within the framework of secular society, they pursued many of the same goals as the cloistered religious. The fourteenth-century English mystic Margery Kempe, a merchant's wife, first turned to God during the period of nervous breakdown she suffered following the birth of her first child. Subsequently she bore thirteen others, and she continued to provide dutifully for her husband's needs, tending him in illness and senility long after they had formally agreed to cease all sexual relations. Her relationships with the deity and the Christians she nurtured were infused with familial feeling. Her Lord exhorted her like her "wedded husband" and (at the same time) her "sweet son"; elsewhere he addressed her as "daughter." Jesus commended her for making every Christian man and woman the child of her soul and for having compassion for them as for her own children. So far are we from the cloister here that this woman, who shed tears for ordinary creatures like herself and devoted her life to them, modeled her relation to both her savior and her charges on the abundant family within which she lived her adult life.

During the same century the Beguines flourished in Belgium, the German Rhineland, and France. Beguine communities attracted poor urban women, offering them security, dignity, purpose, and work. They spun, wove, laundered, cared for the sick, and taught. Institutionally, they occupied a middle world. They were subject to the church but were not an official ecclesiastical body; they possessed no hierarchy and took no lifetime vows. The Beguines offered a unique possibility for great individualism. They also walked at the margin of orthodoxy, and many adherents were suspected of heresy. By the fifteenth century they were in decline. The impulse remained, however, to set up new systems for spiritual enrichment and education that rivaled the traditional institutions. The Sisters of the Common Life, protected by the Brethren and their founder, Gerhard Groote, had similar aims.

Less interested in charitable activity than in contemplation and communion with the divine, some women sought to pursue personal religious goals without formal conventualization. Elena Lucrezia Cornaro Piscopia had already progressed far in her astonishing career as a university scholar and professor (attaining the doctorate in 1678) when she became a Benedictine oblate—a secular, nonresident associate of that ancient order. A learned monk who had served as her spiritual director stood beside her deathbed, and he later directed her funeral, according to the wishes of the deceased, following the Benedictine ritual. This woman who had broken down one of the most obdurate of all the barriers that faced women in their advancement turned away (still young; she was thirty-eight when she died) from the trajectory of her own success to the protection of the religious life that had both comforted and confined so many of her predecessors.

Not merely outside the cloister but outside the accepted norms of religious life, female heretics and witches (according to their accusers) flourished in the Renaissance centuries. The late Middle Ages had been rife with heretical, marginally orthodox, and popular lay movements: Waldensians and Albigensians, Brethren of the Free Spirit, Beguines and Beghards, Lollards and Hussites. Among all these groups, some of which survived into the Renaissance but none of which outlived it, women played frequent and even prominent roles. They figured as well among the victims of inquisition and punishment. The great achievements of art and intellect that constitute the Renaissance did not prevent that age from dissolving into the fear of the unknown and persisting in the violent enforcement of orthodoxy. Indeed, it is in the Renaissance that intolerance reached its height in inquisitorial proceedings (especially in Spain) against lapsed Jewish and Muslim converts, and that fear reached its nadir in the witchcraft terror, most of whose victims were women. If no other indicator were considered at all, the brutalization of the female sex by the inquisitorial church would declare that the Renaissance was no renaissance for women.

Witchcraft was born in the Alps, flourished especially in central Europe in the sixteenth century, and rallied in a last frenzy in seventeenth-century New England before disappearing during the Enlightenment. From 70 to 90 percent of all persons accused and convicted as witches were female (and usually widows or spinsters, women without male protectors). The word *malefica*, it should be noted, is a feminine noun. Women were more prone to be witches, argued the experts Heinrich Krämer and Jakob Sprenger, authors of the witch-hunters' handbook, the *Malleus maleficarum*, because they are credulous, deceitful, frail, unintelligent, passionate, and carnal ("insatiable"). The learned Jean Bodin, historian, jurist, and political theorist, added greed as a seedbed of women's witchery, and he reported that there were fifty female witches for every male witch. Every means was used to prove that a suspected witch was a witch indeed. The accused were questioned. Some suspects confessed at this point, having come to believe (through illness, autosuggestion, or persuasion) that they were in fact guilty of demonic possession. Others did not confess and were tortured. If torture did not elicit confession, they were tortured again, and repeatedly, until they either confessed to witchcraft or made plain their "guilt" by their "obstinacy." They were executed in great numbers and with great pain.

From 1480 to 1700, more women were killed for witchcraft (usually by burning) than for all other crimes put together. Throughout Europe, perhaps 100,000 suspects were brought to trial (the number of the condemned is somewhat below this figure). The kingdom of England, where laws forbade torture, executed fewer than 1,000, but Scotland executed more than 4,000. Twenty-two villages in the territory of Trier burned 368 accused witches in the six years between 1587 and 1593, while in 1577, 400 accused witches were burned in the region of Toulouse. Cardinal Albizzi reported in 1631 from Germany that outside the walls of many towns he had witnessed "numerous" stakes and the binding and burning of many women.

Italian witches were few, but Italian women were suspected and sometimes convicted of other church-related crimes. Sicilian records from 1540 to 1572 show women as prominent offenders among the "crimes" pursued by the Inquisition: as Judaizers (50 percent, but the records for the area stop at 1549), bigamists (39 percent), and practitioners of illicit magic (29 percent).

From 1564 through 1740 in Naples, women constituted 34 percent of those examined for the crime of illicit magic. In the Friuli, women were targeted as practitioners of love magic, various spells, and "therapeutic" magic (here they outnumber men) in the period 1596 through 1685. Surprisingly, however, in a pattern more typical of northern Europe, they are present in overwhelming proportions among suspected witches: there are nearly five women to each male suspect for the period 1506–1610, and six for each male in the period 1611–70. All these figures combine to show that Italians were comparatively mild in the persecution of women in matters of orthodoxy.

In Protestantism, women with the skill and determination to pursue religious goals found new fields of freedom unknown to them in the old church. Protestantism invited each believer to deal directly with God and to find the means for doing so in Scripture. Consulting that wellspring, women readers found in both the Old and the New Testament inspiration for an enhanced female role in the quest of the spirit. They were invited into the churches to read and understand and, as part of the congregation, to sing (all ecclesiastical choral music to this time had been restricted to male voices). They were excluded, however, from theological discussion. It was acceptable that women could receive divine inspiration and share divine compassion; it was unacceptable that they should seek to define doctrine or guide the new institutions of the reformed churches. Men mounted the pulpit while women visited the sick. Catherine Zell, the wife of the former priest and new Lutheran Strasbourger, Matthäus Zell (who was excommunicated in 1527 for having married her), exemplifies the newly active Protestant woman who attempted to exceed the limitations placed on her sex within the new religion. She visited poor and rich alike, tending the sick and burying the dead, while other women adorned their houses and thought of parties. She welcomed Lutherans, Zwinglians, Schwenkfeldians, and Anabaptists to her house, as she defiantly wrote to Ludwig Rabus of Memmingen, an opponent of her ecumenism. The reform had brought freedom and not conformity. At her husband's funeral she spoke publicly, claiming no theological understanding but illustrating her points with scriptural examples.

Anne Hutchinson, an English immigrant to the newly founded Massachusetts Bay Colony, was made to discover the allowed limits of spirituality for women within Puritan Protestantism. She had come to Boston in 1634 expressly to pursue the reformed faith of the self-exiled Puritans, and she believed even more firmly than most in the Covenant of Grace extended by Jesus. So extreme was her theology of grace that she rejected any notion of the efficacy of works in the work of salvation, falling into the heresy of antinomianism. Had her heresy remained her private error, she might have avoided conflict with the community's ministerial fathers. Hutchinson, however, also taught her doctrine, sometimes to as many as sixty or eighty visitors at a time, male and female, in her own small parlor. Brought before the General Court, she defended the public role she had played, citing Scripture and faring well in the war of wits with her male clerical accusers. Only when she professed to having had a direct revelation from God, thereby claiming an extra-scriptural communication of religious truth, did her defense collapse. She was exiled to Rhode Island, an asylum for other victims, male and female, of the defenders of orthodoxy.

Women of some dissenting groups claimed great privileges as a consequence of their special relationship to God. Anabaptists eliminated distinctions based on sex, and their priesthood included women. Quaker women, with the approval of their leaders, sought to preach and teach. Men and women had been created equally in the image of God, such women claimed, and though subjected to men as a result of the Fall, as a consequence of Christ's restoration women were once again raised to equality with men. The secular authorities did not agree. In 1653, two Quaker women who felt they were so gifted dared to preach publicly and, after being called before the mayor of Cambridge (England), they were sentenced and whipped.

Protestantism did not greatly appeal to Italians, male or female. Fewer than 4 percent of all suspected Protestants were female in any of the regions of Italy for which systematic records were kept in the sixteenth century. But to the extent that the reform movement existed in the home of the Church of Rome, it received direct impetus from sympathizing noblewomen. For example, the Duchess of Ferrara, Renata of France (born Renée, daughter and sidestepped successor of King Louis XII of that nation), defended the new faith without openly accepting it. She sheltered Italian believers and French exiles at her court in the 1530s. The poetess Vittoria Colonna, famous for her Neoplatonism and her relations with several learned men, was also attracted to the reform, but was dissuaded from association with it by Cardinal Pole. There were converts to the new faith, however (silenced after 1542, the date of the establishment of the Roman Inquisition). Some chose exile—Isabella Bresegna, for instance, who died in Switzerland, and Olimpia Morata, who died in Germany. Renée and Morata—the Frenchwoman denied by law a throne that was rightfully hers by blood and the Ferrarese scholar exiled to the home of her Lutheran husband—are testimony to the power of Protestantism to appeal to women from the privileged ranks of society.

Of the same bloodline as Renée was Marguerite d'Angoulême (after her marriage, de Navarre), sister of King Francis I of France. Educated alongside her brother, Marguerite was probably more cultured than he, but, like most women of royal or noble rank, was unable to assume the highest tasks available in her nation. Reflective and intelligent, she gathered around her the proto-humanists and proto-reformers of the early sixteenth century in Paris (Jacques Lefèvre d'Etaples, Guillaume Briçonnet, Guillaume Budé), extending her protection (sufficient power for such patronage was hers to exercise) to several potential victims of Catholic orthodoxy. Her daughter, the formidable Jeanne d'Albret, became a champion of the Huguenot cause, as did several noblewomen in France from the 1550s through the 1570s. Of royal blood, she was the mother of Henri de Navarre, later to become King Henry IV of France. Calvinists flourished in her region—Béarn and Navarre—which welcomed visitors from Geneva coming to further the cause throughout the country.

French women below the aristocracy who turned to Protestantism delighted in abusing the clergymen from whose authority the new doctrine released them. Jean Crespin's *Book of the Martyrs* shows Huguenot women disputing with bishops, friars, and theologians. Recruited largely from the artisan and professional classes, these women were not on the whole well educated, and those who could cite Scripture were a minority. Calvinism was well rooted in Lyons in the 1570s, when a large fraction of Protestant women could not write their names. Indeed, the city's most learned women remained faithful to the old religion—most notable among them, the poetess Louise Labé.

Women and the Churches: Freedom and Confinement

In western Christendom, the institutions of the church—Roman Catholic and eventually Protestant—provided a matrix within which women could live alongside the matrix of the family. To a certain extent, women found considerable freedom to express themselves within religious establishments. They wrote and spoke about their experiences, formulated ideas about religious dogma and organization, ran charitable and educational institutions, and gained positions of high visibility and power. On the other hand, religious institutions also reined in human vitality, and the weight of confinement fell disproportionately upon women. Many unwilling nuns were cloistered simply for the benefit of their brothers and sisters—how many there were we do not know, but they were numerous. Many women repressed their own appetites for sex, for food, and for love to a degree that today might be classed as "abnormal" as they redirected physiological urges and spiritual passions to the icons of the church. In many cases this too was entrapment. Many women fought both the church and the social order itself in unconventional and self-destructive activities. Others were innocent even of such resistance, and upon them severe punishments were visited. Women, like men, were martyred to Protestant and Catholic causes and underwent terrible tortures. The religious experience of women in the Renaissance centuries mirrors their conflicted role in that society.

HIGH CULTURE: WOMEN ARMED AND ENTHRONED

The civilization we admiringly call the Renaissance consists of the European high culture of the fourteenth through the seventeenth century. In this high culture of power, beauty, and ideas, only a very few men and even fewer women participated. A few women did gain fame for their exercise of power or patronage, for their learning, and for their writing or other skills. In achieving this fame, however, they encountered the deeply negative view of female capability held by authoritative male figures. Grudgingly they were granted respect by these censorious judges, who created a new model of female existence to define them, an alternate to those of Eve (woman in the family) and Mary (woman in the cloister): the sexless virago, a hybrid of virgin and crone, a dangerously competent female-man—the Amazon.

That model is most clearly seen in the women who sought to exercise military or political power, the ancient prerogatives of the other sex. Clothed in masculine armor, the virgin and mystic peasant woman, Joan of Arc, fought for her king in France to the astonishment and fear of her contemporaries. Here was a woman seizing power in the most direct manner. Honored by later ages, she was condemned in her own to die at the stake as a witch. Given the prevailing norms, it was a marvel that she acted as boldly as she did. Also given the prevailing norms (since her evident purity and piety were no protection), it was inevitable that she would suffer for seeking to perform a male role. In fact, noblewomen in the feudal era had often acted in lieu of their absent husbands in managing and defending a domain. New and striking in Joan of Arc's case was the self-motivation to act, not as a surrogate for a masculine power, but as a free agent. In Italy later in the same century, Caterina Sforza offered a more traditional but still boldly independent figure. Alongside her husband Girolamo Riario and after his assassination, she fiercely defended her family interests and the cities of Imola and Forlì, for which she was ready to sacrifice her six children. She commanded the defense of those strongholds, but in the end she was defeated, possibly raped, and brought captive to Rome by Cesare Borgia.

While these two women assumed military roles, they secured no power. Few women, even those of the most exalted noble and royal families, ever did so. Two major exceptions were the Italian-born Catherine de' Medici, as widow of Henry II, king of France (and as regent for his successors, Francis

II and Charles IX), and Elizabeth, daughter of the Tudor kings of England. Both forged a Renaissance identity for a female sovereign that expressed the ambiguity of their roles. Catherine adopted for herself the emblem of Artemisia, another woman of the armed-and-chaste-maiden type, known also, however, for her dutiful remembrance of her predeceased husband, Mausolus. Wielding this device, she could both act assertively and demonstrate piety to the male rulers between whom she served as a vehicle for the transmission of power. The more independent and bolder Elizabeth, a master builder of her public image, presented herself to her subjects in a variety of feminine identities—Astraea, Deborah, Diana. At the same time, to win support for the unprecedented phenomenon of a female monarch, in moments of crisis she projected androgynous images of her role (man-woman, queen-king, mother-son) and haughtily referred to herself as a "prince" with the body of a woman and the heart of a king. A complete dyad in herself, she took no husband. In and of herself, she insisted on her right to rule, and she was the only woman to hold sovereign power during the Renaissance.

Much of the culture of the late-sixteenth-century Tudor court revolved around this manlike virgin whose name still identifies the age as Elizabethan. Subtly, the poets, playwrights, and scholars of the age commented in their works on the prodigy among them. Foremost among them was William Shakespeare, whose androgynous comedic heroines provide versions of the monarch, sharp-witted and exalted beyond nature. These female characters (boys dressed as women who often dressed as boys to create beings of a thoroughly confused sexuality) charmed and entranced, like the queen herself. The Shakespearean genius also understood how deeply the phenomenon of a queen-king violated the natural order. In the seemingly light-hearted *A Midsummer Night's Dream* he speaks about the abnormality of a political order ruled by a woman when the Amazon queen, Hippolyta, a figure for Elizabeth, is in the end wedded to the lawful male wielder of power. Like Joan of Arc, Elizabeth was perceived (and perceived herself) as an Amazon, and deep in the consciousness of the age she dominated was the discomfiture caused by an armed maiden, a rational female, an emotional force not limited by natural order.

It was rare for a woman to inherit power as did these two queens. It required, in fact, the timely death of all power-eligible males. Most women in the ruling classes did not rule, but shared some of the prerogatives of sovereignty. In the vibrant artistic and intellectual climate of the Renaissance, particularly in Italy, this meant that they exercised the power of patronage. Women who did not rule or direct the forces of destruction with their armies could wield their authority and wealth to shape thought and culture.

Notable among such patronesses was Isabella d'Este, daughter of the rulers of Ferrara, sister of Beatrice, who was to play a similar but paler role in Milan, and of Alfonso, Ferrante, Ippolito, and Sigismondo, whom she was to rival in fame. Trained by Battista Guarini, the pedagogue son of the great humanist Guarino da Verona, she mastered Greek and Latin, the signs of serious scholarship, and she possessed such skills as lute-playing, dancing, and witty conversation. Married to Francesco Gonzaga, the duke of Mantua, she presided at that court over festivities and performances; artists, musicians, and scholars; libraries filled with elegant volumes; and a ducal palace filled with statues, boxes, clocks, marbles, lutes, dishes, gowns, and playing cards and decorated with paintings, jewels, and gold. Ariosto, Bernardo da Bibbiena, and Gian Giorgio Trissino were among those she favored. She studied maps and astrology and had frequent chats with the ducal librarian, Pellegrino Prisciano. Her studiolo and her grotta, brilliantly ornamented rooms in the ducal palace, were her glorious monuments. She designed the allegorical schemes for these and other projects, consulting with her humanist advisers. Ruling briefly when her husband was taken captive during the wars that shook Italy after its invasion by forces of France, Spain, and the Empire, she was repaid with anger for her bold assumption of authority. Her great ability was left to express itself in patronage.

Also dislodged from a brief tenure of sovereignty was the wealthy Venetian noblewoman Caterina Cornaro. Her city had compensated her for the rich island kingdom of Cyprus that she had inherited (and they had usurped) with a miniature kingdom at Asolo. In that court she reigned as queen over a coterie of *letterati*, not the least of them Pietro Bembo, who memorialized the activities over which she presided in his *Asolani*. Cornaro's court is reminiscent of the one in Urbino that Baldassare Castiglione described. There women—the duchess, Elisabetta Gonzaga, and her cousin and companion, Emilia Pia—guided and inspired the discussions of proper behavior for both sexes that make up *Il cortegiano*.

In Italy, where courts abounded as centers of wealth, artistic activity, and discourse, there were many opportunities for intelligent women to perform in the role of patroness. Elsewhere, in nearly every center where wealth and security were sufficient to sustain such activity, the consorts of rulers were patronesses of the arts and culture. Mention has already been made of Margaret of Navarre, sister of King Francis I of France, the author of the *Heptameron*, an original thinker herself, and patroness to a circle of learned men. Before her, Anne of Brittany, the queen of Charles VIII, had ordered Boccaccio's *De claris mulieribus* translated and had filled her court with educated women and discussions of platonic love. In Spain the formidable Isabella guided religious reform and intellectual life. In England, her daughter Catherine of Aragon, King Henry VIII's first discarded queen, supported the work of Erasmus, Juan Luis Vives, and Thomas Elyot. A generation earlier, the proto-figure of the royal patroness and learned woman in England was Margaret Beaufort, already noted as the mother of that country's first Tudor monarch. At the courts of Henry VII's predecessors, Edward IV and Richard III, she had surrounded herself with minstrels and learned men, supported the art of printing (then in its early stages), endowed professorships of divinity at Oxford and Cambridge (where she founded two colleges), supervised the education of her son and grandchildren, and herself translated from the Latin the devotional *The Mirror of Gold of the Sinful Soul*.

WOMEN'S EDUCATION

The women who exercised patronage of arts and letters in the Renaissance had been trained for their roles, and they possessed refined standards of taste. The education these women received was extraordinary. Poor women, like poor men, received no formal education whatsoever, although many men and some women were trained in certain crafts. Middle- and upper-class women were initiated into a particular female culture, however, by which they were taught to perform household functions, and they pursued a regimen stressing needlework and devotional literature, silence, and obedience. The goals of education for these women were twofold: first, to guide the young woman to develop those traits of character most suited to patriarchal marriages; second, to train her in those skills most useful in the domestic economy.

Juan Luis Vives's *De institutione foeminae christianae* (1529), which circulated in forty editions and was translated into Spanish, English, Dutch, French, German, and Italian, became the leading sixteenth-century work on the education of women, and it epitomizes the advice offered on the subject. No defects in women's minds stood in the way of their achieving wisdom, Vives found. At the same time, they had to be carefully guarded from improprieties, for the main aim of their education was honesty and chastity. This paradoxical advice, typifying the male humanist position on the issue of female education, insists that women should be taught but warns that they should not be taught too much. Scripture, good manners, and simple moral tenets were appropriate; science, philosophy, and rhetoric were not. Prayer, reading, and work could fend off idleness, but women could not have a secular goal beyond this. These activities should occupy a girl at home, and she should leave home for no destination other than church. Women were forbidden to break out of the private sphere of the home and into the outer space where in economic and social life, in political and intellectual life, men prevailed. Women were reserved the regime of chastity, decorum, obedience, and silence.

Their personalities rendered desirably flat by this training in negative affect, women were meant to be busy and productive household members. Their work as organizers of the household and as textile workers has already been seen. Training in needlework and spinning accordingly played a conspicuous role in their education. In the fourteenth century, the *Libri di buoni costumi* of a Florentine, Paolo da Certaldo, urged householders to keep a close eye on the females in their houses, making sure they always had work to do to prevent idleness—which was perilous to all, but especially to women. Daughters were to be trained to sew, not to read (reading was suitable only for future nuns), and to bake bread, clean chickens, make beds, weave, embroider, and mend hose. Thus they were prepared for their future roles as wives. According to Alberti, the young wife was prepared properly for marriage by the mother who had taught her to spin and to sew. Learning in women engendered lax housekeeping and marital discord, according to Agrippa d'Aubigné, a French Calvinist, who disapproved of his daughters' quest for an education comparable to their brothers'. In 1683, his compatriot Fénelon urged that (rich) men teach their daughters to read and write, but he did not find it necessary for them to learn Latin as boys did, as they would have no need of it. Writing in the same milieu thirty years later, Madame de Maintenon advised that middle-class students be provided with middle-class information: how to run the household, how to behave with husband, children, and servants, how to cultivate the virtues appropriate to that class, and by no means to consider the enrichment of their minds. In England as late as 1753, the unconventional Lady Mary Wortley Montagu, in a letter advising her daughter on the education of her granddaughter, added to a sound academic curriculum the injunction to learn to sew. It was as important for a woman to be able to use a needle as for a man to use a sword.

So prevalent was the notion that the heart of a woman's education consisted of textile crafts that needles and spindles and such served a new generation of intellectually independent women as emblems of their subjugation. Thus the humanist (and Protestant convert) Olimpia Morata wrote that she had dropped the symbols of her sex: yarn, shuttle, basket, thread. One sixteenth-century French poet, Louise Labé, urged women to raise their thoughts above their distaffs and spindles, while another, Catherine des Roches, expressing more ambivalence, promised her spindle she would love it forever and hold it in one hand while she wielded her pen in the other.

While most women of the elite classes received a traditional education consisting of a combination of character training and needlecraft, some girls went to school. Giovanni Villani reports that in Florence in 1338, eight to ten thousand boys and girls learned to read in elementary schools. Subsequently, the boys alone proceeded to schools that taught calculation, required for business, or logic and Latin, required for university training. Earlier in the same city, a *doctrix puerorum* named Clementia taught Latin. In London in 1390, the orphan daughter of a candle-maker attended an elementary school from age eight to thirteen. In the same city, the Merchant Taylor's School was established in 1561, and it provided elementary education for girls. Other "dame schools" in England were established to teach reading, religion, and the arts of spinning and weaving. Beguine schools gathered boys and girls together in some cities of northern Europe. The town ordinances of Ypres in 1535 providing for the protection of orphaned and abandoned children called for the training of girls in the usual household skills but also, for the able, in reading and writing. In Flanders, Vives offered concrete proposals for the education of poor boys and girls alike. In Lyons from the 1490s to the 1560s, there were five schoolmistresses to 87 schoolmasters (who could teach boys only). Still, in a patchwork of "little" schools, nunnery schools, municipal schools, and neighborhood schools with schoolmistresses and governesses, a few girls of even the lower-middle and working classes began to learn to read, write, and figure.

The Counter-Reformation spurred some educational ventures for women designed to insulate them from the evils of humanism, laxity, and Protestantism. In Brescia, Angela Merici launched a program of Christian education that spread throughout northern Italy to Belgium, France, the Netherlands, and Catholic Germany, and that continued to have great influence into the seventeenth century. As it developed, its emerging goal was not to train professional religious but sound mothers. In some locations, the education was elementary only, with minimal instruction in reading and writing. In some aristocratic Ursuline boarding schools, however, girls received a secondary education including Latin, Italian, geography, composition, and—always—religious training. Other Counter-Reformation schools followed a similar pattern—those established in the seventeenth century by Mary Ward, for instance, and by the Jansenists at Port-Royal under the leadership of Jacqueline Pascal (the philosopher's sister). There all students learned to read, and they read only holy books.

Perhaps the strongest force for women's elementary education lay in Protestantism. If all believers were to make their own peace with God, it was argued, and since God spoke in Scripture, then all must learn to read. Luther had hoped that schools for girls would be established where Scripture might be read for an hour daily either in German or in Latin. In 1533, Elsa von

Kaunitz established such a school in the reformer's own town of Wittenberg. Philip Melanchthon, the executor of Luther's pedagogical program, ordered that schools be set up for girls (staffed by women teachers), which they would attend for one or two hours a day for one or two years. The reformer Martin Bucer also called for the establishment of public schools in all parishes, where girls as well as boys might be taught to read. By the end of the sixteenth century, princely or municipal decrees had established schools for girls in Hamburg, Lübeck, Bremen, Pomerania, Schleswig-Holstein, and Württemberg. The impulse for women's education remained strong in the German states well into the seventeenth and later centuries, but initially the goals were limited. Girls were to be instructed so that their religious duties would be fulfilled, not to attain a general education. Minimally instructed, they returned to their homes and to their spinning. By such advances, at the threshold of the contemporary era women would eventually reach the average level of education of most men. In England at the end of the period that interests us here, one woman to every four men would be literate; in London, five women to every seven men.

A few women began during the Renaissance to strive for a more profound cultivation of the mind than was offered by traditional modes of education or the newer elementary schools. These women turned to the finest curriculum available to men of the day, the one forged by the quattrocento humanists. In the fifteenth century in Italy and in the sixteenth elsewhere in western Europe, that prodigy of Renaissance culture, the learned woman, emerged from this group. Even before the century opened, Maddalena Scrovegni of Padua was admired for her learning (and her chastity) by the Veronese humanist Antonio Loschi. Within a generation, Leonardo Bruni outlined a serious classical curriculum for Battista Montefeltro. These women were the forerunners of a group of women humanists who possessed a genuine Latin erudition (Greek, too, in Scala's case) and were productive in a number of genres. We have letters, poems, orations, and treatises by Isotta Nogarola, Laura Cereta, Cassandra Fedele, Alessandra Scala, and Olimpia Morata (who belongs to the early sixteenth century) that reveal their ability to stand at the side of the humanists of the day. The last four were trained by their fathers, who were professionals, patricians, or both; Nogarola was trained by a professional humanist of the Guarinian school under the supervision of her widowed mother. Aside from the honeyed words of a few humanist admirers, they encountered the massed opposition of the male intellectual community, which seemed to find a little learning in a woman proper and too much masculinizing and abhorrent. These women's anxieties, frustration, and dissatisfaction with the structure of opportunity available to women intrude on their works—conspicuously, in the cases of Nogarola and Cereta. They set a high standard for female academic achievement that was only in rare cases equaled before the modern era.

The Italian phenomenon of the learned woman was to some extent repeated in other settings. She was found in German cities: the patrician nun, Caritas Pirckheimer, for example, forbidden to publish by ecclesiastical authorities, left a collection of private letters. In France, she is found most notably in the person of the Italian-born Christine de Pisan, of whom more later. Christine, however, like the female humanists already named, had origins in the urban patriciate. In the kingdoms of France and England, the learned woman was more commonly of a different type, coming from the highest nobility and even from royalty. Margaret of Navarre, sister of the king, is a case in point. In England, with the exception of the daughters of St. Thomas More (of the gentry), whose learning shone in the early sixteenth century, the classically trained learned women were nearly all connected to the royal line. The Catholics Catherine of Aragon (raised in the court of Queen Isabella of Spain) and her daughter Mary Tudor (taught by Juan Luis Vives) were not without learning of a devotional sort. The Protestant Catherine Parr, Henry VIII's sixth and surviving queen, promoted female scholarship of the same pious mode, and she was herself one of only eight English women writers published between 1486 and 1548. Two figures of the following generation exceed their predecessors and were lustrous representatives of the humanist tradition: Jane Grey, granddaughter of Henry VII and martyr to her family's ambitions for the throne of England; and Elizabeth Tudor, Henry VIII's daughter and successor to that throne.

For Lady Jane Grey as for some of the Italian *erudite* considered, learning offered an opportunity for liberation from a confined existence. The humanist Roger Ascham reports a conversation with Lady Jane, found at her home studying Plato's *Phaedo* (in the Greek) while her kin were out hunting. Asked why she passed up such sport, she replied that Plato afforded her greater pleasure. The reason, Grey confided, was that when she engaged in any other activities, her stern and demanding parents corrected, criticized, or beat her. When she studied, she was free. Limited by her social position and brief life span, she was never able to pursue studies into maturity, but her discovery of liberation in speculative work is reminiscent of the experience of the great Italian humanists. Queen Elizabeth studied in her youth with Ascham, who wrote in 1550 that no learned woman surpassed her. Fluent in Latin, competent in Greek, she read history three hours a day, and she studied theology and philosophy and the other sciences that comprised the advanced curriculum of the day. Unlike her kinswoman Grey, Elizabeth survived to exercise the formidable talents that a man's education had honed.

The humanist education of women that peaked in Italy in the fifteenth century and elsewhere in the sixteenth had declined certainly by the seventeenth century among the upper classes everywhere. The new ideal for women of this category was nonintellectual. At best, young women were supposed to acquire certain "accomplishments" (drawing, dancing, foreign languages, musicianship) for the entertainment of family members and visitors and for the attraction of suitable husbands. Castiglione's *Cortegiano* had pointed the way to this alternate ideal when he required that women know letters, music, dancing, and painting and be capable of witty conversation. He replaced the traditional canon of women's education—spinning, sewing, silence, and chastity—with another as prejudicial to woman's image as a scholar or producer.

THE FEMALE VOICE, THE MALE RESPONSE

Silence was so much enjoined upon women that it is remarkable that they spoke at all. But their voices rise from the near-silence of the Middle Ages to a quiet roar in the seventeenth century. By the end of that century in England, almost 2 percent of all published works had been written by women. During the Renaissance centuries, women always constituted a minority of those who addressed the public with written words, but they were a minority that claimed attention. Lifting their voices, women called to that public to reconsider its evaluation of woman's role in the world.

One of the earliest and possibly the greatest author of this era was Christine de Pisan, born in Venice and widowed in Paris, where she lived by her pen in the early years of the fifteenth century. The author of many works—history, poetry, treatises, and letters—startling in their boldness and originality, she expressed herself most clearly in the *Cité des dames*. Here she describes a self-sufficient society of women leaders, doers, and learners. In the *Livre des trois vertus* (1405), she outlines an appropriate education for female royalty, the aristocracy of courts and countryside, the urban bourgeoisie and artisanate, and agricultural workers. She argues for the education of girls, whose understanding, if properly nurtured, was as sharp as that of boys. It was her own father who furthered her education and took great pleasure in her superior knowledge. Her mother tried to prevent her from such pursuits and urged her to keep at her spinning.

Christine's legacy of serious authorship and feminist argument was continued in the Italian female humanists Nogarola, Cereta, Fedele, Scala, and

Morata, who flourished during the century following Christine's death. Committed scholars, their polished works contain an urgent message as well. Nogarola's assertion of the innocence of Eve, the primal mother, and Cereta's attacks on self-indulgent and purposeless women as traitors to their sex are unforgettable and angry moments in the feminist tradition. In the sixteenth century, learned Italian women moved outside the humanist tradition but continued to treat themes important for their illumination of the female condition. Moderata Fonte's *Il merito delle donne* (composed before 1592) champions female independence through one interlocutor, the polymath Corinna, who would rather die than be subject to men. Lucrezia Marinelli, also from Venice, wrote an immensely popular *La nobiltà et l'eccellenza delle donne* (1600) that argued women's actual superiority to men. A third Venetian, the unwilling nun Arcangela Tarabotti, argued women's essential freedom in her attack on female conventualization, *La semplicità ingannata*.

There were important voices among sixteenth-century poetesses (writing still in Latin but more often in the vernacular) who reflected on their strivings and their loves and illuminated the inner life of women. Among the greatest of them were Vittoria Colonna, Gaspara Stampa, and Veronica Franco in Italy and Louise Labé in France. Franco and Labé, respectively a courtesan and a rope-maker's daughter, openly defied the twin conventions of female chastity and female silence. Direct, beautiful, and bold women, their descriptions of their social and sexual stances are their central message. Both owed the possibility of freedom in their work to the complex, fluid, and pulsating urban context in which they existed and to the fact that their own social identities lay where the interstices between classes were usually drawn. So much for opportunity. These women were also limited by their unique social position. Seeking to pursue their ambitions, they were dependent on male admiration, male attention, and male audiences. Rebels against sexual propriety, they were in the end—ironically—just as dependent on men of high social position as if they had never left the drawing room.

In contrast to these bold seekers, other women vernacular authors of the sixteenth and seventeenth centuries continued to work in the genres that have already received comment in this chapter. Their work revolved around the two poles of family and God. They wrote about, for, and to their children. They wrote to, for, and about God. Beginning with Dhuoda, a ninth-century Frank, for the first genre, and the second-century African, Perpetua, for the second, these are the main genres in which the few women who wrote usually did so. In the seventeenth century, however, some pioneering women would expand the range of female expression to include history and autobiography, genres that until then had been a male preserve (Christine de Pisan is an exception). Especially in England during the period of the Civil War, when chaos permitted independence, women recorded their experiences and left valuable testimony about contemporary events. Even here, however, the traditional habits of female authorship creep in. They may have written in new genres, but they wrote only, or principally, for or about their families.

Thus the genres in which women expressed themselves expanded notably over the centuries, providing ever-increasing opportunities for the projection of the female voice. These centuries that saw the deterioration of women's legal and economic status, the victimization of women by witch-hunters and inquisitions, and the bolting of the door, leaving women at home while men explored and conquered, also heard the voice of protest. These protestors were not merely learned as men were; they dared to speak boldly as men did. To some extent they understood the nature and the consequences of their militancy as much as if they had borne arms. The nun Beatrice del Sera drew a parallel between the sword and the pen (much as others had oppposed the pen and the spindle): if some women had dared to take up arms and fight battles, then why should not others wage not war but peace with their pens? Possibly it is the militancy of some such female wielders of the pen that explains why the literature of the Renaissance bristles with armed and dangerous women. From Ariosto and Tasso to Spenser and Milton, they stalk the pages of the first two centuries of print.

Joan of Arcs, then, these women: armed with pens, invaders of an alien element, committed to a sacred task, admired by a few but hated by most of those whose preserve they challenged by their mere presence. Women whose ambitions or destinies pushed them to adopt an Amazonian role and to stride boldly into the male realms of culture and society took on the burden of confused or illegitimate sexuality. This was the case whether the stage on which they played was political, economic, or cultural. They were perceived or they perceived themselves as masculinized, as fierce, as grotesque. They escaped these labels and these self-perceptions only by the concomitant adoption of the strictest regulations applied to women in their social worlds: chastity, silence, and obedience.

Male authors responded to female aggression in the realm of culture. The long tradition of misogynist literature had already accumulated and was perpetuated in the Renaissance in the agonistic attack-and-defense known best under the French name of the *querelle des femmes*. Defenses of female excellence (by men or women) would provoke new attacks, which in turn would call forth new defenses. The degree to which this argument about the fundamental worth of the female penetrated literary discussion indicates just how profound was male uneasiness, not so much with women's presence as with women's claims for attention. The *querelle* raged in Latin and in the vernacular in Italy, France, England, and the German states and among Catholics, Protestants, and Jews. The original spark of the *querelle* was the attack on women in Jean de Meung's continuation of the *Roman de la Rose,* and it was enthusiastically affirmed in the commentary of Jean de Montreuil (1401). That work, sent directly to Christine de Pisan for her contemplation, in turn elicited a defense of women by that early feminist. A debate carried on by the circle of Parisian literati ensued, and it extended to the threshold of the modern era. The period 1595 to 1655 saw at least twenty-one works for and against women published in France. The "problem of women" was discussed in England in a series of works launched by the misogynistic *The Schole House of Women* (1541), culminating in the famous *Hic mulier* (1620), and fading only after 1639. The *Hic mulier* seems to contain the crystallized hatred of men for women who aspired to literary or public roles: that unsexed "Masculine-Feminine" should throw off her "deformities" and clothe herself properly in the purposes intended for her—chastity, silence, piety, obedience toward her husband, and nurture for her children.

While most men carried forward the age-old misogynist tradition, some men lent their support (in works mostly dedicated to prominent women) to the notion that women possessed valuable qualities. The poet and scholar Giovanni Boccaccio surely meant to praise women when he composed his influential *De claris mulieribus.* This parade of notable women from Old Testament through medieval times helped make all readers aware of a sex usually wholly forgotten in letters. He should not be blamed, perhaps, for the harm he unintentionally inflicted upon women. Most of the women he praised epitomized those traditional virtues of chastity, silence, and obedience. Their example in fact reinforced the misogynistic view. Those few he depicted who were active and productive in the public realm (such fearsome figures as Zenobia, Penthesilea, Camilla, and the like) had violated female sexual norms in some way, for which transgressions they were duly punished. Their example, however tantalizing to new generations of women who yearned to burst out of their chains, served the cause of female oppression.

Boccaccio launched a flood of works by male scholars on excellent women of the biblical, classical, and Christian past and in more recent local history, among them such authors as Filippo da Bergamo, Giulio Cesare Capaccio, Ludovico Domenichi, Jacopo Filippo Tomasini (who also published letters of Laura Cereta and Cassandra Fedele), and Bernardo Scardeone. In quattrocento Ferrara, ruled by Este lords but marked by their consorts as well, the humanist Bartolommeo Goggio wrote *De laudibus mulierum* for Eleanora of Aragon. The arch-humanist and proto-reformer Erasmus was a strong advocate of women's education. The distaff and spindle (those objects again) are useful for women, he argues, but studies, which occupy the whole soul, are more useful. In one of the *Colloquies*, a learned woman argues with an abbot, proponent and opponent, respectively, of female education.

The most remarkable defender of woman's right to study and to progress was the German polymath, Heinrich Cornelius Agrippa von Nettesheim. His *De nobilitate et praecellentia foeminei sexus declamatio* asserted the astonishing proposition that the only difference between male and female was anatomical. Created for the same end, women and men equally possess the gifts of spirit, reason, and words. Adam, not Eve, had been the greater sinner at the beginning of time (he agrees here with Isotta Nogarola), and thus Jesus chose to come as man, not woman, for the redemption of the race. In England, Sir Thomas Elyot was nearly as vigorous an advocate for women. Written not only for a female sovereign but about woman's right to rule, *The Defense of Good Women* (1540) ranked women with men among the rational creatures. The ancient queen Zenobia, one of those militant figures who appear among Boccaccio's heroines and those of his followers in the genre of the collective biography of "women worthies," comes forth here to urge education for women.

EVE, MARY, AND AMAZONS

With so many champions, why did women not triumph in the Renaissance centuries? Let us reduce the matter to its simplest elements. When men praised women *as women*, they praised them for qualities that they could retain only when confined in homes and cloisters, engaged in spinning or weaving or praying and, if literate (they were seen as having the ability to read and write), reading only holy books, writing only for themselves and their families. When men praised women's *accomplishments*, they mixed praise with a sour note: such able women were not really women. Boccaccio's highest commendation of a woman was to say that she was "manly"; Elizabeth's tutor, Ascham, could find no trace of a woman's nature in his pupil. Women could remain imprisoned or renounce their sex; they could choose the model of Eve, of Mary, or of Amazon.

Renaissance man has eight faces in the present book. Woman has three: Mary, Eve, and Amazon; virgin, mother, crone. The first two figures were caught in hopeless opposition as frozen poles of female possibility; the future lay with the third. From the Amazon, that brazen figure glimpsed everywhere in Renaissance civilization, modern woman was born. She bears the Amazon's burden of loneliness, and she has not yet wholly won her freedom.

That freedom may yet come in a renaissance for women, centuries after the Renaissance of men.

BIBLIOGRAPHY

Specialized studies of multiple facets of the lives of Renaissance women have mushroomed in the past twenty years, but no short list of synthetic works can be provided. The following paragraphs name a few of the kinds of sources a student might consult. Romeo De Maio's *Donna e Rinascimento* (Milan: Mondadori, 1987) provides one interpretative overview, in Italian, of woman's condition in the Renaissance; the present author's *Women of the Renaissance* (Chicago: University of Chicago Press, 1991), another. The two-volume work by Bonnie S. Anderson and Judith P. Zinsser, *A History of Their Own: Women in Europe from Prehistory to the Present* (2 vols.; New York: Harper & Row, 1988) examines the conditions of women in various settings—the farm, the city, the salon—from antiquity forward. Several chapters provide valuable material on Renaissance women. Studies of medieval women often reach into the early Renaissance centuries and should be consulted: among them, Frances Gies and Joseph Gies, *Women in the Middle Ages* (New York: Thomas Y. Crowell, 1978); Angela M. Lucas, *Women of the Middle Ages: Religion, Marriage, and Letters* (New York: St. Martin's Press, 1983); and Shulamith Shahar, *The Fourth Estate: A History of Women in the Middle Ages*, trans. Chaya Galvi (London and New York: Methuen, 1983).

Collections of essays on women in the Middle Ages or Renaissance abound, containing focused studies from several disciplines: notable among them are: Derek Baker, *Medieval Women: Dedicated and Presented to Professor Rosalind M. T. Hill* (Oxford: Basil Blackwell for the Ecclesiastical History Society, 1978); Mary Erler and Maryanne Kowaleski, eds., *Women and Power in the Middle Ages* (Athens, Ga., and London: University of Georgia Press, 1987); Margaret W. Ferguson, Maureen Quilligan, and Nancy J. Vickers, eds., *Rewriting the Renaissance: The Discourses of Sexual Difference in Early Modern Europe* (Chicago: University of Chicago Press, 1986); Julius Kirshner and Suzanne Wemple, eds., *Women of the Medieval World: Essays in Honor of John H. Mundy* (Oxford: Basil Blackwell, 1985); Carole Levin and Jeanie Watson, eds., *Ambiguous Realities: Women in the Middle Ages and Renaissance* (Detroit: Wayne State University Press, 1987); Mary Prior, ed., *Women in English Society, 1500–1800* (London and New York: Methuen, 1985); Mary Beth Rose, *Women in the Middle Ages and the Renaissance: Literary and Historical Perspectives* (Syracuse: Syracuse University Press, 1986). The two editions of *Becoming Visible: Women in European History*, ed. Renate Bridenthal and Claudia Koonz (1977) and Susan M. Stuard (2d ed., 1987; Boston: Houghton Mifflin) each include different essays on the period in question.

By one author alone are the essays of two master historians: Natalie Zemon Davis, *Society and Culture in Early Modern France* (Stanford, Calif.: Stanford University Press, 1979), and Eileen Power, *Medieval Women*, ed. M. M. Postan (Cambridge and New York: Cambridge University Press, 1975). *Women, History, and Theory: The Essays of Joan Kelly* (Chicago: University of Chicago Press, 1984) contains that author's classic statements on perceptions of Renaissance women. Julia O'Faolain and Lauro Martines have edited a valuable anthology of documents and texts, and Katharina M. Wilson one of women's works: respectively, *Not in God's Image: Women in History from the Greeks to the Victorians* (New York: Harper & Row, 1973) and *Women Writers of the Renaissance and Reformation* (Athens, Ga., and London: University of Georgia Press, 1987).

The family was the main sphere of women's activity, and it has been the subject of many recent works: Jean-Louis Flandrin, *Families in Former Times: Kinship, Household, and Sexuality in Early Modern France*, trans. Richard Southern (Cambridge: Cambridge University Press, 1975); David Herlihy, *Medieval Households* (Cambridge, Mass.: Harvard University Press, 1985); Christiane Klapisch-Zuber, *Women, Family, and Ritual in Renaissance Italy*, trans. Lydia G. Cochrane (Chicago: University of Chicago Press, 1985); Alan MacFarlane, *Marriage and Love in England: Modes of Reproduction, 1300–1840* (New York: Basil Blackwell, 1986); Michael Mitterauer and Reinhard Sieder, *The European Family: Patriarchy to Partnership from the Middle Ages to the Present*, trans. Karla Oosterveen and Manfred Hörzinger (Chicago: University of Chicago Press, 1982); Steven Ozment, *When Fathers Ruled: Family Life in Reformation Europe* (Cambridge, Mass., and London: Harvard University Press, 1983); and Lawrence Stone, *Family, Sex, and Marriage in England, 1500–1800* (London and New York: Weidenfeld & Nicolson, 1977). On women's work, directly related to women's familial role, see David Herlihy, *Opera muliebria: Women and Work in Medieval Europe* (New York: McGraw-Hill, 1990); Barbara Hanawalt, ed., *Women and Work in Pre-Industrial Europe* (Bloomington: Indiana University Press, 1986); Martha C. Howell, *Women, Production, and Patriarchy in Late Medieval Cities* (Chicago and London: University of Chicago Press, 1986); and Merry E. Wiesner, *Working Women in Renaissance Germany* (New Brunswick, N.J.: Rutgers University Press, 1986).

For women in the convents of Catholic Europe, reprints of the classic studies of Lina Eckenstein and Eileen Power are available: respectively, *Women under Monasticism: Chapters on Saint-Lore and Convent Life between* A.D. *500 and* A.D. *1500* (New York: Russell & Russell, 1963), and *Medieval English Nunneries* (New York: Biblio & Tannen, 1964). At least some of the works of the principal saints and mystics are readily available in modern editions and translations: Catherine of Siena, Bridget of Sweden, Margery Kempe, Julian of Norwich, Catherine of Genoa, Teresa of Avila; see also Elizabeth A. Petroff's anthology, *Medieval Women's Visionary Literature* (Oxford and New York: Oxford University Press, 1986). Roland Bainton's *Women of the Reformation* (Minneapolis: Augsburg Publishing House, 1971, 1973, 1977) presents three volumes of brief biographies of women involved in the Reformation. For England, see also Retha Warnicke's *Women of the English Renaissance and Reformation* (Westport, Conn., and London: Greenwood Press, 1983). A good synthesis of the mountainous literature on witchcraft is provided by Brian P. Levack in *The Witch Hunt in Early Modern Europe* (London and New York: Longman, 1987), and a fine selection of documents by Alan C. Kors and Edward Peters in *Witchcraft in Europe, 1100–1700: A Documentary History* (Philadelphia: University of Pennsylvania Press, 1972).

For women who bore arms and ruled states, such as the visionary Joan of Arc and the queens Elizabeth I of England, Catherine de Médicis of France, and Isabella of Spain, several biographies are available. For women known for their learning, see especially the collections edited by Jeanie R. Brink and Patricia H. Labalme: respectively, *Female Scholars: A Tradition of Learned Women before 1800* (Montreal: Eden Press Women's

Publications, 1980) and *Beyond Their Sex: Learned Women of the European Past* (New York: New York University, 1980). Margaret L. King and Albert Ravil provide an anthology of works in *Her Immaculate Hand: Selected Works by and about the Women Humanists of Quattrocento Italy* (Binghamton, N.Y.: MRTS, 1983). For Christine de Pizan, see in particular Charity Cannon Willard's *Christine de Pizan: Her Life and Works* (New York: Persea Books, 1984), and de Pizan's *Book of the City of Ladies*, trans. Earl Jeffrey Richards (New York: Persea, 1982) and *Treasure of the City of Ladies, or The Book of the Three Virtues*, trans. Sarah Lawson (Harmondsworth: Penguin, 1985). Ruth Kelso's classic on the education of women, *Doctrine for the Lady of the Renaissance* (Urbana: University of Illinois Press, 1956) may be supplemented by Phyllis Stock's *Better than Rubies: A History of Women's Education* (New York: G. P. Putnam, 1978). Male views of women are given general treatment by Vern L. Bullough, Ian MacLean, Susan M. Okin, and Katharine Rogers in, respectively, *The Subordinate Sex: A History of Attitudes towards Women* (Urbana: University of Illinois Press, 1973); *The Renaissance Notion of Women: A Study in the Fortunes of Scholasticism and Medical Science in European Intellectural Life* (Cambridge and New York: Cambridge University Press, 1980); *Women in Western Political Thought* (Princeton: Princeton University Press, 1979); and *The Troublesome Helpmate: A History of Misogyny in Literature* (Seattle: University of Washington Press, 1966).

N I N E
Voyagers and Natives
Tzvetan Todorov

*E*UROPEAN history—indeed, world history—at the end of the fifteenth century and the beginning of the sixteenth century gives the irresistible impression of extraordinarily swift change. A European who lived in 1490 probably had a fair idea of Europe and of the lands surrounding the Mediterranean. He might also have had some vague notions about the rest of Africa and about Asia, but they would not add up to a coherent whole. He might have told himself that doubtless the earth was round, but he would not have been sure of its size.

Everything changed during the next thirty years. In 1492, Christopher Columbus crossed the Atlantic and "discovered" the Antilles; in the following years, he reached the American mainland. In 1498, Vasco da Gama rounded the Cape of Good Hope and inaugurated the sea route to the Indies. In 1500, Pedro lvars Cabral stopped on the coast of Brazil. In 1519, Cortés landed in Mexico and launched the organized conquest of the continent. Finally, in 1522, Magellan's ships circled the world for the first time, after a voyage that had lasted three years. Never have any other thirty years changed the face of the globe as much.

To be precise, the change operated in two directions. On the one hand, the world grew larger, to an extent difficult to imagine. The process had already begun in the preceding years with the rediscovery of the Greek and Roman past—an extended memory that increased the duration of history (hence the time span of humanity) ten- or twentyfold. Now space had expanded as well as time. The Atlantic, the Pacific, and the Indian oceans came to join the Mediterranean, and Europe found itself compared with America, Africa, and Asia. Never had the world been so big, not only in comparison with people's previous idea of it but also because getting from one place to another took so long. Voyages now lasted years, not days (although their length would shorten constantly in the centuries to come).

On the other hand, however, the world began to seem finite, and its unification became imaginable. Before, people may not have gone as far, but the world remained largely unknown and could appear to be infinite. Of course, geographic "discoveries" continued until the nineteenth century, but henceforth they merely eliminated the blank spots in a map whose general outlines had been traced. As for unification of the world, Magellan's voyage was of course only a first timid step, but it enabled people to conceive of and imagine a unity that also grew steadily as communication accelerated.

Lettered Europeans learned the good news through narrations written by men who were either voyagers themselves or chroniclers who had remained home but had noted down oral relations of voyages. Paradoxically, the relations preceded the voyages. From the early Middle Ages, more or less fantastic travel reports met with popular favor and kept curiosity alive. We learn, for example, that the Irish monk, St. Brendan, took seven years to reach the Earthly Paradise after braving a variety of dangers and encountering all manner of supernatural beings. On his return from China, Marco Polo wrote his *Adventures*, which deserves its title even if it does not indulge in the supernatural. Somewhat later, John Mandeville wrote his *Voyage and Travels*, an inextricable tangle of real events and fabulous inventions. He too describes the Earthly Paradise. During the same period, a number of authors compiled inventories of all that was known of the lands and the peoples of the earth in works with such titles as *Cosmography* or *Image of the World*, the most famous of which was the *Imago Mundi* of Cardinal Pierre d'Ailly. These works were well known, and they prepared the way for the accounts of the new voyagers (who, incidentally, took them to be dependable information). Thus Columbus sailed with letters of introduction to the Great Khan, whom Marco Polo had described, and Vasco da Gama with letters to Prester John, a legendary ruler who, according to Mandeville, lived in the Indies.

Thus readers and listeners were not dumbfounded when the first reports of the new discoveries reached them, and we can imagine that the voyagers themselves, who had also read and listened to such relations, were no more thunderstruck. A second reason for this, aside from the popularity of older travel accounts, has to do with a characteristic trait of European history. Geographical conditions in the Mediterranean area assured contact between populations—European Christians, Moslem Moors and Turks, African animists—that differed widely, both physically and culturally. Europeans of the Renaissance became aware not only of geographical heterogeneity but also of their own historical heterogeneity, beginning to see themselves as the heirs of two quite separate traditions, the Greco-Roman and the Judeo-Christian. Furthermore, their Judeo-Christian heritage was not monolithic, since it presented the unique instance of one religion, Christianity, based on another, Judaism. In other words, Europeans had already experienced cultural plurality from their own past and their own present. They had, so to speak, an available category into which they could place newly discovered populations without totally upsetting their overall image of the world.

One place where we can see this clearly is in the course of the Spanish conquest of America. When the conquistadores came upon places of worship, they spontaneously called them "mosques." The mechanism soon caught on and the term began to be used for any temple serving a non-Christian religion. When the Spanish discovered a somewhat larger town, they immediately named it "el grande Cairo." One of the earliest of the Spanish chroniclers, Francisco de Aguilar, called upon his own experience in order to clarify his impressions of the Mexicans:

As a child and youth I began reading many histories and antiquities of the Persians, Greeks, and Romans. I have also read about the rites performed in Portuguese India. (*Chronicle*, trans. Fuentes, *The Conquistadors*, 163)

Contemporary illustrations also testify to the projection of the familiar (or the vaguely exotic) onto the unknown.

There were a great many voyagers and a great many relations of their travels—several hundred in each of the principal countries of Europe during the sixteenth century. Naturally, they differ widely. One reason for this lies in the diversity of the lands visited. Three main destinations emerge, the first of which was America, the strangest and the most "savage" land. In the opposite direction lay China, which was not easily open to foreigners at the time but whose inhabitants were certainly not savages. Finally, there was Turkey, the incarnation of the Moslem world, nearby yet enigmatic, hated and feared. It was Turkey that aroused the most interest, contrary to what we might imagine today.

Another reason for the diversity of travel accounts lay in the nature of the voyage. A conqueror, a missionary, a merchant, or a mere curiosity-seeker did not all see the same land. Whether the traveler left of his own free will or whether he was forced to follow the path of exile also made a difference. There was of course also variation in the personalities of the travelers and in the quality of their writings, thus in their depictions of the natives. Rather than attempt to describe all these travel narratives, I shall limit my remarks to a few representative examples of works that had a particularly large influence and to voyages to America.

CHRISTOPHER COLUMBUS

It is hardly surprising that the first and the most famous of the great voyagers of the epoch is not a perfect incarnation of the new spirit that was coming into being at the time. Christopher Columbus (1451–1506) prompted the change more than he illustrates it. From our point of view today, his figure was double, belonging to the past but announcing the future. The man who contributed so much to the birth of the modern world could hardly already have belonged to it.

The many motives that led Columbus to undertake his voyage are a first illustration of the ambivalence of his figure. His principal motivation had nothing modern about it: his voyage was a religious venture. This theme is somewhat concealed by the obsessively reiterated theme of gold, the symbol of wealth, a goal seemingly totally incompatible with religious aspirations. The incompatibility is only apparent, however. Columbus speaks of gold, promises to find it, and discovers signs of its presence, for this is what was demanded of him by his interlocutors, the sailors in his ships, the rich ship-owners who financed his expeditions, and their Most Catholic Majesties, Ferdinand and Isabella of Spain. He judged the situation correctly: when the newly discovered lands turned out not to contain great quantities of gold, Columbus fell into disgrace.

Columbus's great motivation was of a totally different sort. He wanted to spread the Christian religion throughout the world. He knew because he had read it in Marco Polo that the Great Khan—the emperor of China—wanted to convert to Christianity, and Columbus set off to find him by the "occidental route" in order to help him to carry out this wise resolution. Beyond this immediate project lay another and even more grandiose plan: Columbus dreamed of the reconquest of Jerusalem, and he hoped that his voyage would furnish the money needed to finance a new crusade. He speaks of the project in the journal of his first voyage. He writes that he hoped to find gold and spices

and those things in such quantity that the sovereigns, before three years [are over], will undertake and prepare to go conquer the Holy Sepulcher; for thus I urged Your Highnesses to spend all the profits of this my enterprise on the conquest of Jerusalem, and your Highnesses laughed. (*The Diario of Christopher Columbus's First Voyage to America . . .* , trans. Dunn and Kelley, 291)

Columbus recalled the project during his following voyages and even passed it on to his heirs, who were to use their inheritance to equip an army to conquer the Holy Sepulcher.

The project was anachronistic, to say the least. At the end of the fifteenth century no one else was thinking seriously of crusades, and the laughter of the Most Catholic rulers is understandable. Beside this religious motivation, however, we find another and totally different one that is closer to our own sentiments. Columbus was a lover of nature, and he seems to have found an intrinsic pleasure in the discovery of new lands, new islands, and new sea routes. As with modern man, who finds an object, an action, or a being beautiful only if it contains its own reason for being, for Columbus, "discovery" was an action that contained its own reward. "I want to see and explore as much as I can," he wrote in his journal (ibid., 103). Just as soon as someone tells him of a new island, he is seized with an urge to visit it. This tendency seems even stronger during his third voyage: "He says that . . . he would abandon everything to discover more lands and to probe their secrets"; "He was very eager to [tarry] in the hope of discovering much more land" (*Journals and Other Documents*, trans. Morison, 275, 272). The object of discovery now mattered less than the act of discovery.

Columbus's contact with the remote world that he revealed to Europeans was imbued with the same ambiguity. His submission to traditional prejudices and traditional authorities was in constant conflict with the teachings of experience, and, for the most part, tradition won. His study of prophecies and fabulous travel accounts led him to believe that the mainland lay 750 leagues beyond the island of Hierro in the Canary Islands, and when he had gone that distance he stopped sailing at night for fearing of missing land, which he *knew* was near. When he returned from his voyage, Columbus wrote a *Book of Prophecies* in which he gathered together phrases from Scripture that supposedly predicted his adventure and its outcome. He wrote in the preface:

I have already said that in the execution of my undertaking of the Indies, I have not availed myself of reason, or of mathematics, or of maps of the world. What mattered was the accomplishment of what Isaiah had prophesied. (trans. Thacher, *Christopher Columbus*, 3:461n)

The same was true concerning his identification of the lands he had discovered. By sailing west, Columbus was attempting to reach Cathay (China) and Cipango (Japan). No observation that ran counter to his decision was taken into consideration, and until the end of his life he believed he had been in Asia or the islands bordering it. One day he also decided that Cuba was part of the continent, and he cut short all discussion by forcing all the members of his crew to *swear* that it was indeed *terra firma*. When he reached the coast of South America during his third voyage, however, he pronounced it a third continent because this time he was relying on Pierre d'Ailly, who had declared that there were four continents on the earth occupying the four quarters of a circle. Thus Columbus saw South America as complementary to Asia, somewhat as Africa was to Europe.

This is not the only instance of perception strongly influenced by precon-
ception. Columbus traveled with a list of monsters in mind from his reading,
and we can see him mentally checking off their presence or their absence:
Amazons, yes; two-headed men, no; men with tails, yes; dog-headed men,
no; and so forth. "The day before, when the Admiral was going to the Rio
del Oro, he said he saw three mermaids who came quite high out of the
water" (ibid., 321); "There remain to westward two provinces where I have
not been, one of which they call *Avan*, and there the people are born with
tails" (*A New and Fresh English Translation of the Letter of Columbus Announcing the Discovery of America*, trans. Morison, 11). Columbus had also
read in Mandeville and Pierre d'Ailly that the Earthly Paradise must lie in a
temperate region beyond the Equator, and during his third voyage he was
persuaded that he had found it on the coast of South America.

The same principles governed Columbus's first contacts with the "Indians." At first, communication was nil for the simple reason that they did not
speak one another's language. Rather than admitting this and seeking to over-
come the problem, however, Columbus decided that the natives were telling
him what he wanted to hear. He was persuaded that he was in the Cathay of
Marco Polo: "And the Admiral understood that large ships from the Grand
Khan came there (*Diario*, trans. Dunn and Kelley, 119). As far as he was
concerned, the natives spoke to him about nothing but gold and spices, rich
merchants and noble governors. Columbus was equally persuaded that the
Indians understood everything he said to them, but his own narration proves
the contrary when his gestures of friendship are interpreted as acts of war,
and vice versa.

Columbus appears more modern in his approach to nonhuman nature.
What strikes us first is his veritable cult of nature and his unceasing admiration before mountains and streams, meadows and trees, fish and birds. Of
course, Columbus had every reason to present his discoveries in the best
possible light, but his superlatives surpass simple convention. Furthermore,
on several occasions his sensitivity affected his actions and he interrupted his
travels to admire natural beauty:

Going through it was a wonderful thing [because of] the groves of trees, the freshness, and the extremely clear water, and the birds, and its attractiveness. He says
that it seemed to him that one might not wish to leave that place. (Ibid., 183)

Columbus was not content simply to admire and appreciate nature, however: he also knew how to interpret it. This is what explains his success as a
navigator. He knew how to choose the best winds and the best sails; he
inaugurated navigation by the stars and he discovered magnetic variation. He

knew how to observe plants and animals as well as celestial bodies, which granted him one of his rare successes in communication with other human beings. Stranded on the coast of Jamaica for eight months, he was having trouble persuading the natives to continue to supply him with free provisions. He knew that an eclipse of the moon was imminent, however, and he told the islanders that he would steal the night star if they did not acquiesce to his demands. When his threat seemed on the point of coming true, the chiefs gave in.

One might say that all facets of Columbus's personality contributed to his discovery of America. If he had not been a good observer of nature and a skilled navigator, he never would have reached land. But if he had not lived in the semi-fabulous world of old narrations and prophecies, he never would have undertaken the voyage in the first place. More realistic-minded sailors than he judged the voyage too long (the Americas were not known to exist) and too risky. Columbus's faith was needed in order to carry through such an audacious venture.

What can we say about the natives, not as Columbus found them (for that we will never know) but as he describes them? Columbus was much better at observing nature than observing men and women. Their nudity was what struck him most. True as it was, Columbus had other reasons for insisting on it: if these peoples knew no shame, were they not closer to Adam before the fall? Was this not one more reason to believe that the Earthly Paradise was close at hand? Even if he had to give up this tempting hypothesis, their nudity pleased him. In his eyes, it symbolized their lack of culture, and hence the ease with which they could be led to embrace Christianity.

His image of the Indians changed with time. At first, when he was eager to emphasize the importance of his discovery, he declares everything perfect. The Indians were gentle and agreeable, peace-loving to the point of cowardice, and the most generous creatures in the world, giving without second thought whatever was asked of them. Later, when he was engaged in the colonization of the islands, Columbus gives the opposite impression. Then he saw himself surrounded by cruel enemies, and the Indians who attacked the Spanish seemed to him daring and vindictive. Even their generosity turned out to be a penchant for thievery when he discovered that the Indians took others' belongings as easily as they gave their own. Did this simply indicate different relations to private property? Doubtless, but Columbus's observations are too superficial to say more on the question.

The projects that Columbus conceived for the Indians were just as ambiguous as his image of them. On the one hand, faithful to Christian universalism, he made up his mind that the Indians would convert, and he granted

them the status of free subjects with full enjoyment of rights. In his uncon-
scious ethnocentrism, it never occurred to him to wonder whether they considered that religion as universal as it seemed to him. On the other hand,
however, by definition, the universal expansion of Christianity implied that
funds were needed for the expeditions, since arming a crusade took money.
Thus Columbus hoped that his discoveries would turn a profit. Since he had
no assurance that the Indians would consent to the exploitation of their lands,
it was not long before he envisioned their military occupation. He brought
soldiers and constructed fortresses. The lapse of time between Columbus's
idyllic declarations and his declarations of war was brief.

The profits were slow in coming, however. Gold was rare and rich merchants nowhere to be found. Thus, in a second phase, Columbus decided to
take what was at hand—the Indians—and sell them in Europe as slaves. The
boats bringing goods from Europe were not to return empty: The caravels

might be paid with slaves taken from among the Caribbees, who are a wild people,
fit for any work, well proportioned and very intelligent, and who, when they have
got rid of the cruel habits to which they have become accustomed, will be better
than any other kind of slaves. (*Select Letters*, trans. Major, 84–85)

Thus Columbus distinguished between good Indians—future Christians—
and bad cannibals. The rulers of Spain did not show much enthusiasm for
the idea, but at least a start was made. Columbus sent back several ships full
of slaves, a good half of whom died along the way.

How does it happen that we associate Columbus's name with these two
apparently contradictory images of the natives—"noble savage" and potential
slave? Both views are rooted in ignorance and a refusal to recognize the
natives as fully human but different from himself. Columbus discovered
America, but not the Americans.

AMERIGO VESPUCCI

Why "America" and not "Columbia?" There is no obvious answer. The voyages of Amerigo Vespucci (1454–1512) are dubious and his merits as a navigator contestable. He is the only source of information on his exploits, and
the veracity of his account seems quite rightly open to question. Furthermore, even supposing that the expeditions did indeed take place, Amerigo
was not in command of them, and it is usually the commander who gets the
glory. Even putting aside all these objections, it is clear that Amerigo was not
the first to cross the Atlantic, to reach the mainland, or to have recognized it
for was it is. Why, then? Because Amerigo produced the best travel accounts:
two letters known under the names of *Mundus Novus* and *Quatuor Navi-*

gationes that made a vivid impression on his contemporaries—in particular, on the scholars of Saint-Dié, who published Martin Waldseemüller's *Cosmographiae Introductio* in 1507, in which the new continent was given the name of America. It was the writer who was rewarded, not the navigator. With Amerigo, then, we see a new type of voyager, the intellectual and the artist.

The literary merit of Amerigo's works is clear from a comparison of two letters of approximately the same length, Columbus's letter to Luis de Santangel in 1493 and Amerigo's letter to Lorenzo di Pier Francesco de' Medici of 1503, which is known as *Mundus Novus*. These two works were the most popular publications of the time and the ones most frequently reprinted (Amerigo's letter more than Columbus's, however). Comparisons between them, explicit or implicit, entered into the Saint-Dié scholars' choice of name.

The overall composition of Columbus's letter shows no pre-established plan. He describes his voyage, then the natural features and the flora and fauna of the islands of Haiti and Cuba, then the inhabitants. Next, he returns to geography; then he adds further remarks on the "Indians." He then passes on to a section on monsters, and he concludes by assuring the royal couple that these lands are certainly very rich and by thanking God for having permitted him to make these discoveries.

Amerigo's letter, on the other hand, shows that the writer had some training in rhetoric. It begins and ends with several paragraphs that summarize the essence of what he has to say and make the startling affirmation that this was indeed a new world. The text is clearly divided in two parts within this framework. The first part describes the voyage (with a digression on Amerigo's skill as a pilot); the second describes the new lands and is divided into three subsections—announced as such at the end of the first part—on the indigenous population, the land, and the sky. Amerigo's letter has a quasi-geometric *form*, absent from Columbus's letter, that charms the reader.

In fact, Amerigo caters to his readers, whereas Columbus's letter shows no concern for them. I should add that the position of the two navigator-narrators was radically different. Whether Columbus was writing to Santangel, a high functionary and a shipowner, or to others, he was in fact always addressing the rulers of Spain, Ferdinand and Isabella, whom he wanted to persuade of the wealth of the newly discovered lands and of the need to send new expeditions. His were letter-instruments, written for utilitarian ends. There is none of this in Amerigo, who traveled to acquire glory, not wealth, and who writes for the same reason ("to secure repute for my old age"; or "that my record may live with future generations" (*Letters . . . and Other Documents*, trans. Markham, 51, 52). His letters aim above all at impressing, amusing, and enchanting his friends in Florence. He had *Mundus Novus* translated into Latin so that the cultivated public of all Europe might "know all that is proper to be known" of what had "been discovered touching the greatness of the earth and what is contained in it" (ibid., 52). In his *Quatuor Navigationes*, written in the form of a letter to Piero Soderini, a Florentine notable like himself, Amerigo reiterates and insists upon the notion that his correspondent will take pleasure in reading his letter, and he concludes his introductory remarks with a conventional but significant formula:

It may be that, though your Magnificence is continually occupied with public affairs, you may find an hour of leisure, during which you can pass a little time in frivolous or amusing things, and as fennel usually is served after agreeable dishes to dispose them to better digestion, so, as a change from so many occupations, may you read this my letter. (Ibid., 2, modified)

Columbus was writing documents; Amerigo, literature.

Not only did Amerigo write for a man whom he hoped to amuse rather than persuade to finance further expeditions, but he also had other readers in mind, and he organizes his letter for them. This explains the clarity of his outline and his summaries at the beginning and the end. This attention to clarity and his preoccupation with his readers' understanding are essential to his work. When he touches on cosmographical topics that might be unfamiliar to his readers, he makes his point twice and excuses the repetition ("I will explain this more clearly"; ibid., 51), and he even adds a little diagram. There is nothing of the sort in Columbus. In his *Quatuor Navigationes* Amerigo, now an experienced narrator, shows concern for his readers' interest as well as their comprehension, luring them on with promises of what is to come: "I saw many wonderful things, as your Magnificence will understand"; "We found people who were worse than animals, but your Magnificence must understand . . ." (ibid., 3–4; 36).

Amerigo cultivates his reader in his choice of subject matter as well. The facts observed (or imagined) do not differ much in Columbus and Amerigo, however. Columbus describes the Indians as naked, fearful, generous, without religion, and on occasion cannibals. Amerigo, starting from the same basic information, organizes what he has to say under three headings. Treating together the natives' nudity, lack of religion, unaggressive nature, and indifference to personal property, he associates these with classical representations of the Age of Gold to produce the modern image of the "noble savage." He reports:

They have no cloth, either of wool, flax, or cotton, because they have no need of it; nor have they any private property, everything being in common. They live amongst themselves without a king or ruler, each man being his own master, and having as many wives as they please. The children cohabit with the mothers, the brothers with the sisters, the male cousins with the female, and each one with the first he meets. They break their marriages as often as they like and observe no law in this regard. They have no temples and no laws, nor are they idolaters. What more can I say! They live according to nature. (Ibid., 46–47, modified)

This description inspired Thomas More's *Utopia* and countless authors after him.

Amerigo's second category was cannibalism. Columbus, who understood nothing of the natives' language, reported on cannibalism by hearsay. Amerigo indulges in long commentaries: the Indians took prisoners of war to eat them later; the male was wont to eat his spouse and his children; he had spoken personally with a man who had admitted to having devoured more than three hundred of his fellow men; during a walk among the Indians, he had seen human flesh salted and hanging from the rafters like butcher's meat. Amerigo gives these salty details (if I may be permitted the expression) before he reports the Indians' views on the matter: They find the Europeans' repugnance at such succulent fare incomprehensible. The frequency of this theme in contemporary illustrations and later narrations proves that Amerigo had made a judicious choice.

Third, Amerigo remarks on the natives' sexuality. Columbus limited his comments on the subject to noting that "in all these islands it seems that the men are content with only one wife." Amerigo takes the opposite course, letting his imagination run free. He insists repeatedly on the lasciviousness of Indian women and regales his readers (male Europeans) with details: they have poisonous animals bite their partners' penises, which then swell to such an incredible size that they eventually become eunuchs (we can imagine his readers' shivers and their relief).

Another bonus for European readers comes a bit later, when Amerigo speaks of the European voyagers' success with Indian women (we hope they are not subjected to the same risky treatment as the women's native partners). "When they have the opportunity to copulate with Christians, urged on by an excessive lubricity, they become debauched and turn to prostitution." Amerigo even hints that he has not told all: ". . . which I will not go into for reasons of modesty" or, in the *Quatuor Navigationes*, "I do not further refer to their contrivances for satisfying their inordinate desires, so that I may not offend against modesty" (ibid., 8). This is a time-honored procedure for stimulating the reader's imagination.

These passages of the *Mundus Novus* appealed to the mass of readers (who were, to repeat, exclusively male and European). Other passages are calculated to appeal to the pride of the best among them, the learned, and at the same time to permit all his readers to feel they belonged to the cultural elite. In *Quatuor Navigationes* Amerigo cites authors ancient and modern: Pliny, Dante, and Petrarch. In *Mundus Novus*, after his description of the "good savages," he concludes nonchalantly, "They . . . are more inclined to be Epicurean than Stoic" (ibid., 47). Elsewhere, he takes care to cite the writings of the philosophers. In a significant passage in the first part of the letter, Amerigo complains that the ship's pilot was an ignoramus and that without himself, Amerigo, no one would have known how far they had come. He alone was able to read the stars and make use of the quadrant and the astrolabe. He adds:

These have been much used by me with much honour; for I showed them that a knowledge of the maritime charts, and the rules taught by it, are more worth than all the pilots in the world. For these pilots have no knowledge beyond those places to which they have often sailed. (Ibid., 45)

It is no coincidence that contemporary engravers have also transmitted to us an image of Amerigo as a learned man.

Finally, aside from all other ways in which Amerigo facilitated his readers' understanding, from the outset they found themselves in a familiar universe of references to the Italian poets and the philosophers of classical antiquity. Very few of Amerigo's references are to Christian sources. Columbus's mind, on the other hand, was filled with the sacred texts, along with the fabulous accounts of Marco Polo and Pierre d'Ailly. In this connection, Columbus was a man of the Middle Ages and Amerigo a man of the Renaissance. Amerigo also shows proof of the rudiments of cultural relativism when he transcribes what he knows of the Indians' perception of the Europeans, not merely his own perception of the natives. His readers, avid for novelties, were also part of modern times.

Moreover, unlike Columbus, Amerigo presents a purely human world. The monstrous things he describes are not supernatural. The word occurs, for instance, when he speaks of the personal adornment of Indians who pierced their cheeks or their lips and plugged the holes with stones. The only unlikely elements in Amerigo are exaggerations; they reflect the showman's spiel more than any naive credulity. Thus he reports that the Indians lived to the age of 150 and, in the *Quatuor Navigationes*, he speaks of a native population in which the women were as tall as European men and the men taller still.

The difference between the two men is also clear from their treatment of the Earthly Paradise. Columbus believes in it literally and thinks he has glimpsed it; Amerigo uses it as a simple hyperbole (perhaps returned to fashion by Columbus's ecstatic evocation), and he uses it to put the final touch on a perfectly conventional description of nature in the new world: "If the terrestrial paradise is in some part of this land, it cannot be very far from the coast we visited" (ibid., 48).

One twentieth-century historian, Alberto Magnaghi, has found solid arguments to support a conclusion that Amerigo was not the author of the letters published under his name and that they were instead written by Florentine men of letters and professional writers who took hold of a subject that was in vogue. Magnaghi's conclusions have themselves been contested, but they are intriguing. If we accept them, we might say that these letters were not only written for readers but *by* readers. In this case, they would be emblematic of the triumph of literature.

HERNÁN CORTÉS

After Columbus, the navigator, and Amerigo, the writer, came Cortés, the conquistador (1485–1547). The conqueror of Mexico merits this place not only because he was the first to accomplish a true military conquest but also because his example was to be inescapable. Those who came after him either consciously imitated his behavior or tried to go him one better. Cortés was the first voyager to America who was fully conscious of his political, indeed, his historic, role. Before him, there were inspired navigators like Columbus or curious voyagers like Amerigo; there were above all a mass of adventurers who sought in discoveries a way to get rich quickly and with minimal effort. This may have been Cortés's own frame of mind before he took command of an expedition charged with exploring the territory of Mexico. When he first set eyes on these lands, however, the change in him had already occurred. One of his sailors suggested sending a few armed men to look for gold, "but Cortés said, laughing, that we would not go for so slight a reason, but only to serve God and the King" (Díaz, *True Story of the Conquest of Mexico*, trans. Idell, 43). As soon as he learned of Moctezuma's kingdom, he decided not to limit himself to extorting wealth from it but to subject the land itself. This displeased his soldiers, but he remained firm.

To serve this political aim, Cortés made use of a completely new knowledge of the natives and a well-articulated control over the communications that were established between himself and them. His primary concern as he approached Mexican lands was not to seize gold but to find an interpreter. He first discovered a Spaniard who had been shipwrecked there some years earlier and had learned the language of the land. Later he took to his service an Indian woman who was obviously gifted for languages (but also for politics), the famous Malintzin (also known as Malinche or Doña Marina), who turned out to be of priceless aid to Cortés, efficiently interpreting for him not only what people said to him but their behavior as well.

Thus assured of understanding the language, Cortés neglected no opportunity to gather new information, and he rewarded his informants generously. His military successes cannot be explained otherwise. He soon discovered that there was dissent among the various groups of Indians, and that some of them resisted the central power of the Aztecs. This knowledge was to assume an extremely important role during the war, when Cortés made skillful use of local rivalries, presenting himself as the liberator of one population against a second, then as the liberator of the second against a third, and so on, to gain the active collaboration of the natives. The fall of the Aztec empire was hastened, symbolically, by the efficient collection of information when Cortés learned that Cuauhtémoc, Moctezuma's successor, had fled, and he captured him. Once the king was taken, the kingdom yielded.

Cortés went beyond efficient collection of information; he also made it an important part of his strategy to send unsettling signals to the enemy. He was extremely careful of the impression that his behavior and that of his soldiers made on the Indians, and he punished pillagers in his army with severity—they had taken what they should not (the Indians' personal belongings) and had given what they should not (a poor impression of the Spanish). At another point in the conquest, when Cortés and Moctezuma had climbed the 114 steps to the summit of a temple in Mexico City, the Aztec emperor invited Cortés to rest. "Through our interpreters, who went with us, Cortés replied that neither he nor the rest of us ever got tired from anything" (ibid., 158). One chronicler hints at the reason for this gesture when he reports that in an address to his soldiers Cortés declared, "The outcome of a war depends much upon fame" (Gómara, Cortés, trans. Simpson, 229).

At the same time, Cortés took pains to make sure that the Indians could not understand his own information and communication system. He led them to believe, for instance, that his knowledge of their movements came not from informers but from consultation of his compass. At the beginning, the Indians were unsure whether the Spaniards' horses—an animal unknown to them—were mortal or not. To keep them in doubt, Cortés had the corpses of horses killed in battle buried under cover of night. He deliberately introduced a degree of ambiguity in his acts and led the Aztec dignitaries into impossible choices in which they had reason both to trust and mistrust him. Where he was weak, he gave every sign of force; where he was strong, he let them think him weak, thus leading the Aztecs into murderous traps.

Throughout his campaign, Cortés displayed a taste for spectacular acts and an awareness of their symbolic value. It was essential, for instance, to win the first battle against the Indians; to show his invulnerability by destroying their idols at the first challenge from the priests; to win the first skirmish between Spanish brigantines and Indian canoes; to burn a certain palace well inside the city in order to show how far he had advanced; to climb up to the top of a temple so as to be seen by everyone. He rarely punished, but when he did the punishment was exemplary so that everyone knew about it. He even used weapons with more symbolic than practical effect. He had a catapult built, which did not work, but nonetheless struck fear in the Indians; he used his canons to terrify his interlocutors rather than to destroy walls; his horses were used in similar ways.

Cortés's actions irresistibly recall the teachings of a near contemporary, Machiavelli. Rather than direct influence, what we see is the spirit of the age showing in the one man's writings and the other's deeds. Machiavelli cites Ferdinand, the Most Catholic king, whose actions must have been familiar to Cortés, as a model of the "new prince." The comparison seems inevitable between Cortés's stratagems and Machiavelli's precepts, which placed reputation and dissimulation at the summit of the new hierarchy of values:

It is not necessary, then, for a prince to have all of the qualities mentioned above, but it is certainly necessary that he appear to have them. In fact, I would go so far as to say this, that having them and observing them at all times, they are harmful; and appearing to have them, they are useful. (*The Prince*, XVIII, trans. Musa, 147)

In the world of Machiavelli and Cortés, discourse was not determined by the object it described, nor by conformity with tradition, but was constructed in light of the objective it sought to attain.

The most complex manipulation in which Cortés was involved concerned the myth of Quetzalcoatl. This Indian myth recounted the departure of the god Quetzalcoatl and promised his eventual return. Cortés became aware of the myth and used it to his own profit, affirming to Moctezuma that his own sovereign (the emperor Charles V) was indeed Quetzalcoatl. The Indians later omitted this intervening link and identified Cortés himself with Quetzalcoatl. It was an operation that paid off on all levels: Cortés could boast of his legitimacy among the local population, and it furnished the Indians with a way to make sense of their own history. If Cortés's coming had not fulfilled prophecy, it would have been totally incongruous and, arguably, the natives' resistance might have been a good deal more determined.

All these observations tend to prove that Cortés had a fairly good knowledge of the Indians, a knowledge on which he might not have been able to elaborate in the abstract but which he managed to internalize and to use as a basis for action. The contrast with both Columbus and Amerigo Vespucci is striking. One can even see in Cortés a sporadic but genuine interest in the Indians' culture. Although initially his only thought was to overturn idols and destroy temples (a part of his military strategy), soon after the conquest he was concerned with their preservation as testaments to Aztec culture. "He was very vexed, as he wanted these idols' temples to remain as monuments," one of his adversaries declared.

Cortés is often admiring in his evaluation of the Aztecs. Certainly, like Columbus, he sought to put his discoveries in the best possible light; nonetheless, his esteem for his adversaries seems genuine. "These people live almost like those in Spain, and in as much harmony and order as there" (Cortés, *Letters from Mexico*, trans. Pagden, 108). Their cities were well organized, their houses were beautiful, their markets opulent, their customs refined, and their jewels and textiles admirable. The fact remains, however, that the chief result of the contact between Cortés and the Indians was the destruction, first of their cultural identity, and finally of their very lives. It is thought that by the end of the sixteenth century "microbe shock" had reduced the population that Cortés had found to one-tenth or less of what it had been. Thus it was possible to know and even to admire others and still contribute to their extermination. How was this possible?

The truth is that Cortés admired the objects that Aztec artisans had produced, but he did not recognize them as human beings to be placed on the same level as himself. The Indians might very well have been good workers, valiant warriors, and loyal allies, but Cortés never considered them *subjects* in the strongest sense of the word—that is, individuals gifted with free will. When, on another occasion, he expressed his opinion on the enslavement of the Indians, he saw the problem solely from the point of view of the profitability of the venture, never considering what the Indians themselves might have thought. Symbolically, Cortés's testament mentions everyone deserving of a share in his wealth: his family and his servants, convents and monasteries, hospitals and colleges. Only the Indians, the source of all his wealth, were missing.

BARTOLOMÉ DE LAS CASAS

When they encountered the Indians, Columbus, Vespucci, and Cortés were voyagers who thought above all of themselves, of their own culture, and of the advantages to be gained from the natives. With Las Casas (1484–1566) we see a radical change. Here was someone whose first concern was to protect

the natives from the suffering and the exactions imposed on them by con-
querors and colonizers. He was, after all, known as "the protector of the
Indians." If truth be told, though, Las Casas modified his position several
times during his long career. Without entering into all the details, we need
to distinguish between several stages and several degrees of his "protection."

Born in Spain, Las Casas first arrived in the Antilles in 1502, at the age of
eighteen. He settled on the island of Hispaniola (Haiti) to pursue a dual career
as a planter and a priest. In 1514 his first "conversion" occurred. His own
experience had shown him the extent of the Indians' suffering, but he was
also struck by the Dominican friars' sermons condemning the actions of the
Spanish. One friar refused him communion because he owned Indian slaves,
which was contrary to the spirit of Christianity. Las Casas gave up his Indians
and began to militate in favor of their rights. At the same time, he preached
peaceful colonization, and, at the head of a band of peasants and planters
(rather than soldiers) he embarked on an expedition to colonize lands in what
is now Venezuela. Armed conflict nonetheless broke out, and the expedition
was a failure. Then came his second "conversion": in 1523, he entered the
Dominican order, and for more than ten years he lived in essential retirement
from the world, improving his book culture. From 1535 on, he returned to
active struggle for Indian rights, both on the American continent (with a new
attempt at peaceful colonization in Guatemala) and in Spain, where he sought
to persuade the king and the religious authorities.

Las Casas's best known writings come from this later period. First, he was
indefatigable in his denunciation of the cruelty of the Spanish conquistadores
and colonizers. His *Brevísima relación de la destrucción de las Indias* is the
most famous of these writings but not the only one. Second, he proposed
concrete legal and political measures, which were to contribute to improving
conditions in the American colonies. Third and last, he reflected on the moral
and philosophical foundations of his own acts, and he found their ultimate
justification in the principle (for him, the Christian principle) of the unity of
the human species and the equal dignity of all its members. "The laws and
the natural rules and the rights of men are common to all the nations, Christian and Gentile, and whatever their sect, law, color, and condition, without
any difference." Thanks to this credo, Las Casas appears to us as one of the
first militants for the rights of man.

Things become more complex, however, precisely because Las Casas remained an ardent Christian and a partisan of the conversion of the Indians.
The idea of a universal religion has an internal ambiguity, for the more we
wish religion to be common to all humankind, the more it risks losing its

identity. Conversely, if religion remains faithful to itself, its universality becomes dubious. "The Christian religion is granted to different peoples as the universal way to salvation so that they may leave behind their various sects" (Las Casas, *History of the Indies*, trans. Collard, 14). But what was one to do if these other peoples did not have the same universal ideal? Were they to be constrained by force, once peaceful initiatives had failed?

Las Casas saw only one way to resolve this tension and, without accepting recourse to force, to remain faithful to both the particular nature of the Christian religion and to his ideal of universality. His solution was to minimize the differences between peoples and cultures; to see the Indians according to his own needs—that is, as already furnished with Christian qualities. "Never in other epochs or among other peoples has one seen so many capacities, dispositions, or facilities for this conversion. There is not in the world any nation as docile or less refractory, nor more apt or better disposed than these to receive the yoke of Christ." The Indians, he repeated incessantly, are humble, peace-loving, gentle, generous—in short, already endowed with Christian virtues.

Trapped by his own strategy, Las Casas produces a singularly poor portrait of the Indians, whom he must have known well, however, and for whom he felt sincere love.

This infinite multitude of people was so created by God, as that they were without fraud, without subtilty or malice, to their natural Governours most faithful and obedient. Toward the *Spaniards* whom they serve, patient, meek and peaceful, and who laying all contentious and tumultuous thoughts aside, live without any hatred or desire of revenge." (*Tears of the Indians*, 7)

It is striking to see how Las Casas, faithful in this to the *topos* of the Age of Gold, is led to describe the Indians in almost exclusively negative or privative terms: they are *without* fault; *neither* this *nor* that, and so forth. We might wonder whether Las Casas, who fought against physical violence and military aggression, is not the accomplice of a conceptual violence here, certainly less cruel than the physical variety, but that still had important consequences. He refuses to recognize the Indians for what they were, and he imposes on them an image that originates within himself. The Indians are *assimilated* to Christians.

Something similar occurs with Las Casas's more strictly political ideas. Both during the Venezuelan episode and the later attempt to establish a colony in Guatemala, he does not oppose colonization in principle but simply prefers peaceful and progressive colonization to wars and massacres. The result, he always adds, would be preferable not only for the Indians' well-being but also for the king's finances.

We declare ourselves ready to pacify them and to reduce them to the service of the king our sovereign, and to convert them and instruct them in knowledge of their creator; after which we will work to ensure that these populations pay each year tributes and services to His Majesty, according to the possibilities that their resources permit them: all for the better profit of the king, of Spain and of these lands.

Las Casas had no more desire to stop the expansion of the Spanish empire than to limit the propagation of the Christian faith. He simply dreamed of a "good" colonization carried out under the leadership of the religious orders—thus of a theocratic state in which spiritual power ruled rather than temporal power. On this level as well, then, Las Casas remained an assimilationist. Although assimilation is incontestably preferable to extermination, that does not make it blameless.

Las Casas's metamorphoses did not stop there, however. Although it would be inaccurate to speak of a third "conversion," toward the end of his life his positions became even more radical, leading him to adopt new views on the Indians. This last change occurred around 1550, when a public debate in Valladolid opposed Las Casas to a lay scholar, Juan Ginés de Sepúlveda, who, in the name of Aristotle's doctrine on natural slaves, declared the Indians to be inferior beings and war against them legitimate. Las Casas violently opposed this point of view, and it was in refining his arguments against Sepúlveda that he seems to have reached his final positions. The debate was not decided officially, but its outcome seemed to favor Las Casas.

The topic that impelled Las Casas to clarify his thinking was human sacrifice, which the Aztecs practiced. It struck people's imaginations as much as cannibalism, and authors hostile to the Indians saw in it the best proof of their natural inferiority, and thus of the legitimacy of wars of conquest and their submission to slavery. Las Casas accepted the challenge without avoiding debate. His strategy was dual: first, he did his utmost to render the practice less strange by recalling all the sacrifices that figure in the Bible. Second (and more important), he propounded a new principle regarding different religions, thus taking a position of cultural pluralism.

Las Casas now distinguished between the object of the religious cult and the quality of the religious experience, and he suggested that excellence in the second was preferable to excellence in the first. By practicing human sacrifice, the Aztecs chose the wrong object: the Christian God would never have required the sacrifices demanded by the bloodthirsty Tezcatlipoca. They proved the intensity of their religious sentiments, however, by their readiness to give their god the most precious commodity of human life.

The nations that offered human sacrifices to their gods thus showed, as misled idol-worshipers, the high idea they had of the excellence of the divinity and of the value of their gods and [they showed] how noble and how high was their veneration of the divinity. They showed, consequently, that they possessed, better than the other nations, natural reflection, rectitude of word, and the judgment of reason; better than others, they made use of their understanding. And they surpassed all the other nations in religiousness, for those were the most religious nations in the world who, for the good of their peoples, offered their own children as a sacrifice.

Las Casas's argument is specious, for he presents as suicide what was really homicide. Still, the problem of human sacrifice led him to a new tolerance. Since religiosity was separated from religion, and since the Aztecs were declared more religiously inclined than the Spanish, did it not then follow that conversion to Christianity was not as urgent as it had previously seemed? Las Casas still believed just as firmly in the superiority of his own religion, but because he admits that the ways leading to God are multiple, he comes to respect others' religions.

The same thing occurred on the political level. During the same period (after 1550), Las Casas went so far as to suggest to the king that he give up his conquests and re-establish the old rulers in their prerogatives. Only if these rulers should demand it should the king of Spain then admit them to a sort of federative union in which the highest place was his but local chiefs would keep full autonomy. Needless to say, Las Casas's correspondents did not follow his suggestions.

Thus during the last phase of his life, Las Casas went further in the direction of egalitarianism and recognition of the free will of others. It is legitimate to ask, however, whether he went too far in the direction of cultural relativism (in which case he would be a precursor to more recent changes in our collective mentality). The impulse that led him to recognize the Indians' right to live their religiousness as they understood it also led him to renounce all transcultural judgments and to declare that "barbarity" was purely relative. "Just as we consider the peoples of the Indies barbarians, they judge us [to be] the same because they do not understand us." The fact remains, however, that we consider human sacrifice a truly barbarian act, an act much more barbarian than lighting a candle. It is as if Las Casas accepted extreme positions alone: first he equated the universal ideal with the Christian religion;

then he gave up defending any absolute scale of values. To escape the Scylla of ethnocentrism is it really necessary to throw oneself into the Charybdis of relativism?

BERNARDINO DE SAHAGÚN

Las Casas was above all a militant humanist, even if he also left texts that contributed to a better knowledge of the Indians. During the sixteenth century, another group of authors formed who made this knowledge their principal concern—authors who traveled and studied less for political or humanitarian, religious or artistic reasons than for the express purpose of learning about native Americans. The Franciscan Bernardino de Sahagún (1499–1590), the most remarkable representative of this group, can stand for the rest.

Sahagún's biography is, significantly enough, uneventful. There is nothing comparable to the busy lives of Columbus and Amerigo Vespucci, Cortés and Las Casas. Sahagún was born in Spain, where he entered the Franciscan order at a very early age. He crossed the Atlantic in 1529, and remained in Mexico until his death. His life was spent in learning and teaching, reading and writing. "He was gentle, humble, and poor, very discreet in his speech, and affable toward everyone," one of his companions reported.

He taught principally in the college of Tlatelulco, in Mexico City, initiating the children of Aztec dignitaries into the Christian religion and Latin grammar. Learning was a two-way process, however, and as he taught Latin, Sahagún profited from his contacts to learn Nahuatl, the language of the conquered Aztecs. It was to his interest to do so, of course: with knowledge of the language he could propagate the Christian faith more efficiently. Nonetheless, it reveals a new attitude. Neither Cortés nor Las Casas, not to mention earlier voyagers, had taken the trouble to learn even one of the Indian languages. Whatever Sahagún's ulterior motives may have been, his first act was to adapt to others (or to their language) rather than to demand their submission to him.

Not satisfied with this linguistic apprenticeship, Sahagún also began to learn about the culture of the Mexicans. He collected a number of documents— ritual texts, religious hymns, and accounts of the conquest. When his superior asked him to draw up a description of Aztec culture for the use of the Spanish religious orders charged with converting the Indians to Christianity, Sahagún filled it with his religious fervor and his passion for knowledge, creating a monumental work unique in its genre, a sort of encyclopedia of Aztec culture entitled *História general de las cosas de Nueva España*. This work, which encountered a good deal of resistance from both the religious hierarchy and lay powers, was published only in the nineteenth century.

In its aims, Sahagún's work fit into a familiar category in Christian tradition: the study of the religion, the culture, and the mores of the pagans in view of facilitating their conversion to Christianity. Its novelty lay not in its aims but in Sahagún's serious approach to his task and in the quality of his achievement. Knowledge of others was slowly being transformed from a means to a goal, symbolized by Sahagún's decision to write the work in Nahuatl rather than in Spanish, adding a Spanish translation, rather than the other way around. This bilingual work thus had two prospective readerships, in Spanish religious who sought to hasten the conversion of the Indians, and literate Mexicans who wanted to learn about the history and the ancient customs of their own land. This decision made Sahagún unique even among other religious who had a passionate interest in indigenous culture.

His first problem was to collect information. His method was to alternate between on-the-spot inquiry and summaries he himself provided. His contact with his students enabled him to draw up an outline and questionnaires. He submitted these to the people in the first city where he served who were most familiar with tradition, and for two years he gathered, transcribed, and translated their responses. He then began all over again in a new location, where new experts to whom he submitted the results of his first inquiry provided him with new answers and new commentaries. This took another year. Finally, in a third phase, Sahagún closeted himself with his best students, revised everything, divided the work into twelve books, added the documents he had collected earlier, and, finally, made a free translation of the text into Spanish and had the manuscript illustrated. These tasks kept Sahagún busy, with rare interruptions, for forty years, but the result was exceptional.

It would be a mistake to think, however, that what we find in this work is the word of Indians and free of any admixture of Spanish culture. For all his lively interest in Nahuatl culture, Sahagún's mentality remained Spanish, and although he transcribed his informants' words faithfully, they were still addressed to him, a Spaniard and a Christian, and the person to whom a discourse is directed is just as responsible for its contents as its author, even if he bears less responsibility for it.

Sahagún intervenes in the text in various ways. On occasion, he addresses his informants directly, pleading with them to give up their superstitions or deploring the fate of these misdirected peoples. On other occasions, he compares the Aztec pantheon to its Roman counterpart. On a deeper level, it was

Sahagún who gave the work its basic organization, moving from the highest to the lowest and from the world of the gods to that of stones. Similarly, each individual chapter reflects the organization of Sahagún's questionnaires. The *História general de las cosas de Nueva España* really belongs neither to Spanish culture nor to the culture of the Aztecs. Rather it is the first great monument of Mexican culture, a hybrid culture that arose out of the meeting of two worlds.

The same ambiguity underlies Sahagún's analysis of the Aztec world as a whole. He cannot help noting that the arrival of the Spanish, which in theory brought good (since it introduced Christianity), had effects that were ultimately negative. The corruption, thirst for wealth, and egotism of the Spanish turned out to be contagious. The Indians, he remarks (somewhat like Las Casas), were more religious before the arrival of the Spanish, even if their religion was not the right one. But was not greater religiousness preferable to a better religion? Sahagún's work is imbued with tension between two contrary forces arising out of equally pressing needs: the need to aid in the Christianization of the Mexicans, and the need to admit that conversion had drawn them further away from rather than closer to God.

Sahagún's judgment of the natives proceeded from the same Christian universalism that had been at work in Las Casas. "What is certain is that all these peoples are our brothers, issued from Adam's progeny like ourselves; they are our neighbors, whom we are to love as ourselves." Unlike Las Casas, this principle did not lead Sahagún into idealization. The Indians were neither better than nor worse than the Spanish. Their belonging to a different culture did not automatically entail moral judgment; good and evil could be found everywhere.

It would be anachronistic to see Sahagún as the first ethnologist, not only because of his proselytizing aims but also because he never turned his gaze on himself; he never made the absolutely fundamental comparison between oneself and others. Still, Sahagún and those who followed his example, in America and elsewhere, had the merit of having accepted the challenge of the fabulous expansion in the size of the surface of the globe that followed the new discoveries. An absolutely unknown world opened up before their eyes, a world Europeans knew nothing about and that was destined to disappear rapidly under the combined effects of conquest and physical and cultural contagion. Sahagún and his emulators, who raised ethnographic inquiry to heights previously unknown, give us a glimpse of what this unsuspected world looked like. They enable us to be present as unforeseen spectators at the most remarkable encounter between voyagers and natives known to the entire history of humanity.

BIBLIOGRAPHY

Atkinson, Geoffrey. *Les Nouveaux horizons de la Renaissance française*. Paris: E. Droz, 1935.

Bataillon, Marcel. *Etudes sur Bartolomé de Las Casas*. Paris: Centre de recherches de l'Institut d'études hispaniques, 1965.

Baudet, Henri. *Paradise on Earth: Some Thoughts on European Images of Non-European Man*. Trans. Elizabeth Wentholt. New Haven: Yale University Press, 1965.

Chaunu, Pierre. *Conquête et exploitation des nouveaux mondes (XVIe siècle)*. Paris: Presses Universitaires de France, 1969; 3d ed. rev. and cor., 1987.

Chiappelli, Fredi, ed. *First Images of America*. 2 vols. Berkeley: University of California Press, 1976.

Cline, Howard Francis, ed. *Guide to Ethnohistorical Sources*. Vols. 12–15, *Handbook of Middle American Indians*. Austin: University of Texas Press, 1972–75.

Edmonson, Munro S., ed. *Sixteenth-Century Mexico: The Work of Sahagún*. Albuquerque: University of New Mexico Press, 1974.

Elliott, John H. *The Old World and the New, 1492–1650*. Cambridge: Cambridge University Press, 1970.

Friede, Juan, and Benjamin Keen, eds. *Bartolomé de Las Casas in History: Toward an Understanding of the Man and His Work*. Dekalb: Northern Illinois University Press, 1971.

Gerbi, Antonello. *La natura delle Indie nove: da Cristoforo Colombo a Gonzalo Fernandez de Oviedo*. Milan and Naples: R. Ricciardi, 1975. (*Nature in the New World: From Christopher Columbus to Gonzalo Fernandez de Oviedo*. Trans. Jeremy Moyle. Pittsburgh: University of Pittsburgh Press, 1985.)

Gibson, Charles. *Spain in America*. New York: Harper & Row, 1966.

Hanke, Lewis. *Aristotle and the American Indians: A Study in Race Prejudice in the Modern World*. Bloomington and London: University of Indiana Press, 1959; 1970.

Heers, Jacques. *Christophe Colomb*. Paris: Hachette, 1981.

Julien, Charles-André. *Les voyages de découverte et les premiers établissements (XVe–XVIe siècles)*. Paris: Presses Universitaires de France, 1948.

Keen, Benjamin. *The Aztec Image in Western Thought*. New Brunswick: Rutgers University Press, 1971.

Levillier, Roberto. *America la bien llamada*. Buenos Aires: G. Kraft, 1948.

Magnaghi, Alberto. *Amerigo Vespucci, studio critico . . . .* New ed. rev. and enl. Rome: Fratelli Treves, 1926.

Mahn-Lot, Marianne. *Bartolomé de Las Casas et le droit des indiens*. Paris: Payot, 1982.

O'Gorman, Edmundo. *La idea del descubrimiento de América*. Mexico: Centro de Estudios Filosóficos, 1951. (*The Invention of America: An Inquiry into the Historical Nature of the New World and the Meaning of Its History*. Bloomington: Indiana University Press, 1961.)

Zavala, Silvio. *L'Amérique latine, philosophie de la conquête*. Paris and The Hague: Mouton, 1977.

Index